教育部人文社科重点研究基地中山大学中国非物质
文化遗产研究中心非物质文化遗产保护研究丛书

Intangible Cultural Heritage Safeguarding Research Series
edited by the Institute of Chinese Intangible Cultural Heritage
at Sun Yat-sen University, one of the key research institutes
of humanities and social sciences in universities approved and
supported by the Ministry of Education of China

亚民俗：中美民俗学者交流的故事 第一辑

Metafolklore: Stories of Sino-US Folkloristic Communication · volume 1

张举文　宋俊华　编

中山大学出版社
·广州·

版权所有 翻印必究

图书在版编目（CIP）数据

亚民俗：中美民俗学者交流的故事．第一辑：汉、英／张举文，宋俊华编．—广州：中山大学出版社，2017.11

（教育部人文社科重点研究基地中山大学中国非物质文化遗产研究中心非物质文化遗产保护研究丛书）

ISBN 978 - 7 - 306 - 06231 - 4

Ⅰ．①亚… Ⅱ．①张… ②宋… Ⅲ．①民俗学—文化交流—中国、美国—汉、英 Ⅳ．①K890

中国版本图书馆 CIP 数据核字（2017）第 280695 号

出版人：	徐 劲
责任编辑：	裘大泉 李海东
封面设计：	曾 斌
责任校对：	刘丽丽 赵 婷
责任技编：	黄少伟
出版发行：	中山大学出版社
电　　话：	编辑部 020 - 84110771，84110283，84111997，84110779
	发行部 020 - 84111998，84111981，84111160
地　　址：	广州市新港西路 135 号
邮　　编：	510275　　　传　真：020 - 84036565
网　　址：	http://www.zsup.com.cn　E-mail：zdcbs@mail.sysu.edu.cn
印 刷 者：	佛山市浩文彩色印刷有限公司
规　　格：	787mm×1092mm　1/16　20 印张　468 千字
版次印次：	2017 年 11 月第 1 版　2017 年 11 月第 1 次印刷
定　　价：	118.00 元

如发现本书因印装质量影响阅读，请与出版社发行部联系调换

本文集的完成得到中国教育部人文社会科学重点研究基地
中山大学中国非物质文化遗产研究中心
暨美国民俗学会路思项目的支持

This publication is supported by the Institute of Chinese Intangible Cultural Heritage, Sun Yat-sen University, a Key Research Institute of Humanities and Social Sciences in Universities in China, and the Henry Luce Project via American Folklore Society.

"中国人日常仪式实践研讨会"暨"第十届假日、仪礼、节日、庆祝与公共展示会议"部分参会人员，美国崴涞大学，2006年6月2日至4日。Some participants at the "Conference on Chinese Daily Ritual Practice" in conjunction with "The Tenth Annual Conference on Holidays, Ritual, Festival, Celebration, and Public Display," June 2–4, 2006, Willamette University, Salem, Oregon, USA. Photograph courtesy of Juwen Zhang.

目 录

前 言 ·· 迈克尔·欧文·琼斯 Ⅰ
Preface ·· Michael Owen Jones Ⅲ
序 言 ·· 刘魁立 Ⅶ
Prologue ·· Kuili Liu Ⅹ

亚民俗：学科发展的有机动力 ·· 张举文（1）
Metafolklore: An Organic Development of the Discipline ·················· Juwen Zhang（8）

Ⅰ. 回眸历程，追忆先贤
Glimpses of the Past and Memories of the Distinguished Predecessors

中国记忆 ·· 艾伟（23）
    China Memories ·· Bill Ivey（30）
携手共建国际民俗学会联合会 ·· 朝戈金（37）
    The Collaboration in Initiating the International Federation
    of Folklore Societies ·· Chao Gejin（40）
中美民俗学会合作史略 ·· 罗仪德（42）
    A Capsule History of the AFS-CFS Collaboration ·················· Timothy Lloyd（47）
世界民俗学的两个发展引擎之间的几件信使差事 ·················· 高丙中（52）
    Some Messengers between the Two Developing Engines
    of the World Folklore Studies ·· Bingzhong Gao（58）
丁乃通：醉心于中国民间故事研究的美籍华人学者 ·················· 刘守华（64）

Nai-tung Ting: A Chinese American Scholar Devoted
to Chinese Folktale Studies ··· Shouhua Liu (74)
阿兰·邓迪斯教授访华记 ·· 陈建宪 (84)
Alan Dundes's Visit to China ··· Jianxian Chen (88)
太遗憾了：阿兰·邓迪斯没能收到这本书 ··································· 户晓辉 (93)
What a Pity: Alan Dundes Did Not Receive This Book ·············· Xiaohui Hu (97)

II. 从面对文本到面对面——耕耘友情
From Face-to-text to Face-to-face—Cultivating Friendship

去中国研究，在美国传播 ·· 白素贞 (105)
Researching in China, Disseminating Results in the US ·············· Susan Blader (109)
合作研究中国民俗的一些往事 ·· 马克·本德尔 (114)
Some Recollections of Collaborative Works on Chinese Folklore Studies
·· Mark Bender (117)
中国给我留下的最深刻印象是什么？ ··· 迈克尔·欧文·琼斯 (121)
What Impressed Me Most in China? ······································ Michael Owen Jones (124)
我与美国民俗学界的交流与译事 ·· 李扬 (128)
My Stories of Knowing American Folklorists and Translating their Works ······ Yang Li (132)
中美民俗研究交流的记忆 ·· 萧放 (137)
My Recollections of the China-US Folkloristic Exchange ·············· Fang Xiao (142)
美美与共：我们与美国民俗学界的交往 ···································· 杨利慧 安德明 (147)
Sharing the Beauty: Our Exchanges with American Folklorists
·· Lihui Yang, Deming An (154)

III. 从书本民俗回到生活民俗——共拓新途
From Folklore in Books back to Folklore in
Practice—Opening up New Paths

初识的印象，持久的记忆 ·· 罗伯特·巴龙 (167)
First Impressions, Enduring Memories ···································· Robert Baron (171)

让不让狼死掉 ………………………………………………… 道格拉斯·布兰迪（176）
　　Killing the Wolf ……………………………………… Douglas Blandy（179）
世界平台与本土命题：我与美国民俗学界交往之管见 ……………… 陈泳超（183）
　　World Stage and Local Tasks: A Glimpse of the China-US Folkloristic Exchanges
　　　……………………………………………………… Yongchao Chen（186）
建立关系：中美民间生活与合作 ………………………… 科特·杜赫斯特（189）
　　Building Connectivity: China-US Folklife and Collaborations ………… Kurt Dewhurst（194）
反思合作：中国西南拼布展项目 ………………………… 玛莎·麦克多维尔（199）
　　Reflections on Collaborations: *The Quilts of Southwest China* Project
　　　…………………………………………………… Marsha MacDowell（203）
我的两个故事 ……………………………………………………… 谢沫华（208）
　　My Two Stories ………………………………………… Mohua Xie（211）
十年：中美博物馆合作项目记述 …………………………………… 杜韵红（214）
　　Ten Years: China-US Museum Collaborations in Retrospect …… Yunhong Du（218）
我所参与的博物馆交流项目 ………………………………………… 张丽君（221）
　　My Involvement in the Museum Exchange Projects ………… Lijun Zhang（224）
我的中国之行 ……………………………………………… 萨伦·谢尔曼（228）
　　My Journeys to China ……………………………… Sharon Sherman（232）
我在中美民俗学交流中的两件事 …………………………………… 孙正国（237）
　　My Stories about the China-US Folkloristic Communication ……… Zhengguo Sun（240）

Ⅳ. 从单向离散的到双向机制化的交流——学术交流的新常态
From One-Way and Scattershot to Two-way and Institutionalized Communication—A New Norm of Academic Communication

我的一年美国访学 …………………………………………………… 周星（247）
　　My Year in the US ……………………………………… Xing Zhou（251）
我与美国民俗学的邂逅 ……………………………………………… 王霄冰（254）
　　My Encounters with American Folkloristics …………… Xiaobing Wang（257）
从碰撞到共享：中美民俗学者的交流 ……………………………… 宋俊华（260）

From "Attacking" to "Sharing": Exchanges between the Sino-US Folklorists
　　 ··· Junhua Song（263）
我经历的中国故事 ····························· 安东尼·布切泰利（266）
　　My Narratives of China Experience ················ Anthony Buccitelli（268）
中美民俗学交流对我个人的影响 ···························· 游自荧（271）
　　How China-US Exchanges Influenced Me ················ Ziying You（274）
我与美国民俗学会年会的情缘 ···························· 南快莫德格（277）
　　My Love Affair with the AFS Annual Meeting ········ Namkamidog（280）
第一次参加美国民俗学年会 ·································· 王均霞（283）
　　My First AFS Annual Meeting ······················ Junxia Wang（285）
行走·回首·远望：中美民俗学交流之个人经历 ············ 程　鹏（287）
　　Proceeding, Retrospect, and Prospect: My Experience in the China-US
　　Folkloristic Exchange ····························· Peng Cheng（291）

专有名称 Proper Names ······································（295）

后　记 ··（297）
　　Epilogue ···（298）

前　言

迈克尔·欧文·琼斯

这是一本独具特色的文集。它的完成是基于一系列特定境况，涉及中美两国的学者和机构，及其互动。参与本项目的均是从事民俗学研究的学生和学者，关注的是日常生活中民众的民俗传统和行为表现。

编者用了"亚民俗"这个词来命名这本文集。阿兰·邓迪斯在1966年提出了"亚民俗"这一术语，用来指那些评述民俗的一种"俗"。编者扩展了这个概念，不仅表示民俗学研究者与传统工匠、艺人一起工作的经验，也包含民俗学者之间的思想、观点和价值观的分享。由此，这本非凡的文集聚焦于近年来中美民俗学者之间有关民俗学的互动和交流，延续和发展了在这方面已有200多年的历史。

在本书的开头，张举文首先提供了一个历史大背景。他提到一些由早期的传教士、旅行者，以及民族学家为西方读者所撰写的关于中国的记述，随后介绍了20世纪民俗学研究的发展。他侧重的是现代的变革时期。在上世纪80年代，中国开始对外开放，一些美国人很快展开了对中国乡土史诗叙事的研究。同时，中国民俗学家邀请了一些美国同仁访问和交流，随后多名中国民俗学家在美国一些主要高校学习，将分析传统的新方法带回中国。文集的第一部分是对中美之间近年来的交流的概述，并追忆了两位有关的重要的民俗学家。

2005年标志着一次里程碑式的转变。在北京举办了一届有关传统节日与法定假日的国际研讨会。中国民俗学会邀请美国民俗学会会长和一些美国民俗学家共同参与。美国学者宣读了论文，并在几所大学做了学术报告。来自美国和中国的民俗学家相聚，相互讨论、交流，从只阅读和倾听对方的学术报告发展到面对面的互动。

自2005年中美两国民俗学会的互动以来，后续发生了许多事情。一年后，张举文教授在俄勒冈州塞勒姆的威涞大学组织了关于中国人日常礼仪实践的会议。刘魁立博士作为中国民俗学会会长率团参加，与美国同行交流。由张举文发起成立的美国民俗学会下属的东亚民俗研究分会，引介了许多中国民俗学者参加美国民俗学会的年会。自2007年以来，两个学会之间和个别学者之间的互访已经成为惯例。2013—2014年，分别在美国和中国两地共举办了四届非物质文化遗产保护论坛，每届论坛都吸引了来自两个国家的民俗学者参与。2013

至2016年间,开展了博物馆的跨文化交流项目,也举办了三界民俗影像记录工作坊,并规划了暑期田野学校。目前,一个新的博物馆合作项目正在推进中。至少有100名美国民俗学者通过互访和交流,已经建立了与中国同仁的联系,而中国有200名以上的民俗学者参加过美国民俗学会议,与美国同仁们进行直接互动,从而促进了双方的友好关系,形成有意义的对话。

通过共同参加会议、论坛、庆典等活动,通过在彼此的期刊发表作品,以及访问对方的相关机构,中国和美国民俗学者相互都学到很多东西。在中国,他们运用从美国学习到的方法和理论,并多有评述。在英语世界里,民俗学者已经发现了中国民俗生活世界的显著的多样性和复杂性。

本书还有更多的意义。会议论文和学术文章是有形的产出,而且在很大程度上是客观的。然而,学者们通过学术机构之间的交流、个体间的面对面互动、平等的思想沟通,这些都是个人的和无形的,也是我们的学科持续发展的必要组成部分。

这本书包含了民俗学者在会议和交流时所积累和记录的第一手材料。在四个分主题章节中,共有30多位中美民俗学家讲述自己的交流感受。这些故事记录了为双方注入生机的交流和互动的历史过程:从面对文本到面对真人、从礼节性访问到生动的思想交流。这些故事表达了他们的情感、价值观和世界观。正如编者所说,无论是在国家或国际,甚至包括个人层面,这种"亚民俗"对发展我们的学科至关重要。这本书中的故事,如同那些学术书刊中的文本、描述,以及对民俗传统的分析一样,是民俗学学科的生命线之一。本书既是学术著作,也是对学术的庆祝。

(本文作者为加利福尼亚大学洛杉矶分校荣誉教授,美国民俗学会前会长。湖南大学蒋海军翻译)

Preface

Michael Owen Jones

This is a unique book. It grows out of a set of unusual circumstances involving individuals, institutions, and interactions in China and the United States. The students and scholars participating in events are engaged in folklore studies, that is, research on the traditions and expressive behaviors of people in everyday life.

The editors have entitled this collection of essays *Metafolklore*. Alan Dundes introduced the term metafolklore in 1966 to denote a type of lore that makes statements about folklore. The editors extend the meaning of the term to include stories by folklorists themselves about their experiences working together with traditional artisans and performers but also, beyond that, narratives by folklorists meeting together, connecting with one another personally, and sharing ideas, viewpoints, and values. This extraordinary volume, then, focuses on the interactions and communication between Sino-US folklorists in recent years as the discipline of folkloristics, which is more than 200 years old, continues to develop and diversify.

At the beginning of the book, Juwen Zhang provides a broad historical background and notes some of the documentation by early missionaries, travelers, and ethnographers who wrote about China for Western audiences, and then describes the growth of twentieth-century folklore studies. His survey dwells, however, on the recent era and its transformative processes. China opened its doors to outsiders in the 1980s. Several Americans soon carried out research on epic narratives performed in Chinese villages. In the 1980s, Chinese folklorists invited some of their American counterparts to visit and exchange ideas; a number of Sino folklorists subsequently studied at major universities in the US, returning to China with new ways of analyzing traditions. The following section of the book provides an overview of contacts between West and East in recent years, while commemorating two important folklorists related to this communication.

A milestone event occurred in 2005. An international conference on festivals and calendar customs was held in Beijing to which the China Folklore Society invited the President, along with several other US folklorists. The Americans presented conference papers and gave university lectures. The folklorists from the US and China met, engaged in mutual discussions, socialized, and in other ways went beyond the mere reading of each other's scholarship to truly interface with one another.

Much has happened since the initial meeting of the two national folklore societies in 2005. The following year, Professor Zhang organized and directed a conference at Willamette University in Salem, Oregon on Chinese daily ritual practices to which Dr. Kuili Liu, President of the China Folklore Society, led a delegation to participate and to confer with their American counterparts. The American Folklore Society, which established the Eastern Asian Folklore Section initiated by Juwen Zhang, has brought Chinese folklorists to the U. S. to take part in its annual conferences. Since 2007, mutual visits between the two Societies and between individual scholars have become routine. Forums on Intangible Cultural Heritage were held in 2013-2014: two in the US and two in China, each with participants from both countries. Between 2013 and 2016, an intercultural project on museums was developed; three Folklore and Film workshops were conducted, and a Summer Field School has been planned. Now a new joint museum project continues. At least 100 American folklorists have established relationships with their Chinese counterparts through visits and exchanges to China, while upwards of 200 folklorists from China have directly interacted with those from American and attended folklore society meetings in the US, thereby promoting the formation of cordial networks and meaningful dialogue.

By taking part in conferences, forums, and ceremonies together, by publishing in one another's journals, and by visiting each other's institutions, Chinese and American folklorists have learned much from one another. Folklorists in China often remark on the American methods and theoretical issues they have learned and applied to their own research. The Anglophone folklore circles have discovered the remarkable diversity and complexity of living traditions in the Sino folklore world.

There is more. Conference papers and scholarly articles are tangible outputs, and also to a great extent impersonal. However, the exchanges of people between institutions, the firsthand interactions of individuals, the communication of ideas between equals: these are personal and intangible. They are also a necessary component in the continued growth of our field of study.

This book, then, is about people's experiences in meeting and communicating firsthand with one another. In four sections about thirty Chinese and American folklorists address their own experiences in exchanges, their stories grouped according to common themes. The accounts reveal the process of contacting and interacting with one another, from text to person and from cordial visits to the lively exchange of ideas that energized participants from both countries. Their stories express feelings, values, and worldviews. As the editors contend, this kind of "metafolklore" is essential to developing our field of study, whether nationally or internationally and certainly on a personal level. The stories in this volume, like the texts, descriptions, and analyses of lore and traditions in books and journals, are a vital part the discipline of folkloristics. This volume is simultaneously scholarship and celebration.

(University of California, Los Angeles, Emeritus Former President of American Folklore Society)

2006年6月中国民俗学会会长刘魁立与美国民俗学会会长迈克尔·琼斯在美国俄勒冈州崴涞大学举办的"中国人日常礼仪实践研讨会"期间握手留念。China Folklore Society President Kuili Liu and American Folklore Society President Michael O. Jones shaking hands during "the Conference on Chinese Daily Ritual Practices" held at Willamette University, Salem, Oregon, June 2006. Photograph by Juwen Zhang.

序　言

刘魁立

张举文教授立意编辑这本文集，主题是中美民俗文化学界的学术交流，这让我联想到中国民俗学发展过程中整个国际联系的情况。举文教授执意要我为这部极有意义的大书作序，我诚惶诚恐，谨把个人在对外交流进程中的若干场景回忆起来，捧献给举文教授和各位读者，权当是代序吧。

20 世纪 50 年代以前，民俗学领域谈不上有组织的学术性国际交流。50 年代以后，在当时的社会主义阵营中，文化交流固属频繁，但是民俗学作为一个被冷落的学科，在这方面也没有什么让人特别瞩目的活动。一个时期的消歇之后，随着国家的改革开放，学术自身的发展获得了新的机遇，队伍日渐壮大，成果激增，国际交流日渐频繁。就我个人而言，在国际学术交流方面也有一些值得回忆的瞬间。

一个特殊的机缘，1955 年我被派往苏联莫斯科大学学习苏联的民间文艺学，有机会接触到一大批当时苏联最著名的民俗学方面的专家托卡列夫、米列金斯基、普洛普、契切洛夫、托尔斯泰、保加特廖夫、奇思托夫、保米兰采娃等。应该说苏联的民俗学和民间文艺学界的圈子并不大，他们相聚的机会却不少。我作为少有的国外研究生，被导师契切洛夫和保米兰采娃带领着去学习和旁听。我的民俗学知识基础多半是那个时候打下的，学习的心得潜移默化地在我后来的工作中有所体现。那个时候在苏联，也在一些场合介绍过中国口头传统和民间习俗的情况。例如在学校、在电台电视台讲解过中国的传说故事、中秋节和端午节。我发表在 50 年代、60 年代之交的两篇关于收集工作的文章，也是那个时候在苏联农村进行田野考察之后根据实践心得写成的。

进入 80 年代，为了总结智慧之光已经照亮的科学发展道路，包括中国学者和外国学者的探索历程，我开始研究欧洲民间文化研究史问题，并着手撰写这方面的系列论文。评论神话学派、流传学派等文章就是这样写成的。

为了认识和分析当代外国的五光十色的新理论、新观点，我认为有必要以简捷的办法和较快的速度追视其历史，明了其根源，这样才不至于在这些新学说的炫目的光彩面前感到困惑莫解。于是，1985 年开始，我策划主编了一套《原始文化名著译丛》，希望能把欧洲民间文化研究最基本的理论著作介绍给国人，尽快填补这一空白，免去学人再在二三流著作上花费更多的精力和时间。我希望我国学界能在较短时间内迎头赶上，充分利用我国的优越条件，做出我们出色的贡献，在广泛的国际学术对话中发出更高更强的声音。

策划和组织《原始文化》和《金枝》等一系列名著的翻译，花去我很大精力，但我觉得是值得的。我还认为，我有责任把自己关于这些著作的认识和分析陈述出来，供读者参考。《泰勒和他的〈原始文化〉》与《论〈金枝〉》等文章写出后便以序言的形式刊印在各部著作之前。

80年代初，日本民俗学界由臼田甚五郎带队，日本民俗学界以及汉学研究界的知名学者悉数来华参访，由此开始了两国之间的学术交流。随后，我和王松先生组团回访，在东京、大阪等地进行学术交流，关敬吾先生亲自参会，听取我们关于中国民俗学会、中国民俗学的学术报告。以后的交往就日渐频繁。1985年，在庆祝《卡列瓦拉》成书一百五十周年的时候，我不仅在中国对外友协的庆祝会上作了报告，还在赫尔辛基作了报告，为此获得了芬兰政府颁发的银质奖章。1988年，我在南斯拉夫作《关于今日中国的民间歌手》的报告，在芬兰作关于《中国民俗学发展成就》的报告。此外，多次赴俄罗斯莫斯科、埃利斯塔、乌兰乌德、赤塔等地以及芬兰、冰岛、南斯拉夫、匈牙利、韩国、日本等国和我国台湾地区参加国际学术会议，发表论文，就民间文学问题进行学术交流。

1994年，我与日本、韩国口头传统研究领域最著名的学者稻田浩二、崔仁鹤两位教授，共同创立了亚细亚民间叙事学会，为研究东亚民间故事传统搭建了一个交流平台，我曾多年担任会长和中国方面的负责人。不包括特别会议，三国轮流召开了十余届学术年会。在多次年会上，我都有研究论文发表。《民间叙事的生命树》一文引起了三国学者的特别注意。稻田浩二教授曾经对这篇论文给予了极高的评价，开玩笑说，"朝闻道，夕死可矣"。会后还来信说："我在11月7日研究生的课上给学生们介绍了您发表的论文《民间叙事的生命树》，同时与大家一起学习。我已经拜读过好几次了，每次都有新的发现和该学习的地方。"我自知，这一研究成果为中国民间故事形态研究仅仅提供了一种范式，对其内在规律的深层挖掘还不够，还有许多问题等待进一步深入探讨。在两个世纪之交，我曾有近一年的时间受日本斯拉夫研究中心之邀，研究俄罗斯北方民间文学传统问题。当时同在的还有美国、俄罗斯、加拿大、匈牙利等国的俄罗斯问题专家，大家通用俄语，交流切磋愉快而有效。2001年初，我在形态学研究最发达的俄罗斯，在由米列金斯基和涅克留多夫主持的高级讲座中作了《民间叙事的生命树》的学术报告。当时在场的还有李福清等学者。

在苏联解体之后，我除了继续保持着和俄罗斯科学院高尔基世界文学研究所、莫斯科人文大学的紧密联系之外，还把在苏联时代举全国学术界的力量完成的一件重要文化工程《世界文学史》介绍给中国。经我请求，当时的世界文学研究所所长把版权无偿转让书交给了我。我和外国文学研究所前所长吴元迈作为主编，该书2014年在上海文艺出版社出版发行，共计8大卷16册。苏联解体之后，我曾经担任独联体各国民间文学协作委员会的学术委员会顾问。另外，我现在还担任俄罗斯科学院《传统文化》杂志的编委会委员。

国家之间的交流，是靠领袖互访，是靠政治、经济、外交、军事等方面的协议来完成的。而学术交流，则是靠不同国家学者群体的学术观点的介绍和借鉴来完成的，体现在翻译介绍、交流互访、国际学术会议等多种形式的交流来完成的。

进入21世纪，我主持中国民俗学会领导工作期间，经学会同仁以及美国张举文教授的共同努力，与美国民俗学会建立了组织联系。此后，两国的学术交流纳入了正常的轨道，增多了互访，有了一个交流的机制和平台。

近三十年，一大批中青年学者在对外文化交流方面发挥了特别积极的作用，成绩卓著。他们不仅是国际学术交流方面的文化使者，同时也是中国民俗学界的才俊、精英。例如，本书编者张举文和宋俊华，参与本书撰稿的朝戈金和高丙中等，以及在国内外生活和工作的民俗学者巴莫曲布嫫、董晓萍、黄永林、叶涛、何彬、简涛、康保成、纳日碧力戈、王晓葵、尹虎彬等。由他们所组成的多维度的网络联系着世界各国的民俗学界，形成一支学术大军，互相学习、借鉴，推进着人类民间文化的探索和研究，唱响着人类智慧的颂歌。

在所有学者的个人交往中，有非常多的让人心动的故事和让当事者永远难忘的场景。在这些故事和场景当中，有那么多闪光的思维碰撞，激发彼此。后来这些交流的火花点燃起他们创作的激情，使他们的文章、使他们的创意隐含着国际对话的精神。国际学术交流不是一种大家参与的合影，而是彼此的敬重、心声的互映、智慧的交换。如果把每个学者、每一个学派的学术贡献看成是人类文化历史的一个印痕，那么，国际交流作为共享、共进的过程，其结果将是世界民俗学界的发展和繁荣。

我衷心祝愿中美两国民俗学界的学术交流日益繁盛，促进两国人民的友谊长存！

（本序作者为中国社会科学院研究员，中国民俗学会前会长）

Prologue

Kuili Liu

This collection of essays focuses on Sino-US folkloristic communication, but I could not help associating the topic with the development of Chinese folkloristics against the international background. Professor Juwen Zhang has designed this significant volume, and urged me to write a preface for it. I felt overwhelmed, as well as honored. I humbly present to him and the readers, as a prologue, some recollections of my involvements in international exchanges.

Prior to the 1950s, there was no organized world-wide communication in the field of folklore studies. Although there were frequent cultural exchanges among the socialist countries after the 1950s, folkloristics was a forgotten discipline. With the Opening-up and Reform in China in the 1980s, Chinese academic communication with the outside world has broadened and intensified. An increasingly strong team of folklorists in China has not only made tremendous progress in defining and developing the discipline, but also had made a great contribution to the world of folkloristics. Some of my own memories in this regard may be worth mentioning.

In 1955, a special opportunity brought me to Moscow University to study Russian folkliterature and arts. I was able to learn from and meet with many famous folklorists including S. A. Tokarev, E. M. Meletinsky, V. Propp, V. Chicherov, N. I. Tolstoy, P. G. Bogatyrev, K. V. Chistov, and E. V. Pomerantseva. At that time the circle of folklore and folk literature in Russia was not big, but the folklorists met frequently. As one of the few foreign graduate students, I was brought by my advisors, Dr. Chicherov and Dr. Pomerantseva, to meetings. I gained most of my folkloristic knowledge during that time, which was reflected in my later works. I also had opportunities to introduce some Chinese oral traditions and folk customs through local radio and TV stations and schools. Two of my articles about fieldwork, published in the early 1960s, were the result of my experience in the rural areas in Russia.

In order to better understand our disciplinary history, I began early in the 1980s to intensively examine European history of folk culture studies, and eventually published my results on myths and related schools of thought. With similar intention, that is, to find a shortcut to sort out this complex history of ideas and introduce it to Chinese scholars, I began, in 1985, to design and edit the series, *Translations of Famous Studies on Primitive Cultures*. I hoped that Chinese scholars could catch up with the rest of the world in a short time, make unique contributions, and proudly present their strong and clear voices in international academic discourse.

Designing and editing such a series, which included such masterpieces as *Primitive Culture* by Edward Tylor and *The Golden Bough* by James Frazer, took a great deal of my time and energy. I believed that the effort expended was worthwhile, and that I had a responsibility to state my own views about those works to Chinese readers. My articles, "Tylor and his *Primitive Culture*" and "On *The Golden Bough*," were published as prefaces to those translations.

In the early 1980s, the Sino-Japan folkloristic communication began with a delegation from Japan to China led by Dr. Usuda Jingoro. Subsequently, Mr. Song Wang and I led a Chinese delegation to Tokyo and Osaka, Japan. Dr. Seki Keigo, a respected leading folklorist in Japan, attended one of my presentations about the China Folklore Society and the development of Chinese folklore studies. Thereafter the communication increased in scale and frequency. In 1985, at the celebration of the 150th anniversary of the *Kalevala* in Finland, I gave a speech in Helsinki, and I was awarded a Silver Medal by the Finnish government. I also gave a similar talk at a celebratory event in China. In 1988, I gave a talk on "The Folk Singers in China" in Yugoslavia, and a talk on "The Achievements of Chinese Folkloristic Development" in Finland. In addition, I made multiple visits to Russia, Finland, Iceland, Yugoslavia, Hungary, South Korea, and Japan attending international conferences on folk literature.

In 1994, Japanese folklorist Koji Inada, Korean folklorist Choi In-ryul and I launched the Asian Folk Narrative Studies Society as a forum of exchange on folktale studies in East Asia. This society has held annual meetings ever since, in addition to special conferences. I was honored as the President representing China for many years. My article, The Life Tree of Folk Narrative (2010), attracted great attention in East Asia. Professor Inada commented on it, citing Confucius's story, and said, "Now that I learned the Dao in the morning, I will not regret to die in the evening." In one of Inada's letters to me, he said, "I introduced your article, 'The Life Tree of Folk Narrative,' to my graduate students, and studied it with them. I have read it several times, and each time I made new discoveries." This article has provided a basic model for the morphological study of Chinese folktales. At the turn of this century, I was invited to go to the Center for Slavic Studies in Japan to work on Northern Russian folk literature. At the Center, scholars were from several countries: the US, Russia, Canada, and Hungary. Everyone was speaking Russian. It was a very pleasant and effective exchange. In early 2001, I presented my work on "The Life Tree of Folk Narrative" in Russia, where morphology is studied at the highest level. The lecture was chaired by Dr. S. Neklyudov, and Dr. V. L. Riftin, the best-known Sinologist in Russia, was among the attendees.

After the disintegration of the Soviet Union, I still maintained close contact with the scholars and Institute of World Literature in Russia, and introduced the monumental Russian academic project, *World Literature History* to Chinese readers. At my request, the Russian authors gave us the copyright for free to translate their works. Eventually, after more than ten years of hard work, we published the series in 16 volumes in 2014. I am still on the editorial board of the journal *Traditional Culture*, published by the Russian Academy of Sciences.

The diplomatic relationship among countries depends upon their leaders through political, economic, diplomatic, and military agreements. However, academic communication depends upon sharing different opinions by scholars from different countries, and is reflected through mutual translations and visits, as well as international conferences.

Entering the 21st century, I was elected the President of China Folklore Society. During my tenure (2002-2010), with the efforts from other CFS colleagues and Professor Juwen Zhang in the US, CFS and the American Folklore Society established an institutional relationship. Afterwards, the exchange between Chinese and American folklorists became routinized, and their increasing mutual visits have built a mechanism and a platform for communication.

In the past thirty years, a large group of middle-aged and younger folklorists have played a unique positive role in China's international outreach. Theyare, to name only a few, Qubumo Bamo, Xiaoping Dong, Yonglin Huang, Tao Ye, Bin He, Tao Jian, Baocheng Kang, Naribilige, Xiaokui Wang, Hubin Yin, and others, as well as the editors and contributors to this collection. They are not only cultural ambassadors in international interactions, but also the main force of Chinese folkloristics. They have built a network connecting folklorists all over the world.

The individual and personal experiences of scholarly cross-cultural exchange presented in this volume includes many touching and unforgettable stories and moments. During those clashing or sparkling moments, scholars' ideas and thoughts are generated. Those sparks will later ignite their passion and will eventually be reflected in their writings and in international discourses. Engaging in international academic communication is not like taking a group picture. Rather it consists of the genuine exchange of respect, ideas, and wisdom. If each scholar's ideas and each school of thought can be seen as separate footprints in the history of human cultural development, then international communication is the process of connecting and sharing them, and it will lead the discipline to prosperity all over the world.

I sincerely wish continued prosperity in Sino-US folkloristic exchanges, and a long friendship between the two peoples!

(China Academy of Social Sciences
Former President of China Folklore Society
Translation by Juwen Zhang)

亚民俗：学科发展的有机动力

张举文

I. 亚民俗：民俗研究中不可忽视的学者个人角色

民俗学者了解和阐释的不应该只是"他者"，而同样重要的是去关注"自己"，讲述自己的故事。毕竟，民俗学者也是"民"（folk，即广义的"人；民众"people），正如乔治斯和琼斯（Georges and Jones 1980）曾提出的，民俗学研究是"人研究人"，所以，民俗学者有必要"记录我们自己"（谢尔曼/Sherman 2011［1998］）。这也是构建一个学科共同体的必要和有益的一部分。

因此，本文集记录的便是中国和美国部分民俗学者在相互了解和认识的过程中，在这个特殊"田野"、特殊时代所经历和反思的"故事"。有理由相信，作为学者，只有建立在共同认可的概念和逻辑上，才可能有学术对话；只有建立在互相了解世界观和价值观的基础上，才可能有和谐的交流；只有建立在平等基础上的交流，才可以有助于人类文化的多元发展。民俗学正是因为关注不同文化传统，鼓励和协调人类文化的多元交流，才成为"人文研究的核心"（Wilson 1988：157）。

"亚民俗"这一概念首先由邓迪斯界定和使用，"指的是有关民俗的民俗学评述"（Dundes 1966：505）。他强调的是对有关民俗的"评论"，而不是有关的"思想"或"概念"等层面的意义（Lemon 1983：191n）。当然，这个概念可以被理解为"有关民俗的民俗"，并作为"口头文学批评"研究"文本""亚文本"和"语境"的重要定理（Narayan 1995：244）。半个世纪过去了，虽然邓迪斯这个概念被偶尔提到（Lichman 1982，Shenhar 1987，Narayan 1995，Brown 2005），但这个概念没得到足够的重视（Lemon 1983：191）。其实，可以公正地说，这个概念对民俗学的分析方法有着"极大的推进意义"（Tangherlini 2005：218）。

作为民俗研究的必要部分，亚民俗体现的是学者对所研究的民俗的一种"宏观"影响。在具体的民俗事项研究中，亚民俗的意义和作用体现在各自的概念上，例如，在"言语民族志"（Hymes 1964）的研究中的"亚语言交流"（Hays 1973，France 1976，Briggs 1993，1984，Wilce 1995，Berger and Del Negro 2002），在叙事研究中的"亚叙事"（Hill 1990，

Cunningham 1991，Ciosain 2004），在影视与民俗研究中的"影视民俗"（Zhang 2005），等等。其实，这些都是对民俗活动中的"亚文本"（texture）（Dundes 1980 ［1964］）和"乘启关系"或"语境"（Ben-Amos 1971）的强调，是"表演论"（Bauman 1977）关注的，也是早期学科的"文本"为核心的范式所忽视的。但是，还有必要将这种"乘启关系"从表演本身扩大到更广泛的社会和文化以及历史的"乘启关系"（Ben-Amos 1993）。这便是"亚民俗"所包含的意义。

在此，我们借用并扩延这个概念，用"亚民俗"指那些民俗活动的参与者（实践者和研究者）有关自己所参与的活动的感受和反思的交流，从而使自己的行为和思想不仅成为研究该民俗传统的必要语境成分，而且也成为该民俗传统的传承机制的一部分。其实，民俗传统传承的规律始终是：（各种）参与者本身就是在传承中创造新的传统。虽然可以说没有民俗研究者的参与，民俗活动会以其自身的规律延续，但是，一旦有了研究者的参与，该民俗传统所受到的外力影响就绝不可忽视。曾几何时，研究者把"自己"与所研究的对象分隔开来，形成了一个时代的"民族志"风格，而那也正是"写文化"（Clifford and Marcus 1986）所批判的、缺失"自我反思"的殖民时代的学风。说白了，那就是学者不把自己当作"民"的做法。

无疑，理性的学术交流与感性的人情世故及其社会背景是不可分隔的。学者之间在非观点问题上的交流也是基于理性的对人的全面认识。民俗学作为学科在中国（和美国）已有百年历史了，但是，直到1980年代，中国民俗学界一直是以翻译"文本"来"引进"各种理论方法。而在此后三十多年中，中国民俗学者开始"请人"和"交朋友"。由此而获得的不仅是一份"人情"，而更重要的是对一种思想观点的来龙去脉的全面了解，再也不是干巴巴的文字了。同时，他们也开启了"走出去"的时代。这期间，中美民俗学者有了日益加深的交流。从中，也许中国方面对美国方面的影响才刚开始，但是，美国方面对中国方面的影响可以说难以衡量，无论是在教材的编写、学科理论和方法的构建，还是在中国民俗学会和民俗学者的日常行为上。总之，经过面对面交流之后的学术观点对其个人和学科的影响有时是难以做量性评判的，但会点点滴滴浸入整个世界观和学术观的演变和发展中。因此，关注亚民俗将有益于对学科发展的历程的认识和反思。

Ⅱ. 中美民俗研究交流史上的几个节点

从1980年代起，中美民俗学交流开启了一个新阶段。而在进入21世纪后，更是走上了前所未有的新时代，在多个层面都充分体现了双方交流的密度、频度和深度，例如，两个学会的互动，学者个人之间的交往，高校民俗学项目点之间的交流，双方召集和参与的各种会议的规模，以及双方的出版物中有关题目的文章数量，等等。的确，中美民俗学交流开始了全面和健康的发展。但是，有必要将这三十多年中美民俗学者的交流置于更大的历史背景中来认识。

1)"去中国"时间线上的几个重要节点

将马可·波罗(Marco Polo 1254—1324)在 13 世纪所讲述故事作为"西方"(指欧美)对中国民俗生活的兴趣的开始似乎是可行的。在其后的两个世纪里,那些故事激发了无数幻想和历险,最终开启了一个新的时代:传教士与中国。最突出的当然是利玛窦(Matteo Ricci 1552—1610)。他在中国的经历,包括他的日志,通过在欧洲的出版,掀起了基督世界对中国传教的高潮,但最终也引发了中国皇帝与梵蒂冈教皇的互不妥协,导致了此后三百余年的"礼仪之争"。传教士们对中国的记述对西方的思想影响,包括对哲学家和数学家莱布尼兹的影响,也是不可忽视的。而今天在北京的数百个耶稣会传教士的墓地似乎还在讲述着那个时代的故事。到了 19 世纪,以理雅各(James Legge 1814—1897)为代表的许多传教士翻译了大量的中国古代文献,包括《诗经》(两千多年前民歌搜集的典范)。当然,那些经过文人整理的民间文学和诗歌也同样激发了西方的想象。例如,唐朝的诗歌就激发了音乐家马勒(Gustav Mahler 1860—1910)的创作(如《大地之歌》),进而影响了西方音乐自身的发展。

那些更直接描述中国民俗生活的著作对西方形成有关中国的定势思维起了至关重要的作用。这个时代的代表性人物及其作品是美国传教士明恩博(Arthur Smith 1845—1932)的《中国人的人性》和《中国的农村生活》(或译《中国乡村生活》)。有趣的是,前一本书近些年出现多个中文译本,如《中国人德行》《中国人的性情》《中国人的气质》《中国人的性格》。在此,需要指出,大量的传教士对中国民俗生活的描述和阐释的确有其客观描述的一面,但我们有必要去想想那些信息是从哪里来的(是普通百姓吗?),也必须注意到其描述和阐释的动机是什么(是对多元文化的平等认识吗?)。反之亦然。百多年前有关中国的各种故事传说和记述这些年来不断翻印,在英文世界里继续对儿童和大众产生极大的影响(如,菲尔德 1885,1894;皮特曼 1910,1919)。这也正是我们今天特别关注的问题,即文化交流和学术交流中的出发点,以及话语权问题。

直到 1930 年代,非传教士的记录,或者说学者式的研究才开始出现。当然,这并不意味着传教士式的(思想)模式的彻底结束,因为其影响还很大。这也是今天的中国在努力的方向:从被内化的"殖民"心态走出来,发现自己的文化之根,重建文化自信。

从民俗学意义来说,美国的"民俗学者、汉学家"(Greenway 1960:153)詹姆森(R. D. Jameson 1896—1959)于 1920—30 年代到中国的学术交流,例如,在北京国立清华大学担任教授,发表《中国民俗学三讲》(1932,1987)开启了美国民俗学者到中国进行民俗学研究和交流的新时代。尽管之前美国的卡林(Stewart Culin)对中国的游戏民俗很关注,但他的研究主要是基于对美国的华裔群体的考察,只到中国搜集过一些博物馆藏品。在 1930 年代中期,艾伯华(Wolfram Eberhard 1901—1989),作为从德国移民到美国的民俗学家,对中国民间故事的田野调查,以及之后对中国文化的研究,不仅影响了美国民俗学界,也培养了一批对中国文化思想有深刻研究的学者(如艾兰 Sarah Allan,其对中国古代的宇宙观和信仰的研究非常有助于民俗学研究)。

从 20 世纪 40 年代到 70 年代,世界性的战争和中国的特殊历史阻隔了中国学者与外界的交流,也停滞了内部的学科建设。值得一提的是短暂但有意义的《民俗学志》。该刊 1942 年由德国人叶德礼(Matthias Eder)神父创办。由于战争,该刊物几年后便搬到了日本,后来改名为《亚洲民俗研究》(Asian Folklore Studies),再后来改为现在的《亚洲民族学》(Asian Ethnology)。该刊物激发了一批中国学者,包括赵卫邦(Chao Wei-pang 1942, 1943),去关注中国近代民俗学的发展。

直到 80 年代,中国的大门才真正地打开,中国民俗学者和世界各地的民俗学者才有机会进行交流,包括从其他学科角度对民俗的关注。例如,研究中国俗文学的白素贞(1981 年)较早来到中国,与北京大学的汪景寿和段宝林等学者交往,跟踪记录金声伯和孙书筠等曲艺家的表演。类似的还有马克·本德尔(见本文集)的故事。再如,丁乃通(1978—1985 年,四次)和邓迪斯(1990 年)受邀访问中国。他们分别推动了中国民俗学者对故事类型、神话等的研究。这些美国民俗学者带去的不仅是学术思想,更是一份平等交流的心态(见李扬、陈建宪、户晓辉的故事)。同时,诸多学者开始了不同程度的交流。至 2000 年,格拉西也访问了北京大学。再后来,便是本文集所记录的故事。

2)"留学海外"时间线上的几个重要节点

在此无需赘述中国历史上"走出去"的民俗文化交流历史,而只需几个例子就足以说明民俗交流的丰富多彩。从两千多年前的"徐福徐贵东渡日本"的故事,到唐朝(618—907)的鉴真和尚在日本建立"唐招提寺"和玄奘去西天取经,再到明朝(1368—1644)的郑和下西洋以及之后的几个世纪的大批"下南洋"移民,再到 19 世纪到美洲的"苦力"劳工,直至今天持续的"留学"和"小留学生"浪潮,中国的民俗生活与移民一起融入了各国文化之中,同时又反射回中国,影响着今天中国人对自己的传统的认知和传承。

其实,"民俗"一词,虽是汉字,却经过日本文化概念化后再被中国精英引介到中国的术语。那也正是 20 世纪初中国精英们发现了可以救国的"民族主义"及其最佳载体的"民俗"后,所倾力要灌输到国民教育中的思想。(这与今天的"非遗"浪潮有许多相似点。)这也说明了"民俗学"何以诞生于北京大学这样的精英摇篮的原因。曾经担任北京大学校长的蔡元培(1868—1940)就对欧洲民族学情有独钟,因而鼓励北京大学的民俗歌谣运动,并在全国展开了"走向民间"的活动。留学美国的吴文藻(1901—1985)对"社会学"的关注以及留学美国的江绍原(1898—1983)对"迷信"等民俗的关注,都成为当代中国民俗学的根基。

20 世纪的前三十年里,中国知识分子在爱国救国的追求中,将"民族主义""民俗学"与"社会学""民族学"一同介绍到中国。此后,欧洲的浪漫主义思潮与美国的实用主义思想都影响了之后一个世纪的中国社会和人文学科的思维范式。当时,一批精英留学欧洲、美国和日本,不断翻译引介新的思想。例如,日本的柳田国男的民俗学思想就被介绍到中国。欧洲"进化论"和"自繇(由)"等思想也被(严复)介绍进来。许多民俗学著作也被翻译介绍到中国。从事这些工作的几乎都是留学海外的知识分子。例如,留学菲律宾的林惠祥译介了英国的博尔尼（C. Burne）所著的《民俗学手册》，留学法国的杨堃译介了范热内普的"过渡礼仪"概念，周作人和刘半农等译介了丹麦的安徒生童话，周桂笙和魏以新等译介了德国的格林童话，等等。这期间的一个特点是针对文本的互动，而不是面对面的互动。

这期间，几个重要的节点是：1922 年在北京大学创办的《歌谣周刊》，1928 年在中山大学创办的《民俗周刊》。随后，在几个大学都出现了类似"民俗学研究会"的组织。另外还有上面提到的《民俗学志》。这些刊物和组织鼓舞着一批中国民俗学者在艰难的战乱期间坚持做民俗调查，不仅积累了珍贵的民俗记录，更延续了民俗学这个学科的种子。

这些历史的积淀也使得 1980 年代的中国民俗学重建如雨后春笋，迅速成长。从此开始了中国民俗学者与国外民俗学者面对面交流的时代，包括越来越多的学者走出国门。但是，直到 2006 年，中国民俗学会会长刘魁立率领代表团（包括副会长高丙中、理事萧放和陈泳超）首次赴美参加民俗学会议，才奠定了与美国民俗学会的机制化交流。随后，在 2007 年，双方学会进行了互访（叶涛秘书长因未得到签证而没能随团访问美国），开启了多方位的互动，即本文集所讲述的故事（见高丙中、萧放、罗仪德的故事）。

Ⅲ. 开启真正的民俗学交流，展望更丰富多彩的未来

正如前面所述，良好的学术交流要基于平等的人与人的交往，对一个学者个人的了解和对其理论思想的了解同样有意义。可喜的是，这样的新时代之门已经打开。例如，在过去的三十多年里，中国建立了几十个民俗学硕士和博士学位点，其中的每一个学生都可以轻易说出所了解的十几个甚至更多的美国民俗学家的名字及其思想。但是，美国方面对中国同行的了解则无法相比。这一点美国同行也有所注意或呼吁。比如，在美国各个民俗学学位点中，有关中国或亚洲的民俗课程寥寥无几。罗伯特·巴龙在他 2008 年第一次到北京与中国民俗学者交流时便感叹道："在这儿，民俗学者在探讨高深理论，从事的是批评民俗学，而这些很不幸还没被翻译到美国。鉴于近年民俗学理论匮乏，中国民俗学者的理论概念需要被介绍到美国。"

对中国民俗学者来说，真正的学术交流是在建立了自己的根、体现出自己的特长之后而进行的平等对话。中国民俗学者通过近三十年对自己传统的自觉，吸收了来自不同学科和理论背景的思想，并通过非遗运动，开始展露出自己的学科生机。而美国民俗学在近年与中国的交流中也已经获得了很多新的力量。例如，越来越多的民俗学学科点开始有来自中国的学生和访问学者，各种学术会议都有来自中国的案例分析和观点，这些无疑都有助于开阔美国民俗学者的视野，也同样有助于中国民俗学者成为有国际视野的新型学者。

在此，我们可以用邓迪斯通过他的中国经历所提出的希望来看看我们所取得的成就和要走的路有多远。当然，丁乃通在通过多次与民俗学者的面对面和书信交流中也表达了类似的感受，并为他自己能帮助培养新一代民俗学者的成长和参加翻译交流而感到欣慰（详见刘守华在本文集中讲述的故事）。

邓迪斯在从1990年的中国行回到美国后不久，便在《美国民俗学会通讯》上以"有关中国的民俗研究"为题，呼吁学会成员以邮寄民俗学出版物的方式帮助中国同行了解外界。他写道："在中国，我们所见过的许多民俗学者和学生给我们留下深刻印象。他们极其渴望更多地了解欧美的民俗理论与方法……我希望美国民俗学者能够给他们寄些书籍，我敢肯定，他们会很感激的……很难表达他们是多么如饥似渴地盼望更多地与西方接触……我之前根本没意识到在中国有那么多活跃的民俗学者……"（另见陈建宪在本文集中的记述）

邓迪斯简单描述了他所访问的三个民俗学点及所会见的学者：华中师范大学的陈建宪（当时翻译了他的《世界民俗学》）、北京师范大学的张紫晨和钟敬文、华东师范大学的陈勤建和上海文联的吴宗西，也提供了三个民俗学点的地址。他强调道，"美国民俗学会会员捐赠书籍的慷慨之举定会受到他们的赞赏"。那时，互联网刚开始在美国使用，在中国还不为人所知。

邓迪斯在写给《世界民俗学》（1990）的中文版序言说，"民俗学研究已逐渐成为一个跨学科和国际性的学科领域"，而在《民俗解析》（2005）的中文版序言中则特别强调了"民俗学（有关民俗的研究）真正是一门国际性学科"。在1990年，邓迪斯感到遗憾的是"中国的民俗学家至今还没有参加民俗学研究方法的国际间协作，同时欧美民俗学家也不知道中国民俗学家们所取得的成就"。大约十年后，邓迪斯依然在期待着，"中国民俗学家们做两件事情。首先是就相互感兴趣的话题更主动地参与到民俗学家的国际对话中去。其次是从民俗的收集和记录转移到分析和解释的批评场域"。在两个序言中，邓迪斯都提到，中国民俗学者可以芬兰和爱尔兰民俗学者为例，要"发表两次"自己的成果以便有更多的读者。同时，他感叹道："可悲的事实是，西方民俗学家们相对极少向中国民俗学研究的世界敞开的窗口。"

倘若邓迪斯看到今天中国民俗学者之间的交流，他一定会感到些许欣慰，但他一定还会希望我们的交流要从广度发展到深度。今天，我们的面对面和借助互联网的交流已经成为日常。当我们在"搜集"的同时走向"阐释"，我们还要确知我们的世界观与方法论出自哪里，要将我们的心态直面目标：在相互分享文化与观点中互相学习，做到平等理解和尊重。

进入21世纪，中美民俗学交流从个人或单向的交流转向了机制性和多向性的互动。双方的民俗学会无疑至关重要，但学者们的个人努力是必不可少的。这其中便有着无数有趣和有意义的"亚民俗"故事。同时，在国际性的学术交流中，中国学者的声音越来越清晰，观点越来越成体系。例如，2015年《亚洲民族学》的特刊是中美学者共同对中国民俗学学科成长与成熟的反思，2015年《美国民俗学刊》刊发了首个有关美国华裔和亚裔民俗的特刊，2016年《美国民俗学刊》的有关神话特刊突出了中国的学术成果，2017年《西部民俗》发表了有关中国非遗的特刊。另外，还有中美学者合作的英文版的学术和普及书籍，如杨利慧、安德明、特纳合著的《中国神话手册》（2008）等。

总之，在过去的十多年里，中美民俗学界的交流为各自的学科发展都注入了极大的生机。作为记录日常生活的学科，民俗学不仅要记录"他者"，也更要记录"自己"。因此，记录这十年来学会、学科以及自己的学术发展，对双方民俗学今后的发展无疑会有益处。一个学科，如果没有自己学科发展史中的"亚民俗"，就不是一个完整健康的学科。

  这本"亚民俗"故事集便是在延续目前中美民俗学界的广泛交流，使个人的故事为学科发展史注入有生机的血肉。这里仅收入了部分民俗学者的故事，还有不少有着亲身经历和感人故事的学者这次没来得及写下自己的故事。相信这样的故事会继续讲下去，也希望今后有关的亚民俗也会与学术研究一样得到延续发展，将亚民俗作为民俗研究的重要组成部分。从这层意义来说，中美民俗学者之间的"人研究人"的亚民俗交流，为民俗研究的"人研究人"打下了良好基础。

Metafolklore: An Organic Development of the Discipline

Juwen Zhang

I. Metafolklore: The Inseparable Folklorists' Personal Roles in Folklore Studies

Folklorists should not only try to understand and interpret the "other," but also to document their "self" (or themselves) by telling their own stories about their participation in folklore events with the "other." In the past, in the field of "ethnography," researchers tended to separate themselves from the "other" people being described or studied. Such efforts, based on the colonialist mentality, were criticized for their lack of "reflexivity" in "writing culture" in the post-colonial period (Clifford and Marcus 1986). Simply put, it was the era when folklorists did not consider themselves as "folk." We have now come to understand that folklorists are also the "folk" ("common people," or "people" in the broad sense) and that folkloristics is about "people studying people" (Georges and Jones 1980). Therefore, as folklorists, we should "document ourselves" (Sherman 1998).

In this volume, we present the "stories" and "experiences" reflected upon by a group of folklorists from China and the United States. Some of them have conducted fieldwork in each other's country since the 1970s and 1980s. It is reasonable for scholars to believe that academic discourse can be established only on the basis of mutually recognized concepts and logic; meaningful communication is possible only on the basis of mutually understood worldviews and values; and the harmonious development of diverse human cultures can happen only when all are considered equal. Folkloristics emerges out of "the very center of humanistic study" (Wilson 1988: 157), precisely because it pays attention to diverse cultural traditions and encourages and mediates communication among them.

The concept of "metafolklore" was first defined and used by Alan Dundes to mean "the folkloristic statements about folklore" (1966: 505). What he emphasized was the practitioners' "comments" on folklore, but not the "ideas" and the "concepts" within the practice of folklore (Lemon 1983: 191n). In general, metafolklore is understood as "folklore about folklore," and is important for studying "text," "subtext," and "context" in "oral literary criticism" (Narayan 1995: 244) and in the text-centered folkloristic approach. Over the past half century or so, the concept of metafolklore has not been given sufficient attention (Lemon 1983: 191), although it is mentioned occasionally (Lichman 1982, Shenhar 1987, Narayan 1995, Brown 2005). Despite this relative lack of attention, it is fair to say that metafolklore has enabled a "significant advance" in folkloristics (Tangherlini 2005: 218).

As a component of folkloristics, metafolklore reveals the "micro-influence" of practitioners upon the folklore studied. Different aspects of metafolklore are appropriate to specific kinds of folklore studies. We talk about "metacommunication" or "metalanguage" (Hays 1973; France 1976; Briggs 1993, 1984; Wilce 1995; Berger and Del Negro 2002) in the "ethnography of speaking" or the "ethnography of communication" (Hymes 1964); we use the term "metanarrative" (Hill 1990, Cunningham 1991, Ciosain 2004) in narrative studies; and "filmic folklore" in film and folklore studies (Zhang 2005). In fact, some aspects of metafolklore have gone beyond Dundes' original definition, including his concept of "texture" (Dundes 1980 [1964]), or "subtext," and "context" (Ben-Amos 1971), even the "performance-centered" approach (Bauman 1977), with the result that the immediate context of a folklore event has to be examined within a broader social, cultural, and historical "context" (Ben-Amos 1993). This is what metafolklore means in this collection.

We therefore wish to borrow and extend the concept of metafolklore *to refer to the mutual communication among participants—researchers and practitioners alike—in folklore events in such a way that their own experiences and reflections become not only part of the context of the event, but also part of the mechanism of the transmission and transformation of the folklore tradition.* Although some may believe that a folklore tradition develops with its own internal logic, without being influenced in any way by the outsider (e.g., the researcher/observer of that tradition), in fact, folklore in practice assumes that all participants in any folklore event play a part in its transmission, while, at the same time, are part of the creation of a new tradition. The impact of the researcher's participation in the event must no longer be ignored.

Modern folkloristics has a history of over one hundred years in Europe, the US and China. Throughout most of this history, perhaps until the 1960s, folklorists were engaged in text-centered study. Texts were translated or interpreted either from "ancient" or "foreign" sources. This textual emphasis was true for those who studied Chinese folklore either as Western missionaries or scholars, or as Chinese domestic folklorists. However, in the past thirty years, Chinese folklorists both have been inviting foreign folklorists to China to collaborate, and have been studying abroad.

These practices have helped establish a foundation for human exchange, and, equally important, a comprehensive understanding of the history of various ideas, that is, where certain ideas originated and in which direction they are now going. Departing from the "face-to-text" communication age, Chinese folklorists have now entered an era of "face-to-face" communication.

Chinese and American folklorists have strengthened their communication on a daily basis in the past three decades. During this period, the Chinese impact upon American folklore studieshas been minimal, if at all; the American impact upon Chinese folklore studies, while recognized, is difficult to measure, whether in the compilation of textbooks, constructions of theory and methodology in the discipline, or in the everyday activities carried out by the China Folklore Society and Chinese folklorists. By using the term "metafolklore" as we have here, we hope to capture the importance of cross-cultural scholarly exchanges in the development of the field.

II. A Few Key Turning Points of Sino-US Folkloristic Communication

In the 1980s, Sino-US folkloristic communication began a new era. Then, upon entering the 21st century, communication reached an unprecedented level in terms of the scale, frequency, and depth of interaction. This was the case between the two Societies, among individual scholars, between folklore programs, at the meetings held or attended by both Americans and the Chinese, and the number of publications produced on related topics. Indeed, Sino-US communication has developed to a comprehensive and healthy stage. To better understand the current situation, however, one must put these thirty years into an historical perspective.

1) "Going to China"

The West's (broadly speaking, Europe and the US) interest in Chinese folklife dates back to the travels of Marco Polo (1254-1324). Those travel stories inspired fantasies and adventures for the next three centuries, when Western missionaries arrived in China. The Jesuit Matteo Ricci (1552-1610) was certainly the most extraordinary foreign individual to enter China up until the early 20th century. His published experiences exerted a huge influence on both China and Europe and led to waves of missionary activity in China, which eventually led to an unresolvable argument—the "Chinese Rites Controversy"—between the Pope and Chinese Emperors that lasted nearly three hundred years. The massive number of writings by the missionaries, both positive and negative, on Chinese everyday life and thought shaped how the West "looked at" and "thought of" China and Chinese people, and the influence of the missionaries can be easily discerned even today. Historically, the philosopher and mathematician G. W. Leibniz (1646-1716), an influential European thinker, was influenced by the missionary records of Chinese language and thought. Today, hundreds of graves of Jesuit missionaries in the middle of Beijing remain a continual reminder of missionary influence. By the 19th century, numerous Chinese classics, including the *Book of Songs* (*Shijing*), the first collection of poems/songs/ballads from over two-thousand five-hundred years ago, were translated into European languages by missionaries. James Legge (1814-1897), the first Professor of Chinese at Oxford University, was, perhaps, the most productive among them. Of course, other genres of literature by Chinese writers were also introduced to the West and inspired many great Western writers, composers, and dramatists to create works based on Chinese literary and musical art. Two outstanding examples are Gustav Mahler (1860-1910) and Bertold Brecht (1898-1956). Gustav Mahler, who never visited China, composed "*Das Lied von der Erde*" (The Song of the Earth), based on poems by Li Bai (701-762) and music of the Tang Dynasty (618-905). Bertold Brecht's play, "The Caucasian Chalk Circle," was based on a 14th century Chinese mixed drama. In turn, these Western works influenced Chinese art.

Descriptions by missionaries of Chinese folklore and folklife played a key role in the creation of Western stereotypes of Chinese people. For example, the writings of an American missionary, Arthur Smith (1845-1932), *Chinese Characteristics* (1894) and *Village Life in China* (1899), were greatly influential. In the past twenty years in China at least four different versions of translations and reprints of Smith's works appeared. While many such descriptions might be partially accurate, one must ask: Were such descriptions complete enough to describe the subject? Who were the informants? Were they from common people? Further, we must also understand the standpoint from which this culture was described and interpreted: did the observer consider the observed culture "equal" to his? Unfortunately, those accounts of Chinese daily life from a hundred years ago, without historical context, are still being reprinted, with new illustrations. They still exert great influence on the children and general public today in the English speaking world (Fielde 1885, 1894; Pitman 1910, 1919), and are available through online sources. The question just given are precisely the questions we need to ask in paying attention to such reflexive metafolklore, that is, how researchers influence the continuity of a tradition and its practitioners (e.g., how they change their views about their own traditions and practices).

A new era of "academic" studies dawned in the 1930s. At the same time, the missionary "ethnographies" of the past were still influencing both academic and public spheres. What China has been attempting to accomplish since then is, precisely, to destroy the feelings of inferiority internalized by foreign powers, to rediscover its own cultural roots, and to restore its cultural self-confidence.

The beginning of academic communication between American and Chinese folklorists can be traced back to J. D. Jameson (1896-1959), who went to China as a folklorist and published many articles and entries on Chinese folklore. For example, his *Three Lectures on Chinese Folklore*

(1932) and over one hundred signed entries on China in the *Standard Dictionary of Folklore, Mythology, and Legend* (1950) (Greenway 1960), along with many publications in the *Journal of American Folklore* and *Western Folklore*, were a crucial beginning. Although Stewart Culin (1858-1929) also published many pieces on Chinese folklore (gaming, in particular), he collected the information mostly from Chinese American communities; he had little contact with China. In the mid-1930s, Wolfram Eberhard (1901-1989) lived in China for about two years, which laid a firm foundation for his scholarship on China's folklore (e. g., Chinese tale type index, ethnicity and folklore, and origins of Chinese culture), and his works influenced American folklore circles and Sinology for decades (e. g., his role in working with Paul Radin (Buccitelli 2017), his role in UC Berkeley training sinologists, like Sarah Allan whose work on ancient Chinese thought and life has influenced Chinese scholars).

China's special situation from the 1940s to the 1970s made Chinese academic communication with the outside, as well as within its own circle, impossible. What is worth mentioning is, despite the hiatus in academic communication, the journal *Folklore Studies* (*minsuxue zhi*) was launched in Beijing in 1942 by Father Matthias Eder of Germany. Due to China's internal conflicts, the journal was soon moved to Japan and was transformed from a multilingual journal to an English language one and renamed *Asian Folklore Studies*; this was later changed to the current *Asian Ethnology*. The journal inspired some Chinese folklorists, such as Wei-pang Chao (1942, 1943), to devote attention to the development of folklore studies in China.

In the 1980s China again opened its door to the world and enabled Chinese folklorists to have face-to-face communication with the West. It was this happy new era of the exchange of ideas that is the focus of this volume.

2) "Studying Abroad"

A few examples will suffice to prove the point that the history of Chinese "going abroad" and spreading their folklore and culture has been rich and colorful: 1) The story about the journey of Xu Fu and Xu Gui to Japan over two thousand years ago; 2) Two Tang Dynasty (618-907) Buddhist Monks: Jianzhen (688-763) to Japan and Xuanzang (c. 602-664), who walked from China to India and back (15 years); 3) Admiral Zheng He's seven expeditions to Southeast Asia, South Asia, and even East Africa during the Ming Dynasty (1368-1644); 4) The massive migration to Southeast Asia in the centuries following the Ming; 5) The "*coolies*" to South and North America in the 19th century; and 6) Today's wave of "studying abroad" among college students, and even secondary schoolers. During these waves of migration and folklore exchange, Chinese folklore was absorbed into many foreign cultures, while, at the same time, many "foreign" cultural elements became "Chinese."

In fact, the Chinese term "folklore" (*minsu*), was introduced from the Japanese *minzoku* by

Chinese exchange students studying in Japan at the turn of the 20th century. At that time, the Chinese educated elite found that the concept of "nationalism," represented best by media presentations of "folklore," could save their country from being colonized; thus the idea of nationalism through folklore was integrated throughout public education in China. This explains why "Chinese folkloristics" was created by the Chinese educated elite at Beijing (Peking) University. Cai Yuanpei (1868-1940), one of China's most brilliant and revolutionary educators and President of Beijing University (1917-1922), who supported the New Culture and May 4th Movements, founded Academia Sinica, and the Shanghai Conservatory of Music (formerly "National College of Music"). He was particularly keen on "ethnology" as a result of his studies in Europe. He thus encouraged the "ballad" (*geyao* collection) movement on campus, which eventually became a national campaign of "going to the people" to search for important items of folklore. The establishment of the journal *Ballads Weekly* (*Geyao Zhoukan*) at Beijing University in 1922 and the *Folklore Weekly* (*Minsu Zhoukan*) at Zhongshan (Sun Yat-sen) University in 1928 greatly helped expand the field. As a result, "folklore associations" were founded in several universities. Wu Wenzao's (1901-1985) interest in "sociology" and Jiang Shaoyuan's (1898-1983) interest in "folklore" were also influential, as were Kunio Yanagita's ideas on national folklore and European ideas of "evolutionism" and "liberty." A great number of folklore studies were also introduced to China by those who studied abroad, including Charlotte Burne's (1850-1923) *The Handbook of Folklore* (1914) partly translated by Lin Huixiang; Arnold van Gennep's (1873-1957) concept of *rites de passage* (1909) introduced by Yang Kun (1901-1998); Danish Hans Christian Andersen's fairy tales translated and introduced by Zhou Zuoren (1885-1967) and Liu Bannong (1891-1934); and Jacob and Wilhelm Grimm's Märchen (or Hausmärchen) translated by Zhou Guisheng (1873-1936) and Wei Yixin (1898-1986). All this work was done in the first three decades of the 20th century.

Such a foundation built in the early decades of the 20th century enabled a speedy restoration—like "bamboo shoots after a rain"—of Chinese folkloristics in the 1980s. Thereafter, the expanding face-to-face communication between Chinese and American (or international) folklorists began, while increasingly greater numbers of Chinese folklorists were able to go abroad. For example, Nai-tung Ting was invited China four times from 1978-1985; Alan Dundes was also invited to three Folklore Programs in China in 1990. (See the essays by Shouhua Liu, Jianxian Chen, and Xiaohui Hu in this volume.) However, in 2006, when Dr. Kuili Liu, CFS President, led a delegation, including Bingzhong Gao, Fang Xiao, and Yongchao Chen, to participate in a folklore conference in the US, institutionalized communication with the AFS began, which led to the mutual visits of a AFS delegation to China and a CFS delegation to the US in the following year (CFS Secretary General Tao Ye was unable to join the delegation due to the US rejection of his visa application). Subsequently, interactions at all levels and in all areas followed, as we learn from the stories in this volume.

III. Beginning genuine folkloristic communication and looking for a promising future

As emphasized earlier, genuine academic communication should be based on a shared sense of mutuality and equality. We, in this volume, have attempted to open the door to such communication. In the past thirty years, dozens of graduate folklore programs have sprung up in China. Whereas any student in these programs can easily discuss the ideas of American folklorists, it was a rare American folklorist who was truly engaged with the ideas of Chinese folklorists. However, this was not because there were no folklorists in America who were educated in the ideas of Chinese folklorists, but courses and lectures on Chinese folklore among the folklore programs in the US have been too few. As Robert Baron noted in his story, in this volume, of his first face-to-face conversation in Beijing in 2008, "Here were folklorists practicing high theory, engaged in a critical folkloristics unknown and, unfortunately, yet untranslated in the United States. Given the dearth of folklore theory in recent years, the conceptual work of Chinese scholars needs to be known in our country." This situation must be improved.

For Chinese folklorists, genuine and equal academic communication should be achievable, continual, and rewarding to all. After all, they have begun to establish their own roots and to demonstrate their differences from other cultures with self-confidence. Chinese folklorists have adopted various theories from, for example, philosophy, linguists, and semiotics; they have gained self-awareness of their traditions and have displayed their disciplinary vitality and vigor through, for example, the current movement on safeguarding Intangible Cultural Heritage. American folklorists have also gained new energy through interactions with the Chinese: increasingly more folklore programs have begun accepting Chinese students and hosting visiting scholars from China; many more Chinese folklorists have given presentations of their research and are participating in conferences in the US. The result is a broadening of horizons for American folklorists and deepening of Chinese folklorists' understanding of the international scene.

Alan Dundes already noticed this historical turn when he visited China, while returning home from India, during the summer of 1990. He wrote a note to the *AFS Newsletter*, entitled "On Folklore Studies in China" (see Jianxian Chen's story in this volume):

In China, we [Alan Dundes and his wife] were impressed by the large number of folklorists and folklore students we met. These scholars were most anxious to know more about folklore theory and method as practiced in Europe and America. …I would hope that American folklorists will consider sending them copies of books and offprints which I can assure you will be most welcome. ...It is hard to convey how starved they are for increased contact with the West. ...I had previously had no idea there were so many active folklorists in China.

Dundes also briefly described his meetings with Chinese folklorists in three places: in Wuhan with Jianxian Chen [who translated Dundes's *The Study of Folklore* (1990) and *The Flood Myth* (2013) into Chinese]; in Beijing with Zichen Zhang and Jingwen Zhong; and, in Shanghai with Zongxi Wu and Qinjian Chen. He also made known the addresses of the three folklore programs, along with one in India, which he visited prior to arriving in China. He emphasized, "The generosity of those members of AFS who take the time and trouble to send one or more books or offprints to any of the above folklore centers will be very much appreciated."

In his preface to Jianxian Chen's Chinese translation of *The Study of Folklore* (1990), Dundes wrote, "Folklore studies has gradually become an interdisciplinary and international discipline." He also lamented, "Chinese folklorists have thus far never participated in international communication on folklore studies, while European and American folklorists know little about the achievements by the Chinese folklorists." About eleven years later, in 2001, in a communication with Xiaohui Hu on translating Dundes' *Interpreting Folklore*, Dundes was still expecting, "Chinese folklorists to do two things. First, to participate more actively in the international dialogue of folklorists on subjects of mutual interest. And second, to move from the collection and documentation of folklore to the critical arena of analysis and interpretation." Four years later, in his preface to the completed Chinese version of *Interpreting Folklore* (2005), he wrote, "Folkloristics, the study of folklore, is truly an international academic discipline." Dundes mentions the example of "double publishing" of the Finnish and Irish folklorists to reach a wider audience, and lamented, again, "The sad truth is that Western folklorists have relatively few windows opening to the world of Chinese folklore scholarship."

If Dundes could see the current communication between Chinese and American folklorists, he might feel slightly comforted. But, he would certainly expect that such communication would continue to develop even further. Today, our face-to-face communication and Internet sharing of publications have become routine. As we move on to "interpreting" while "collecting," we also need to be sure where we stand ideologically and methodologically, and to adjust our mentality to the goal of equal understanding and mutual respect in learning from each other while sharing our cultures and views.

This is where we need to return to Dundes's initial concept of "metafolklore." More than fifty years have passed since then, what progress have we made and how much is left to do in the field of "metafolklore"?

In the second decade of the 21st century, Sino-US folkloristic communication has been transformed from individual (or one-way flow) to institutional and multiple-level interactions. While AFS and CFS have certainly played a key role, individual folklorists are the central moving force. Precisely for this reason we have put together this volume of meaningful and interesting metafolklore stories. On the international platform, the voices of Chinese folklorists are becoming heard, and their theories and methods are maturing, as exemplified in some recent publications: a special issue on the discipline of Chinese folklore in the journal *Asian Ethnology* (2015), a special issue on Chinese and Asian American folklore in the *Journal of American Folklore* (2015), a special issue on Chinese epics in the *Journal of American Folklore* (2016), a special issue on Chinese intangible cultural heritage in *Western Folklore* (2017), and collaborative works for both academic and public readers such as the *Handbook of Chinese Mythology* by Yang, An, and Turner (2008).

This volume on metafolklore is designed to help continue and promote extensive communication between Chinese and American folklorists, thus enabling the individual folklorists' stories about folklore to become an integral part of this discipline. Although only a small number of stories is offered in this volume, a great number of individuals and their stories will surely emerge and be documented in the future. We believe that the field of folkloristics in China and the US will acknowledge "metafolklore" as an important, even crucial, component of folklore studies. It is our hope that this volume of Chinese and American metafolklore will lay a good foundation for "people studying people" in folkloristics.

References Cited:

Asian Ethnology. A special issue on Chinese Folklore Studies toward Disciplinary Maturity. 74 (2), 2015. Guest edited by Jing Li.

Briggs, Charles L. 1993. Metadiscursive Practices and Scholarly Authority in Folkloristics. *Journal of American Folklore* 106 (422): 387–434.

—1984. Learning How to Ask: Native Metacommunicative Competence and the Incompetence of Fieldworkers. *Language in Society* 13 (1): 1–28.

Bauman, Richard. 1977. *Verbal Art as Performance*. Waveland Press.

Ben-Amos, Dan. 1971. *Toward a Definition of Folklore in Context*. *Journal of American Folklore* 84 (331): 3–15.

—1993. "Context" in Context. *Western Folklore* 52 (2/4): 209–226.

Berger, Harris M. and Giovanna P. Del Negro. 2002. Bauman's Verbal Art and the Social Organization of Attention: The Role of Reflexivity in the Aesthetics of Performance. *Journal of American Folklore* 115 (455): 62–91.

Brown, Tom. 2005. "The Hunting of the Earl of Rone." The Emergence of "New" Folklore Motifs: Individual Creativity and Group Control. *Folklore* 116 (2): 201–213.

Buccitelli, Anthony Bak. ed. 2017. *Telling Chinatown, Writing America: Jon Y. Lee's WPA Manuscripts*.

Special Volume of *Folklore Historian*. (Forthcoming)

Chao, Wei-pang. Modern Chinese Folklore Investigation（中国近代民俗学研究概况）. Part I. The Peking National University. *Folklore Studies*, Vol. 1 (1942), pp. 55 – 76; Part II. The National Sun Yat-sen University. *Folklore Studies*, Vol. 2 (1943), pp. 79 – 88.

Ciosáin, Niall Ó. 2004. Approaching a Folklore Archive: The Irish Folklore Commission and the Memory of the Great Famine. *Folklore* 115 (2): 222 – 232.

Cunningham, Keith. 1991. "It Was the (Untranslatable)": Native American Contemporary Legends in Cross-Cultural Perspective. *Folklore* 102 (2): 89 – 96.

Dundes, Alan. 1966. "Metafolklore and Oral Literary Criticism," *The Monist* 50: 505 – 516.

—1980. *Interpreting Folklore*. Bloomington: University of Indiana Press. [First published in *Southern Folklore Quarterly*, 1964.]

Fielde, Adele M. 1885. *Pagoda Shadows: Studies from Life in China*. (3rd ed.) Boston: W. G. Corthell.

—1894. *A Corner of Cathay: Studies from Life among the Chinese*. NY: Macmillan & Co.

France, M. N. 1976. Metalanguage and Category Acquisition. *Philosophy and Phenomenological Research* 37 (2): 165 – 180.

Georges, Robert and Michael O. Jones. 1980. *People Studying People: The Human Element in Field Work*. University of California Press.

Greenway, John. 1960. R. D. Jameson (1895 – 1959). *Western Folklore*. 19 (3): 153 – 154.

Hays, David G. 1973. Language and Interpersonal Relationships. *Daedalus* 102 (3): 203 – 216.

Hill, Jane H. 1990. Weeping as a Meta-Signal in a Mexicano Woman's Narrative. *Journal of Folklore Research* 27 (1/2): 29 – 49.

Hymes, Dell. 1964. "Introduction: Toward Ethnographies of Communication". *American Anthropologist*. 66 (6): 1 – 34.

Jameson, R. D. 1932. *Three Lectures on Chinese Folklore*. Peiping: The San Yu Press. (Chinese version in 1987.)

Journal of American Folklore. A special issue on the New Perspectives on the Studies of Asian American Folklore. 127 (510), 2015. Edited by Juwen Zhang

Journal of American Folklore. A special issue on the Living Epics of China and Inner Asia. 129 (513), 2016.

Lichman, Simon. 1982. The Gardener's Story: The Metafolklore of a Mumming Tradition. *Folklore* 93 (1): 105 – 111.

Limón, José E. 1983. Legendry, Metafolklore, and Performance: A Mexican-American Example. *Western Folklore* 42 (3): 191 – 208.

James, Clifford and George E. Marcus, eds. 1986. *Writing Culture: The Poetics and Politics of Ethnography*. University of California Press.

Narayan, Kirin. 1995. The Practice of Oral Literary Criticism: Women's Songs in Kangra, India. *Journal of American Folklore* 108 (429): 243 – 264.

Pitman, Norman H. 1910. *Chinese Fairy Stories*. NY: Thomas Y. Crowell.

—1919. *A Chinese Wonder Book*. Illustrated by Li Chu-T'ang. NY: E. P. Dutton & Co.

Shenhar, Aliza. 1987. Metafolkloristic Additions to Stories by the Artistic Narrator. *Folklore* 98 (1): 53 – 56.

Tangherlini, Timothy R. 2005. Alan Dundes (1934 – 2005). *Folklore* 116 (2): 216 – 219.

W*estern Folklore*. A special issue on Intangible Cultural Heritage in China. 76 (2), 2017. Edited by Juwen Zhang and Xing Zhou.

Wilce, James M. Jr. 1995. "I Can't Tell You All My Troubles": Conflict, Resistance, and Metacommunication in Bangladeshi Illness Interactions. *American Ethnologist* 22 (4): 927 – 952.

Wilson, William A. 1988. The Deeper Necessity: Folklore and the Humanities. *Journal of American Folklore* 101 (400): 156 – 167.

Yang, Lihui, Deming An, Jessica Turner. 2008. *Handbook of Chinese Mythology*. Oxford University Press.

Zhang, Juwen. 2005. Filmic Folklore and Chinese Cultural Identity. *Western Folklore*. 64 (3/4): 263 – 280.

艾伯华 (Eberhard, Wolfram). 1999.《中国民间故事类型》(*Typen Chinesischer Volksmärchen*). 王燕生、周祖生译. 商务印书馆.

邓迪斯 (Alan Dundes). 1990.《世界民俗学》(*The Study of Folklore*). 陈建宪、彭海斌译. 上海：上海文艺出版社.

——2013.《洪水神话》(*The Flood Myth*). 陈建宪等译. 陕西师范大学出版社.

——2005.《民俗解析》(*Interpreting Folklore*). 户晓辉译. 广西师范大学出版社.

丁乃通 (Ting, Nai-tung). 2008.《中国民间故事类型索引》(*A Type Index of Chinese Folktales*). 春风文艺出版社，1983.（再版. 郑成威等译. 华中师范大学出版社.）

谢尔曼 (Sherman, Sharon). 2011.《记录我们自己》(*Documenting Ourselves* 1998). 张举文等译. 华中师范大学出版社.

严复. 1930 [1903]. 群己权界论.（译述 *On Liberty*. By John Stuart Mill). 上海：商务印书馆.

詹姆森 (R. D. Jameson). 1987.《中国的"灰姑娘"故事》, 载于《民间文艺学探索》, 钟敬文主编. 北京师范大学出版社.

I. 回眸历程，追忆先贤

  中美民俗研究的交流其实早于两国民俗学会的成立，也不局限于两会的交往。民俗生活，不论是从"局内人"还是"局外人"的角度来看，无论是为了政治还是文化或其他目的，也无论是出于家族延续还是社会和谐，都是建立和了解人类日常生活的基础，与学科的形成发展是无关的。但是，对民俗生活的学科性研究则有助于我们对自身的文化生活在更深层面"知其然亦知其所以然"。由此而论，这样的学科的健康发展离不开来自多文化背景的学者的平等交流。

  纵观一百多年来中国自身对民俗的研究，以及外界对中国的研究，一个明显的事实就是，中外交流中的两个不平等：一个是对自己和对别人在观念（包括理论）上的不平等；一个是语言上的不平等。或者说，平等的交流应该是观念上的平等（对自己和对别人）和语言上的平等（彼此能懂或用对方的语言）。美国民俗学科的发展史也证明了它经历着从"向内看"转到"向外看"和"从外看"的过程。百年来，双方虽然在两个方面都有了很大的进步，但是，要达到这样的平台，各自都有很长的路要走。可喜的是，双方对此开始有了共同的认识和同舟共济的追求，这一点可以从每篇故事中感受到。

  张举文在对"亚民俗"的定义扩展时，也提供了对一个多世纪的中美民俗研究的历史回顾，由此衬托出今天的前所未有的局面。从中可以概括中美（包括中外）民俗学交流经历的几个（交叉或重叠的）阶段：1）从介绍引进到模仿套用；2）从研究译文到面对面聊天；3）从请进来到走出去；4）从被翻译到翻译自己；5）从听者到说者；6）从追随到领头；7）从去中国特色到显中国特色；8）从眼光向外到眼光向内；9）从个别交往到多重的机制化交流。当然，对中国学者来说，还有"向外看齐"（或"与世界接轨"）的倾向，因而忽略挖掘自身文化之根及其特色和优势，不利于构建符合自己文化实践的理论体系。这样的情结也可以从本文集中的一些叙述中读出来。

  这部分的七篇文章体现了两个主题。一个是对近十多年来以两国民俗学为主体的交流历程的反思：艾伟、罗仪德和高丙中讲述的是近十多年的交流背景和内容，勾勒出了两个民俗学会在交流中的推动作用；朝戈金的故事突出体现了中国民俗学界"从请进来到走出去"和"从追随到领头"的转折，或者说走向平等合作的开始。另一个主题是对两位帮助中国民俗学者走向世界的民俗学家的缅怀和追忆：刘守华回忆了丁乃通的故事，陈建宪和户晓辉分别讲述了邓迪斯的故事。他们的故事不仅是对前辈的追忆，而且也让我们更珍惜今天的现实和成果，重视我们今天对学科的传承的作用。但有趣的是，这三位对美国民俗学和民俗学家颇有研究的中国民俗学家至今还没有到过美国。

I. Glimpses of the Past and Memories of the Distinguished Predecessors

Communication in folklore studies between Chinese and American folklorists began long before the establishment of the two folklore societies in the two countries, and has now gone beyond the two societies. Whether from an "insider" or "outsider" point of view, whether for political or cultural purposes, whether for the continuity of the family or social order, folklife is the very foundation for building communication among peoples of different cultures. Regardless of how academic disciplines have been formed, academic studies of cross-cultural interactions indeed help us understand why we do and what we do. In this sense, the healthy development of such a discipline is inseparable from equal communication between scholars of diverse cultural backgrounds.

Looking at studies of Chinese folklore in the past century, whether from an insider or an outsider view, one can recognize two obvious facts: the unequal attitude and viewpoint (or theories) between studying one's own culture and studying other cultures; the equal use of (native vs. foreign) languages in academic discourse. In other words, equal communication should be based on an equal attitude and viewpoint toward self and other, and an equal level of comprehension (or capability) in using each other's language.

American folkloristics has gone through a process from "looking inside" to "looking outside," and to today's "looking from outside" (i.e., reflective and reflexive). Nowadays, there has been great progress in both areas in both China and the US, but there is still a long way to go. What is encouraging is that both sides have come to a common understanding of these issues and, together, have begun to seek new paths, as demonstrated in many stories in this volume.

In extending the definition of "metafolklore," Juwen Zhang has provided an overview of past Sino-US folklore communication, which serves as a background to highlight today's unprecedented accomplishments. These stages in the history of Sino-US (or Sino-foreign) exchanges may be seen from a Chinese perspective as follows: 1) from introducing to mimicking; 2) from studying texts to chatting face-to-face; 3) from inviting guests to becoming guests; 4) from being translated to translating; 5) from being listeners to being speakers; 6) from being followers to being leaders; 7) from de-characterizing to re-characterizing Chinese traditions; 8) from looking out to looking in; and 9) from individual to multiple and institutionalized communications. Certainly, among Chinese views there is still a tendency to "keep abreast of foreign studies" (or "converging with the world," so-to-speak) while ignoring unique Chinese cultural roots and their distinctive merits. This tendency will hinder Chinese scholars in their attempts to establish theories that derive from their own cultural practices. Some of the stories within this volume implicitly show such a sentiment.

The seven pieces in this section focus on two themes. One theme is the background/history of Sino-US folkloristic communication in the past ten years, centering primarily on the two folklore societies, AFS and CFS. Bill Ivey, Tim Lloyd, and Bingzhong Gao tell their stories of how the individuals and institutions on both sides have benefited. Gejin Chao's story highlights the transition of Chinese folkloristics from "inviting the foreign scholars to China" to "going abroad," and from "being followers" to "being leaders;" in other words, the beginning of equal collaboration on the world stage. The other theme is the commemoration of two folklorists who played important roles in pioneering the communication between the two countries: Shouhua Liu tells the story of Nai-tung Ting; Jianxian Chen and Xiaohui Hu tell the story of Alan Dundes. These stories are told not only to commemorate those who came before us, but also to remind us to cherish current accomplishments and to value our role in the continuity of our discipline. Interestingly, the three Chinese folklorists mentioned above have good knowledge of American folkloristics, yet have never been to the US.

中国记忆

艾 伟*

美国政府因其对文化事务的缺乏关心而臭名昭著。美国并不像大多数主要国家一样设有文化部或文化事务部。相反，政府将具有文化意义的政策放置在很多部门和机构，并且通过一些小机构为艺术和人文项目提供资金支持来直接促进文化的活力。当美国国务院需要参加文化部长的国际会议时，政府机构就会邀请这些小机构中的某位主管作为特别代表出席。

在克林顿政府的第二个任期，我是国家艺术基金会的主席，任期从1998年到2001年末。在2000年的秋季，美国政府要求我代表美国出席将在10月底举办的首届上海国际艺术节①，来自世界各地的文化部长们将出席艺术节的开幕式。我被要求作为"适当的最高权威"——一个没有部长头衔，但是被政府授权可以具有那个能力的人代表政府出席。我热情地答应这次旅行，并听取了一位熟悉中国情况的国务院官员的介绍。

1990年代后期，我所在的机构，国家艺术基金会，曾经为中美艺术交流中心的一个小项目提供资助，这个中心位于纽约市的哥伦比亚大学。该项目由周文中教授创建和领导。周教授是一位非常著名的古典音乐作曲家，他被云南省的乡村传统音乐深深吸引。周教授从福特基金会得到了大量的资金资助，但是那个资助即将被用完，而他正在计划去昆明、丽江和云南其他地方的最后一次旅行。

我决定将去上海艺术节的行程和去云南省南部和西部的行程结合起来，在那里我将与周教授和他的同事，还有社会学家郝光明会面，并且参观博物馆、乡村和历史遗迹。柏瑞·博杰，国家艺术基金会民俗艺术项目的主任，将陪同我一起前往。

这次旅行的第一部分包括对上海文化场所的正式参观以及和来自世界多个国家的文化领导人的正式会议。这些会议都非常的"官方"。我记得和中国文化部部长的一次会议（我记

---

* 编者注：艾伟现为印第安纳大学民俗学与民族音乐学系访问研究员，美国民俗学会高级中国顾问。2006年至2007年，他在担任美国民俗学会会长期间为中美民俗学交流发挥了至关重要的作用。在过去的十多年里，他组织和参与了诸多合作项目。他有着丰富的学养、从政的历练，以及从事公共服务经历，为民俗学者在社区、国家和国际层面贡献于人类文化理解树立了一个典范。他在此所讲述的故事不仅是他个人参与中美民俗学会的交流体会，也表明了什么是"正确的"时候的"正确的"行动，从而创造"正确的历史"，即中美民俗学的交流。

① 译者注：据上海国际艺术节网站http://www.artsbird.com显示，第一届上海国际艺术节于1999年举办，2000年举办的是第二届。

得他姓孙)。那次会议包括来自不同国家的八个代表,我们坐在大的扶手椅里,扶手椅的排列就像理查德·尼克松总统和毛泽东会见时的场景一样,翻译们蹲伏在每个椅子后面。开幕式当晚的演出在全新的上海音乐厅里举办,当宾客们攀爬着长长的楼梯出现在宾客入口的时候,我们耳朵里响起由数组豪华钢琴所奏出的小夜曲。表演结束后,显要人物们转移到海滨现场欣赏精致的焰火表演。不幸的是,雨下了一整夜,不管我们在政府中的地位有多高,所有的宾客都被同等对待了。我们站着观看美丽的烟花,雨水首先淋湿了我们的头,然后是西装和领带,最后是我们的鞋子。

第二天,博杰和我飞到了昆明。那是中国航空旅行的"旧时代"。我们乘坐的是"祥鹏航空",在短暂的飞行中,我们享受了一顿不错的餐食,当离开飞机的时候每位乘客还得到了一份礼物。对一个美国人而言,飞机着陆时特别令人兴奋,因为即使飞机还在跑道上滑行的时候,很多乘客已经站起来,打开头上的行李架,迅猛地拿出行李箱和其他行李。当我透过窗户观看昆明老化的候机楼时,我竟然看到了在跑道边整齐排列的俄罗斯米格-21战斗机。

我们入住昆明一个西式风格的旅馆。作为一位到访的美国政府高官,我被安排住进一个具有中国特色的顶楼的豪华套房里,房间里的每一盏灯、每一个设备、每一盏顶灯都被床边的一个大面板上的旋钮和开关控制。套房入口附近的一个落地灯无法关闭,灯具是硬装进墙里的。最后,我只能用一条毛毯盖住落地灯,然后享受了一个倒时差的好睡眠。

接下来的一天,我们参观了一个空间有两个餐厅那么大的非常好的艺术画廊/画室,我立即发现中国的画家们处在国际影响力的顶端(这确实发生了)。下午晚些时候,周教授、郝光明、博杰和我被一辆中国产的、大的、外交风格的豪华轿车接到另外一个宾馆参加一场新闻发布会,详细介绍美中艺术交流中心在云南开展活动的影响。周教授注意到这是云南省召开的首批具有西方风格的新闻发布会之一,记者的问题是试探性的,而且非常有礼貌。对于周教授和光明而言,这是一个很好的总结他们的阶段工作的方式。

我们参观了云南民族大学,我被多种民间传统与美术、大众表演相融合的方式所打动。大学里的学生来自多个民族,每个人都被要求精通多民族的音乐、舞蹈和服装,而不仅仅是他们自己的。西方音乐和视觉艺术也是课程的一部分。一位年轻的老师给我演示了传统的剪纸,我发现她的专业是教当代绘画。将西方艺术制作和传统实践轻松地同时呈现出来似乎在云南是很正常的,而在美国我却闻所未闻。

我们乘坐一个短程航班到了丽江,这是在一个漂亮的古镇周边发展起来的小城市,早前被联合国认定为世界文化遗产。现代化丽江的旁边,一个由粗糙的花岗岩岩石铺成的小广场经过了几个世纪的磨洗,城中蜿蜒的街道旁边是从山上融化而来的清澈、湍急的溪水在不断流淌。丽江是纳西人的家,多数生活在临街商店中的商人都穿着染成靛蓝色的棉服来凸显自己的民族身份。这是真实的中国!

我们参观了一个致力于展示纳西文化和他们的哲学以及东巴宗教的博物馆,然后乘坐一辆小货车离开城市去参观一个有几百人居住的乡间村落。我们被村民们和来自广州中山大学的人类学家邓启耀教授热情接待。我们和乡村领袖坐在一个古庙中喝茶,这个古庙在中国的

"文革"中曾经被用作村镇中心和学校。一个脸戴面具、手持刀剑的东巴祭司在社区里六位青年的帮助下表演了一个仪式,在仪式中祭司和邪灵打斗并最终击败了他们。全城的人都见证了我们代表团的特殊待遇,这是对周文中教授的特别认可。听取说明需要三个过程的翻译,从纳西语到当地汉语方言再到英语。这是令人兴奋的事实,一个真实的、几个世纪以来功能很少发生变化的乡村:工作在美国的民俗学家难以得到的探索、学习和研究的语境。

当时我并不知道,在很多方面我正在看到的是古老、传统中国的余晖。在丽江附近,农村人仍旧在使用牛耕作,在田野里,在高高的电线杆上的喇叭每天播放着来自北京的全国广播。中国的首都依然是一个满是自行车的城市,我的西方人特征和灰色的头发得到了足够的关注,尤其是在云南西部。2000年的时候,很多学生能说流利的英语,但是对于更早的一代人和宾馆、机场、火车站中的大多数服务者来说,他们只能说中文。

我的第一次中国旅行的经历紧张而精彩。大城市的发展和农村生活的反差惊人。云南的村庄提供了通向古老过去的一个连接。传统的宗教实践和民俗研究都因为中国的"文革"而中断了,但是现在它们似乎都回归了。我的第一次到丽江和云南乡村的经历使我确信:中国是民俗学家的天堂。

华盛顿有紧急的事务。总统竞选已经结束,当我从昆明飞回上海,再从上海飞到纳什维尔的途中,我一直为选举结果担心着。我是在选举日当天抵达的。阿尔·戈尔选举失利,很遗憾,我在政府的工作也结束了。我的工作把我带到了中国,第一次访问表明,中美合作共同研究民俗具有很大的潜在价值。每个国家的研究环境都是独一无二的,民俗学家的工作带来了独特的视角,友善的精神激励每一位参与者。我决定找个机会再次访问中国。

* * * * *

七年之后,我的理想变成了现实,当时我正在担任为期两年的美国民俗学会会长。美国民俗学会执行理事长罗仪德已经和中国民俗学会的领导们有了对话。2007年10月,中国民俗学会代表团参加了在加拿大魁北克召开的美国和加拿大民俗学会联合年会,然后去了纽约和华盛顿。

美国民俗学会做了回应。我们的代表团,由张举文教授、阿果兹诺博士和我组成,于12月3日到达北京。我们立即在北京三个不同的地方参与了三场对话,这确定了我们整个行程的快节奏和激情参与。第四天,我们在叶涛教授的陪同下到了济南,参加在山东大学举办的一个研讨会,然后我们在曲阜呆了一整天,接下来的一天是纪念山东民俗学会成立20周年研讨会。中国民俗学会刘魁立会长接下来加入了我们的代表团,我们到了武汉,在华中师范大学我做了一场演讲。接着我们飞到云南,参访昆明和丽江的民俗学家和博物馆。旅行、会面、演讲、会议,都伴随着极好的膳食、对名胜古迹的引人入胜的参观和大量的为民俗和友谊干杯。在昆明的一个晚上,晚饭后唱歌开始前,我和举文发明了一个现在流行的"出击敬酒":从你的座位上站起来,围着桌子移动,举起杯中的美酒,向你尊敬的同事直接敬酒,"我敬你!"

在丽江，我们代表团住在一家不错的家庭旅馆里，早餐是煮鸡蛋、热牛奶还有臭豆腐。我们在丽江古镇散步，欣赏小商店和纳西妇女在沿着石头铺成的街道欢快流淌的雪山融化的水中洗衣服。我们走在环绕着商业区的山坡上，叶涛敲开了一个村民的门。我们受到了欢迎并被以茶招待。非常的舒服，非常的好客！

我们的最后一站是广州，这也是重要的一站。我们的东道主，中国非物质文化遗产研究中心，是中山大学一个新的国家级研究中心。坐落在校园里一个最现代化的建筑中，这个研究中心是一个中国在全球非物质文化遗产保护和保存运动中所处领导地位的巨大标志。中心主任康保成教授，宋俊华教授，硕士研究生陈熙和中心全体职员将成为把中国和美国的民俗学家合作推向一个更高水平的参与者。

《保护非物质文化遗产公约》通过只有几年的时间，但是中国已经成为早期的、热情的签约国。非物质文化遗产工作使政府和民间机构参与到民俗和传统社区中，为民俗学者提供了大量新机遇和挑战。虽然美国参与了该公约的制定，但美国政府几乎没有兴趣参与这个世界范围内的认定和保护工作。思想的种子已经被种下：或许我们可以运用非物质文化遗产作为我们的比较框架，建立一个项目比较美国和中国在保护民俗方面的理论和实践？这样一个项目将会允许我们超越教师和学生的交流以及偶尔在会议上的会面和出版，两国的学者和学生都将从项目中获益。

到了2011年，北京、广州和昆明都成了满是汽车和摩托车的城市，丽江有了一个新的机场航站楼，昆明机场跑道边的退役米格战斗机也不存在了。来自中国和美国的民俗学家已经用了很多年来交换思想、出席会议、建设对国际合作来说最基本的信任和友谊。现在是时候开展基于共同理解和善意的真正项目了。罗仪德从亨利·路思基金会获得一个可能的许可，支持召开一系列会议来建构非物质文化遗产工作的基础理论。现在是再次访问中国的合作伙伴的时候了，这次是为一个真正的国际倡议获取支持。

* * * * *

到2011年，陈熙已经成了我们美国民俗学会在中国的代表，利用她在中山大学工作的业余时间来协调交流活动。我于2011年3月11日飞到广州，正是可怕的海啸侵袭日本的第二天。到处都有关于这场悲剧的讨论，这给我的工作带来了一个悲伤的背景。我的工作是讨论建立一个可能的项目，这需要很多中国参与者的帮助。陈熙翻译我们的对话，我和康教授以及中心的全体成员在九楼的会议室里讨论罗仪德的具体建议：如果美国民俗学会获得资助，中山大学非物质文化遗产研究中心能否作为关于非物质文化遗产比较研究的一系列会议——论坛——的参与者？康教授和他的同事问了非常多的问题，但是最后我们约定：我们将一起举办四个论坛，两个在中国，两个在美国。第一个论坛将于2012年秋天在广州举办。

第二天陈熙和我从广州出发，首先赶到昆明，去和云南民族博物馆的谢沫华馆长会面。在昆明市中心下榻后，我们与谢馆长和他的高级助理杜女士在一家离昆明翠湖宾馆几条街的餐馆里共进晚餐。晚上非常冷，餐厅的服务员将一些小炭火盆放在我们桌子的周围，但这热量只能保持我们的脚暖和。我们紧靠着桌子，品尝着美酒，在陈熙的帮助下解释我们的项目："谢馆长能否与美国民俗学会和中大非遗中心合作，把与中国博物馆的合作远景带入我们的论坛？"谢馆长询问了许多问题。晚餐后，陈熙和我一致认为，谈话是积极的。

第二天早晨，陈熙和我去了一个商业区，购买了暖和的外套。然后我们参观了民族博物馆并继续在博物馆里和谢沫华馆长茶叙。我们最终达成一致，他和他的机构将成为我们项目的一部分。

然后是到丽江，我们和丽江纳西东巴文化博物馆的李馆长谈论了一天。又一次，陈熙和我解释了我们系列论坛的想法，并且强调博物馆将在我们的会议和出版当中作为一个特别受关注的领域。我们在一个很好的、简单的临街餐馆里通过一顿美味的午餐解决了所有事情。那天晚上，我们走在丽江老城区山坡上的狭窄小路上，这个区域已经因密集的复古，欧洲流行的舞蹈俱乐部、许许多多的国际游客的入侵而发生了转变。我们在山顶附近发现了一个小酒吧，既可以俯瞰老城区，又能看到新城区。老板为我们提供了他家酿的美酒，非常的可口。

我们的最后一站是北京，我忧心忡忡。美国和中国民俗学家的关系开始于2007年，四年后人物角色都发生了变化。美国民俗学会也有了一位新的会长Diane Goldstein；在中国，刘魁立不再担任中国民俗学会会长，新会长是中国社会科学院的资深成员朝戈金。陈熙和我入住新族酒店后，乘坐出租车到了中国社会科学院办公地。叶涛教授，依然是中国民俗学会的秘书长，在六楼的一个会议室里和我们一起等待。朝教授进来了，他是蒙古口头文学的高级专家，曾在美国学习并讲一口流利的英语。他坐在巨大的会议桌旁，问了很多有关会议的问题。中国民俗学会是这个项目所必需的，会长会同意参与吗？

是的，他将提供帮助。我们通过一场丰盛的晚宴和许多杯美酒确定了彼此的承诺。第二天，陈熙和我与约翰·菲茨杰拉德共进午餐，他是福特基金会在中国的代表。像朝会长一样，菲茨杰拉德问了许多关于美国民俗学会、中国民俗学会以及我们合作举办会议和出版物的计划的问题。我们学到了重要的一课：许多团体和个人来到中国希望发展文化事业。中国的学者和官员们总是热情好客，但是酒宴后去开展真正的工作和维持长久的友谊却并不容易。菲茨杰拉德非常谨慎，他问陈熙的问题似乎还不太礼貌，但是他很快分派了一些福特基金来帮助设计我们的项目。

我学到了重要一课。中国学者比在美国的教授工作更加努力。当学术生涯呈现出相似时，中国的民俗学家必须做出小心的选择来确保他们时间上的投入能够产生实际效益。想法和机会要谨慎把握，详细的计划和准备才是关键。陈熙和我被参与我们论坛的每一位伙伴详细地询问。一旦问题被答复，任务被分配，财政问题得到解决，一个项目一定会成功进行。

第二天早晨陈熙返回广州，下午晚些时候我也离开北京返回美国。美国民俗学会罗仪德执行理事长给路思基金会精心地制作了一份完美的建议书，我们共享的召开国际非物质文化遗产论坛的"中国—美国梦"变成了现实。

＊　＊　＊　＊　＊

　　据说，如果你在中国生活一个星期，你可以写一本书；如果生活一个月，你可以写一篇文章；但是如果你一次又一次地体验中国，你甚至连一张贺卡都写不出来。这个说法是有道理的，因为刚开始，中国似乎是清晰的——它是欢迎的、友好的、精力充沛的、雄心勃勃的、拥挤的、紧张的。当一个访问者在一个熠熠生辉的新机场降落，乘坐快车去一个西方风格的宾馆，体验一种"现代化冲击"，"哦，我理解中国"，访问者说，"它是一个具有越来越多现代西方特征的古老文化。我要写一本书。"

　　现实要复杂得多，新访问者的自信会很快一扫而空。但经验带来了一个重要的事实：中国和美国的民俗学者特别适合研究和比较形成世界上两个最伟大国家的多种传统、社区、民族和文化财富。

　　所以，今天，多次访问中国之后，我可以写我的贺卡了。贺卡封面是一张广州龙舟节的照片，贺卡里面的信息是："我们建立了一个以友谊和信任为基础的相互学习和研究的国际模式，我们现在有能力把比较民俗研究的独特价值带给未来几代学者。"

（青岛理工大学张成福翻译）

美国民俗学会会长艾伟与中国民俗学会长刘魁立相互敬酒，北京，2007年12月。AFS President Bill Ivey and CFS President Kuili Liu toasting to each other, Beijing, December 2007. Photograph by Juwen Zhang.

徐金龙、叶涛、黄永林、艾伟、刘魁立、陈建宪、阿果兹诺、韩成艳、桑俊、孙正国（自左向右），2007年12月于武汉华中师范大学。Jinlong Xu, Tao Ye, Yonglin Huang, Bill Ivey, Kuili Liu, Jianxian Chen, Mable Agozzino, Chengyan Han, Jun Sang, Zhengguo Sun (from left to right), Central China Normal University, Wuhan, Dec. 2007. Photograph by Juwen Zhang.

蒋明智、康保成、阿果兹诺、艾伟、张举文、叶涛、刘晓春（自左向右）在美国民俗学会代表团访问中山大学期间，2007年12月。Mingzhi Jiang, Baocheng Kang, Mable Agozzino, Bill Ivey, Juwen Zhang, Tao Ye, Xiaochun Liu (from left to right), at Sun Yat-sen University during the first AFS Delegation visit, Dec., 2007. Photograph courtesy of Juwen Zhang.

China Memories

Bill Ivey*

The US government is notorious for not paying much attention to cultural matters. Unlike most major nations, the US does not have a cultural ministry or department of cultural affairs. Instead, the government places policies with cultural significance in many agencies and departments, and directly addresses cultural vitality through a few small agencies that provide financial support for arts and humanities projects. When the US Department of State needs to participate in international meetings of cultural ministers, the department extends an invitation to one of the small agency's directors to serve as a special representative.

I was chairman of the National Endowment for the Arts in the second Clinton-Gore Administration, serving from 1998 until late 2001. In the fall of 2000, the Department of State asked me to represent the US at the first Shanghai International Arts Festival, scheduled for late October. The festival opening would be attended by cultural ministers from around the world, and I was asked to attend representing the US as the "Highest Appropriate Authority" —someone without the rank of "minister" but authorized by the government to act in that capacity. I enthusiastically agreed to take the trip and was briefed by a State Department official familiar with China.

In the late 1990s my agency, the National Endowment for the Arts, had provided grant support for the Center for US-China Arts Exchange, a small program administered by Columbia University in New York City. The project was created and directed by Professor Wen-chung Chou, a famous classical music composer who had become fascinated with the traditional music of villages in Yunnan Province. Professor Chou had received major funding from the Ford Foundation, but that support

---

* Bill Ivey is Visiting Research Scholar of the Department of Folklore and Ethnomusicology, Indiana University, and Senior China Advisor to the American Folklore Society. During his tenure as the AFS President in 2006 – 07, he played a vital role in shaping AFS-CFS exchange relations. He has also organized and participated in a number of exchange projects in the past ten years. With academic, government, and public service experiences, he has exemplified how folklorists can contribute to nurturing human cultural understandings at local community, national, and international levels. His story here reveals not only his personal experience and the recent history of AFS-CFS exchange, but also how a "right" decision at "right" time can make a "right" history, in this case, for many folklorists in China and the US.

was winding down and he was planning a final trip to Kunming, Lijiang, and other Yunnan locales.

It was decided that I would combine my visit to the Shanghai festival with a trip south and west to Yunnan Province, where I would meet Professor Chou and his colleague, sociologist Ken Hau, and visit museums, villages, and historic sites. I would be accompanied by Barry Bergey, director of the NEA's Folk Arts Program.

The first part of the trip included formal tours of cultural sites in Shanghai, and ceremonial meetings with cultural leaders from many nations. These conversations were very "official." I recall a meeting with China's then-cultural minister (I recall that his surname was "Sun."). The meeting included eight representatives from different countries, seated in big armchairs that resembled those that appeared in the meetings between President Richard Nixon and Mao Zedong; an interpreter crouched beside each chair. The opening-night performance was held in a brand-new Shanghai concert hall. As guests ascended the long stairway that rose to the venue entrance, we were serenaded by an array of grand pianos. Following the performances, dignitaries relocated to a waterfront site to observe an elaborate fireworks display. Unfortunately, rain fell throughout the evening; no matter how lofty our government posts, all guests were made equal. We stood watching beautiful fireworks as the rain first drenched our heads, then suits and ties, and finally our shoes.

Barry and I flew to Kunming the next day. These were the "old days" of air travel in China. We flew on "Lucky Air," were served a nice meal on a short flight, and when departing the plane every passenger was handed a gift. The landing was exciting for an American, because even while the aircraft was rushing down the runway after touching down, dozens of passengers were already on their feet, yanking suitcases and bundles out of overhead storage compartments. When I looked out the window toward Kunming's aging airline terminal, I couldn't help observing line of Russian Mig-21 fighter jets lined up beside the runway.

We stayed in a western-style hotel in Kunming. As a visiting US government dignitary, I was housed in a top-floor suite-one of those distinctively-Chinese luxury rooms in which every lamp, every device, every overhead light is controlled from a vast panel of knobs and switches beside the bed. One floor lamp near the suite's entrance just would not turn off; the fixture was hard-wired into the wall. In the end, I covered it with a blanket and fell into a jet-lagged sleep.

The next day we visited a very nice art gallery/studio space that doubled as a restaurant, and I could immediately see that Chinese painters were on the cusp of global impact (this has certainly happened). In the late afternoon Professor Chou, Ken Hau, Barry Bergey and I were chauffeured in a big, Chinese, diplomatic-style limo to another hotel for a press conference detailing the impact of the Yunnan activities of the Center for US-China Arts Exchange. Professor Chou noted that this was one of the first Western-style press conferences ever held in Yunnan Province, and reporter questions were tentative and very, very polite. For Professor Chou and Ken this was a good way to "tie a bow" around their work.

In the morning we visited the Yunnan University of Nationalities, and I was struck by the way multiple folk traditions intermingled with the fine arts and popular performance. Students at the university are drawn from multiple nationalities, and each is expected to master the music, dance, and costume of multiple groups, not just their own. Western music and visual art are also part of the curriculum. A young instructor presented me with a traditional paper cutting; I discovered that her faculty post was in teaching contemporary painting. Easy, simultaneous engagement with western art making and traditional practice—almost unheard of in the US—seemed the norm here in Yunnan.

Then we took a short flight to Lijiang, a small city that grew up beside a beautiful ancient village that early-on was recognized by the UN as a World Heritage Site. Positioned slightly above modern Lijiang, a small plaza made up of rough-cut quarried granite, worn down over the centuries, gave way to tight, winding streets that worked their way downhill beside clear, rushing water melted from mountain glaciers and channeled through the village. Lijiang is home to Nashi people, and most of the merchants who lived above their streetfront shops dressed in the indigo-dyed cotton outfits that distinguished the nationality. This was real China!

We toured a small museum dedicated to the Nashi and to their philosophy and Dhongba religion, and then left town in a small van to visit a rural village, home to a few hundred. We were hosted by villagers and by anthropologist Qiyao Deng, a professor at Sun Yat-sen University in Guangzhou. We sat for tea with village leaders in an old temple that had been converted into a town center and school during China's "Cultural Revolution". A Dhongba priest, costumed and equipped with mask and sword, assisted by a half-dozen young men in the community, performed a ritual in which the priest battled—and ultimately defeated—evil spirits. The whole town turned out to witness this special treat for our delegation—a special recognition of Chou Wen-chung. Explanation required a three-part process of interpretation, from Nashi language to a regional dialect into Chinese and finally to English. This was exciting stuff-a real, functioning rural village little-changed from centuries past: a context for exploration, learning and study that wasn't available to folklorists working in the US.

I didn't know it then, but in some ways I was seeing the last of old China. Near Lijiang, farmers still plowed behind oxen, in fields where now-silent loudspeakers on tall poles recalled daily national broadcasts from Beijing. China's capital was still a bicycle city, and my western features and grey hair got plenty of attention, especially out-west in Yunnan. In 2000 many students spoke good English, but for faculty of an earlier generation, and for most service providers in hotels, airports, train stations it was Chinese only.

My first China experience was intense and exciting. The contrasts between big-city development and rural life were striking. Yunnan villages provided links to an ancient past. Both traditional religious practice and folklore scholarship had been interrupted by China's "Cultural

Revolution", but both seemed to be coming back. My first contact with Lijiang and rural Yunnan convinced me that China was a paradise for folklorists!

There was pressing business back in Washington. A presidential campaign had just ended; I worried about the election as I flew from Kunming to Shanghai and on to Nashville. I arrived onElection Day. Al Gore lost; sadly, my government job was at an end. But my work had taken me to China, and that first visit provided evidence of the great potential benefits to folklore studies that would come from a China-US collaboration. The research environment in each country is unique; folklorists brought distinctive perspectives to their work; a spirit of friendship energized every encounter. I was determined to find a way to visit again.

My hope became reality seven years later, when I was completing a two-year term as president of the American Folklore Society. AFS director Tim Lloyd had participated in conversations with leaders of the China Folklore Society. In October, 2007, a CFS delegation attended the AFS annual conference in Quebec, Canada, and traveled to New York City and Washington, DC.

The AFS responded. Our delegation—Professor Juwen Zhang, Dr. Mabel Agozzino, and I—traveled to Beijing on December 3. We immediately presented three talks in three different Beijing locations, which established a fast pace and intense engagement that lasted the entire trip. By day four we were in Jinan, accompanied by Professor Tao Ye, participating in a seminar at Shandong University, then a full day in Qufu and the next day a seminar honoring the 20th anniversary of the Shandong Folklore Society. CFS president Kuili Liu then joined our delegation and we were on to Wuhan, where I gave a speech at Central China Normal University. Next was a flight to Yunnan Province to visit folklorists and museums in Kunming and Lijiang. Traveling, meeting, speaking, conferencing—all were accompanied by excellent meals, fascinating visits to historic places, and extensive toasting to folklore and friendship. Late one night in Kunming, after a meal and before the singing began, Juwen and I invented the now-famous "attack toast": rise from your seat, move around the circular table, raise your cup of liquor and deliver a personal toast directly at a respected colleague. "I attack you!"

In Lijiang our delegation stayed at a wonderful family inn; breakfasts were boiled eggs, warm milk, and "stinky" tofu. We walked the old village of Lijiang admiring small shops and Nashi women washing clothes in the icy mountain water that raced along the stone-paved streets. We walked the hillside surrounding the commercial district, and Tao Ye knocked on a villager's door. We were welcomed in and served tea. Very comfortable and hospitable!

Our last stop was in Guangzhou, and it was an important one. Our host, Institute of Chinese Intangible Cultural Heritage, was a new, national research center on the campus of Sun Yat-sen University. Housed in one of the most modern buildings on campus, the Institute was a strong symbol of China's leadership in the global movement to protect and preserve intangible cultural heritage. Institute Director/Professor Baocheng Kang, Professor Junhua Song, graduate student Xi

Chen, and Institute faculty would become important partners as China and US folklore colleagues took our collaboration to a higher level.

The convention of the Safeguarding of the Intangible Cultural Heritage had only been around for a few years, but China had been an early and enthusiastic signer. ICH work had engaged government and the private sector in folklore and traditional communities, offering a host of new opportunities for folklore scholars along with many challenges. While the US had participated in planning the ICH convention, the American government exhibited almost no interest in participating in this worldwide recognition and preservation effort. The seed of an idea was planted: perhaps we could construct a program that would compare Chinese and American theories and practices for engaging folklore, using intangible cultural heritage as our comparative frame? Such a project would allow us to move beyond faculty and student exchanges and occasional meetings to present conferences and publications that would benefit scholars and students in both countries.

By 2011, Beijing, Guangzhou, and Kunming were car-and-motorbike cities, Lijiang had a new airport terminal, and the sagging Mig fighters were no longer beside the runway at Kunming. Folklorists from China and the US had now spent several years exchanging ideas, attending conferences, and building the strong bonds of trust and friendship that are essential to international cooperation. It was now time to build real projects upon shared understanding and goodwill. Tim Lloyd approached the Henry Luce Foundation about a possible grant to support a series of meetings constructed around elements of ICH work. It was time to visit China partners again, this time to obtain support for a real international initiative.

By 2011, Xi Chen had become our AFS representative in China, working extra time from her base in the SYSU Institute to coordinate Society activities. I flew to Guangzhou on March 11, 2011, the day after the terrible tsunami struck Japan. The talk of this great tragedy was everywhere, forming a sad backdrop to my work discussing a possible project that would require the help of several China partners. With Xi interpreting our conversation, I met with Professor Kang and faculty in the Institute's 9th-floor conference room to discuss the specific proposal developed by Tim Lloyd: If the AFS secured funding, would the Institute be a partner in a series of meetings—"forums"—on comparative approaches to Intangible Cultural Heritage? Kang and colleagues had many questions but in the end it was agreed—we would together produce four forums, two in China and two in the US. The first would be held near Guangzhou in the fall of 2012.

The next day Xi Chen and I set out from Guangzhou, traveling first to Kunming, to meet with Mohua Xie, director of the Yunnan Nationalities Museum. After settling in downtown Kunming, we met for dinner with Director Xie and Ms. Du, his senior assistant, at a restaurant a few blocks from the Green Lake View Hotel. The night was very cold, and the restaurant staff placed small charcoal braziers around our table, but the heat only kept our ankles warm. We huddled close to the table sipping good liquor and with Xi's help, explained the project: "Would Director Xie cooperate with the AFS and the Institute to bring the perspective of China's museums into our forums?" Director Xie asked many questions. Following the dinner conversation Xi and I agreed that the conversation seemed positive.

The next morning Xi and I went to a shopping district and purchased warm coats. We then toured the Nationalities Museum and joined Mohua Xie for tea in the museum; it was agreed that he and his institution would be part of our project.

Then it was on to Lijiang, and a day with director Li of the Dhongba Nashi Museum. Once again Xi and I explained the idea of our series of forums, and stressed that museums would be an area of special attention in our meetings and publications. We settled things over a good lunch at a very nice, simple neighborhood restaurant. That evening we walked the narrow hillside pathways above the old district of Lijiang—an area now transformed by intensive restoration and by an invasion of Euro-pop dance clubs and hundreds of international tourists. We found a small bar near a hilltop overlooking both the old and new city. The proprietor offered up his own homemade liquor. It was delicious.

Our final stop was Beijing, and I was apprehensive. The relationship between folklorists in the US and China began in 2007, and over four years the cast of characters had changed. The American Folklore Society had a new president—Professor Diane Goldstein; in China, CFS president Kuili Liu had been succeeded by Professor Chao Gejin, a senior faculty member at the Chinese Academy of Social Sciences. Xi and I checked into the Sunjoy Hotel and took a cab a mile or so west to the CASS offices. Professor Ye Tao, still secretary general of the China Folklore Society, waited with us in a 6th-floor conference room. Professor Chao came in. A tall expert in Mongolian oral literature, Chao had studied in the US and spoke good English; he sat down at the big conference table and asked many questions about the proposed meetings. CFS was essential to the project; would the president agree to participate?

Yes, he would help. We sealed our commitment over an excellent dinner and many cups of liquor. The next day Xi and I had lunch with John Fitzgerald, China representative of the Ford Foundation. Like Chao, Fitzgerald asked many questions about the AFS, CFS, and our plans for cooperative meetings and publications. We learned an important lesson: many groups and individuals came to China hoping to develop cultural programs. China scholars and officials were always welcoming and hospitable, but moving beyond dining and toasting to real work and lasting friendships was not easy. Fitzgerald was properly cautious and to Xi Chen his questions seemed impolite, but he soon allocated some Ford money to help plan our project.

I learned important lessons. China scholars work harder than professors in the US. While academic careers present similarities, folklorists in China must make careful choices to make certain their investment of time will produce real benefits. Ideas and opportunities are approached with caution and careful planning and preparation are critical. Xi Chen and I were closely questioned by each of our Forum partners. Once questions were answered, responsibilities assigned, finances figured out, a project could proceed successfully.

The next morning Xi Chen returned to Guangzhou, and in the late afternoon I left Beijing for the US. AFS director Tim Lloyd crafted an excellent proposal to the Luce Foundation, and our shared China-US dream of international ICH forums became reality.

It is said that if you spend a week in China you can write a book; spend a month and you can write an article, but experience China again and again and you can't even write a postcard. There is some truth in this saying, for at first China seems clear—it is welcoming, friendly, energetic, ambitious, crowded, intense. A visitor who lands in a shiny new airport, takes a fast train to a western-style convention hotel, experiences a kind of "modernity shock." "Oh, I understand China," the visitor says, "it is an old culture with more and more characteristics of the modern West. I will write a book."

Reality is much more complicated, and the confidence of the new visitor is quickly swept away. But experience has brought an important truth: Chinese and US folklore scholars are especially well-suited to study and compare the multiple traditions, communities, nationalities, and cultural treasures that define the world's two greatest nations.

So, today, after many visits, I can write my postcard. It has a photo of the Guangzhou Dragon Boat Festival on the front; on the back this message: "We have built an international model of learning and research based on friendship and trust; we can now have the ability to bring the unique value of comparative folklore studies to future generations of scholars."

携手共建国际民俗学会联合会

朝戈金*

过去的这几年中,美国民俗学会和中国民俗学会一道组织了若干学术活动,大大增加了彼此的了解;与日本民俗学会和学界,也有一些互动和交流。这些活动为随后共同发起成立国际民俗学联合会奠定了重要的基础。

中美日三国民俗学会共同发起成立国际民俗学联合会(IFFS)的动因,是想扩大民俗学在国际人文社会科学学界的影响力。但具体的契机,是首届世界人文大会的筹备。在连任了两届副主席后,我是 2014 年 10 月当选为"国际哲学与人文科学理事会"(ICPHS)主席的。我的前任是非洲马里的阿达玛·萨玛赛库先生。他在任时就极力推动召开首届世界人文大会,以提升人文学术的国际影响力。我接手主席工作后,这也就成了我任期内最重要的事情。我上任前,在比利时的列日就已经举行了多次会议筹划主办这届大会的事宜。随后,在巴黎的联合国总部和比利时,我们分别召开了新闻发布会和数次协商会议,组委会的若干核心成员多次讨论这次人文学科的首次全球大亮相——人文科学的奥林匹克应该是个什么样子。民俗学学科在国际人文和社会科学界的阵营中,声音一直不够响亮,这局面令人深感遗憾,也就想做点事情,让民俗学在国际人文科学的大合唱中发出我们的声音。根据大会的规程,只有成为国际哲学与人文科学理事会的成员组织,才更方便在大会框架中申请本学科的"分会",于是就想到应该成为该理事会的成员组织。根据理事会的章程,只有跨国区域性组织或国际性学术组织,才具有成为其成员组织的资格。我们就顺理成章地想到应该成立一个国际性的民俗学学术组织,随后成为其成员单位。

共同创立民俗学联合会这个想法首先需要得到中国民俗学会的支持,在北京召开的中国民俗学会常务理事会上,这个提议得到与会者的一致支持;美国方面则随后利用召开年度大会的机会,在执委会上经讨论获得赞同意见;日本民俗学会也经过会议程序,同意加入其中。

---

* 编者注:朝戈金是中国社会社学院民族文学研究所所长,民俗学博士。自 2010 年担任中国民俗学会会长以来,他不但大力推动和发展中美民俗学交流,而且也为中国民俗学的建设做出重大贡献。近年来,他代表中国民俗学界在国际民俗学交流中发挥了核心作用,体现了中国民俗学从"引进来"到"走出去"的转折。朝戈金不仅自身参与了中美民俗学交流的诸多活动,翻译介绍国际民俗学理论,在中国组织国际会议,也培养和帮助了许多年轻民俗学者加入这一国际交流中。他对蒙古史诗和口头传统的研究成果,丰富了口头程式理论。

通过电子邮件之间的反复讨论后，利用 2016 年 7 月在内蒙古呼和浩特举办中美民俗学暑校预备班的机会，日本民俗学会时任会长小熊诚教授、负责联合会事宜的桑山敬已教授，以及岛村恭则教授一行三人专程赶来与中美民俗学会负责人会商推动成立联合会事宜。这次会议上，三方就联合会的章程和筹备工作中的若干具体环节和步骤，特别就人员配置和工作分工达成高度一致的共识。其间美国民俗学会的罗仪德先生的贡献卓著，在联系兄弟学会、起草联合会章程、联络国际哲学与人文科学理事会商议成立事宜等方面，出力尤多。中国民俗学会方面参与联合会事务的代表，目前是副会长安德明研究员。

眼下，国际哲学与人文科学理事会对于接纳国际民俗学联合会的态度比较积极。要加入这个顶级国际学术组织，需经过其执委投票通过，所以还要一些时日。不过，对于最终成为这个国际人文学术大家庭中的一员，我们还是信心满满的。

那么，加入国际哲学与人文科学理事会（ICPHS），会给民俗学带来什么样的益处呢？这里是该理事会的简要介绍：它由联合国教科文组织筹建于 1948 年 10 月，并于 1949 年 1 月召开第一次全体会议予以正式确认。它是与国际科学理事会（ICSU）、国际社会科学理事会（ISSC）同为隶属联合国教科文组织的三大顶级国际学术机构（目前 ICSU 和 ISSC 正在筹划合并）。当前 ICPHS 有近 20 个成员组织，包括国际学术院联盟、国际哲学学会联合会、国际历史科学委员会、国际语言学常设委员会、国际古典研究学会联盟、国际人类学与文化人类学研究联盟、国际宗教史协会、国际现代语言与文学联盟、国际东方与亚洲研究联盟、国际史前史及古代史科学联盟、国际音乐理论研究学会、国际非洲学研究学会和国际科学史与科学哲学联盟—科学技术史分会、国际美学学会等。理事会的刊物《第欧根尼》在学界具有很高的学术声望。

【编者注：国际民俗学会联合会于 2017 年 8 月在比利时宣布成立】

中国民俗学会会长朝戈金（站立者，左为美国民俗学会前会长艾伟，右为时任美国民俗学会会长杜赫斯特）以蒙古民歌欢迎客人，北京，2011 年 7 月。China Folklore Society President Chao Gejin singing a Mongolian folksong to welcome guests (AFS President Kurt Dewhurst on the right, AFS Past President Bill Ivey on the left), Beijing, July 2011. Photograph by Juwen Zhang.

The Collaboration in Initiating the International Federation of Folklore Societies

Chao Gejin[*]

The American Folklore Society (AFS) and China Folklore Society (CFS) have together organized a number of academic activities in the recent years which have greatly increased mutual understanding. Meanwhile both Societies have also engaged in some interactions with the Japan Folklore Society. All of these activities laid important foundation for the joint effort to launch the International Federation of Folklore Societies.

The International Federation of Folklore Societies (IFFS) was established in 2016 by the joint effort of the AFS, CFS, and Japan Folklore Society (JFS), with the purpose of expanding the impact of folkloristics in international academic worlds. The intention was to prepare for joining the World Humanities Conference. After being the Vice-Present of that Conference for two terms, I was elected the Chairperson of the International Council for Philosophy and Human Sciences (ICPHS) in October, 2014. My predecessor was Mr. Adama Samassekou from Mali. During his tenure, he actively supported the development of the World Humanities Conference in order to elevate the influence of humanities in academia. This task has been my priority since I became the Chairperson. In fact, before my term, some preparatory meetings had been held in Liege, Belgium. Soon after my taking office, a number of discussions and press conferences were held at the UN headquarters in Paris and Belgium. Image how it would be like to have a gathering for the representatives of humanities from all over the world—an Olympic Games for the humanities! The

---

[*] Chao Gejin (Chogjin) is Director of the Institute of Ethnic Literature, CASS, with his Ph. D. in Folklore from BNU. Since becoming the President of China Folklore Society in 2010, he has not only engaged in and further developed Sino-US folkloristic communication, but also has contributed tremendously to the reconstruction of Chinese folkloristics. In recent years, on behalf of the CFS, he has played a key role in the international folkloristics communication, indicating a change of Chinese folkloristics from the stage of "introducing into China" to "going abroad." In addition to his personal involvement in various Sino-US exchanges, translating international folkloristic theories, and organizing international conferences in China, Chao Gejin has also trained and helped many young folklorists to join this international communication. His own research achievements on Mongolian epics and oral tradition have enriched the oral formula theory.

voice of folkloristics in the international humanities and social sciences has never been loud enough. It is unfortunate. This situation urged me to do something to help sing louder in the international chorus of humanities. According to the rules of the ICPHS, one has to be its member in order to apply for a symposium or session during its conference. Also, the rule requires that an organization has to be cross-regional or international in order to be its member. As a result, we naturally began to think of founding such an organization to become its member.

This initial idea needed to be supported by the CFS as the first step. At the CFS Standing Committee meeting in Beijing in 2015, it received unanimous approval. On the AFS side, its Board also agreed with this initiative. On Japan side, it also went through its necessary procedure. All sides jointly agreed to launch a folklore association—IFFS.

Through numerous discussionsvia emails, taking the opportunity of preparing for the Summer Field School by the CFS and AFS in Huhehot, Inner Mongolia in July 2016, the representatives of the JFS—President Makoto Oguma, Professors Kuwayama Takami and Shimamura Takanori, made a special trip to meet with us and discuss the details for the establishment of the IFFS.

At this meeting, the three parties reached an agreement regarding details such as the articles of the Society, staffing, and division of responsibilities for the future organization. Timothy Lloyd's contribution was particularly important in connecting other societies, drafting the articles, and contacting ICPHS. The current China Representative is Deming An, Vice-President of CFS.

Currently, the ICPHS supports receiving new member such as the IFFS. We still need to go through the process of approval by its executive committee in order to join this top academic organization in the world. We are, however, full of confidence that we will become a member of this international family of humanities.

After all, what are the advantages for folkloristics to be a member of the ICPHS? According to its own introduction, ICPHS was founded in January 1949 after a preparation by the UNESCO from October 1948.

ICPHS is one of the three top academic organizations under the UNESCO, and the other two are International Council for Science (ICSU) and International Social Science Council (ISSC), which are under construction. ICPHS has nearly 20 member international organizations or associations, and its journal is *Diogenes*, with high reputation in the academic world.

[Editors' note: The International Federation of Folklore Societies (IFFS) was established in Bdlgium in August, 2017.]

(Translation by Juwen Zhang)

中美民俗学会合作史略

罗仪德[*]

无论是在学术领域还是公共领域，许多民俗学家，包括阿兰·邓迪斯、亨利·格拉西、迈克尔·琼斯、理查德·鲍曼、比尔·艾伟、莎伦·谢尔曼都曾更早来到中国访问和做学术报告，或者是像艾伟那样，作为美国政府高级官员主持会议。但是，中美两国民俗学会之间的正式合作关系，可以说肇始于2007年4月2日。那天，美国崴涞大学的张举文发给我和俄亥俄州立大学的民俗学家、中国西南口头诗歌专家马克·本德尔下面这封邮件，邮件的标题是"一个大胆的想法"：

> 考虑到你提到的美国民俗学会有兴趣在未来与中国民俗学会合作，我有一个大胆的想法：组织一个美国民俗学会团队，和中国同仁们一起开展关于中国非物质文化遗产保护运动的联合调查和会议。这个团队可以和中国民俗学者一起在中国旅行，去看一些被列入国家级非遗名录的地方，然后讨论旅途中的所见所想……总之，这个想法很大胆。你是否有兴趣继续探讨？

我对这个想法很感兴趣，很大程度上是因为美国民俗学会执行理事会也致力于扩展国际联系。接下来的几天我和举文又进行了进一步探讨。自从2004年中国认可联合国教科文组织的《非物质文化遗产保护公约》以来，中国政府对于非物质文化遗产的保护越来越重视，所以近年来中国的民俗学学术项目不断增加，我们对此颇感兴趣。比如，2011年，不算省级和地市级政府的财政支持，仅中国中央政府就为非物质文化遗产工作提供了将近3亿美元的财政支持，这项财政支持相当于美国政府在同一年为美国国家艺术基金会和人文基金会提供的全部财政支持。但这种支持附带有政府条件，其中许多与发展文化旅游机会有关，所以

---

[*] 编者注：在过去的十多年中，罗仪德在中美民俗学会的交流中发挥了重要作用。自2001年担任美国民俗学会执行秘书长以来，他尽心尽责促使美国民俗学会取得了稳步发展，同时也将美国民俗学会和其他国家以及国际性的组织联系起来，以此来肯定民俗学在学术领域的学科地位。他是美国研究博士，主要研究领域包括：美国饮食民俗、职业文化和民俗的公共实践历史。他多次来访中国，结识了很多朋友，也发表了演讲和访谈，并且有一个广为人知的中文名字，罗仪德，是中国民俗学会会长刘魁立在2007年的互访后为他取的名字。他的有关中美民俗学会合作项目背景以及美国公共民俗学和学术现状的访谈，发表于中文期刊《民俗研究》（2013年第6期，30—41页）。

中国非物质文化遗产领域的民俗学家和中国的政府机构参与的形式复杂而多变，并不都是具有积极意义的。我们作为局外人，更多的是羡慕这些参与的机会。

一个月后，北京大学教授、中国民俗学会副会长高丙中来访俄亥俄州立大学（当时也是美国民俗学会所在地），并在俄亥俄州立大学民俗研究中心举办的"民俗档案与国家"会议上提交了一篇论文。会议期间的一个下午，高教授和我畅谈了一个小时，他告诉我中国民俗学会想与美国民俗学会展开合作。我表明了我们在此项合作推动方面兴趣相同。通过谈话，我们决定通过以派两国的正式代表团互访这一典型的外交行动来开始我们的伙伴关系。

2007年10月，中国民俗学会派出一支五人代表团，由会长刘魁立教授带队，出席并参加了美国民俗学会年会，这次年会是和加拿大民俗协会联合举办的。会议结束后，当时的美国民俗学会会长、范德堡大学的艾伟和我陪同这些中国同事去纽约和华盛顿，与这两个城市的美国学者与公共民俗学家会见和交谈。六周后的12月初，美国民俗学会派出一支三人代表团（美国民俗学会会长艾伟、副秘书长梅布尔·阿果兹诺以及张举文）飞赴中国，开始为期两周的访问。访问期间，代表团走访了北京、济南、武汉、昆明、广州，与各地的民俗学机构会晤并演讲交流。（因为我妻子的家人突然离世，所以很遗憾我没能参与其中。但是在2008年5月，我独自到访中国两周，与北京、济南、广州和深圳的中国民俗学者们见面和交流。）

接下来的三年，我们一方面继续互派代表团参加彼此的会议，同时我们也开始讨论更多形式的合作方式——包括在中美两国举办关于民俗学、非物质文化遗产理论和实践的会议，交换年轻民俗学者，这些都需要大量的外来资助。尽管美国民俗学会和中国民俗学会已经支持我们的计划，并超出了我们自己的预算，但是，任何一个社团都很难以独自的项目获得更多基金。所以，当我与张举文和美国学术团体协会副会长史蒂夫·惠特利谈起如何争取尽可能多的资金支持时，他们都推荐路思基金会。张举文其实在几年前就已经受到路思基金会的资助，作为基金会的青年教授到访中国并做研究。

亨利·路思，1898年生于中国山东省，他的父亲是一个长老会传教士，他在中国生活到15岁。他是一个出版商，创办了标志性的美国杂志，如《时代周刊》《生活》《财富》和《运动画刊》。他对于中国和亚洲有着强烈的感情，于是，他创办了一个亚洲项目，致力于支持美国与东亚和东南亚国家文化与学术上的交流。2010年夏，我开始了与路思基金会亚洲项目负责人海伦娜·科伦达持续七年的对话。她为我们提供了三项基金，这成为我们和中国民俗学会合作的有力后盾。在我们工作展开的过程中，她还为我们提出了明智的建议。这对于我们而言都是非常珍贵的。

2011年路思基金会为美国民俗学会提供了两年的赞助。通过交流实践，建立了进一步的互相理解，扩展了我们与中国民俗学会的关系，并使这种合作关系更加正式化。2011年至2013年之间，除了路思基金会之外，我们又得到福特基金会、岭南基金会、美国国家人文基金会、亚洲文化协会、中国教育部的资金支持。我们在广州、纳什维尔、武汉和华盛顿举办了一系列的四个双语论坛来比较中美两国的民俗与非物质文化政策、个案研究、田野方法和档案实践。同时我们也为两国的年轻民俗学者组织了两年的互访交换项目。

2013年路思基金会又继续为美国民俗学会提供了三年资助。在2013年至2016年这三年中,美国民俗学会再次与中国民俗学会合作,并扩展到两国的诸多机构,共同致力于组织一系列的会议和专业交流,以此来增加中国和美国民族志博物馆从业人员之间的互相交流(在中国分别是广西民族博物馆、贵州民族博物馆、云南民族博物馆。在美国分别是马瑟斯世界文化博物馆、密歇根州立大学博物馆和国际民间艺术博物馆)。我们还发展了许多新的网络资源来支持两国的民俗学术研究。2016年12月我们得到了第三期的资助,用来在中国和美国民族志博物馆合作者之间开展一个长期的研究合作,合作内容是研究中国西南地区的纺织传统,并且还为年轻的民俗学学者以及来自中国、美国和亚洲其他地区的非物质文化遗产学者举办三年的暑期田野培训班。

这个项目将中美两国许多有才能和敬业的民俗学者组织到一起。中国民俗学会从一开始就是我们的主要合作者。该学会起初是在刘魁立教授的领导下,现在是在朝戈金会长的领导下。他们都是中国社会科学院的研究员。中国民俗学会秘书长叶涛和副秘书长朱刚协助朝戈金教授工作。此外,中山大学非物质文化遗产研究中心的前任领导康保成教授、现任领导宋俊华教授,还有美国民俗学会在中国的代表陈熙,也都是我们计划伊始的主要合作者。

在所有这些活动中,以路思基金会的基金为主,我们也得到福特基金会的支持,同时还有岭南基金会、美国国家人文基金会、亚洲文化协会、中国教育部、华中师范大学、中国社会科学院、内蒙古师范大学、六个与我们合作的博物馆,以及一些中国当地的大学和政府提供的资源和资助。

这些活动继续用民俗学和非物质文化遗产的视角去比较、分析并在中美两国之间开展广泛的实践活动,从而通过研究、记录、教育、呈现和保存等诸种方式来保护传统文化。中美民俗学会所组织计划的合作项目是在中美两国的官方渠道之外,以非官方的、学者对学者、机构对机构等小规模的合作项目,让每一个活跃的参与者在职业生涯的各个阶段,来共同分享学术、教学以及公共民俗学工作中的理论和实践,从而努力推动两国民俗学领域的发展。

一直以来,在美国民俗学会的中国学者专家对于发展中美民俗学会的工作和联系帮助巨大,我们的计划主要聚焦于组织广泛的各个领域的美国民俗学者与中国同仁们合作。基于共同的利益和方法,迄今为止,已经有100多位美国民俗学家和200多位中国民俗学家共同参与到我们的项目中,他们彼此交流了理论和最佳实践,这不仅推动了他们彼此的工作,而且还通过与同仁们合作,并向同仁们学习观念和课题,加深了他们自身的理解。

作为结语,我想讲一个小故事。在2007年年底的一个晚上,我与艾伟,还有刘魁立和萧放教授,在纽约格林尼治村的一个饭馆共进晚餐,这是纽约的同事罗伯特·巴龙推荐给我们的。饭后,按照一个中国的流行风俗,我们决定唱歌。刘教授先唱。和许多与他同时代的中国学者一样,他在苏联完成研究生学业,所以,他的俄语说得非常好。他宣布他要唱一首中国人家喻户晓的俄语歌——20世纪50年代非常流行的《莫斯科郊外的晚上》。艾伟和我也学过俄语,也知道这首歌,所以,当刘教授唱起来的时候,我们也加入进来和他一起合唱。或许是我想得太复杂了,但是,我想这种巧合的文化互动——一个中国人和两个美国人,都是刚刚相识,却因为在曼哈顿下城一个饭后的夜晚一起唱一首熟悉的俄文歌曲而分享着充裕的文化知识——至少在某种意义上巩固了我们和中国民俗学同仁的同事关系和友谊,并在此后加快了我们同中国民俗学者以及民俗学机构的联系。

最后,我诚挚地感谢,在过去这十多年里,为中美民俗学会合作而在各个方面为我们提供援助的每一个人。

(天津大学史静翻译)

刘魁立、罗仪德、罗伯特·巴龙、张英敏、萧放（自左向右），2007年10月于纽约。Kuili Liu, Timothy Lloyd, Robert Baron, Yingmin Zhang, and Fang Xiao (from left to right), New York, Oct. 2007. Photograph courtesy of Fang Xiao.

美国民俗学会执行秘书长罗仪德在北京的一次晚宴上唱美国民歌，2011年7月。AFS Executive Director Timothy Lloyd (standing; Xi Chen in the middle, Bill Ivey on the right) singing an American folk song at a dinner in Beijing, July 2011. Photograph by Juwen Zhang.

A Capsule History of the AFS-CFS Collaboration

Timothy Lloyd[*]

Although a number of US folklorists in the academic and public spheres, including Alan Dundes, Henry Glassie, Michael Owen Jones, Richard Bauman, Bili Ivey, and Sharon Sherman, had made earlier visits to China to give talks—or in Ivey's case to hold meetings, as a senior US government official, with Chinese government representatives—the AFS-CFS partnership can be said to have begun in earnest on April 2, 2007, when Juwen Zhang of Willamette University sent me and Ohio State University folklorist and southwest China oral poetry specialist Mark Bender the following email, the subject line of which read "A Wild Idea":

> Having thought of your mentioning that AFS is interested in future work with CFS (China Folklore Society), I have this wild idea: Having an AFS team hold a joint investigation and conference [with Chinese partners] on China's intangible cultural heritage protection movement. The team could travel in China to see some of the places listed on the National Name List with CFS scholars and then discuss what is seen and thought along the route.... Anyway, it is wild. Would you have an interest in exploring it?

I was interested in the idea, in large part because the AFS Executive Board had noted their interest in expanding our international connections, and Juwen and I discussed it further in the

---

[*] Timothy Lloyd has played a central role in the AFS-CFS communication in the past decade or so, and in the steady growth of AFS since 2001 when he became Executive Director of AFS. During his tenure as director he has connected AFS to a number of other national and international organizations to help affirm the disciplinary status of folklore studies in the academic world. He is a scholar of American foodways, occupational culture, and the history of public practice in the field of folklore, with a Ph. D. in American Studies. He has many friends in China through his visits, published lectures and interviews, and is better known by his Chinese name, 罗仪德 Yide Luo, given by the then CFS President Dr. Kuili Liu in 2007 after their first meeting. His provides a broader background for the AFS-CFS projects as well as the situation of academic and public folklore in the US through an interview published in the *Folklore Studies* [2013 (6): 30–41] in Chinese.

following days. We were particularly interested in China because of the recent increase of the number of academic folklore programs in China, which itself was in large part due to the rapid growth of Chinese governmental attention to matters of intangible cultural heritage since China ratified UNESCO's Convention on the in 2004. For example, in 2011 the Chinese national government alone—to say nothing of the support offered by government at the provincial and local level—provided financial support to ICH work that totaled around $300 million US, about the same amount as the US government provided that same year to support the entire National Endowment for the Arts and the National Endowment for the Humanities. But this support comes with strings attached that connect to government priorities, many of them having to do with the development of cultural tourism opportunities, so the forms of engagement of Chinese folklorists with the ICH domain, and the government agencies that administer it in their country, are complicated, varied, and not always positive. We outside China have much to learn from, and there is much to admire in, these engagements.

The next month, Prof. Bingzhong Gao of Peking University's sociology department, who at the time was a Vice-President of the CFS, came to the Ohio State University, AFS's institutional home at the time, to present a paper at the "Folklore Archives and the State" conference produced by OSU's Center for Folklore Studies. Prof. Gao and I spent an hour talking one afternoon of the conference, during which he informed me that the CFS wanted to initiate a partnership with the AFS. I indicated our shared interest in such a move, and from our conversation grew the idea of starting our partnership through a typical diplomatic move: exchanging visits by official delegations to each other' countries.

In October 2007, a five-person delegation from CFS, led by the President Professor Kuili Liu, attended and participated in the AFS's annual meeting, which that year was a joint conference with the Association Canadienne d'ethnologie et de folklore/Folklore Studies Association of Canada in Québec City. After that conference, our Chinese colleagues accompanied AFS President Bill Ivey of Vanderbilt University and me to New York City and Washington DC for meetings and conversations with US academic and public folklorists in both cities. Six weeks later in early December, a three-person delegation from AFS (AFS President Bill Ivey of Vanderbilt University, AFS associate director Maria Teresa Agozzino, and Juwen Zhang) made a two-week visit to China, with stops for meetings and lectures in the Folklore Programs in Beijing, Jinan, Wuhan, Kunming, and Guangzhou. (Because of a death in my wife's family immediately beforehand, I was not able to take part in this trip, so I made a two-week visit to China in May 2008 for meetings with CFS leaders and lectures in Beijing, Jinan, Guangzhou, and Shenzhen.)

Over the next three years, as we continued our exchange of delegations to conferences in the other country, we began discussing more involved forms of partnership—including conferences on folklore and ICH theory and practice in both countries, and exchanges of early-career folklorists—

with the leadership of CFS. Any such effort would require significant outside funding, and although AFS and CFS had supported our work to date out of our own budgets, neither society was in a position to fund much more on its own. When I talked to Juwen Zhang, and to my colleague and American Council of Learned Societies Vice President Steve Wheatley, about possible sources of support, they both suggested the Henry Luce Foundation. Juwen, in fact, had received support to visit and conduct research in China as a Luce Junior Professor a few years previously.

Henry Luce, the publisher of such iconic American magazines as *Time*, *Life*, *Fortune*, and *Sports Illustrated*, was born in 1898 in Shandong Province, China, where his father was a Presbyterian missionary, and he lived in China until he was 15. His strong feelings for China and Asia generally have been translated into a major program of support for cultural and intellectual exchange between the US and the countries of East and Southeast Asia. In summer 2010 I began what has now become a seven-year ongoing conversation with Helena Kolenda, Director of the Luce Foundation's Asia Program, which has provided three grants to AFS that have been the backbone of support for our work with CFS. Helena's wise counsel to all of us has also been invaluable as our work has developed.

In 2011 AFS received a two-year grant from the Luce Foundation to expand and formalize our CFS relationship through the exchange of best practices and the building of greater mutual understanding. Between 2011 and 2013, with this Luce Foundation funding supplemented by support from the Ford Foundation, the Lingnan Foundation, the National Endowment for the Humanities, the Asian Cultural Council, and the China Ministry of Education, we produced a series of four bilingual conferences (in Guangzhou, Nashville, Wuhan, and Washington, DC) comparing folklore and ICH policy, case studies, field methods, and archiving practices in both countries. We also managed two years of an international exchange program for younger folklorists from both countries.

Then in 2013 the Luce Foundation awarded AFS a further three-year. Between 2013 and 2016, AFS—again working in partnership with the China Folklore Society and in collaboration with a number of institutions in both countries—managed a program of conferences and professional exchanges to increase mutual understanding between staff at China and US ethnographic museums (in China, the Guangxi Nationalities Museum, the Guizhou Nationalities Museum, and the Yunnan Museum of Nationalities; and in the US the Mathers Museum of World Cultures, the Michigan State University Museum, and the Museum of International Folk Art), and the development of a number of new online resources to support folklore studies scholarship in both countries. In December 2016 we received a third grant, also for three years, to carry out a long-term research collaboration of our China and US ethnographic museum partners on textile traditions in southwestern China, and to produce three annual summer folklore institutes for early-career folklore and ICH scholars from China, the US, and elsewhere in Asia.

This project has brought together many able and committed people and organizations in both China and the US. The China Folklore Society, originally under the leadership of its President Professor Kuili Liu, and now led by President Chao Gejin, also of the Chinese Academy of Social Sciences, has been our primary partner from the start. Professor Chao has been ably assisted by CFS Secretary-General Professor Tao Ye and by Dr. Gang Zhu, CFS's assistant secretary. The Institute of Chinese Intangible Cultural Heritage at Sun Yat-sen University in Guangzhou, first under the leadership of Professor Baocheng Kang and now of Professor Junhua Song, and with the assistance of our AFS China Representative Xi Chen, has also been our major partner from the start. Professor Yonglin Huang of Central China Norman University in Wuhan and another Vice President of the CFS, and the directors of three Chinese provincial ethnographic museums (Wei Wang of the Guangxi Nationalities Museum, Cong Gao of the Guizhou Nationalities Museum, and Mohua Xie of the Yunnan Nationalities Museum) have all been important participants in our work. AFS 2006 - 2007 President Bill Ivey, first of Vanderbilt University and now of Global Cultural Strategies, has been our Senior China Advisor since 2007.

In all of these activities, Luce Foundation funding has been supplemented by support from the Ford Foundation, the Lingnan Foundation, the National Endowment for the Humanities, the Asian Cultural Council, the China Ministry of Education, Central China Normal University, the Chinese Academy of Social Sciences, Inner Mongolia Normal University, our six museum collaborators, and a number of local university and government sources in China.

These activities continue to use the lenses of the field of folklore studies and intangible cultural heritage (ICH) to compare, analyze, and carry out a wide range of best-practice activities in China and the US intended to sustain tradition-based culture through research, documentation, education, presentation, and conservation. By design, the AFS-CFS program works at a small scale, outside of official government channels in both countries—unofficially, scholar-to-scholar, institution-to-institution—and strives to advance the field of folklore in the US and China by sharing theory and practice in scholarship, teaching, and public folklore work among active participants at all stages of their careers in our field.

While China specialists in the AFS membership have been helpful in developing AFS-CFS projects and relationships, the primary focus of our program has been on engaging a diverse group of American folklorists of all interests in collaborations with China partners. Building on shared topical interests and approaches, the more than 100 US folklorists and 200 Chinese folklorists who have participated in our project so far have exchanged their own theories and best practices with their colleagues from the opposite country, and have advanced their own work and deepened their own understanding by engaging with and learning from their colleagues' concepts and projects.

To close, I'd like to tell a brief story. On the first night in late 2007 when Bill Ivey and I were in New York City with Professors Kuili Liu and Fang Xiao, the four of us had dinner at a restaurant in Greenwich Village that our New York colleague Robert Baron had recommended to us. After dinner, following an important and widespread Chinese custom, we decided to sing songs. Professor Liu went first. Like many Chinese academics of his generation, he had done his graduate study in the Soviet Union; as a result, he knew Russian well, and he announced that he would sing a song in Russian that many Chinese people know. The song he sang was a Russian popular song from the 1950's, called "Podmoskovnie Vechera" ("Moscow Nights"). As it happens, Bill Ivey and I had studied Russian too and knew that song, so we joined in with Prof. Liu on the chorus. Maybe I'm making too much of it, but I'd like to think that this coincidental cultural transaction—one Chinese and two Americans, all new acquaintances, sharing sufficient cultural knowledge to be able to sing a Russian popular song together in Lower Manhattan one night after dinner—made at least some contribution to the early cementing of our friendship and collegiality with our Chinese folklore-studies peers, and the rapid development of our relationships with Chinese folklorists and folklore institutions since then.

My sincere thanks go to everyone everywhere who has had a hand in this work over the past ten years.

世界民俗学的两个发展引擎之间的几件信使差事

高丙中*

民俗学是一门世界性的现代学术，它一方面深植于具体的国家获得发展的动力，另一方面建立一些国际的和世界的研究对象和议题，奠定与提升它的世界性和人类关怀的学术基础。比较神话学、故事类型学等是这个方面早期的最重要的成就。由联合国教科文组织在1980年代开始推动、到2003年以《保护非物质文化遗产公约》为标志的人类非物质文化遗产保护，是民俗学的世界性发展的最新成就，也是它的一个高峰。

要说世界民俗学的国家队伍，中国和美国不仅在从业和兼业的人数上是最庞大的，而且在学术产出和公众影响上也应该是最前列的。中美两国的民俗学无疑是当前世界民俗学最有活力的两个方阵，发挥着世界民俗学的发展引擎的作用。中国与美国的民俗学，就像两国所有其他领域一样，学术交流与合作在过去四十年不断增长着。尤其是最近十多年，代表民俗学学人的两国民俗学会建立了会际合作关系，让两个引擎能够在一定的协调中发挥作用，推动人才培养，在公共民俗与非物质文化遗产保护等议题上引领世界民俗学的前沿课题。我本人有机会参与了其中一些事件，受益良多，深感荣幸，也深怀感激。

中国现代民俗学是在引入英国、法国、北欧多国、日本、苏联、德国、美国的学术资源的过程中发展起来的，因此它的世界性是从学科兴起之初就与之俱来的。在相当长一个时期，中国学人到国外大学学习，译介国外的论著在国内传播。期间也有一些国外学者陆续前来中国交流。

我在2002年夏天由中国民俗学会理事长刘魁立先生提名担任学会秘书长，有机会参与策划、组织学会的国际学术交流。此前，美国民俗学者个人与中国同仁有一些交流，如

---

* 编者注：高丙中现任北京大学社会学和民俗学教授，北京师范大学民俗学博士。作为中国民俗学在1980年代重建后的第一批民俗学者的代表，他基于中国文化有关民俗的定义和研究方法的论述影响着目前中国的民俗学界。例如，他提倡的民俗学对生活世界和日常生活的研究，将民俗生活回归于民（即普通公民）的思想，以及跨学科的研究方法等，都得到中国民俗学者的极大响应。同时，他也派学生到海外做民族志研究，开创了中国人类学者研究异域文化的先例。在北京师范大学获得民俗学博士学位后，高丙中一直在北京大学工作，沟通民俗学、人类学和社会学等学科的交流。作为中国民俗学会的中坚之一，他极其关注民俗学学科的建设和发展，努力开拓学科的新领域，寻找学科的新方向，强调中国民俗学会与外界的交往，也是开启中美民俗学界交流之门的主要推动者，更是中美民俗学交流的一名主要信使。

1985 年丁乃通先生受华中师范大学刘守华、陈建宪和黄永林等学者邀请到该校讲学，并保持了多年的往来。1990 年，阿兰·邓迪斯受陈建宪邀请来武汉访问、讲学。在北京，邓迪斯主要由北京师范大学接待。钟敬文先生与他举行了会谈，安排他做讲座、游览长城和故宫。这些活动由我和我师弟 Jay Dautcher 负责担任翻译，我们也是他们夫妇游览的导游。邓迪斯先生是一个幽默风趣的大学者。我们陪他们夫妇一起在百盛百货购物，他们看到一对作为工艺品的巨大花瓶，非常欣赏。他兴致勃勃地对我说，如果你能够把它们放到我肩上，我想我能够把它们扛回去。我曾在 2001 年 2 月至 2002 年 7 月到加州大学伯克利分校做访问学者，选修了邓迪斯先生的民俗学理论课程，受益匪浅。期间，安德明和杨利慧来伯克利访问，我们一起做了邓迪斯的学术访谈。

2005 年初，中国民俗学会借北京市朝阳区文委之力，与北京民俗博物馆合办"民族国家的日历：传统节日与法定假日国际研讨会"（2005 年 2 月 14—15 日，北京），邀请美国、日本、俄罗斯、马来西亚等国民俗学学者参加。这次会议邀请的美国学者有美国民俗学会会长、加州大学洛杉矶分校教授琼斯，世界著名民俗学家、在中国有重要影响的表演理论代表人物、美国印第安纳大学杰出教授鲍曼，以及美国印第安纳大学人类学教授斯托尔姬，另外还有美国南卡大学历史系杰出教授史密斯。这种研讨会由中国学者根据国内现实需要设置议题、筛选多国学者参加，既吸引国际民俗学的学术资源为国内的重大议题所用，也为国际民俗学增加了一个民俗学参与一国公共事务的成功经验。这次国际节假日研讨会是我们学会努力推动主要传统节日成为国家法定假日的系列活动之一。接下来文化部在 2006 年把除夕、清明节、端午节、中秋节列入国家级非物质文化遗产代表作名录；国务院在 2007 年颁布法令，确定这四个传统节日成为国家假日。在后续多年的中美民俗学同仁的交流中，中国同行的这一成绩一直为大家津津乐道。

鲍曼和琼斯在北京举行了一系列讲座，北京大学、北京师范大学、中国社会科学院民族文学所、中央民族大学的多个单位都安排了他们的讲座。鲍曼关于表演理论、互文性的讲座，琼斯关于物质民俗的讲座，至今还令人记忆犹新。在这期间，中国民俗学会设立了"民俗学成就奖"，颁发给乌丙安、段宝林、陶立璠等中国民俗学家，以及日本的福田亚细男和美国的邓迪斯、鲍曼等著名的民俗学家。他们在中国学界有比较大的名望，对中国的民俗学发展有比较大的影响。最近这些年，在中国民俗学界被引用最多的外国民俗学者是鲍曼、邓迪斯和德国的鲍辛格。

2005 年夏天，我和几位民俗学朋友在北京见到了张举文博士，相互谈得十分投机，真的是相见恨晚。我和他都没有喝酒，但是短时间内能够成为好朋友，实在难得。他十分热心在世界范围内为民俗学寻找发展的热点和动能，对中美民俗学的交流与合作充满期待。我说，在这个历史时期，中国民俗学更需要向美国民俗学同仁学习。我们一致同意在接下来的几年共同推动两国民俗学会的会际交流和会议交流。他在美国民俗学会参加东亚民俗学的联络工作，和美国民俗学会的行政会长罗仪德先生沟通便利，从此他在两个学会之间发挥了一个重要的桥梁作用。

2006 年 6 月 2 日至 4 日，举文在自己学校做东，举办"中国人日常仪式实践研讨会"

暨"第十届假日、仪礼、节日、庆祝与公共展示会议",邀请中国民俗学会会长刘魁立、两名副秘书长萧放和陈泳超以及作为副会长的我参加。我很荣幸在会上做了题为《地方节日、国家知识分子与公共文化》的主旨发言。

在会议上第一次见到了桑迪诺教授,他是美国节日研究的著名专家,有多本美国节庆研究著作出版。那个时候正是中国国内对节假日议题情有独钟的时期,我有心邀请他访问中国参加会议,给我们传授他做节假日研究的成果,但是不凑巧,没有成行。这么些年,我还有一个遗憾是未能促成加州大学伯克利分校的布里格斯教授到中国讲学。我曾经安排了他的访问,但是最后没有成行。不过来日方长,希望有机会弥补遗憾。

张举文所在的崴涞大学坐落在俄勒冈州的州府塞勒姆市,夏天非常凉爽宜人。对于我这个在夏天素有"火炉"之称的湖北长大的人来说,生活在这个夏天是太美好了。举文安排我们游览了森林公园,还到太平洋沿岸欣赏了沙滩风光,在海边品尝了海味。我这次印象最深的是看到一望无边的田畴种植着不同年龄的圣诞树。它们将逐年进入市场,进入千家万户装点圣诞节。"年"是非常基本的时间节点,人们有一个惬意的欢度仪式,对于人们追求幸福生活至关重要。美国社会一直平稳地传承着自己从圣诞节期到新年的传统,而中国在现代的大多数时间都是由"国家"出来否定传统新年仪式的。好在我们遇上了中国社会重新重视传统新年习俗的时期,民俗学同仁能够为国家重新建立尊重传统习俗的现代时间制度发挥作用,而美国社会与美国民俗学界都为我们提供了宝贵的参照。

2007年5月3—5日,我受诺耶斯教授之邀到俄亥俄州立大学参加文化保护的会议,第一次有机会见到了美国民俗学会的行政会长罗仪德先生及其夫人芭芭拉女士。罗仪德先生十分真诚、宽厚、朴实,芭芭拉给人非常亲和、友好的印象,总是用温暖的微笑对待客人。我们晚上在诺耶斯教授家的后花园聚会,来自七八个国家的年轻学者用自己的母语唱歌,大家也一起手舞足蹈,真有天下民俗学者是一家的感觉。我们中国人对于美国居家的美好想象,一多半来自他们的后花园——无论是开放,还是用植物半遮蔽,都是用精心布置的植物和小装饰所点缀,各有情趣,魅力无限。我这是第一次感受到美国后花园的乐趣。后来,我们在印第安纳的"中镇"做民族志研究,就安排一个研究生专门做了中镇的后花园研究。中国也曾经是一个有后花园文化的社会,从孟姜女故事、西厢记故事到鲁迅故家的百草园,都是我们熟悉的。但是在过去六十多年(两代人的时间),我们的私人生活萎缩了,后花园文化消失了,甚至大多数的后花园也消失了。

2007年10月,美国民俗学会与加拿大民俗学会联合召开年会,会址在加拿大的魁北克市。中国民俗学会刘魁立会长应邀组成代表团参加这次年会,萧放、王霄冰和我加入其中。同年12月,美国民俗学会会长艾伟率学会代表团回访中国,与北京师范大学、北京大学、中央民族大学、山东大学、华中师范大学、中山大学等民俗学博士点的师生交流,也访问了云南大学、云南民族博物馆,以及丽江等地。从此,两个学会开始了越来越多的互访和合作。

在10月的会议上,美国民俗学会会长艾伟教授、行政会长罗仪德博士非常热情地款待了我们,在会议期间专门宴请我们,举办以我们为主宾的座谈,把中国学者组成一个专门的小组发言。艾伟教授曾经在克林顿政府时期担任国家艺术基金会主席，掌管对于包括公共文化、民间文化在内的各种艺术团体的资助。因为美国没有文化部，这个基金会实际上部分发挥着类似中国的文化部的作用。他和我们交流，给我最大的触动是他对于非物质文化遗产保护的支持。他后来一直热心于参与非遗的研究与学术会议，在与中国民俗学会的合作中也包含了相关的内容。这在中国同行看来是十分难能可贵的，因为美国并没有加入《保护非物质文化遗产公约》。在2015年夏天的成都非遗节期间，他也来参会。我们一起愉快地回忆了这些年两国民俗学同行的合作与交流，我非常诚恳地对美国同行带给我们的帮助与启发表达了谢忱。

魁北克的秋天是色彩斑斓的季节，我们游湖观云，欣赏枫叶，在小镇体验法语区的传统文化，在旧战场追忆英法战争的经历，真切地认识到自然风景、人文情趣与历史故事、宜居小城的兼容并包是多么可贵。北美的魅力在小城市，信然。会后，刘老师率领代表团继续访问华盛顿等地，我则赶往威斯康星州的阿特金森堡，试探在美国做一个小镇的社会生活的民族志研究的可能性。我在那里停留了两周，想做的是正式的田野作业之前的预调查。虽然我们后来选择印第安纳州的"中镇"作为田野作业点已是2010年的事情了，但是这次的预调查还是发挥了预备的作用。

我在中镇调查期间再次到印第安纳大学做了一次讲座，鲍曼教授和斯托尔姬教授夫妇拨冗来听讲座，之后他们请我喝咖啡。我们谈了中美民俗学、人类学的一些现状问题。他说，你2005年冬天来这里做讲座，你讲到的"非遗"对我们很多人都是陌生的；但是今天你看，我们没有人不谈非遗了。我说，非遗只是现象，你贡献甚巨的表演理论是非遗话题之前的理论，也是非遗实践中仍然受重视的理论。

美国在意识形态上坚持文化是社会事务，不设文化部，所以就没有一个专门的政府部门负责文化事务，也就没有加入《保护非物质文化遗产公约》。但是这并不妨碍美国民俗学界参与国际合作，并不妨碍中美民俗学在相关议题上的交流与合作。

实际上，我们与尼克·斯皮泽和罗伯特·巴龙的合作是在我们的所有国际合作中占分量最重的。他们二位2008年1月受我们邀请到北京和云南等地访问、讲学，传播他们对于美国公共民俗的长期观察与研究。2012年的美国民俗学会年会在新奥尔良召开，主办方邀请我作为嘉宾在会上做一个主旨发言，我讲了《非物质文化遗产保护与"文化革命"的终结》。会议期间，尼克安排我们游览了新奥尔良的天主教墓园。我第一次见识了像楼房公寓一样的坟楼，一座坟楼里一间间房子安葬一个个家人的尸体。我感觉好奇而惊悚。他还安排我们观摩卡特里娜飓风后重建的社区如何传承本地的音乐文化，与民间音乐家进行了现场表演与面对面交流。这是尼克最津津乐道的音乐文化在救灾、疗伤、社区恢复中的创新与传承项目。我们还参观了新奥尔良最有特色的音乐巡游团体的服装博物馆。而罗伯特作为客人仍然热心做向导，带我们参观了曾经役使奴隶耕作的大庄园。当然，我们也见识了李将军的铜像，一个内战中战败的首领能够以铜像为后世所纪念，这似乎是美国所特有的内战观才能够包容的。这对于中国人似乎难以想象。这是我第一次见识美国南方，深感它处处不同于东北部的清教徒传统。我还是犯了老毛病，见到有意思的地方都会想安排学生来做民族志研究。

好在有热心而可爱的尼克，他慷慨地接待我的一个博士生在本地完成了一年的田野作业，让他见证了多人种、多文化在一个地方混合、演进的现实。

年会之后，尼克安排我在杜兰大学人类学系做一个讲座，介绍我们的美国社会的民族志研究。这是我第一次向美国听众讲中国学者对于美国社会生活的认识。我讲，我们现阶段并不会设置过高的目标，我们更倾向于针对中国国内对于美国社会的认识标签，提供一种更丰满的叙事。我们的民族志在一种社区公共生活的背景中讨论美国的个人主义，在慈善公益、互助团体发达（如 Habitats for Humanity）的背景下认识资本主义，在活跃的宗教生活条件下认识美国作为最发达的现代社会，等等。

在与尼克和罗伯特的多次交流中，我们把美国的公共民俗视为中国的非遗保护的对应物。美国的体制认可文化在社会之中，各种社团、社区可以把市民、居民的文化视为地方的公共文化。中国的非遗保护在现阶段所达成的后果，也就是选择性地承认社会中原有的文化或传统能够成为公共文化，而此前多少年，这些项目要么是被忽略的，要么是被从政治上反对的。

后续我们一起召开了两个会议，一个在新墨西哥州的圣塔菲（2013 年 4 月），一个在云南的昆明和红河（2014 年 12 月）。前一个会议是中美民俗学家对于公共民俗和非物质文化遗产保护的比较研究，后一个是东亚文化遗产保护的研究。在这两个地方都参观了地方特色的传统建筑和民间手工艺。中国民俗学者对圣塔菲的爱杜比建筑（adobe）有一种惊艳的感动，美国学者对于云南的宗族、信仰与村落留下了深刻的记忆。

中美民俗学者的一个大规模合作是 2014 年的华盛顿国家广场的民俗生活节。这年的主题国家是中国和肯尼亚。中国的组织方是文化部下属的对外文化合作公司，美国的组织方是史密森学会，直接负责的是 Jim Deutsch 和 Sojin Kim 女士，但是参与志愿服务的专业工作者都是中美两国的民俗学者。美国学者有尼克·斯皮泽、罗伯特·巴龙、杰西卡·特纳、李靖、张巧运等，中国学者有安德明、黄龙光、韩成艳、王立阳和我等。期间，国会图书馆民间生活中心负责人皮特森女士还接待我们参观了国会图书馆，也分享了民俗生活节的一些历史资料。

在广场展示的中国项目有舞狮、侗族大歌、蒙古长调、羌族古歌、甘肃和青海的花儿、苗族蜡染和刺绣、扬州风筝、哈式风筝、陕北剪纸、杨柳青年画、景德镇陶瓷、鞡鞨绣、朝鲜族拼布、陈氏太极、浙江婺剧等。当然还有中国食品，如饺子、麻婆豆腐。一份麻婆豆腐配一份米饭，就是 10 美元，同样的搭配在北大食堂花 3 元人民币就能够买到。在两周时间里，共有 100 多万人参访民俗生活节的活动，我们这些志愿者互相合作，为美国观众讲解民间文艺与技艺及其人物和背景知识。我们也有机会登上华盛顿纪念碑顶部俯瞰全城，并在 7 月 4 日的美国国庆焰火中与市民和游客一起惊呼天女散花般的璀璨。我们坐在林肯纪念堂前，看着远处的华盛顿纪念碑倒映在林肯纪念堂前的水池里，一波波的焰火既在天空与华盛顿纪念碑缠绕在一起，也连同纪念碑倒映在水池里，天上与水中交相辉映，与我们在北京国庆节期间看到的焰火不同。

华盛顿广场应该比三个天安门广场还大吧？从国会山以下的绿地和林荫道，两侧十几家博物馆，到华盛顿纪念碑，再到长长的水池与林肯纪念堂相连，两边是多个球场、历史和历史人物纪念建筑。所以，华盛顿广场能够容纳各种活动，既包括国家主题的纪念活动，也包括市民和游人的体育和休闲活动。

民俗生活节铺开各种项目，只是占据了华盛顿广场小小的一角。我看到一辆大巴士多少天都停在广场上，展示着反核的标牌，一点不碍事的样子。我们聊天说到中美两国的政府与社会在公共空间的不同关系时，尼克曾经问我，你估计天安门广场会在某个时候允许民族民间文化的项目在那里展示吗？我说，美国安置文化与政治的关系更老道一些。当中国在1966年开始"文革"破"四旧"，清除各种传统文化的时候，美国开始在华盛顿国家广场兴办民俗生活节，展示各地、各民族的传统生活文化；但是，中国现在通过非物质文化遗产保护的方式重新设置社会中的文化与国家的关系，后续应该能够更好地安排政治与文化的关系。

在中美民俗学的交流中，我自己比较满意的是，近年来年轻一代学者已经开始到对方的社会开展以实地调查为基础的研究。例如，印第安纳大学的博士生 Curtis Ashton 曾到北京东岳庙做调查，并以此完成博士学位论文；我的学生王立阳也利用中美民俗学的合作项目在美国做了一年的交流和田野作业。另外，还有不少博士生和年轻学者通过会议和访学在不断加深双方的交流。我相信，从他们开始，中美民俗学的交流将进入一个更有深度的时代。

Some Messengers between the Two Developing Engines of the World Folklore Studies

Bingzhong Gao*

Folkloristics is a modern international discipline. It rooted in each country's unique development history, as well as in topics of international interest, and has credibly established itself as a vital discipline within the humanities. Comparative mythology and tale studies were among its early achievements. The 2003 Convention on Safeguarding Intangible Cultural Heritage initiated by the UNESCO in the 1980s was a recent new level on world folkloristics.

Concerning folkloristic strength at state level, China and the US are undoubtedly the two leaders in terms of the number of folklorists, and the academic and public influences. They are clearly the two frontiers in world folkloristics, and thus should play the leadership role in the world. Like some other fields, folkloristic communication between China and the US has been increasing for the past four decades or so. In particular, the past ten years have witnessed great accomplishments in training young folklorists, reaching out to public folklore, safeguarding Intangible Cultural Heritage (ICH), and in exploring cutting edge topics. I am grateful to have been involved in some of these events, from which I have benefited tremendously.

Chinese folkloristics have drawn upon English, French, German, Russian, Japanese, and American experiences, and gained an international character since its inception. In the early days, Chinese scholars had to study abroad and then introduce works back to China, or, some foreign

---

* Bingzhong Gao is Professor of Folklore at Beijing University. As a representative of the first generation of folklorists after the restoration of Chinese folkloristics in the 1980s, he has greatly influenced Chinese folklorists with his definition of folklore and discussion of research methods. For example, he promotes studies of the "living world" and of "everyday life," which has been well-received in the Chinese folklore circles. Meanwhile, he has sent many students abroad to conduct fieldwork, and has pioneered the field of Chinese anthropological studies of "others." After receiving his Ph.D. in Folklore from BNU, Gao has taught at Beijing University, bridging folkloristic, anthropological, and sociological discourses on Chinese culture studies. As one of the leading scholars in Chinese folkloristic studies, he devotes attention to the development of the discipline, to expanding the scope of the field, to seeking new directions, and to communicating his results with the world. He is also one of the main initiators of Sino-US folkloristic exchanges, and, certainly, a main messenger between the two sides.

scholars had to come to China in order to have an exchange.

In 2002, I was nominated by the President of China Folklore Society (CFS), Dr. Kuili Liu, as the Secretary General, and began to strategize on enhancing international communication. Previously, there were individual folklorists who communicated with American folklorists. For example, in 1985 Dr. Nai-tung Ting of University of Western Illinois was invited to lecture at the Central China Normal University (CCNU). In 1990, Alan Dundes was invited by Jianxian Chen to CCNU. During his visit, Dundes also visited Beijing and Shanghai and met Chinese folklorists. In Beijing Dundes met with Dr. Jingwen Zhong, the distinguished founder of the first doctoral program of folklore in China. Dundes and his wife also toured the Great Wall and Forbidden City, accompanied by Jay Dautcher and me. Professor Dundes had such a refreshing sense of humor. On one occasion in a department store, he and his wife showed interest in a giant vase. He said to me, if you could put it on my shoulder, I believe I can carry it back to the States. I later studied in UC Berkeley in 2001-2002, and benefited greatly from taking his course on folkloristic theories. During that time, Lihui Yang and Deming An also visited Berkeley, and together we conducted an interview of Professor Dundes.

Early in 2005 (Feb. 14-15), China Folklore Society, in collaboration with the District of Chaoyang in Beijing and Beijing Museum of Folklore, organized an international conference on "National State Calendar: Traditional Festival and Legal Holidays." Among the invited international scholars were Professor Michael Jones, AFS President, and Professors Richard Bauman and Beverly Stoeltje from Indiana University. This conference effectively influenced the Chinese central government's policy regarding legal holidays. In the following year, the State Council issued the law to set the Traditional New Year's Eve, Qingming (Tomb Sweeping) Festival, Dragon Boat Festival, and Mid-Autumn Festival as the ICH item at State Level, and made them national festivals with days off from work. This event has been a frequently mentioned topic among Chinese and American folklorists in terms of what folkloristics can achieve.

During their visit to Beijing, Professors Jones and Bauman also lectured in several universities, and left deep impressions on many Chinese folklorists. At that time CFS also established the Folklore Achievement Award. Among the recipients were a few Chinese folklorists, a Japanese folklorist, and Professors Jones and Bauman.

In summer 2005, I met Dr. Juwen Zhang in Beijing, along with a few other folklorists. Our conversations were so congenial that we all felt that we should have been known to each other earlier. He and I did not drink any alcohol, but became good friends in a short time. This friendship is indeed precious. At that time, he was genuinely seeking the opportunity to engage Chinese and American folklorists inexchanges. I told him that Chinese folklorists were particularly in need of learning from American folklorists at that time. We both agreed to do something together to move the communication forward. He initiated communication with Timothy Lloyd, the Executive

Director of AFS, and since then, he has played an important role in bridging CFS and AFS.

On June 2-4, 2006, Juwen Zhang hosted the Conference on Chinese Daily Ritual Practice and the Tenth Annual Conference on Holidays, Ritual, Festival, Celebration, and Public Display, Willamette University, Salem, Oregon. He invited Dr. Kuili Liu, CFS President, the two Vice Secretary General Fang Xian and Yongchao Chen, and me as the Vice President to participate. I was honored to give a keynote speech entitled "Local Festivals, National Intellectuals and Public Culture."

At the conference I also met Professor Jack Santino for the first time. I had known his work and wanted to invite him to China. However, it did not work out due to his schedule. This remains a regret for me. Another regret I have is that my wish to invite Professor Charles Briggs to China did not come true. I hope there still is a chance to do so.

The university where Juwen Zhang teaches is located in Salem, Oregon. It is particularly cool and comfortable in summer there. Spending a few days there was a special treat for someone like me who grew up in a place in Hubei known as "furnace." Juwen arranged trips to Forest Park in Portland and the Pacific coast introducing me to local clam chowder and other seafood. What impressed me most was the endless Christmas tree fields with varying heights. They would enter many houses as Christmas decorations. The junction of "year" is a very important turn in everyday life as a rite of passage. This tradition has been steadily continued in the US. But in modern China, most traditional festivals were denied by the "State." It is fortunate that now we are in a good period of history when the traditional New Year can be revived.

In May 2007, I attended a conference at the Ohio State University at the invitation of Dorothy Noyes. There I was able to meet, for the first time, the AFS Executive Director Tim Lloyd and his wife, Barbara, and both of them made a deep impression on me. Professor Noyes held a party in her backyard for the conference attendees. Some young scholars, who were from seven or eight countries, began to dance and sing in their mother tongues. It was the moment when one would feel that all the folklorists in the world were one family. The beautiful imagination that we Chinese have about American family life is mostly based on their backyard—either wide open or half hidden in plants, every single thing being carefully decorated and full of interest and charm. It was my first time to enjoy the pleasure of being in a backyard in the US. Later on, I arranged one graduate student to work on the topic of "backyard" in Middletown in Indiana. China once was a society with backyard culture, which generated the famous folktales that we are familiar with, for example, Mengjiang Girl (whose tears destroyed the Great Wall in order to find her husband buried underneath), West Chamber (a romantic drama written in the 13th century), and the Hundred-Flower Garden (by Lu Xun, the greatest Chinese writer of the 20th century). But in the past two generations, about sixty years, our private life withered; the backyard culture disappeared, and most backyards even vanished as well.

In October 2007, CFS President, Dr. Kuili Liu led a delegation to participate in the joint AFS annual meeting with Canadian Folklore Society in Quebec City in Canada. The delegates included Fang Xiao, Xiaobing Wang, and me. In December, AFS President Bill Ivey led a delegation to China and visited BNU, Beijing University, Minzu University of China, Shandong University, CCNU, and Sun Yat-sen University, meeting folklore faculty and students. They also visited Yunnan University and Yunnan Nationalities Museum. From then on, more and more mutual visits and collaborations began.

During the 2007 AFS meeting, Bill Ivey and Tim Lloyd held a special forum and reception for us. What I sensed from Bill Ivey was his great support to safeguarding ICH, perhaps due to his experience as NEA Chairman during the Clinton Administration. He attended a series of meetings in the later years with great enthusiasm toward ICH. That was very precious from the perspective of a Chinese folklorist, because USA has not adopted the ICH Convention. At the meeting in Chengdu in 2015, we met again, and shared our memories of the past, and I sincerely thanked my American colleagues for their collaboration and illuminous practices in cultural conservation.

After the 2007 meeting, our delegation made visits to New York and Washington, D.C. (see Fang Xiao's stories), and I left for Fort Atkinson, Wisconsin, seeking to do some ethnographic work about a small town. I stayed there for two week to do some preparation, but we later decided to do the project in Middletown, Indiana, starting in 2010.

While I was in Middletown, I gave a talk at Indiana University, and Professors Bauman and Stoeltje attended. At the coffee afterwards, we talked about the status of folklore and anthropology in China and the US. He commented that when I talked about ICH in 2005, the term was new to them, but now everyone talked about ICH. I said that ICH was only the surface, and that his great contribution about performance theory was the premise, which was still emphasized in dealing with ICH practice.

In American thought, culture belongs to the domain of social affairs. As a result, there is no Department of Culture or a special government branch to deal with culture affairs. Thus the US government did not ratify the UNESCO's ICH Convention. However, this does not hamper American folklorists in international collaborations, or our Sino-US folkloristic communication.

In fact, our collaboration with Nick Spitzer and Robert Baron was the most important part of the international projects that I have been involved in. We invited them to Beijing and Yunnan to lecture in 2008, to share their experience and observations in American public folklore sphere. At the AFS 2012 in New Orleans, Nick Spitzer invited me to give a panel talk on "The Protection of ICH and the End of 'Cultural Revolution.'" During the meeting, he arranged tours to the Catholic cemetery, which was like apartment buildings to me. I felt surprised and frightened. He also took us to the rebuilt community after Hurricane Katrina to see how music was used among folk musicians for face-to-face interaction. There was also the bronze bust of General Lee from the Civil War. It was surprising to me to see that a defeated general could still be there; it would be unimaginable in China. It was the first time I experienced the Southern US, different from the Protestant tradition in the Northeast. I again wanted to have my students work on this place. Nick hospitably hosted one of my students to do a year of fieldwork there, and helped him to document the practice of multicultural interactions.

After the annual meeting, Nick arranged for me to give a lecture at Tulane University about how we did ethnographic work in the US. It was my first time talking about how Chinese do fieldwork in the US. I said that we would not aim too high at the initial stage, but were inclined to provide some general understanding of American society so as to enrich our studies on Chinese domestic issues.

Through our communication with Nick and Robert, we take American public folklore as the equivalent of Chinese ICH protection. The American system allows various communities to develop their own local public culture. What China is doing at this stage with ICH is to achieve the goal of recognizing selected cultures or traditions in local communities as public culture. Prior to this movement, such local cultures were either ignored or dismissed by political authorities.

We continued our effort on this with two more meetings: one in Santa Fe, New Mexico (April 2013) and one in Kunming and Honghe, Yunnan (Dec. 2014). The first was to compare public folklore with ICH, and the second was to look at the culture heritage protection in East Asia. Attendees visited local sites of traditional architecture and art craftsmanship. Chinese folklorists showed great amazement at the adobe building; American folklorists were impressed with the clan and beliefs in the villages in Yunnan.

One large scale collaboration between Chinese and American folklorists was the Smithsonian Folklife Festival in Washington Mall in 2014. The theme of that year was China and Kenya. With the involvement of China's Ministry of Culture, and under the direct leadership of Jim Deutsch and Sojin Kim from the Smithsonian Institute, many folklorists from China and the US volunteered to participate. On the US side, there were Nick Spitzer, Robert Baron, Jessica Turner, Jing Li and Qiaoyun Zhang; on China side, there were Deming An, Longguang Huang, Chengyan Han, Liyang Wang, and me. During the festival, Betsey Peterson, who was in charge of American Folklife Center at the Library of Congress, gave us a tour to the library and shared some historical materials.

At the Mall, there were many traditional Chinese performances: lion dance, singing from of the Dong people, Mongolian long tone singing, ancient songs from the Qiang people, and other crafts works such as embroidery, kite-making, paper-cutting, and ceramic work. Of course, there were various regional foods. One share of *mapo tuofu* was $10.00, but would be RMB3.00 ($0.40) in the student dining hall in Beijing University. As volunteers, we had the chance to get on top of the Washington Monument. We also experienced the celebration of the Fourth of July, watching the fireworks, very similar to those at the Tiananmen Square during the National Day (Oct. 1) in Beijing.

The Washington Mall is about three times bigger than the Tiananmen Square. Along the Mall, there were many museums and monuments, as well asathletic fields. Clearly, the Mall holds both events with national themes and common people's daily sports and leisure activities.

The Folklife Festival only occupied a small corner of the Mall that year. I saw a bus parking there for several days with anti-nuclear signs, and it did not affect traffic or other activities. Nick and I chatted about how different the two governments might use such public spaces. Nick once asked me whether the Tiananmen Square would allow different minority nationalities in China to have their cultural events. I said that the US had more experience in dealing with culture and politics. When China began the "Cultural Revolution" to sweep away the "traditions," the US began to use the Mall to hold folklife festival, demonstrating different cultural traditions. However, China now is resetting the relationship between culture and government through the ICH movement, and it should be able to handle the relations between culture and politics well in the near future.

What I personally feel satisfied with, in the process of Sino-US folkloristic communication, is that the younger generation of folklorists from both sides have begun to conduct fieldwork in each other's society. For example, one doctoral student from Indiana, Curtis Ashton, did fieldwork in the Dongyue Temple in Beijing and completed his dissertation on it. My own student, Liyang Wang, did fieldwork in the US for one year through the AFS-CFS joint project. Also, many young folklorists from both sides have visited each other and participated in various folklore meetings, deepening and broadening our communication. I believe, from their generation on, the Sino-US folkloristic communication will enter a new era of greater depth and fruitfulness.

(Translation by Juwen Zhang)

丁乃通：醉心于中国民间故事研究的美籍华人学者

刘守华*

以编撰《中国民间故事类型索引》而知名于海内外的丁乃通教授，于1989年4月因突发心肌梗塞在美国西伊利诺大学溘然长逝，距今已有15年了。他是1915年4月22日在杭州出生的，已达百岁冥诞。他在上世纪80年代中国改革开放热潮中曾几次回国访问，并于1985年应聘为华中师范大学客座教授，驻校授课，传播芬兰学派的故事学研究方法，使中国民间文艺学同国际接轨，给师生以深刻有力的教诲启迪。音容笑貌，历久弥新。现特撰此文，以寄忆念之情。

先从他由研究英国文学转向研究中国民间故事说起。他早在1936年即毕业于清华大学西方语言文学系，并于1938年获得美国哈佛大学英国文学硕士学位，三年后又在哈佛大学获得博士学位。随后开始了他在高校讲授英国文学的漫长生涯，先在国内之江大学、河南大学、中央大学、岭南大学任教；从1957年起客居美国，任教于泛美大学和西伊利诺大学。他是怎样转向民间文学特别是中国民间文学研究的呢？他在1985年应邀到华中师范大学讲学时写成的一篇短文中告诉我们：

> 我是一个美籍华人，本来是研究和教授英国作家文学的，完全不懂民间文学。60年代初期，研究一个比较文学上的题目，发现民间文学不但是好些作家文学的基础，而

---

* 编者注：刘守华是华中师范大学教授，是新中国的第一代民俗学者之一，从1950年代就开始搜集研究民间故事，成果卓著，并为中国民间文学和民俗学发展培养了骨干力量，受到整个学界的极大敬重。他的"故事学"研究代表了中国学者在民间叙事理论上的成就，也亟待传播出去。这里他讲述了丁先生在中国的故事，继续着与丁先生的对话，体现了一位学者对事业和对同行的忠诚和敬意，也为学科树立了一个榜样。这个故事标志着中美近三十多年来的交流的开始。正如中国俗语所说，前人栽树后人乘凉，我们这些还在世的后人也要为我们的后人栽树。这也正是延续亚民俗的核心意义所在。

在此，我们也缅怀一位为中美民俗学交流做出了卓越贡献的美籍华人学者丁乃通（1915—1989）。刘守华老师将珍藏多年的丁先生的信件在此首次公开，更显出这份学术友情的纯洁。丁先生在美国民俗学界长期受到冷落，其有关中国民间故事的学术成就常常被带有政治观点的学术所排挤。但历史总能澄清什么样的学术成果会延续下去。丁先生有关中国故事类型等著述依然是研究中国故事的重要的理论基础。本文集中李扬也讲述了与丁乃通先生的交往故事。这些故事无疑会勉励更多的人沿着这条路走下去，栽下更多的树。

且是比较两个或更多的文化背景上不同民族文学作品的最有用的工具,这才开始认真地阅读关于民俗学和民间文学的书籍和杂志。至于我和中国民间文学所以结下不解之缘,主要的原因是看不惯美国自命为中国通的右翼分子和以反共自豪的从台湾去的学人,勾结起来攻击谩骂中国的民间文学工作者。我不但和他们发生争论,而且决心要用具体材料证明他们曲解了中国的民间文学。因此花了几年的心血,写了一部《中国民间故事类型索引》,看了许多中国各民族的故事,认识了中国人民的智慧和才能,深刻了解到中国民间文学在世界上占了一个不但是重要而且是领先的地位。①

《中国民间故事类型索引》是丁先生经10年艰辛劳作而写成的巨著。他依据580多种故事资料,归纳出843个类型,涵盖故事7300余篇。在索引编撰体系上,它借用芬兰学派的AT分类法来处理中国民间故事,其优点是便于人们将中国故事纳入国际通用编码体系而进行比较。但是,这一框架并不完全适合扎根于独特历史文化土壤之中的中国故事,因而在某些方面难免有削足适履之缺陷。难能可贵的是,该书将1966年"文革"之前的中国故事资料几乎搜罗殆尽。

在身处异国他乡又和国内同仁隔绝的情况下,他克服困难,利用世界各国藏书,不仅拥有的故事超出德国学者艾伯华的《中国民间故事类型》一倍多,而且对许多故事类型的情节梗概及其变异形态的描述也精细得多。当它于1978年列入"FFC 223"由芬兰科学院出版之后,立刻就作为关于中国民间故事最为适用的检索工具书而深得各国学者的好评。

丁乃通先生长期居留海外,而且一直专攻英国文学,晚年却转向中国民间故事研究,显然同他身上固有的中国情结有关。当中国结束"文革"动乱迈入改革开放的历史新时期之后,他关切中国的民间文学专业,并倾注心力全力促进其发展。他在上述短文的另一段中告诉我们:

> 我在最近七年中,已经来中国四次:1978年、1980年、1981年和今年(1985年)。1981年是受民间文艺研究会的邀请。那时民间文学工作正在复苏,虽然确知前途光明,总以为能恢复"文革"以前的情形便很好了。不想此次到中国,看到的蓬勃热烈现象,比原来想象的高出了许多倍。据北京民研会说,几乎每一个县市,都出了自己地区的故事集子,而且往往不止一册。好几个省还出了一种或多种中国民间文学杂志。这些故事,我虽因忙,只看了极少数,可是已经发现它们的忠实性,比以往的高很多。另外有的同仁,还找到了好多从前大家都认为在中国缺乏的长篇叙事诗,最长的一部,有150万行左右,比别的国家最长的叙事诗都长得多。这种事实,在世界上采录民间文学最彻底最成功的国家之一的芬兰,也感到惊奇,在报纸上特别登载。可是据好些同仁指出,目前所已经找到的资料,还只是极表面一层,越发掘下去,越会感到中国口头文

---

① 刘守华:《一位美籍华人学者的中国民间文学情结》,见《中国民间故事类型索引》,华中师范大学出版社2008年版,第364页。

学传统深厚广阔，令人有取之不尽、用之不竭的感觉。只要是中国血统的人，无论现在国籍怎样，都应该对于自己民族伟大文化传统和劳苦大众（尤其是农民）想象力之丰富、艺术创造力之强盛，感到骄傲。

我们邀请丁乃通先生来华中师范大学讲学，从1985年9月16日接他进校，到10月17日送别，持续了整整一个月。他每周给我们的本科生和研究生讲一两次课。我们平时还可随时向他请教，或不拘形式地展开讨论。他带来一纸箱外文书刊，其中有阿兰·邓迪斯的《世界民俗学》、斯蒂·汤普森的《世界民间故事分类学》以及《世界民间故事母题索引》等。他主要参照汤普森的著作给我们讲故事学，常拿着英文原著边译边讲。由于我们的英语水平差，对国外学术又很陌生，他只能慢条斯理地讲，话语却沁人心脾，使听者有如沐春风的感受。以这一个月的讲学为中心，我们的交往从1983年5月开始到1988年4月，前后达5年之久，书面通信近20次。他满怀热烈的中国民间文学情结，不止一次地给我有力的冲击和感染。1985年10月17日讲学结束，我校举行简短仪式表示感谢，由章开沅校长聘请他为客座教授。他当即将所携带的外文书刊，还有付给他的讲课酬金640元，全部捐赠给我们。后来，连学校报销的机票款也给了我们，叮嘱我们买两个书柜，多搜购一些民间文学资料，建立自己的资料室。

他以极大的热忱指导听课的陈建宪和黄永林两人，将自己的成名之作《高僧与蛇女》从英文译成中文在国内发表。怎样着手？他细致周到地给予辅导："先一段一段地念，把意思弄懂了，再一句一句地看。不懂时多查字典，多想一想，不要拘泥于每一个字都要译，而是把意思尽量忠实地译出来，再把译稿寄给我改。"在审阅他俩的试译稿时，丁先生和夫人许丽霞就像批改小学生作文似的，用红笔在原稿上改写得密密麻麻，几经反复才得以定稿。1986年10月21日，他在给我的来信中特地写道："小陈和小黄翻译的我写的白蛇传论文的手稿，已经由我和丽霞改好了，即日寄给你，请你转交给他们。这稿子可真的花了丽霞好多时间修改。最大的原因是他们二人英文程度不够；次之是其中材料涉及西方文学、文化史、宗教等，都是他们不懂的；三者是以前写的时候知道论文太长，不易出版，力求紧凑，有些地方没有专门知识不容易懂；四者那是多年前的作品，当时用的资料很不好，我不知放到哪里去了。所以自己写的东西，修正译本时才这样困难，这论文最后那一段我已经全部改写了。因为那时我对民间故事知道得还是不多，所以有失误处。请你把这一封信给陈黄二人看，希望他们赶快誊清寄到上海。"他还就此写道："希望在国内研究自己民族文化的学人，快快多学外文走向世界。"在丁先生的言传身教和各自艰苦磨炼下，这批学生正走进中国高校民间文学专业中坚行列，如陈建宪、黄永林、林继富、覃德清、肖远平等。他对这些学生的出路与业绩极为关心，在一次来信中就写道："从前在我班上的同学中，有好几位已有良好的成绩，使我十分欣慰。"

至于他对我研究故事学的指导，这几年更倾注了大量心血。在初次通信中，他就表示，从信中"深深了解你对故事学的热诚，在这一点上，我们真是志同道合"。他在多次面谈和来信中，希望我就AT461即"求好运"这个世界性故事类型作深入系统的研究，首先对中国材料做透彻研究,"先把中国的说法整理成一组,用历史地理法探测传播地区及方向、起源民族及地域、原始形式及意义,尤其要查找古书里有没有这样的故事";再做艰苦努力,"搜集和研究全世界的说法",特别是和印度故事进行比较。"可是了解中国的传统,在我看来并不需要把印度的说法作为前提",而是要着力研究这个故事在中国传承变异的特征,如"问三不问四"的情节设置,在印度就没有。

为了帮助我完成这项研究,他寄来了汤普森《世界民间故事分类学》一书中的有关论述,还有德国学者蒂勒早在1919年就已刊出的长篇论文《一个命运之子的童话》。他还告诫我不要急于求成,"这种工作中有价值的著作,很多都是许多年或甚至终生的成果"。阅读这些论著之后,使我眼界大开,以数年时间写出《一个故事的追踪研究》[①]《一个蕴含史诗魅力的中国民间故事》[②] 等论文,在故事学研究上向前迈进了一大步。

丁先生在华师讲学时,生活十分简朴,他谢绝宴请,我和老伴常用小白菜、黄花菜拌的素面给他作为中餐,他十分中意。他在中国出书不但不要稿酬,还自己出钱购书送人。他喜爱中国民间故事,深为故事朴实优美的民族文化内涵而自豪(如指出中国称赞女性聪明的故事特别多而格外引人注目),因而在研究和评说中国故事时常常达到痴迷境地,从而以他对中国民间文学的一往情深给予我们师生以终身滋润心田的深切感染。

丁乃通先生在这几年中还为促进中国民间文学事业做了许多事情:

首先,作为一位献身于中国民间文学研究的海外华人学者,他渴望尽可能多地了解中国民间文学事业发展的实际状况。因此,当湖北大冶县文化部门于1985年9月举行民间文学工作现场会议邀请他参加时,他虽腿有病行走不便,还是十分高兴地准备参加。后来,他因故未能成行,我便将会上所得资料——主要是一批喜爱民间文学的农民自费编印的本村或自家的故事、歌谣、谚语集转交给他。他十分珍惜这些用土纸油印的小册子,经过认真研究,以《民间文学民间办——一个新生事物在中国》为题,用英文写成长篇论文刊于日本出版的《亚洲民俗研究》1997年第2期。后经黄永林译成中文,刊于《中南民族学院学报》1988年第3期。湖北省文化厅还将它转发给全省文化部门学习参考。此文不仅对这些保持了民间文学朴素本色的作品如《土地菩萨的故事》的学术、文化价值给予很高评价,还特别赞扬了农民自己动手,参与搜集、保存民间文学的新鲜经验。文章写道:"一些热爱民间文学的农民像雨后春笋般相继投资,自费编印已搜集的民间文学作品专集。""尽管这些集子在版本上没有很高的地位,但它们仍显示出值得注意的发展趋势。它们迅速而持续地出现,证明了中国民间文学工作者在唤醒中国无限丰富的口头文学遗产方面取得了初步成果。"他把这一经验和国际上通常只将农民作为搜集对象的做法进行比较之后,特别感到兴奋,认为大冶的做法"即使不能说是空前的,也是极不寻常的"。作为一个科学工作者,他自然也看到了这一工作由于缺乏专业指导所存在的问题。最后,他语重心长地呼吁,由于中国既拥有丰富的口头文学,同时又拥有大量关于民间故事、风俗和信仰的书面记载,"如此

---

① 刘守华:《一个故事的追踪研究》,载《民间文学论坛》1989年第2期。
② 刘守华:《一个蕴含史诗魅力的中国民间故事》,载《光明日报》2012年2月27日。

独特的遗产,值得以特别的注意力去调查、保护和研究。我真诚地希望中国政府为民间文学的研究提供更多的资助,认识到民间文学的研究是一门独立的学科,同意在中国的高等院校中开设更多的关于民间文学的课程。"此文刊出后,他在来信中还一再表示:"我那篇关于大冶的报告,主要的目的是为中国民间文学界打气。希望中国别的省市,也能传来一样好的消息,使中国民间文学工作成为全世界的模范。"

他还想以鄂西故事家刘德培为对象撰写一篇关于民间口头叙述风格的论文,请我们将刘德培口述故事的录音,一字不动地记下来给他使用,"材料必须完全忠实,比较忠实是不够的"。对我们提供的材料,他认为"可以用来代表上好的口头叙述的风格"。可惜此文后来未能完成。

其次是编辑出版他的比较故事学论文集。他的《中国民间故事类型索引》一书虽蜚声于海内外,而历年发表的论文却散见于欧美各学术刊物,没有结集成书,特别是未译成中文,不能为中国学界所参阅。因此,当我们提出编译他的论文集时,立即获得他的热烈响应。经反复商定,从他发表的论文中选出研究"白蛇传""黄粱梦""灰姑娘"和"云中落绣鞋"这几个故事类型的四篇论文,由李扬、陈建宪、黄永林等年轻学人译成中文,再经他校订成书,以《中西叙事文学比较研究》①作为书名,交华中师范大学出版社于1994年10月推出。他在来信中特别地申明:"这一本书我决不能要稿费的,为了引起国内同仁的兴趣,也一定可买200册,请代转赠愿意接受的同仁。等到书价决定之后,请你告诉我所需确数,我便能请舍弟乃时,汇钱给您。"此书是丁乃通先生用芬兰学派的历史地理方法对中外故事进行深入比较研究的代表作,各篇规模都达到几万字,其学术价值不仅在于对芬兰学派方法的娴熟运用,还在于他是以30年时间研究西方作家文学之后又转向民间文学研究的,因而他研究那几个故事不限于使用口头传承材料,而是把口头材料和中外古典文献以及作家文学融为一体,作深入的跨文化比较。他懂多种语言,治学态度又十分严谨,不惜花费巨大精力在世界范围内广泛搜求资料加以融会贯通。这里试举一例,为了查考美女蛇故事是否源于印度,他曾以半年时间在香港通读《大藏经》,最后将《大藏经》中有关蛇意象的叙说及其出处共148处一一注明。这样,文章就有了震撼读者心灵的说服力。

再次是筹划续编《中国民间故事类型索引》。当此书的英文版已成为国际学界检索中国民间故事通用工具书之时,中国学者对此还一无所知。我从1979年开始从事中外民间故事比较,却见闻有限,后来承蒙日本东京都立大学的饭仓照平教授给我复印了英文版本从遥远异国邮来。为了使这一重要成果为中国学人所把握,丁先生首先帮助乌丙安教授门下的几位研究生将它的情节梗概译成中文。限于当时条件,有关索引没有译出。后来又由段宝林教授约请另外几位学人将它全文译出,由丁乃通及夫人许丽霞仔细校订,终于由中国民间文艺出版社于1986年7月印行。书市脱销后经华中师范大学出版社于2008年再版。但此书所收录的材料限于1966年"文革"之前,此后的几年,特别是民间文学事业复苏的80年代的材料亟待补充,丁先生对此一直耿耿于怀。他几次回到中国,都要花很大精力搜购故事资料。在

---

① 丁乃通:《中西叙事文学比较研究》,华中师范大学出版社1994年版。

华中师范大学讲学期间，我们就帮他弄了两个纸箱的新故事资料邮寄到美国。只要有伏案工作的条件，他就把新出版的故事集拿在手里，一边揣摩它的内容，一边随手在书上画出它的AT编码。关于续编故事类型索引问题，我们无拘束地进行过多次讨论。

他特别谈到编撰民间传说类型索引一事。在1984年1月29日的信中说："中国的传说似乎比任何国家都多，古代文献中的资料，更是浩瀚如海，很可能别国有的类型，中国都有。如能大家合编一部中国传说类型的书，可以给别的国家作为参考模范。如果你们有兴趣把传说整理起来，我可以把西方已有人建议的分类方法，翻印了，寄给在主持这个工作的同仁，供他参考。"

在丁乃通先生看来，关于将神话、传说、故事融为一体，编撰一部大规模的故事类型索引，目前尚不具备条件，然而对传说学作开拓性研究是富有远见卓识的倡议，有待于我们对这一课题给予高度重视，以促其取得真正具有突破性的重大成果。至于将他所撰的类型索引一书加以改进，是切实可行而又为研究者所急需的。长期在台北中国文化大学任教，多年来深受丁乃通先生教益的金荣华先生，在沿用丁乃通类型框架的基础上加以改进，对《中国民间故事集成》地方卷本中收录的故事进行分类编码，已奋力完成一部新的《民间故事类型索引》①，经反复增补修订的四卷本已于2014年在台北问世，对丁乃通学术成果作了重要补充与拓展。

最后，丁乃通先生还做了许多工作，沟通中国学人和欧美学术界特别是和芬兰学派的关系，帮助他们走出国门，走向世界。作为国际民间叙事文学学会的资深会员，他介绍贾芝、乌丙安、段宝林、刘守华、陈建宪、过伟等许多人加入了这个学术团体，并帮助他们参加每四年举办一次的国际研讨会。他在信中曾不厌其烦地告诉我们如何发表论文，如何准备就有关问题进行答辩，还说必要时他可以出来"帮些小忙"等。他抱定一个明确的宗旨：中国民间文艺学要打开国门，走向世界，必须保持自己的特色与尊严。他还同贾芝同志多次商洽，要在海外出版一个研究中国民间文学的英文刊物。他自告奋勇，提出担任开头几期的编辑工作。但限于各种条件，此事未能及时落实。所以，他在1987年6月6日的来信中表示，如一时定不下来，就将此事委托另一位海外华人学者何万成先生负责。由此可见丁乃通先生对此事的筹划真可谓煞费苦心。

丁乃通先生是在20世纪80年代改革开放伊始多次回国，积极参与中国的民间文学事业的。那时正是民间文艺学发展的黄金季节之一。他谆谆教诲、悉心培育的一批民间文艺学者如今已成为学术中坚力量。在中国民间文艺学界走向世界、汇入世界学术大潮的历史性转折中，他发挥了重要的桥梁作用。他的学术成果及严谨学风，不愧为中国学界的楷模之一。在中外学校交流迈进到又一个新阶段的今天，重温他的感人事迹，将会给我们以新的启迪和推动。

---

① 金荣华：《民间故事类型索引（共四册）》，台北市口传文学学会，2014年版。

附录（所附信札均用中文写成）：丁乃通学术信札

（一）

守华：

今天收到来函，当然是非常高兴的事。AT460 和 461 是一个故事圈或集团，流传极广，若能查出来龙去脉，对国际民间故事研究可能是一个大的贡献。可惜我对这些故事，从来没有深入探讨过，所以我能供给你的资料，都是阿尔奈和汤普森的《民间故事类型》第二版和那两本书上的资料，芬兰大师阿尔奈于 1915 年便写了专文讨论这类故事，名学者蒂勒于 1919 年也有文章讨论过。

我本人对此题的初步概念是：中国的说法不可能全是脱胎于印度的，因为中国的 461 型，开始是主角为了向小姐求婚，才非得觅宝不可。这种开端是欧洲的典型，在印度是没有的。中国的 461A 型宗教意味较浓，可是它的特征"问三不问四"，在印度似乎也没有。你假若要比较中印两国的说法，当然是好的，可是了解中国的传统，在我看来并不需要把印度的说法作为前提。此故事圈在印度的说法，似乎只有二十一个，但在中国流传的，拙作（《中国民间故事类型索引》）上已列出四十多个，加上你发现的，已有一百个左右。再过几年，你一定会有更多的收获，足够写一篇有价值的研究论文了。假如我是你的话，一定会先把中国的说法整理成一组，用历史地理法探测传播地区及方向、起源民族及地域、原始形式及意义，尤其要查找古书里有没有这样的故事。先把中国的来龙去脉弄清楚了，再研究别国的传统也不迟。搜集和研究全世界的说法，恐怕要费时间精力，因为这些故事流传最多的地域是波罗的海四周的国家……这样艰苦的工作，像我这样年龄的人已做不动了，像你那样年富力强，不妨尝试一下，欧洲的专家可能会有人帮助你的。

乃通　1984.5

（注：他随即寄来一些欧洲学者的研究成果，其中有汤普森《民间故事概论》中的一节，我请张秋丽女士译出，发表在《民间文学研究动态》上。还有蒂勒的论文《关于命运之子的童话》，我请杨才秀女士译出，摘要在 1989 年第 2 期《中国比较文学》上刊出。经过几年的搜求资料和酝酿构思，于 1988 年写成《一个故事的追踪研究》。）

（二）

守华：

你去年给我们信，我始终没有回复，非常感到抱歉。你的来信来到时，我正在忙着准备去欧洲。可是主要的原因，是你说有人邀你同编一本中国民间故事类型索引，问我要用什么方法。我不知道你们要编的是怎样性质的书，无法回答。好几次问北京民研会的同仁，总是不得要领。直到年底，收到段宝林先生的信，方才了解诸位计划编一部把所有的中国故事全部包括进去的索引。你信上所提的是不是这样的大规模的索引？这种索引，别的国家还没有能出版过。因为除了（或可译为童话）之外，还没有人有那么许多时间、精力和财力，把传说、神话、杂谈等，也有系统地分成详细的类型。当然用来分析童话的 AT 系统，需要改进的地方，非常之多。美国学者因为美国本国已很少有真的民间童话，他们专长的印地安人和非洲土人的故事，很少有轻松讲着好玩的。俄国的学者，也因自己国内的故事中，有许多用不上 AT 制度，因此这两个超级大国的学人，批评芬兰学派的最多。可是他们自己写作研究时，一牵涉到童话，仍往往不免用 AT 类型的数目和名称。童话研究所以能有一个虽非完善，却已相当稳定的分类法，是因为童话的故事，往往比较整齐，轮廓明朗。十九世纪和二十世纪初年的大学者，好多专注重童话，把它的性质弄得相当清楚。童话的变异比较容易追踪了解。其他两种比较严肃的故事——神话和传说——因为和宗教、政治、社会情形、生产方式、风俗、历史背景等等，都有极严密的关切，不但许多同时因地而完全不同，并且常是零零碎碎的，情节的条纹不清楚，所以到现在还只有零星的分类法，没有广泛地应用的系统。一般学者都认为大家对它们的性质，还没有懂得够，所以西方的民俗学家，目前还在热烈地讨论传说的根源、意义和本质之中，他们讨论出一个名堂之后，也许也会有国际性的分类制度出来。我感到这样的探讨，没有做完之前，便不妨先把传说试分起类型来，将来有需要时，再大规模修改，也还不迟。中国的传说似乎比任何国家都多，古代文献中的资料，更是浩瀚如海，很可能别国有的类型，中国都有。如能大家合编一部中国传说类型的书，可以给别的国家作为参考模范，这点意见我已向北京民研会的同仁提出了两三次，没有答覆。如果你们有兴趣把传说整理起来，我可以把西方已有人建议的分类方法，翻印了寄给在主持这工作的同仁，供他参考。

乃通　1985.1.29

（三）

守华：

上星期收到你二月二十八日来函，深深了解你对故事学的热诚。在这一点上，我们真是志同道合。中国大学里除了贵校之外，还有其他院校，有这样的一门学问或课程的？西方无此课。虽然十九世纪有个英国学者提议过，可是二十世纪初期，虽然民间故事（童话）的研究大步迈进，以后却反不谈这样一门学问。主要的原因，是小说的发展倾向心理分析和个性描写，情节越过越不注重。而民间故事成了民俗学的附庸，民俗学家有兴趣的是文化人类学，嫌故事发展的研究工作不够科学化（事实上人类学的理论，不断的变更及自相矛盾，表示他们也不太科学化）。加以在美国念文学和民俗学的学者互相诽谤、怀疑，现在除了西德少数学人外，简直没有人从事这门重要的工作了。事实上这种研究工作，正应该大大推进和发展才行，这一点我和你面谈时，会作具体的建议的，希望我们至少能在中国把这门学问推广，弄成一门许多人都承认是有价值的学问。

我今年已70岁，八月后便自我在美国的学校西伊大退休。我的太太许丽霞，得了美政府的福布莱特奖金，下学年要到武汉大学教图书馆学。我大概和她于九月一日同到武汉，或明年一二月到别的大学（可能是西南师大），转一下后，再到武汉。承你邀请我为贵校兼任教授，非常感激，可是你说的故事学博士研究生班，好像仍然在设计中，不知道有没有得到教育部的批准？据说现在中国教育部对聘请外国专家，尤疑很多，所以你如真的想办，希望你早日去教育部打听，或正式提出建议。专心要研究这一门的学生，除英文外，还需要能阅读德文或法文。这些学生，将来在中国就业，有无问题？在美国是任何文科的博士，找事都很困难。这两点特此提出作为参考。我非常希望中国研究民间文学（或文学）的同仁，能达到国际水准。你如要我帮你的忙，我一定可以的，只是要在武汉做良好的研究工作，贵校或武大图书馆，一定要有基本的参考书，这一点请你先和图书馆谈妥，我可以寄书目给你。录音机我一定送你，只是我膝盖里有的软骨破碎，不能多提东西，所以要向旅行社设法，在这里买了请他们运到武汉取货，希望能成功。

关于461型，你有没有在中国古书或佛经里找到同样的故事？关于460和461型的文章（多半是德文的大部分列在了　里）你有没有看过？这故事类型好像西方的古文献里没有记载，你如在中国的古典文献中发现，便是一个重要的发现。我的书上除了461型，还列有中国特有的461A型，这个故事（问三不问四）很像是和佛教有关。希望你能在佛经里找得到。

乃通　1985.3.31

(四)

守华：

  研究"幸运儿故事"的权威论文，终于拿到复制本了，即日另邮寄给你。希望你好好的阅读后，加上春天寄给你的那书印证，可以开始做有系统的研究工作，为中国其他学者设一个运用国外资料，求取有科学价值成果的良好模范。小陈和小黄翻译的我写的白蛇传论文的手稿，已经由我和丽霞改好了，即日寄给你，请你转交给他们。这稿子可真的花了丽霞好多时间修改。最大的原因是他们二人英文程度不够；次之是其中材料涉及西方文学、文化史、宗教等，都是他们不懂的；三者是以前写的时候知道论文太长，不易出版，力求紧凑，有些地方没有专门知识不容易懂；四者那是多年前的作品，当时用的资料很不好，我不知放到哪里去了。所以自己写的东西，修正译本时才这样困难，这论文最后那一段我已经全部改写了。因为那时我对民间故事知道得还是不多，所以有失误处。请你把这一封信给陈黄二人看，希望他们赶快誊清寄上海，赶上原定出版日期。

乃通　1986.10.21

(五)

守华：

  看到你十一月一日的信，里面没有提起我复印后寄给你的一篇论文，你有没有收到？假如你还没有收到，请告诉我一声，对研究460—461型，这是很重要的资料。

  你写了蛇郎故事的研究，非常之好。这故事组成的单元，是国际性的，可是故事完全是中国的，对于不容易找到外文资料的人，确是个好的题目。你编写的故事学教材，一定能起很大的作用，希望不久便能看到你这些大作及《民间故事比较研究》。

  在武汉听过我讲课的学生，好几个都能有美满的职业，为民间文学服务，异常高兴。小陈小黄有大进步真是难得，我应邀写了一篇关于大冶的英文报告，柯小杰在丽霞离中国前和她通过信，送给她自己的著作，其中有一本叫《经济谣谚选辑》，里面附了他的两篇论文，表示他头脑清楚，思路灵活，是个可造之才。他现在正在读业余大学，假如他愿以民间为终生职业的话，不知道你能不能把他收入华中师大，将来做研究生。以他那样的经验和热心，将来可以做你的大帮手，也可以对民间文学研究有大的贡献。祝你研究成功！

乃通　1986

(六)

守华：

  谢谢您十二月十四的长信和美丽的贺卡。白蛇传论文已在国内发表，当然是大好事。报酬我当然不能要的，如果有的话，请您转赠小陈和小黄，或留着贴补出版拙作论文集的费用，请您代为决定，谢谢。

  我的论文选集，如定名《中西叙事文学比较》，当然对于谈者，把内容表示得明显很多。可是我不便寄给您和小黄的论文中，有一篇是关于童谣，另一篇是没有什么比较的角度的，能否也包括在这个题目底下？此外，我写的关于大冶的报告，是否也能译后在这集子里出版？那报告倒是有个比较角度的。这一本书我决不能要稿费的，为了引起国内同仁的兴趣，也一定可买二百册，请代转赠愿意接受的同仁。等到书价决定之后，请您告诉我所需确数，我便能请舍弟乃时，汇钱给您。那本书能有您写一篇序，便已够了，我毋需再加上一篇。文章排列次序，我也没有什么意见。通常像这样的选集，多半是按各篇出版时间的先后排列的。可是那样一来，论白蛇传的一篇也许会列在最先。那又刚在上海发表，似不太妥。能否请您在序言里指出，凡已出现于中国刊物的，都列在最后，或干脆不包括在内？那样我的301型研究，便成为第一篇，比较适宜。此信内附了我一篇很短的、最近在美国出版的论文，对分类方法有所解释，小陈可以先译出来。和此信同时，我们又邮寄了三篇长的论文给您，请转交小黄。其中关于童谣的一文，是丽霞和我合写的。她在1979年爱丁堡的民间诗歌研究会国际大会上宣读后，在《民间文化与语言》上出版，可是那刊物上的字太小，复印本看不清楚，又没空白加中文字，所以便把原来的稿子寄一份给您。《中国民间叙事中的西方人》一篇情形类似，是我写给1978年在印度召开的国际民间文化讨论会，请别人代读的。据主办人说已在该会的论文集中发表，我因那集子大而价贵，没有买，加以这种集子用的字都太小，寄给你们也没有用，所以便寄原稿给您。

您要在国际叙事文学研究会大会上念的论文，题目非常之好。匈牙利有几个一流的汉学家，一定能欣赏大作的。我因近来健康不太好，明年能否去参加，还没有决定。

从前在我班上的同学中，有好几位已有良好的成绩，使我十分欣慰。

祝您安好，并祝贵校蒸蒸日上，前途无量。

乃通　1988.1.8

（七）

守华：

读您四月五日来函，颇感欣慰。

我那关于大冶的报告，主要的目的，是为中国民间文学界打打气的，希望引起了国际注意之后，中国别的农民，也能照大冶的样子，自动起来搜集和出版民间文学，真的做到民间文学民间办。湖北省赞成我的论文，祝振善表示高兴，当然都是好事。可是最重要的，是要中国别的省市，也能传来一样好的消息，使中国民间文学工作，成为全世界的模范。

您能替印度的Dao写文章，当然很好，他答应我所有的论文一定会出版，希望他说的话能实现。他们用的纸张，质料很差，印刷也常有错误。假如您对这些事介意，可以婉言谢绝他。匈牙利开会的情形不同，去会的真的有许多是权威，可是念的论文，那里大概不会负责出版的。

乃通　1988.4.27

Nai-tung Ting: A Chinese American Scholar Devoted to Chinese Folktale Studies

Shouhua Liu [*]

Professor Nai-tung Ting, recognized at home and abroad for compiling *Type Index of Chinese Folktales*, passed away in April 1989 as a result of a heart attack suffered at the Western Illinois University. He was born on April 22, 1915; his 100th birthday was recently celebrated. He visited China several times during the beginning of the Economic Reform in the 1980's, and was invited to be a visiting scholar at CCNU to teach Finnish folklore research methods, and to introduce Chinese Folk Literature to the world stage. His teachings enlightened faculty and students alike; his voice and countenance left lasting impressions. I now dedicate this essay to his memory.

Let me begin with the story of his transition from studying British literature to studying Chinese folk literature. He graduated from Tsinghua University with a degree in Western Literature in 1936, and obtained Master's and Doctorate degrees in British Literature from Harvard University by 1941. After that, he began lecturing in British literature at Chinese universities; in 1957 he started

---

[*] Shouhua Liu, Professor of Chinese Folk Literature at CCNU, is one of New China's first generation folklorists (since the 1950s). He has been collecting and studying folktales since the 1950s, and has outstanding accomplishments in the field. He has also trained some leading scholars in the field of Chinese folk literature and folklore studies, making him a highly respected figure in academia. His *History of Chinese Folktales* and *Chinese Folktale Studies* are excellent representative of Chinese scholars' achievements in folklore narratology, and is deserving wide attention. Here he recounts Dr. Ting's story in China, followed by their correspondences, showing a scholar's loyalty and respect for the career and work of his older colleague. The story of their interactions marks the start of nearly 30 years of Sino-US exchanges. As a Chinese proverb says: Predecessors plant trees so that successors can enjoy their shade. But we as successors must also plant trees for our descendants. Such is also the core significance of the metafolklore emphasized in this volume.

This article honors Nai-tung Ting (1915 – 1989), a Chinese American scholar who made remarkable contributions to Sino-US folkloristic exchanges. His letters, kept by Liu for many years, make their first public appearance here, demonstrating the sincerity of their scholastic comradery. Dr. Ting was neglected for a long time in the US folklore field; his academic accomplishments concerning Chinese folktales were often excluded by the politically-biased academia. But history always clarifies what accomplishments get passed down. Now, Dr. Ting's writing on Chinese folktale genres and other subjects continue to serve as bases for research on Chinese folktales. This volume also includes Yang Li's account of his interactions with Dr. Ting. These stories will undoubtedly encourage many more people to continue on this path, planting trees for the future.

teaching in America, first at University of Texas, Pan American and then Western Illinois University. How did he come to study folk literature, especially Chinese folk literature? He wrote the following in an essay during his visiting lectures at CCNU:

"I am a Chinese American who used to study and teach British literature. I did not know a thing about folk literature. At the start of the 1960's, while studying the subject of literature comparison, I found that folk literature was not only the foundation for much high (authored) literature, but also the most effective tool for comparing two or more literary works with different cultural backgrounds. That was when I began reading books and magazines on folk studies and folk literature. As for how I formed an indissoluble bond with Chinese folk literature, the main reason was that I could not bear the sight of Right-wing scholars from Taiwan, who prided themselves in being anti-communist, ganging up to attack Chinese folklorists. Not only did I debate with them, I was determined to prove, by using concrete evidence, how distorted their understanding of Chinese folklore was. Therefore I spent several years writing *Type Index of Chinese Folktales*, read many stories from different Chinese ethnicities, learned the wisdom and talents of Chinese people, and gained a deep understanding of Chinese folk literature's importance and unique role in the world."

Type Index of Chinese Folktales was a monumental work that took Dr. Ting 10 years to complete. He included 834 folktale types covering over 7300 stories and using more than 580 references. He used the Aarne-Thompson classification system to index Chinese folktales. The advantage of this system was that it allowed people to easily compare Chinese stories with other works in the Universal Index System. However, this type of framework was not completely suited for Chinese stories that were rooted in a unique historical culture. Thus, it has unavoidable defects in certain aspects. Yet what is commendable is that *Type Index* includes almost all Chinese folklore stories that appeared prior to the "Cultural Revolution" in 1966.

Despite being isolated from colleagues back home, he doggedly pursued and finally completed his research. He referenced books from all over the world, more than twice the amount used by German scholar Wolfram Eberhard in *Types of Chinese Folktales*, and was more detailed in his descriptions of plot devices and variations of such in different story types. When *Type Index* was published by the Academy of Finland in 1978, it received immediate favorable reviews as the best index reference book for studying Chinese folktales.

Dr. Nai-tung Ting lived in the US for many years, and focused on British literature until transitioning to Chinese folktales in his later years. This is clearly related to his inherent ties with China. When China ended the "Cultural Revolution" and advanced into its new era of economic reform, he became concerned with China's folk literature field, and dedicated himself to its development. In another segment of the same essay he writes:

> "In the past seven years, I have visited China four times: once in 1978, another in 1980, a third time in 1981, and again this year (1985). I came in 1981 because of an invitation from the Society for Folk Literature and Art Studies. Folk literature was in recovery at that time, and although I knew it had a bright future, I thought it would be good enough for it to simply return to the state it was before the "Cultural Revolution". I was pleasantly surprised when I saw that it came back with a vigor many times more than I imagined. According to the Beijing Society of Folk Literature and Arts Studies, nearly every district had published an anthology of local folktales, often in multiple volumes. Several provinces even came out with one or more Chinese folk literature magazines. Although I had time to read very few of these stories at the time, I could tell that they were faithfully told. In addition, some folklorists found epic poems that many thought China lacked. The longest one is about 1.5 million lines long, much longer than epics from other countries. This news surprised even Finland, one of the most successful countries in folklore collection, and made their papers. But many folklorists pointed out that the materials found so far are only the tip of the iceberg. The more we delve into it, the more amazed we'll be at the extensiveness of Chinese oral literature traditions, as if it were inexhaustible. Anyone with a Chinese heritage, regardless of nationality, should be proud of this great home cultural tradition and the imagination and creativity of the toiling masses (especially peasants) who produced it.

We invited Dr. Nai-tung Ting to lecture at CCNU for a month, starting on September 16, 1985. Every week, he gave one or two lectures to our undergraduate and graduate students, and we were free to consult him anytime outside of class. He brought a box of foreign books and periodicals, including Alan Dundes's *The Study of Folklore*, and Stith Thompson's *The Folktale* and *Motif-index of Folk-Literature*. His lectures on narratology were mainly based off Thompson's works, often translating the English text in his hand throughout the class. Since we were bad at English and strangers to foreign academics, he had to go at a slow pace. With the month-long lecture at the midpoint, our interactions lasted 5 years from May 1983 to April 1988, with almost 20 mail exchanges. His enthusiasm for Chinese folk literature made a great impact on me. On October 17, 1985, the lectures ended. Our university held a brief ceremony of appreciation, and the University President Kaiyuan Zhang asked him to be our visiting professor. He donated all the foreign books he brought and the 640 yuan he got for his service to us. Later, he even donated the flight reimbursement issued by the school, and urged us to buy a couple bookcases to collect materials on folk literature and establish our own reference room.

He instructed Jianxian Chen and Yonglin Huang with great enthusiasm, who translated his well-known work, *The Monk and the Snake* into Chinese for publication. How did they go about it? He gave meticulous guidance: "First read passage by passage, and get an idea of the full picture. Then examine it line by line, and look up unfamiliar words in the dictionary. Put a little thought into it, don't limit yourself to word-for-word translations, and try to translate it so that the meaning remains faithful to the original work. When you're done, send me your translations for revision." Dr. Ting and his wife, Lee-hsia Ting, reviewed the translations meticulously, filling the spaces with red pen marks. This process was repeated many times before the draft was finalized. In his letter to me received on October 21st, 1986, he wrote, "Lee-hsia and I have finished revising Chen and Huang's draft. I'll mail it to you within a few days, please deliver it to [the publisher]. This draft took forever to edit, one reason being their English level was not high enough; another was that the materials used touched upon Western literature, cultural history, and religion, all things they don't know about; the third is that at the time I wrote it, I knew that long thesis papers were hard to publish, so I tried to condense the content, which made it hard to understand for those without professional knowledge; finally it is a work from many years ago, the references I used were subpar and I can't remember where I placed them. I rewrote the last part of the thesis completely, because I knew very little about folklores back then, so there were some mistakes. Please show this letter to Chen and Huang, I hope they can mail out a clean copy soon." He also wrote: "I hope scholars studying Chinese folktales can learn foreign languages and go global." With Dr. Ting setting an admirable example, many of his students have become key educators in China's folk literature field. Dr. Ting kept his students' careers and achievements at heart; in one letter he said "Among the students in my class, several already have remarkable accomplishments, I am deeply gratified."

He has also put painstaking effort into instructing me on my narratology studies. In our first letter exchange, he said that from my letter "I deeply felt your passion for narratology, in this, we are kindred spirits." In our many correspondences, he hoped that I would conduct a systematic study on AT461, a type of "luck-wishing" stories. "Organize the Chinese ones first and use historical geographical knowledge to pinpoint which ethnic group and territory they originated from, where they were spread, and the direction of propagation. Pay special attention to similar stories found in ancient books." After that, he wanted me to "collect and study storiesfrom all over the world," especially those from India with which to compare. "But knowing Chinese tradition, I don't think Indian stories have to be the prerequisite." Instead I should focus on studying how these stories morphed through generations. For example, the trope of asking a limit of three questions or favors is not used in Indian folktales.

To help me with my research, he sent relevant excerpts from Thompson's *The Motif-index of Folk-Literature*, and a long thesis "Fairytale of Destiny's Child" written by the German scholar Václav Tille in 1919. He also warned me not to be hasty, "The valuable works in this field are often works that took many years or even a lifetime. " The theses and books opened my mind to a whole new world, and I wrote a number of papers, including "The Tracking of a Story" and "A Chinese Folktale with the Charms of an Epic" within the next couple years. I felt I was making huge progress on my narratology studies.

While Dr. Ting was lecturing at CCNU, he lived very simply. He rejected banquet invitations, and my wife and I often made him plain meals of noodles with bok choy and daylily. He enjoyed those very much. When he published in China, not only did he not want royalties for his authorship, he paid for books himself to give to others. He loved Chinese folktales, and was proud of the impressive minority cultures reflected in them (pointing out there is an outstanding number of stories praising the intelligence of women). He often loses himself in studying and evaluating Chinese stories, and has motivated us all with his dedication to Chinese folk literature.

Dr. Nai-tung Ting made many contributions to the development of Chinese folk literaturein the past three decades:

First, as a foreign scholar who has dedicated himself to Chinese folk literature studies, he longed to understand the reality of the development of Chinese folk literature. Therefore, when the Cultural Department of Daye, Hubei invited him in September, 1985 to attend the Folk Literature Studies Conference, he was overjoyed and prepared for it excitedly despite having a leg impediment. He was unable to attend in the end, so I delivered the material from the conference—mainly self-published compilations made by peasants interested in folk literature consisting of local folktales, songs, and proverb collections—to him. He treasured these little mimeograph booklets. Through careful analysis, he published his English thesis in Japan, titled "Folk Literature Run by the Folk: A New Development in the People's Republic of China" in the second edition of *Asian Folklore Studies* in 1997. It was later translated into Chinese by Yonglin Huang and published on the third edition of *Journal of South-Central University for Nationalities* in 1988. The Hubei Agency for Cultural Affairs forwarded it to cultural departments throughout the province for reference. This thesis not only appraised the academic and cultural values of stories such as "Tale of the Ground Buddha" that conserved the plain nature of folk literature, but it also commended peasants for being hands-on in the whole process of collecting and preserving folk literature. In the paper he wrote: "Now, things are looking up. The peasants are carrying on the operation themselves.... Some lovers of folk literature invest funds to edit and publish works of folk literature collected by themselves.... Although these publications are not very respectable in format, they nevertheless show developments worthy of attention. First of all, the rapid succession of their appearance bears witness to the initial success leading Chinese folklorists have achieved in awakening the nation to China's immensely rich oral heritage. " He was extremely excited after comparing this with the past global practice of using peasants only as subjects for collection, and thought that although what Daye did "wasn't unprecedented, it was still rare. " As a scientific facilitator, he naturally saw the problems in the project that resulted from lack of professional instruction. He concludes by calling for action. Since China has a rich oral tradition and plenty of written records of customs and traditions, "Such a unique heritage deserves extraordinary attention to investigation, preservation, and research. Before aid from private sources can become a substantial factor, it is earnestly hoped that the Chinese government will finance folkloristic studies more adequately, realize that the study of folklore is an independent discipline, and approve the introduction of more courses in folklore in Chinese universities." After this article was published, he continued to express in his later letters that "the main goal I had for writing the report on Daye was to encourage the Chinese folk literature community, so that in the future, other cities in China will bear the same good news, setting an example for folklore studies around the world."

He also wanted to write an article on the style of oral narration with Depei Liu, a storyteller from West Hubei, as the subject. He asked us to transcribe a recording of Depei Liu's storytelling word for word, saying that "the material must be entirely authentic, mostly authentic is not enough." He thought that the material we provided "could be used to represent superior oral narration styles." Unfortunately, this article was never completed.

Then, he wanted to publish an anthology of articles on comparative narrative studies. Although *Type Index of Chinese Folktales* was renowned at home and abroad, the articles he published were scattered throughout different European academic journals, not collected into a book. More important, they were not translated into Chinese, and therefore could not be referenced by the Chinese academia. Thus, when we suggested that we publish a translation of his articles collection, he responded enthusiastically. After repeated consultations, we decided to translate four of his published articles: "Legend of the White Snake," "Perfect Dream," "Cinderella," and "Embroidered Shoes from the Cloud." The translation was completed by Yang Li, Jianxian Chen, Yonglin Huang and other young scholars, and checked by Ting himself. The anthology was published under the title *A Comparative Study of Chinese and Western Literature Narratology*. It was published by CCNU Press in October, 1994. He stressed in his letter, "I will not take any royalty for this book. To attract the interest of colleagues, please buy 200 copies and gift them to colleagues who are willing to accept it. When the cost of the book is finalized, please let me know the exact price, and I'll ask my brother to reimburse you." This book was a representative work of Dr. Nai-tung Ting's comparative research on Chinese and foreign stories using the Finnish historical geographic method of examination. Each piece reached several tens of thousands of characters. Its academic value lies not only in the adept use of Finnish methods, but also in the extensive comparison he was able to carry out because of his unique academic experience. He studied Western authorial literature for 30 years before turning his attention to folk literature. This allowed him to study those four stories using a combination of oral tradition materials, classical bibliographies, and authorial literature. He was knowledgeable in many languages and had a strict attitude in scholarly pursuits, so he was determined to amass extensive reference materials from all over the world to achieve comprehensive mastery at all costs. To give an example, to ascertain whether tales on snake-beauties originated from India, he spent half a year reading *Great Treasury of Sutras* in Hong Kong, and annotated all 148 places in the text where snake-related motifs appeared. In this way, his writings had the authority to impact readers' hearts.

Additionally, he planned to write a sequel for *Type Index of Chinese Folktales*, whose English version had become a universal reference for all Chinese folklore studies conducted by the international academia, but remained little-known in China. I had been comparing Chinese and foreign folktales since 1979, but had limited knowledge of the type index. Thanks to Dr. Ikura Shohei from Tokyo Metropolitan University, I was able to get a copy of the English version of *Type Index*. In order for Chinese scholars to make use of this important resources, Dr. Ting assisted Dr. Bing'an Wu's graduate students in translating its outline into Chinese. Due to the conditions at that time, the translation was never completed. Later, Dr. Baolin Duan invited several other scholars to translate the full text, which was carefully proofread by Ting and his wife Lee-hsia and finally printed by the Chinese Folk Literature Association in July, 1986. After the book went out of print, CCNU came out with a second edition in 2008. However, the references sourced in the book all preceded the Cultural Revolution in 1966; materials regarding the following years, especially during the revival of folk literature studies in the 1980's, have yet to be added. This remained on Dr. Ting's mind for years. Every time he visited China, he would spend a lot of energy collecting story material. During his visiting lecture period at CCNU, we gathered two boxes full of new story material to mail to the U.S. Whenever he was able to, he was bent over his desk with newly published anthologies, studying their contents and recording each tale's AT code. We often discussed the continuation of the *Type Index*.

In a letter he sent on January 29th, 1984, he talked particularly about writing a type index for folklore: "China seems to have more myths than any other country, with a vast amount of material in ancient literature. It's likely that China has all the lore types found in other countries. If everyone can collectively compile a book on Chinese folklore types, it can serve as a model for other countries. If you're interested in organizing the myths, I can send a categorizing method suggested by Western scholars to the colleague who'll direct this project for reference."

In his opinion, at that time we did not have the conditions to compile an extensive type index that integrates myths, legends, and tales. But to do pioneering research on the topic of mythology is a timely proposal; it's a topic we should attach great importance to in order to promote breakthroughs in the field. As for improving his *Type Index*, it is both a feasible and much-needed task. Dr. Ronghua Jin, who has been teaching at the Taipei Chinese Culture University and benefited from Dr. Nai-tung Ting's guidance for many years, improved upon Ting's type framework, classified stories from *Chinese Folklore Anthology*, and has successfully completed a new *Type Index of Chinese Folktales*. After repeated revisions, the fourth volume came out in 2014 in Taipei, making important supplements and expansions to Ting's academic work.

Finally, Dr. Nai-tung Ting worked diligently to connect the Chinese and Western academia, especially with the Finnish school, in order to help Chinese scholars engage the world. As a senior member of the International Society for Folk Narrative Research, he introduced Zhi Jia, Bing'an Wu, Baolin Duan, Shouhua Liu, Jianxian Chen, Wei Guo and others into this academic organization. He also helped them participate in the International Research Conference held once every four years. In his letters, he patiently told us how to publish articles, how to prepare for questions related to our research, and even said that if needed, he can "give a little help." He had a clear mission: in order for Chinese folk art and literature to step onto the global stage, it must retain its unique characteristics and dignity. He also discussed many times with Mr. Zhi Jia about publishing an English-language periodical on Chinese folk literature. He volunteered to take charge of editing the first few publications. But because of circumstances, this ambition was never realized. Thus, in his letter on June 6th, 1987, he expressed that if it cannot be finalized within a short time, the task should be entrusted to Wangchen He, another overseas Chinese scholar. It's easy to see the pains Dr. Nai-tung Ting took to plan this project.

Dr. Nai-tung Ting began coming home often after the Economic Reform in the 1980's, involving himself enthusiastically in China's folk literature studies. That was one of the golden ages of development in folk literature studies. The folklorists he instructed and nurtured have become the backbone of academia. He served a crucial bridging role in the historic turning point of Chinese folk literature academia integrating into the global academic current. His academic accomplishments and rigorous style of study was certainly a worthy model for the Chinese academia. Revisiting his impressive accomplishments today, as Chinese and foreign schools enter a new phase of development, will continue to provide us with enlightenment and motivation.

(Translation by Eurydice Chen)

Appendix: Letters from Nai-Tung Ting to Shouhua Liu

(Professor Shouhua Liu has preserved the letters, all in Chinese, from Dr. Nai-tung Ting, from May 1984 to April 1988, and decided to publish seven of them here for the first time. Given the nature of these letter and the space limit of the volume, we hereby provide only a synopsis of each letter in English. These letters clearly demonstrate the collaborative spirit between two sincere and serious folklorists. —Juwen Zhang)

Letter 1 (May 1984):
In this letter, after receiving Professor Liu's article, Dr. Ting talks about his opinion about tale types AT460 and 461. He was delighted that Liu found over sixty variants in addition to his over forty variants. He encourages Liu to focus on Chinese versions, but not the idea of Indian origin, and to apply the historic-geographic method to explore

the origin of the tale in the Chinese minority nationalities as well as in ancient texts. It would be good to look at its variants in other countries after knowing its Chinese development. Along with this letter, Ting includes two articles, which were eventually translated and published in Chinese.

Letter 2 (Jan. 29, 1985):
Dr. Ting replies to the inquiry from Liu about editing an index of tale types of all Chinese folktales, and notes that such a project would be unique to China. He also points out how American and Russian scholars have worked on fairy tales, but not all folktales, with the AT types because the categorization of fairy tales is relatively easier than other types of tales. Ting suggests that Chinese folklorists/scholars could first work on the categorization of legends because they are numerous in Chinese texts, and thus set an example for other countries.

Letter 3 (March 31, 1985):
Dr. Ting replies to Professor Liu's letter about teaching a course on folktales and feels that they both indeed have common interest. Ting points out that folktales were a hot topic in the 19th century, but declined in the 20th century due to the increasing interest in fictional literature and in cultural anthropology from the folklorists. He hopes to work with Liu in China to promote this topic so that it would become a valuable field.

Dr. Ting mentions that he is 70 years old and retires that year. His wife will be on a Fulbright fellowship to work in Wuhan, and he will be going along. He is grateful to be invited to teach a graduate course in CCNU, and hopes that the students could learn to read foreign texts. He also asks about the future employment of the students in folk literature. He is willing to help to do more research in Wuhan, and hopes that library can be equipped with basic references. He also promised to give them some books and a tape recorder. Finally, he asks about the development of Liu's study on tale types 461 and 460, saying that that he does not see such types in Western literature, and hopes that Liu could find more variants in Buddhist classics.

Letter 4 (Oct. 21, 1986):
Dr. Ting is happy to have found materials on the tale type 461, and is ready to mail them to Professor Liu. He hopes that this would set an example for other Chinese scholars to use foreign materials. He also mentions that his wife has revised the translation of his article on the "White Snake" done by Liu's two students.

Letter 5 (1986):
Dr. Ting receives the letter from Professor Liu dated in Nov, but asks to confirm whether his previous letter with materials on tale types 460 – 461 was received because they are important. He praises Professor Liu's article on the snake groom because it has international elements, but is completely a Chinese tale. He is happy to learn that the students in his class in the previous year are now at good work posts.

(Note: The two students mentioned in this and the previous letters are Dr. Jianxian Chen and Dr. Yonglin Huang, who both became professors at CCNU and are still at work there. —J. Z.)

Letter 6 (Jan. 8, 1988):
Dr. Ting is happy to learn that his article on the "White Snake" has been published in China, and insists on giving the royalty to Jianxian Chen and Yonglin Huang for their use in future publications. He then discusses possible

inclusion of a few fairy tales in the new book on comparison of Chinese and Western tales, as well as his other articles written in China. He also insists that he would not accept the royalty, but to use it to buy books for other folklorists. He then discusses his work on tale type 301 and related translation and publication issues. He further mentions sending an article written by his wife and him, and another manuscript by him because the published volume is too expensive to buy. Finally, Dr. Ting is delighted to see the topic on which Professor Liu would present at the international conference in Hungary. Once again, Dr. Ting is happy to learn the achievements of his former students at CCNU.

Letter 7 (April 27, 1988):

Dr. Ting is happy to receive a letter from Professor Liu. He says that his article about how the local peasants collect and publish folktales in Daye, Hubei Province was intended to encourage Chinese folklorists and to attract international attention. He hopes that such good things could be taking place in other provinces in China and thus setting an example in the world. He then comments on whether Professor Liu should send this article to India for publication, and how the conference in Hungary could have some authorities attending.

阿兰·邓迪斯教授访华记

陈建宪[*]

1990年5月15日晚，我与华中师范大学外事处办事员高卓献一起，在武汉南湖机场，迎接首次访华的美国加州大学阿兰·邓迪斯教授和他妻子卡罗琳女士。当我与他握手时，心里不禁涌出一丝感叹：好事还真是多磨啊！

邀请邓迪斯教授访华，是一个很偶然的机缘。

1985年9月，我考入华中师范大学攻读民间文学硕士，正巧赶上美国伊利诺斯州立大学的华裔学者丁乃通教授来校讲学。丁先生讲了一个多月课后，又指导我和师弟黄永林翻译他的论文《高僧与蛇女》，还把他带来的一些英文专业书籍赠给了我们。在他赠送的这批书中，就有邓迪斯教授主编的《民俗学研究》。

1988年元月，我毕业留校担任助教。当时中国开放时间不长，对西方民俗学了解甚少，于是我想把丁乃通先生留下的英文书译一本过来。最初想译丁先生的《中国民间故事类型索引》，但北京大学的段宝林教授告诉我，他们已在翻译此书。于是我选择了邓迪斯这本《民俗学研究》，很快得到上海文艺出版社徐华龙先生的支持。6月13日，徐先生寄来了约稿合同，约定当年12月31日交稿。我看时间很紧，加之我的英文水平是个半吊子，就把在武汉大学读研的好朋友彭海斌拉来，两人一起翻译此书。

由于我们对西方民俗学了解不多，加之英文水平不高，翻译中遇到了许多困难。不过我们终于按时完成了译稿。这年12月23日，我写信给邓迪斯的学生白薇莉，托她转一封信给邓迪斯，想请他为中文版写篇序言。1989年1月28日，白薇莉在回信中寄来邓迪斯的简历，还附了邓迪斯本人的一封信。在信中，邓迪斯提出了想访华的愿望，并说自己可以在美

---

[*] 编者注：陈建宪现任华中师范大学文学院教授。他是1980年代中国民间文学和民俗学重建后的第一代民俗学者之一。他的《论中国洪水故事圈——关于568篇异文的结构分析》独具特色。过去外界只知道几个中国洪水神话，而他证明了有568个之多，而且遍及中国40多个民族。他的有关神话母题的研究，以中国的神话为依据，比较了世界不同神话，发展了邓迪斯等有关神话母题的研究，也体现了中国民俗学在神话母题上的理论突破。他所翻译的邓迪斯的两部重要著作（《世界民俗学》和《洪水神话》）为中国民俗学开阔了视野。

在此，我们也缅怀一位属于世界民俗学者敬仰的前辈，阿兰·邓迪斯（1934—2005）。户晓辉在本文集中的故事也是讲述邓迪斯对中国民俗学成为世界民俗学一部分的厚望。陈建宪和户晓辉之所以能够在这里讲述邓迪斯的故事，也是因为我们今天在一定程度上实现了邓迪斯当时的愿望——中国的民俗学者对外界了解的越来越多了，也越来越多地被外界所知，并开始为世界民俗学做出贡献。

国申请资助解决经费问题。

我向导师刘守华教授汇报了这些情况，刘老师很支持。我们给学校外事处打了报告，并寄信给邓迪斯、加州大学出版社以及美国大使馆，办理邓迪斯来华和《民俗学研究》中文版权的事。正当一切顺利进行时，没想到发生了八九政治风波，学校所有外事活动全部停止，邀请邓迪斯访华的事自然搁下来了。

半年多后，邓迪斯寄来《民俗学研究》中文版序言，重提访华的事。几天后，我们再次向学校提交了邀请邓迪斯访华的报告。12月11日，上海文艺出版社寄来了译稿清样，清样中收入了邓迪斯寄来的照片和序言。责编秦静告诉我，为便于销售，书名改成了《世界民俗学》。

邓迪斯在给中文版的序言中写道：

> 民俗学研究已逐渐形成为一个科际的（interdisciplinary）和国际性的学科领域。遗憾的是，中国民俗学家们对中国以外的情况却知之甚少。中国的民俗学家至今为止还没有参加民俗学研究的国际间协作，中国的学者们不了解欧美民俗学家所采用的新的理论与方法，同时，欧美民俗学家也不知道中国民俗学家们所取得的成就。正因为如此，人们希望中国民俗学家的研究成果能以英文、法文、德文或其他国际学术语言出版。当然，同时也应以中文出版一些欧美学者的著作。（这也是我对我的书以中文出版感到如此高兴的原因）

> 中国是世界上人口最多的国家，有人就有民俗。所以，中国的民俗比任何其他国家都更为丰富。中国还有许多迷人的少数民族——每一个少数民族都有自己的民俗。因此，中国民俗学家参加国际民俗学共同体，使这一人类创造力与想象力的丰富宝藏为全世界对此感兴趣的人共同分享，这是绝对必要的。

1990年春节后，学校批准邀请邓迪斯教授访华。2月25日，我给邓迪斯寄出正式邀请函。收到他的回信后，我又与北京师范大学的董晓萍老师和华东师范大学的陈勤建老师联系，请他们协助安排邓迪斯夫妇访问武汉后顺访北京和上海的事，得到了他们的积极响应。从这时起，我的工作重心就放在了接待邓迪斯教授访问的事上。我找到了武汉测绘科技大学英语系的胡孝申副教授做翻译，同时认真进行学术准备以便向邓迪斯教授请教。

没想到事情又起波澜。4月29日，中国民间文艺家协会通知刘守华老师去泰国访问，时间正好与邓迪斯访华相冲突，这样接待任务就由我全盘负责了。这还不说，系领导告诉我，由于处于敏感时期，中央有文件，外国人不得与大学生接触，不得给学生讲课。原来的日程安排中，邓迪斯教授所有的讲演，全都改为座谈。

5月14日，我生病高烧，在家休息。忽然接到学校通知，原来邓迪斯5月5日发给我一个电传，告诉我他们乘坐的班机15日到武汉，由于译员从英文译不出我的名字，险些误事。我忍着高烧到学校安排车子，终于在15日晚顺利地接到了邓迪斯夫妇。

5月16日上午,邓迪斯与我校研究生和省内专家共二十余人座谈,主要由他介绍西方民俗学的历史与现状。下午由我向邓迪斯介绍中国民俗学的情况。我发现邓迪斯对中国一无所知,我讲的一切对他都是新闻。他的情绪非常昂奋,对什么都好奇。交谈中,我发现邓迪斯教授是一个相当爱笑的人,很有幽默感。当我谈到中国对各民族民间文学进行调查和记录时,他大加称赞,但他同时又特别关心种族歧视问题。我告诉他:中国对少数民族有很多优惠政策,可以生两个孩子,上大学可以加分。他还是不太理解,说不应该强制实行计划生育,并说所有民族的学生都应该平等。

5月17日上午,小高带邓迪斯夫妇去参观黄鹤楼、归元寺和湖北省博物馆,我则向王庆生校长和中文系三个主任汇报接待情况,提出的主要问题是:一、外事处认为接待规格不够,我只是一个刚留校的助教,邓是国际知名学者,地位不对等。二、能否授予邓迪斯为本校客座教授?三、能不能有更多学生来听邓教授的课?除了第三个问题外,另两个问题学校都同意解决。

这天下午,仍由我与邓迪斯座谈,研究生和本科民间文学小组参与。由于相互了解更多,且准备得比较充分,交谈气氛很放松,涉及神话研究、生殖崇拜和荤故事等话题。他告诉我说,他曾研究过厕所文学,即在男厕所墙壁上涂抹的那些文字与图画,并运用心理分析方法写过一篇论文。他还说他写过一篇关于足球的文章,他认为那是一种同性恋的表现。他给我介绍了他的博士学位论文《北美印第安人民间故事结构分析》,我对他这种从故事中抽取"母题素"的方法,当时没听明白,他当即将这篇论文送了我一份。这天晚上,我们专业的几个研究生陪邓迪斯夫妇去中南民族大学博物馆去看扎染,我得空回家。三天没回家了,两岁多的儿子见了我,高兴得哇哇直叫。

5月18日上午,学校为了弥补接待身份不对等的礼节,由王庆生校长亲自出面,在校长办公室会见了邓迪斯夫妇。王校长向邓迪斯教授赠送了一幅中国山水画,同时颁发给他一个聘书,聘任他为我校民间文学专业的客座教授。中文系安排了外国文学专业的王忠祥、彭端智两教授和文艺学专业的邱紫华教授,与邓迪斯先生座谈。邓迪斯夫妇非常高兴。这天下午,仍是我和民间文学的研究生们与邓迪斯座谈,邓一直问他什么时候可以给学生讲课,并表示他早就准备好了。我委婉地告诉他说,考虑到他从美国老远飞来,又连日劳累,因此没有安排他给学生上课。他很不高兴,连连说:"I'd like to work!"

5月19日,仍是我和研究生们陪同邓迪斯夫妇。几天来谈话很多,似乎觉得该说的都已说了。这时我想试探与美国民俗学界进行合作的可能性,我向邓迪斯提出将来两校是否可以派研究生互访。他比较谨慎,说经费问题无法解决。我又提出希望他能帮助我们得到FFC丛书,他说很困难。不过他答应,回美国后,他会将他自己出版的书籍送一套给我们民间文学专业。这天下午,由于刘守华老师不在家,我还陪同他去看望了师母陈老师。

5月20日中午,我和高卓献一道将邓迪斯送上飞机,董晓萍老师在北京接机,由钟敬文教授亲自主持接待。在北京成功访问后,邓迪斯教授又去了华东师范大学,与上海民俗学界交流,然后从上海返回美国。

这次从翻译邓迪斯的著作到邀请他们夫妇访华,历时近两年,中间几经波折,最终顺利完成。我作为一个刚参加工作不久的年轻人,从中学到了许多东西。举一个好笑的例子,当时我们的收入很低,我不知道给初次见面的邓迪斯先生送点什么礼物好。后来看中了武汉一位著名老书法家傅金龙先生的一幅字,那是一个草书的"龙"字,非常有气魄,我花了半个多月的工资把它买下来,送给邓迪斯先生。但我却不知道应该将它精致地包装起来,只是用了张废旧报纸草草地包着,在邓迪斯夫妇出门吃饭前匆匆给他。既没有介绍这幅字的价值也没说明书法和"龙"字的含义,以致邓迪斯完全不知道这幅字的价值,随手就扔在一边了。除了这类礼节性的事情外,这次活动全程的组织工作,让我体验到了什么叫做"事非经过不知难",这为我后来组织各种集体性的活动提供了经验。

邓迪斯教授的访华,在中美民俗学界建立了直接的学术联系,加深了两国学者在学科理论与活动方面的交流。邓迪斯夫妇回国后,对在中国访问的印象非常深刻。他不仅给我们专业寄来了十几本他的著作,而且满怀热情地在美国报刊杂志上介绍中国民俗学的情况。直到他去世前几年,他或他夫人每到圣诞节都给我寄来新年贺卡。而我的博士学位论文《论中国洪水故事圈》,就是在他赠送的《洪水神话》启发下确立选题并展开研究的。

2013 年,邓迪斯主编的《洪水神话》也译为中文出版了。遗憾的是,邓迪斯先生没能亲眼看到这本书的中文版。这里,我用该书《后记》中的一段话,作为本文的结束:"对于我个人来说,这本书除了给我留下与学生、与朋友相处的美好记忆外,还是献在阿兰·邓迪斯教授灵前的一束鲜花。对一生钟情于学术的邓迪斯先生来说,学术是无国界的,学问是代代相承的,我似乎看到了九泉之下他那迷人的微笑。"

陈建宪与邓迪斯于武汉,1990。Jianxian Chen and Alan Dundes in Wuhan, China, 1990.

Alan Dundes's Visit to China

Jianxian Chen*

On the evening of May 5th, 1990, Zhuoxian Gao of the Foreign Affairs department of CCNU and I went to the Wuhan Nanhu Airport. We were there to meet Dr. Alan Dundes and his wife Carolyn who were on their first visit to China. When I shook hands with him, I couldn't help but think: good things truly are a long time in coming!

It was by coincidence that I invited Dr. Dundes to visit China.

In September of 1985, I was accepted into CCNU for the Folk Literature graduate program, and it happened that at that time Chinese folklorist Dr. Nai-tung Ting was a visiting lecturer at CCNU from Western Illinois University. After lecturing for a month, Dr. Ting instructed my peer Yonglin Huang and me to translate his paper, "The Monk and the Snake." He also gave us some English folklore books he brought. Among the books he gave us was Dr. Dundes's *The Study of Folklore*.

By January 1988 I had graduated and was kept at my university as a teaching assistant. It was not long after China's reform, and I knew little about Western folklore studies. Thus I was eager to try translating one of the books Dr. Nai-tung Ting left us. At first, I wanted to translate Dr. Ting's *Type Index of Chinese Folktales*, but Dr. Baolin Duan from Beijing University informed me that they were already in the process of translating it. Therefore, I chose Dundes's *The Study of Folklore*. I

---

* Jianxian Chen is Professor of Folk Literature at CCNU. He is one of the first generation folklorists from the 1980s when Chinese folk literature and folkloristics were restored. His groundbreaking work is *On the Circle of Flood Myth in China: Structural Analysis of* 568 *Variants* (2005), which shows that there are at least 568 variants of the flood myth in China emerging from 40 minority groups. Very few of these myths were previously known. His studies on myth and motif, based on Chinese materials with comparisons from the rest of the world, not only developed Dundes's ideas, but also constituted a breakthrough on the topic by the Chinese folklorists. His translations of Dundes's two important volumes [*The Study of Folklore* (1990), and *The Flood Myth* (2013)] broadened the horizon for Chinese folkloristics.

This essay honors the memory of a renowned world folklorist, Alan Dundes (1934 – 2005). In this volume Xiaohui Hu also tells the story of how Dundes had great hope for Chinese folkloristics to become part of world folkloristics. That Chen and Hu can tell these stories here is precisely because we have, to a great extent, realized what Dundes hoped for—Chinese folklorists to know more about the world folklore; world folklorists to know more about Chinese folklore; and Chinese folklorists contributing to world folkloristics.

soon won the support of Mr. Hualong Xu from the Shanghai Literature and Art Publishing House. On June 13th, Mr. Xu mailed a book contract, setting the deadline on December 31st of that year. Because I saw that I was on a tight schedule, and my English level was subpar, I dragged my friend Haibin Peng into the project, and we translated the book together.

Since we had a limited understanding of Western folklore studies, and our English wasn't very good, we faced many difficulties during the translation process. However we eventually finished the translated manuscript on time. On December 23, I wrote to Dundes's student, Beverly Butcher, and asked her to deliver a letter to Dundes, with the hope that he would write a preface for the Chinese edition. On January 28th, 1989, Beverly mailed back Dundes's resume, along with a letter from Dundes himself. In the letter, Dundes mentioned his desire to visit China, and said that he could apply for grants in America to cover the costs of the trip.

I reported the situation to my teacher, Shouhua Liu, who was very much in support of it. We reported to the Foreign Affairs department of the university, and mailed Dundes, the University of California Press, and the U. S. Embassy to resolve issues regarding Dundes's visit and the copyright of *The Study of Folklore*. Just as everything was going smoothly, the Political turmoil of 1989 happened, and all foreign activities of the university were brought to a halt, naturally postponing Dundes's visit.

After more than half a year, Dundes sent the preface for *The Study of Folklore*, and brought up the visit again. A couple days later, we submitted another report to the university regarding inviting Dundes to China. On December 11th, the Shanghai Literature and Art Publishing House mailed the edited copy of the translated manuscript, including the preface and photos Dundes sent. The editor, Jing Qin, told me that for the purpose of marketing, the book title was changed to *The Study of World Folklore*.

In the preface for the Chinese edition, Dundes wrote:[①]

> Folklore studies has gradually become an interdisciplinary and international academic field. Unfortunately, Chinese folklorists know very little about the state of affairs outside of China. Up to this point Chinese folklorists have not yet participated in any international folklore study collaborations, and they haven't kept up with the new theories and methods developed by Western folklorists. Meanwhile, Western folklorists also don't know about the achievements of Chinese folklorists. That is why people hope Chinese folklorists' research accomplishments can be published in English, French, German, or other international academic languages. Of course, Western works should also be published in Chinese. (This is also the reason I was so happy about this book being published in Chinese.)

---

① This quote is translated from the Chinese translation since the original English could not be located—Translator's note.

China is the most populous nation in the world; with folk, comes folklore. Thus, China has richer folk customs than any other country. China also has many fascinating ethnic minorities—each minority has its own customs. Therefore, it is absolutely necessary for Chinese folklorists to join the international folklore study community, and share these treasures of human creativity and imagination with all who are interested.

After Lunar New Year of 1990, the university approved of Dr. Dundes's visit. On February 25th, I sent Dundes an official invitation. Upon receiving his answer, I contacted Dr. Xiaoping Dong from BNU and Dr. Qinjian Chen from CCNU, requesting their assistance in arranging Mr. and Mrs. Dundes's trip which would start in Wuhan and then go to Beijing and Shanghai. I received their enthusiastic response. Since then, the focus of my job was on the matter of meeting Dr. Dundes. I asked adjunct professor of English Department at Wuhan Technical University of Surveying and Mapping, Dr. Xiaosheng Hu, to be my interpreter, and I also made serious academic preparations for Dr. Dundes's visit.

I did not expect yet another conflict to arise. Yet, on April 29th, the China Association for Folk Literature and Art Studies notified Dr. Shouhua Liu that he was to visit Thailand during Dundes's visit to China. This meant I would be responsible for the entire reception. In addition, the department chairperson told me that the country was in a sensitive period, and the central committee ordered that foreigners were not to come in contact with students, nor to lecture to them. All the lectures we had planned for Dr. Dundes were turned into seminars.

On May 14th, I came down with a fever and was resting at home when I suddenly received a notice from the university. Apparently Dundes sent me a telegraph on May 5th, saying that their flight would arrive in Wuhan on the 15th. The interpreter at the post office nearly caused a delay because he couldn't translate my name in Dundes's telegraph back to Chinese. Eventually they found the message was for me. I arranged a car at the university while enduring my fever, and finally met Mr. and Mrs. Dundes on the evening of the 15th.

On the morning of May 16th, Dundes held a seminar with more than twenty graduate students from the university and experts within the province. He introduced the history and current state of Western folklore studies. In the afternoon I introduced the state of Chinese folklore studies, and I realized Dundes was completely clueless about China. Everything I said was news to him. He was high-spirited and curious about everything. During the discussion, I found Dr. Dundes to be a fun-loving, humorous man. When I talked about how China was investigating and recording folk literature from different ethnic groups, he praised it immensely. But at the same time he was worried about racism. I told him: China has many preferential policies for ethnic minorities, for example they can have two children and get a point boost on their college entrance exam. He still didn't quite understand, and said family planning should not be executed forcibly, and students of all ethnicities should be equal.

The next morning, Gao took Mr. and Mrs. Dundes to the Yellow Crane Tower, the Guiyuan Temple, and the Hubei Provincial Museum. Meanwhile I reported the reception situation to Principal Qingsheng Wang and three directors from the Chinese department. The main problems raised were: 1) the Foreign Affairs Department thought that the reception was not up to standard—I was only an adjunct professor while Dundes is an internationally-renowned scholar. Thus, we were not equal in status. 2) Could we appoint Dundes to be a visiting professor for our university? 3) Can we have more students attend Dr. Dundes's lectures? The University could only resolve the first two.

This afternoon, Dundes and I had another seminar, joined by graduate and undergraduate students studying folk literature. Since we knew each other better and were more prepared, the atmosphere was very relaxed. We talked about myth studies, reproductive worship, and erotic stories. He told me that he studied bathroom literature, which are writings and drawings on the walls of men's bathrooms, and wrote a paper analyzing it from a psychological perspective. He said he also wrote an article about soccer, which he thought was a display of homosexuality. He recommended me his doctoral dissertation, "Structural Typology in North American Indian Folktales." I did not understand his method of extracting motifemes from stories at the time, but he immediately gave me a copy of the dissertation. That night, a couple graduate students from our major went with Mr. and Mrs. Dundes to the South-Center University for Nationalities Museum to watch them tie-dye. I was finally free to go home. It had been three days since I'd been home, and my two-year-old son cried happily when he saw me.

On the morning of May 18th, to make up for the inequality in status of reception, Principal Qingsheng Wang personally met Mr. and Mrs. Dundes in his office. Principal Wang gave Dr. Dundes a Chinese landscape painting, and also presented him with a letter of appointment, naming him a visiting professor of our Folk Literature major. The Chinese Department arranged for Dr. Zhongxiang Wang and Dr. Duanzhi Peng from the Foreign Literature major and Dr. Zihua Qiu from the Literature and Art major to talk with Dr. Dundes. Mr. and Mrs. Dundes were delighted. This afternoon, folk literature studies graduate students and I had another seminar with Dundes, and he kept asking when he could start lecturing, expressing that he was all prepared. I gently told him that considering he flew all the way from the US and hasn't gotten much rest in the past couple days, we did not arrange for him to lecture yet. He was very displeased, and kept asserting: "I'd like to work!"

On May 19th, it was still the graduate students and I who accompanied Mr. and Mrs. Dundes. We discussed a lot in the past few days, and felt as if everything had been said. By this time I wanted to probe the possibility of a collaboration with the American folklore academics, and proposed the question of whether our universities could have graduate exchange programs. Dundes was quite cautious, and said that it would be impossible to get it funded. I then brought up that I hoped he could help us obtain the FFC book series. He said it was difficult, but agreed that after he returns to the States, he would give our Folk Literature major a set of his own published books. This afternoon, since Dr. Shouhua Liu wasn't home, I went with him to see Dr. Liu's wife, Dr. Chen.

Midday of May 20th, Zhuoxian Gao and I saw Dundes off at the airport, and Dr. Xiaoping Dong was waiting to pick him up in Beijing. Dr. Jingwen Zhong managed the reception himself. After a successful visit to Beijing, Dr. Dundes went to CCNU again, and exchanged with the Shanghai folklore academia, then returned to the US from Shanghai.

The entire process of translating Dundes's book and hosting him in Wuhan took two years. It was full of twists and turns but ultimately concluded with success. As a young person who had just entered the workforce, I learned a lot from the experience. To give an amusing example, we had very low incomes at the time, and I didn't know what to give Dr. Dundes for our first meeting. Then I took a fancy to a calligraphy piece by a renowned Wuhan calligrapher Mr. Jinlong Fu. It was the character "dragon" written in the grass script, and had a lot of character to it. I spent half a month's worth of my wage on the piece as a gift to Dr. Dundes, but I didn't know how to wrap it nicely, and I carelessly wrapped it with a couple pieces of scrap paper. I gave it to Mr. and Mrs. Dundes hastily before we went to dinner, without introducing the value of this piece or explaining the symbolism of the character "dragon," so that Dundes had no idea what value this piece held and cast it to the side. Besides these types of situations concerning courtesy, through the organization of this entire event, I understood the meaning of "one does not know the difficulty of a job until one has done it himself." This gave me the experience for all sorts of group event organizations I did in the future.

Dr. Dundes's visit to China made a direct scholastic connection between Sino-US academia, increasing conceptual and activities interactions between scholars from the two countries. After Mr. and Mrs. Dundes returned to the US, their visit left a deep impression on them. Not only did he send us major copies of his works, he also introduced the state of Chinese folklore studies enthusiastically in American periodicals. Until a few years before his passing, he or his wife sent me greeting cards every Christmas. My doctoral dissertation, "On the Circulation Circle of the Flood Stories in China," was inspired by *The Flood Myth* which he sent to us.

In 2013, *The Flood Myth* edited by Dundes was also published in Chinese. Unfortunately, Dr. Dundes couldn't see the publication of this book. Here, I use an excerpt from the epilogue of that book to end this essay: "This book to me, besides leaving me with pleasant memories of times spent with my students and friends, is a bouquet I lay on Dr. Alan Dundes's grave. To Dr. Dundes, who dedicated his entire life to learning, learning is without national border, and knowledge is passed down through generations. I seem to have seen him smiling charmingly down on us."

(Translation by Eurydice Chen)

太遗憾了：阿兰·邓迪斯没能收到这本书

户晓辉[*]

2001年，我在中国社会科学院文学所启动了一个科研项目——"民俗学理论与方法的跨文化对话"。我把对邓迪斯的研究作为该项目的核心部分。有两个原因令我对他的思想着迷：对民俗刨根问底的精神，即使结果可能是错误的；视学术研究无禁区的态度。

我当时的计划是遴选邓迪斯的一些理论著述翻译成中文，于是，便与他通过电子邮件联系上了。他不仅与我讨论了所选的文章和翻译时可能遇到的问题，而且还寄给我一些书，并为翻译他的《民俗解析》写下了中文版的序言。他写道：

> 作为热衷于民俗学（有关民俗的研究）真正是一门国际性学科（Dundes，1999）这种观念的一个民俗学家，我非常高兴也很荣幸我的一本论文选集被译成中文，我想感谢户晓辉为实现这个翻译计划所做的一切努力。
>
> 我希望这些文章会激励中国民俗学家们做两件事情。首先是就相互感兴趣的话题更主动地参与到民俗学家的国际对话中去。其次是从民俗的收集和记录转移到分析和解释的批评场域。对于第一个目标来说，中国民俗学家一定像他们之前的芬兰民俗学家和爱尔兰民俗学家那样认识到：不幸的是，世界上多数民俗学家阅读中文决不比他们阅读芬兰语或盖尔语更多。因此，中国的民俗学家和芬兰民俗学家及爱尔兰民俗学家一样，不得不"发表两次"，即用母语为他们自己的民族发表他们的材料和研究成果，又要用一种欧洲语言如法语、德语或英语发表这些文章，以赢得更广泛的读者。芬兰民俗学家如果只用芬兰语发表就不可能成为世界知名的民俗学家。可悲的事实是，西方民俗学家们相对极少有向中国民俗学研究的世界敞开的窗口。虽然有一些概述（参看下文参考书目中引用的那些篇目），但绝大多数中国的民俗和民俗学对西方人来说基本上是一本合着的书，尤其是中国五十多个少数民族的民俗。在理论上，我们可以等到有更多的西方

---

[*] 编者注：户晓辉是中国社会科学院文学所的研究员，文学博士。他从文学、美学和哲学等视角对民俗的研究拓宽了中国民俗学的学科领域。他相信他目前所倡导的"未来民俗学"是人的核心理性的实践民俗。他曾访问过东亚和欧洲，但还没去过美国。2015年他受邀访美，但因手续等原因而未能成行。然而，他与美国民俗学界的联系展示了中美交流中的亚民俗的独特的一页——一个和著名民俗学家的一段鲜为人知的故事。而且，他是用英文写的这篇故事！在此，我们可以相信邓迪斯是会对中美目前的交流感到欣慰的。（另见本文集陈建宪有关邓迪斯的故事。）

民俗学家获得了阅读中文的知识，但从现实考虑，对于中国最出色和最聪明的年轻民俗学家来说，更明智的是在《亚洲民俗研究》（*Asian Folklore Studies*）或任何重要的民俗学杂志上发表文章，以成为世界范围内正在进行的民俗学思想对话的一部分。

关于第二个目标，我的印象可能不对，即中国的民俗学家和世界各地如此众多的民俗学家一样，欣赏并真正喜爱民俗，但他们倾向于收集传说、迷信和民歌等诸如此类的材料，却不能以任何有意味的方式分析它。材料收集当然是重要的，但民俗学不可能只是由文本构成。还必须关注语境。谁在其他人面前把笑话讲给谁？接受者对某个民俗的反应是什么？最重要的是，这条民俗的意义或多种意义是什么？它可能对于故事的讲述人是一个意思，对于听众又是另一个意思，因此，它是否对不同的听众成员具有不同的意思呢？男人和女人是否以同样的方式理解某个民俗呢？有没有关于男人和女人对某个民俗所讲述的不同异文的研究呢？（关于一个颇具启发的例子，参看 Taggart，1990）一个足够简单的问题却需要认真的田野作业才能得到一个有意义的答案。民俗的文学研究和历史研究早就有了，但民俗的心理研究却非常罕见。可是，民俗（包括中国民俗）包含许多幻想的材料，而幻想就需要对心理因素给以一定的关注。是否存在着对中国民俗的深层心理学研究呢？如果没有，为什么会没有呢？

我真诚地希望我这些文章的中译文将激发中国民俗的进一步研究。我要再次感谢户晓辉博士承担了这项有抱负的计划。

我在收到这个序言后，于 2004 年 4 月 26 日回复道："亲爱的邓迪斯教授，感谢您写的序言！我打开了文件。我赞同您的这些观点。这也是我翻译您的文章的目的。我觉得语言问题是中国学者参与国际民俗交流的障碍。如您所说，西方很少有人能读懂中文，我们只好用英文交流。总之，我认为中国学者需要做更多的工作来开启这个对话交流，因为他们学英文比西方人学中文要容易得多……的确，您说您的印象可能是"错误的"，您知道，从 1980 年代至今，中国民俗学者（特别是年轻一代）其实是读过心理分析、原型、以及仪式等有关理论的，尽管可能有些禁忌题目，如有关性的问题。但我认为，他们的，或者说我们的分析和阐释还不够好，还需要更多的学习，包括您的著作。我正在翻译您的序言，感到其中是否有个笔误，有一个 than 是否应该是 that？"

同一天，邓迪斯回信，"亲爱的晓辉，好眼力！的确，那个 than 应该是 that。之后的那句话有点特别，但其目的是要说，中国学者也必须二次发表。你可以把这个意思加入中文的翻译。至于你对中国民俗学者运用那些理论的评述，我认为原型理论是毫无用途的。荣格对原型的神秘概念是无法用经验验证的。其实，不存在所谓的荣格式的原型。对人类来说，不存在普适的泛人形象。至于所谓的仪式理论又是一个理论陷阱，属于 19 世纪末那些古典学者的幻想，他们错误地认为，每个神话后面都有一个共质仪式。可是，有许许多多的神话与仪式没有任何关系。所以，如果有年轻的中国民俗学者运用原型理论和仪式理论，他们的确有必要重新考虑一下如何对待民俗素材。"

由于有了邓迪斯的帮助和支持，翻译的文章于 2005 年 1 月出版了。我立刻告诉了他这个消息,并通过电子邮件传给他书的封面和封底。邓迪斯回复道:"绝妙的设计!谁找到的那些图像?我真希望马上看到纸质的书。万分感谢你传来这些图像。"2005年3月,他写道:"亲爱的晓辉,寄来的书还没收到。是陆运还是海运?我很渴望见到这本书,哪怕只是一本。我知道这个拖延不是你的错,但我希望至少有一本可以是航空邮寄的。"我回复道,"亲爱的邓迪斯教授,我又给编辑打过电话了。他告诉我是一个多月前海运的。我让他航空邮寄一本,可是他说那样对这边来说太贵了。他也说,那些书会很快到的。所以请再等几天"。

4月2日,我从一位同事那里得知邓迪斯3月30日在给研究生上课时突然倒下,去世了。我想到他还没能亲自收到那本书,心中感到极大的遗憾。但令我感到宽慰的是他知道也欣赏我的翻译工作,正如约翰娜·雅可布森博士在2005年4月5日写给我的信中所说的那样,"我觉得邓迪斯博士的遗产之一是他把学者们联系到一起了。我只是想在邓迪斯博士去世后这个悲伤的时候向你表示问候。他会被大家怀念的。我希望你别的都好——祝贺你翻译出版邓迪斯的著述;我知道,他的主要关注点之一是翻译和协调国际学者之间的联系,我很高兴你的项目结出了硕果。"

我为新版的《中国大百科全书》(2009)撰写了"邓迪斯"和"民俗研究"两个条目。我曾与邓迪斯保持通信往来直到2005年3月22日。作为极有幽默感的学者,邓迪斯曾经引用另一位民俗学者的话来描述自己,"邓迪斯是在没有追随者的领域里的带头人!"可是,我相信,他的确有过,而且还将会有追随者——追随他的学术方法、他的学术精神,以及他的国际视野。邓迪斯曾描述自己是"图书馆里的民俗学者",我也是一位扶手椅里的民俗学理论学者。尽管邓迪斯不是职业哲学家,但是我敬佩他对理论和方法的审慎意识。他把民俗视为"人民的传记。你在触及日常生活中的真人真事"。的确,作为民俗学者的我是人民中的"民"之一,可是在中国,一位传统的"民"还需要成为一个(现代的)公民。

理查德·道尔逊曾说,"一个学科的成功依靠的是它所能吸引到的人的心智。通过吸引邓迪斯,一位口才出众的演说家,一位卓越的教师和学者,民俗学再次证明了它的品性气质。"我认为邓迪斯的确是一位伟大的学者、献身的教师,也为中国民俗学者所敬爱。

(张举文翻译)

中文版《民俗解析》封面（户晓辉译，广西师范大学出版社，2005年）。The cover of the Chinese translation of *Interpreting Folklore* (*Minsu Jiexi*), translated by Xiaohui Hu, Guangxi Normal University Press, 2005).

邓迪斯给户晓辉的手书赠言。Dundes' autography for Xiaohui Hu.

Holy Writ as Oral Lit

What a Pity: Alan Dundes Did Not Receive This Book

Xiaohui Hu[*]

In 2001, I embarked on a key project of the Institute of Literature, Chinese Academy of Social Sciences (CASS), "Cross-Cultural Dialogue of Folkloristic Theories and Methods." I took Alan Dundes to be the core of this project. I was fascinated by his thought for at least two reasons: 1) his spirit to get to the bottom of folklore, even though the solution he had found might be wrong; and 2) his idea that there was no forbidden zone in the sphere of learning.

In undertaking the project, I planned to select some of Dundes' theoretical articles and translate them into Chinese. Thus I contacted him via email. He not only discussed with me about the list of articles and the possible problems in translation, but also sent me several of his books and wrote a short "Preface" for the Chinese translation of his *Interpreting Folklore*. Here is what he wrote:

> As a folklorist dedicated to the notion that folkloristics, the study of folklore, is truly an international academic discipline, I am very pleased and honored to have a selection of my essays translated into Chinese and I want to thank Hu Xiaohui for all his efforts to make this translation project a reality.
>
> It is my hope that these essays will encourage Chinese folklorists to do two things. First, to participate more actively in the international dialogue of folklorists on subjects of mutual interest. And second, to move from the collection and documentation of folklore to the critical

---

* Xiaohui Hu is Senior Research Fellow at the Institute of Literature, Chinese Academy of Social Sciences, with his Ph. D. in Literature. He has been active in the Chinese folklore world through his folkloristic works from literary, aesthetic and philosophical perspectives. His current interest is in "Folkloristics of Future" which he believes is the practice of folklore with rationality and to the core of humanity. He has visited East Asia and Europe, but has never been to the USA. He had an opportunity to attend a seminar in Oregon in 2015, but was hindered by internal paperwork. However, his connection to and understanding of American folklore circles present a unique story in the Sino-US metafolklore communication—an unknown story of this well-known folklorist. Furthermore, he wrote this piece in English! We could imagine that Dundes would feel pleased to see the current Sino-US exchanges. (See also, Jianxian Chen's story about Dundes.)

arena of analysis and interpretation. For the first goal, Chinese folklorists must realize as have Finnish and Irish folklorists before them than [that] unfortunately the majority of the world's folklorists do not read Chinese any more than they read Finnish or Gaelic. Hence just as Finnish and Irish folklorists have had to 'double publish,' that is, publish their data and research results in their native languages for their own peoples but also publish essays in one of the European languages: French, German or English so as to reach a wider audience, [so Chinese scholars must do the same]. The Finnish folklorists would never have become world-famous if they had published only in Finnish. The sad truth is that Western folklorists have relatively few windows opening to the world of Chinese folklore scholarship. There are several useful surveys (see the titles cited under References below), but most of Chinese folklore and folkloristics remains essentially a closed book for the West, especially the folklore of the more than fifty minority peoples of China. In theory, one might wait until more Western folklorists acquire a reading knowledge of Chinese, but realistically, it makes more sense for the best and brightest younger Chinese folklorists to publish articles in *Asian Folklore Studies* or any of the leading folklore journals to become part of the ongoing intellectual worldwide conversation in folkloristics.

With respect to the second goal, it is my impression, perhaps a false one, that Chinese folklorists just like so many folklorists all over the world have an appreciation and genuine love of folklore, but they tend to collect legends, superstitions, and folksongs and other such data, but then fail to analyze it in any meaningful way. Data-gathering is of course essential, but folkloristics cannot be a matter of just texts alone. There must also be attention to context. Who tells the joke to whom else in the presence of which other persons? What is the addressee's response to the item of folklore? And most important of all, what are the meaning (s) of the item of folklore? It may mean one thing to the story teller and quite another to the audience, and for that matter it may mean different things to different members of the audience. Do men and women understand an item of folklore in the same way? Are there any studies of the different versions of an item of folklore as told by men and those versions told by women? A simple enough question but one that requires serious fieldwork to get a meaningful answer. There have long been literary and historical studies of folklore, but psychological studies of folklore are rare. Yet folklore (including Chinese folklore) include much fantasy material and fantasy requires some attention to psychological factors. Are there in-depth psychological studies of Chinese folklore? If not, why not?

It is my sincere hope that the Chinese translation of these essays of mine will stimulate further research in Chinese folklore. Again I reiterate my thanks to Xiaohui Hu for undertaking this ambitious project.

After I received this preface, I wrote back to him on April 26, 2004:

Dear Prof. Dundes, Thank you for your preface! I have opened the attached file. I agree with you about these ideas. They are also my goals as I translate your essays into Chinese. I think language is a problem for Chinese scholars to participate in dialogue of world folklorists. As you said, few folklorists in Western countries can read Chinese, we have to communicate in English as a common language. Anyway, I think Chinese folklorists ought to do more work to promote this dialogue, because they learn English more easily than Westerners learn Chinese…You are right because you said your impression "perhaps a false one." You know that from 1980' till now, Chinese folklorists (especially those young scholars) indeed have used psychoanalytical theory, archetype theory, ritual theory among others to study folklore, even though there are some taboo topics, e. g. , sexual problems. But I think their or our analysis and interpretation is not good enough, we need to learn a lot, including learning from your essays. I am translating the preface, and I wonder in "For the first goal, Chinese folklorists must realize as have Finnish and Irish folklorists before them than unfortunately…" the "than" ought to be "that"?

On the same day, Dundes replied:

Dear Hu, Good eye! Yes, "than" ought to be "that". The next sentence is a little peculiar. The point is that at the end, it ought to say that Chinese folklorists must also double publish. You might want to add that thought in the Chinese translation. As for your remark about the theories used by Chinese folklorists, I consider archetype theory to be totally useless. Jung's mystical notion of the archetype is not empirically verifiable. There is no such thing as an archetype in the Jungian sense. No universal pan-human images built into the human species. And so-called "ritual theory" is another specious theory belonging to classicists in the late nineteenth century who wrongly assumed that behind every myth lay one foundation ritual. But there are many, many myths which have no connection whatsoever to ritual. So if archetype theory and ritual theory are being used by young Chinese folklorists, they very much need to reconsider how to approach folklore data. AD.

Because of Dundes's help and support, my translation was published in January, 2005. I told him the news immediately and sent the images of the front and back cover of the book via Email. He replied, "A stunning design. Who found the images? I can't wait to see the actual book. Many, many thanks for sending the images."

On March 2005, he wrote again, "Dear Hu, The books still haven't arrived. Were they sent by mule or by sea-mail? I am anxious to see at least one copy of the book. I realize the delay is not your fault, but I wish at least one copy had been sent by air-mail. AD."

I replied, "Dear Prof. Dundes, I have called the editor here again, and he told me that he sent the books by sea-mail more than one month ago, I asked him to send one by air-mail, but he said it is very expensive here. He also told me the books might arrive soon. So please wait for some days."

On April 2, I heard from my colleague that Dundes collapsed and died suddenly while giving a graduate seminar on March 30, 2005. What a pity! I regretted that Dundes had not personally received the book! But I were gratified at his knowing and appreciating my translation, just as Dr. Johanna Jacobsen wrote to me on April 5, 2005:

"I think one of Dr. Dundes's legacies is that he brings scholars together—I thought I would write to you and just say hello after the sad event of Dr. Dundes's death. He will be truly missed. I hope you are otherwise doing well—congratulations on your translation project with Dundes; I know that translation and facilitating international scholarly contact was one of his key interests, and I am glad that that project saw fruition."

I wrote the entries "Dundes" and "The Study of Folklore" for the new edition of the *Chinese Encyclopedia* (2009). And I had kept correspondences with him until March 22, 2005. As a scholar with good sense of humor, Dundes once quoted one folklorist who said, "Dundes is a leader in the field without any followers!"[①] But I believe that he did have and will have some followers because of his research methods, his academic spirit and his international perspective. Dundes had referred himself as a "library folklorist."[②] I am also an armchair scholar of folkloristic theory. Even though Dundes was not trained as a philosopher, I admire his strong consciousness of theory and methodology. He called folklore "the autobiography of a people. You're dealing with real people in everyday life." That is right, because I, as a folklorist, am a "folk" among people, and in China, a traditional "folk" needs to become a citizen.

Richard M. Dorson once said, "The success of a discipline depends upon the quality of the minds it attracts. In attracting Alan Dundes, a brilliant speaker, teacher, and scholar, folklore has again proved its mettle."[③] I think Alan Dundes was really a great scholar and a devoted teacher, and also was loved by Chinese folklorists.

---

① Rosmary Lévy Zumwalt. "Alan Dundes: Folklorist and Mentor." In *Folklore Interpreted: Essays in Honor of Alan Dundes*. New York and London: Garland Publishing, Inc., 1995, p. 23.
② *ibid*, p. 21.
③ Richard M. Dorson. "Foreword." In Alan Dundes, *Analytic Essays in Folklore*. Mouton Publishers, 1975.

Ⅱ. 从面对文本到面对面——耕耘友情

　　如同中国的其他现代学科，中国民俗学的发展历程始于对西方民俗学的翻译介绍。那些零星译本，虽然都在不同程度上扩大了中国知识分子的视野，但毕竟有"管窥一斑"或"一叶障目"的现象。当然，西方早期对中国的了解也是通过传教士对中国儒家典籍的选择翻译，以及他们的日志札记等文本。无疑，这些文本中的中国人的生活展示的不但是片面的中国人的生活和文化传统，而更重要的是，这些片面的文本构建了历史的扭曲，产生了影响深刻而长远的"心理定势"（刻板印象）。显然，这样的事在各个社会和文化中都还在继续。

　　同样，中国对西方的了解也经历过类似的过程。对民俗学者来说，我们只需稍微考证一下这些词语的出现背景及其在日常生活中的使用，就可以明白中国人的民俗生活及其观念的演变历程："洋人""洋鬼子""红番""鬼佬""外宾""外国人""老外"，直到今天的"老美"和"老中"等。而北京（还有一些其他城市）的"友谊商店"则记录了一段更扭曲的历史（其实只有三四十年而已）：从只有"外宾"可进入、只有用"外汇券"购买中国百姓买不到的商品，到"老外"和中国人都可以随便进入、用同样的人民币买任何其他地方都可以买到的东西。这难道不也正是中国知识分子在经历的变化过程吗？

　　改变这种局面的途径似乎只有大规模的面对面的交流。随着人类多元文化的多重互动，特别是学者的互动，这个问题正在发生历史性转变，正朝着积极的方向发展，令人鼓舞。对中国来说，这个转变始于1980年代：中国民俗学得以重建，对外界的了解不再是"盲人摸象"了。

　　此部分的故事继续讲述中国民俗学界所经历的历史性转折：从面对文本转向面对面的对话。以时间顺序，白素贞和本德尔以自己在1980年代初期来到中国的体验讲述了自己的学术历程和学术观点的变化。虽然白素贞和本德尔都不是以民俗学者的身份来到中国的，但是他们此后对两国民俗学的贡献是可贵的。李扬则代表了较早走出去的新一代民俗学家，由此获得世界眼光，并开始搭建学术桥梁。迈克尔·琼斯以自己经历的一个普通而又珍贵的故事展示了人与人交流中有意义的东西，注释了他自己的"人研究人"的理论观点，也讲述了2005年中美民俗学会"第一次握手"的故事。萧放则以日记形式真实地展现了一位中国民俗学者在十多年来"走出去"的历程，也展示了中国学者在对外交流中的"关注点"的变化。这部分的故事不只是说明了交流方式的改变，更是交流观念的改变。有了这个转变，才会有从不平等的学术研究到平等的学术交流的转变，才会有真正的学者与学者的交流。

II. From Face-to-text to Face-to-face—Cultivating Friendship

Like other modern disciplines in China, folkloristics began with translations of Western folklore studies. To a certain degree, those sporadically translated texts enriched the work of Chinese intellectuals; but they also caused the problem of "seeing a speck through a pipe" (as a Chinese saying goes) or "can't see the forest for the tree" (as an English saying goes). The West's understanding of China began through missionaries' journals, with their interpretations of Chinese people and culture, and translations of Confucian classics. There is no doubt, however, that the missionary texts revealed a limited and one-sided description of Chinese culture and tradition, which resulted in stereotypes of the Chinese which remain prevalent even today. However, such a practice of stereotyping one people by highlighting certain aspects without providing context is still continuing in all societies.

China has also undergone such a process in trying to understand the West. To folklorists, it is sufficient just to consider the changes of the terms used to refer to foreigners throughout history: *yangren* for (remote overseas) foreigners; *yangguizi* for foreign demons; *hongfan* for red-haired barbarians; *guilao* for foreign devil; *waibin* for foreign distinguished guests; *waiguoren* for foreigners; and today's *lao-wai* for Foreigners or *lao-mei* for Americans (just as *lao-Zhong* for Chinese for themselves (particularly in contrasting circumstances where both are mentioned), in the same ways as Lao Wang for "old buddy Wang") in everyday life (certainly, the usage is highly situational). The evolution of the Friendship Stores (*youyi shangdian*) in Beijing and other big cities also demonstrates gradual changes in policy and attitude until late 1980s: from the period when only "foreign distinguished guests" could enter and use "foreign currency coupons" to purchase things that the average Chinese could not purchase (and certain things that were simply not available to Chinese nationals/natives anywhere), to the current situation allowing *lao-wai* and Chinese citizens to enter and purchase the same things with the same paper currency. Doesn't this also demonstrate the changes over time for Chinese intellectuals?

Stories in this section continue to focus on the historical turn in Chinese folkloristics: from face-to-text to face-to-face academic discourse. Chronologically, Susan Blader and Mark Bender talk about the academic paths they followed and how their approaches to the field evolved during their Chinese experiences in the early 1980s. Neither Bender nor Blader went to China as a folklorists; however, their contributions to folkloristics are precious. Michael Jones tells about something very ordinary, yet very precious, in people-to-people communication that illustrates the concept of "people studying people"; he also made the first handshake on behalf of AFS with CFS in 2005. Yang Li represents the new generation of folklorists who went abroad relatively early and thus gained a vision of world folklore that allowed them to better bridge academic exchanges. Fang Xiao, through his diaries, gives a personal account of how a Chinese folklorist feels when "going abroad" in the past dozen years thus revealing how things have changed. Lihui Yang and Deming An demonstrate how Chinese folkloristics has grown through cross-cultural communication, how its role in international discourse has changed, and, as a result of this, how their personal intellectual growth has been enhanced.

Stories in this section show that the changes that have occurred are not only in the means of communication, but also in attitudes and points of view. Only with these changes can there be truly equal communication between scholars.

去中国研究，在美国传播

白素贞[*]

  虽然我受到的是汉学训练，而没有受过民俗学或人类学的专业训练，但我在过去的四十多年里却一直从事着对中国口头表演艺术的田野调查和研究。

  我在完成宾夕法尼亚大学东方研究学院的博士课程和考试后，于1971年前往台湾，开展关于李白和杜甫两位唐朝诗人的学位论文研究。假如我一直专注于这个题目，我到现在估计还在努力完成这篇论文的路上。我到台北书店试着寻找一个力所能及的新的论题，那期间我无意中看到一本装帧有趣的小说《三侠五义》。这本小说出版于1879年，[①]作者石玉昆是一位19世纪的著名表演艺术家，从文本中交替的唱词和说话的风格看，很有可能是满族人。虽然对说书人、说书和口头传统一无所知，我当场就决定对《三侠五义》的研究将是我的新论题。这就是天意。在一位导师的建议下，我读了一些关于口头传统的书籍，逐渐了解了为什么说《三侠五义》的作者是一位说书人，为什么说它的起源是口头传统。我从未以这样的眼光看待"文学"。我的研究和我的人生从此都发生了戏剧性的转变，而后接下来的事，大家就都知道了！

  在《三侠五义》的介绍部分有几篇文人的序言，他们在序言里介绍了他们是如何把一本唱本的手稿[②]进行修订：他们删除了唱词部分，内容一下子就缩短了，然后对一部分语言进行改写，使之不那么"粗俗"，更书面化，例如，他们把绝大多数带有口语化特点的语句删除了。多伦多大学的凯特·史蒂文斯教授敦促我去访问位于台北郊区的"中央研究院"，在那些从大陆带过来的海量手稿中搜索这部说书的早期的版本。"中央研究院"慷慨地准许我利用傅斯年善本图书馆，我阅读了一本名叫《龙图公案》（包公审案）的手稿，一本名为

---

[*] 编者注：白素贞是美国达特茅斯学院的荣退中文教授，在宾夕法尼亚大学获得了博士学位，致力于中国口头艺术表演研究。她曾于20世纪80年代初来到中国，对中国民间表演艺术开展田野调查，成为美国这方面研究的先驱者之一。在民俗学研究方面，她能够把书面文本和口头表演结合起来，通过访问、讲座、表演和观光的方式为无数的中美学者搭建了交流的桥梁。她最近完成了一个项目，公开了一些中国的已故的口头演唱表演艺术家好几十个小时的表演视频。这些视频是她在过去的几十年里录制的，是极富价值的可供日后进一步研究的资料。她的研究证明民俗学本身就具有交叉学科性质，民俗学的学术阵地因为非民俗学专业背景学者的加入而巩固，并例证了在中美交流过程中的亚民俗的丰富。

① 《三侠五义》的英文书名取自杨宪益、戴乃迭英译的鲁迅《中国小说史略》。

② 手稿名为《龙图耳录》（用听觉记录下的神圣的帝王图景），即宋代皇帝仁宗在梦里看到一个人影，原来是包公。

石派书［石（玉昆）派别的说书］的歌书（唱本）。古代书会雇佣抄写员抄写，这个手稿便是由抄写员把说书人的表演听写记录下来的，这就是阿尔伯特·洛德（Albert Lord）所谓的"指令性表演"①。

在1977年，我在没有观看过任何一位说书人的任何一场演出的情况下，完成了我的学位论文《〈三侠五义〉的研究及其与〈龙图公案〉唱本的关系》。② 直至1981年的秋天，在美国国家科学院委员会的中国学术交流项目的资助下，我终于有机会前往中国大陆寻找尚存的会说包公的说书艺术家。我的接待人是北京大学（北大）中文系的汪景寿教授。1981年10月我到访的时候，他正在斯坦福大学做访问学者，1982年1月才回来。但是，他一回来，之前紧闭的大门一下子就敞开了。我发现汪教授很特别：即使和外国人合作很有风险，他还是大胆地想办法帮助他接待的学者，而且总是表现得那么得体。他总是为我和凯特·史蒂文斯提供一切便利的条件。凯特·史蒂文斯是一名执着的曲艺研习者，从20世纪50年代起，她就在跟一些表演艺术家和民族音乐学家学习曲艺。因此，汪教授和凯特无疑是我的良师益友，有了他们我才得以顺利地进入令人痴迷的中国说书领域。

在过去的35年里与中国说书表演艺术家合作的经历，是我人生中最有意义、最激动人心的时光。我有幸见到和采访到这些说书艺术家们，他们能够诚恳而自如地谈论自己的人生和艺术。其中最坦率和慷慨的是：孙书均，钟玉杰——京韵大鼓；钟德海，白慧谦——三弦；陈少武——二胡；曹宝禄，马增惠——单弦牌子曲；韩德福——三弦；梁厚民，李润杰，张志宽，王学义——快板书；刘司昌——山东快书；常宝华、李金斗、陈涌泉、李伯祥、杜国芝——相声；关学增——北京琴书；史文秀——梅花大鼓；马玉萍——河南坠子；钟喜荣——西河大鼓；高辉——天津时调；金声伯，唐耿良——苏州评话；蒋云仙——弹词（说唱交替）。他们帮助我理解了作为一位说书艺人到底意味着什么。

说书人对故事烂熟于心，然后为我们说唱；只有通过民间职业艺术家完美精湛的技能，我们才有幸在舞台上看到那样的表演，而他们完全凭一张嘴。中国多数传统的说书人不能解释他们自己的说书艺术。他们只是单纯地从师父那里"口头传承"那些故事，把故事烂熟于心，再原封不动地传承下去。但是，我们知道，那些最伟大的说书艺术家能够在口头传统的基础上创作，使他们的故事充满活力、连贯性和便于理解，以适应他们不断变化的听众、表演时间和环境。

从1981年10月到1982年8月，我真正走进这个领域，主要是在北京。日后我几次来到中国，最后一次是在2000年11月，我受汪教授之邀参加一个"国际故事节"。那里有国际学者们的报告，每天晚上有说书人的表演，也有业余国际表演者的表演。在2000年以前，

---

① "指令性表演"的译法来自阿尔伯特·贝茨·洛德《故事的歌手》（尹虎彬译，北京：中华书局，第180页）——译者注。
② "中央研究院"慷慨地准许我利用傅斯年善本图书馆查阅了大量的手稿，那是20世纪40年代从大陆带到台湾去的。对我的论文来说，最重要的就是名叫《龙图公案》（包公审案）的手稿（有50册，将近30页大纸缝合在一起的中国式书卷），一本名为石派书［石（玉昆）派别的说书］的歌书（唱本）。石派书还有两本很有趣的唱本：《风波亭》和《青山石》。

在达特茅斯学院迪吉基金会的慷慨资助下，我邀请了数位来自中国的说书艺术家到美国访问，在美国知名的学院和大学里开展讲座、展览和表演活动。最近，达特茅斯学院的校友大卫·马丁送了一个大礼，他促成了来自中国艺术研究院曲艺研究所的两位中国民族音乐学家蔡源莉和包澄洁从 2016 年 3 月到 6 月底为期四个月的美国之行。他们与我密切合作，完成了《中国说唱艺术纪录》（这是一份在 1981 年到 2000 年期间录制的说书人表演的宝贵录像，有 30 个小时。很快这部纪录片将被发布在网上）。

在过去，关于"口头传统"或"口头说唱表演"，民俗学研究者的主要工作是搜集文本，对它们进行分类；如果是外文还要对它们进行翻译。在这些方面，我自愧不如。当然，在来到中国、见到说书人和观看表演之前，我只有文本这一条研究路径。但是，我的兴趣点由关注口头说唱文本，首先，转移到了关注"评"，即关注故事人物及其行为和说书人是怎样传达文化价值的——说书人会对故事人物及其行为进行评论，就是"评话"和"评书"；其次，转移到了关注"变"，即一个故事的事件和人物，经历不同的朝代和语境，有哪些变化对故事产生影响；最后，转移到了关注在什么程度上的变化使这个故事变成了一个不同的故事，传达了不同的价值。

虽然我知道在口头传统中不存在"最早的"或"权威的"版本，但是，在我和《三侠五义》的苏州评话表演艺术家金声伯经过多次讨论之后，我总是会回归到"变"的话题。1982 年 5 月，在一次关于"变"的讨论中，金先生告诉我，在他说书的时候，他只允许自己在两个方面进行改变：1. 使故事更加精致和丰富（丰富）；2. 使故事更加清晰、有逻辑和合乎情理（改造）。但是，当我问他这类"变"会不会真的把一个故事变成不同的故事时，和许多其他文献记载中的说书人一样，他坚持声称他永远不会改变"书"（故事本身；事件），有些东西可以改变，但有些不能。他在石玉昆作品的基础上作一些改变，但是他的这些改变不会影响或真正改变故事的意义。然而，在 1983 年 11 月对金先生的访谈中，他的表演艺术团领导在场（好像他需要她的保护），金先生调皮地对我说："如果非要用一个字来定义我的说书，那就是'变'！"

在一位杰出的口头说书艺术家和一位天真的研究者之间有一次讨论，我节选了两段作为结束。我相信，这两段节选能够直击说书艺术的核心。看到最后，它们会让你捧腹大笑！①

> 金：我根据石玉昆先生的书变化。应该有变化。它里面讲的不多，我就想，我必须加进去。那是我大胆，因为他的东西不多嘛，留下来的不多嘛。所以这里面必须加东西，加东西就是加思想跟小细节。他有个一，我看还不够，应该加二、三，够了，行了。或者还该发展，那就到我死了以后，我的学生，我的徒孙，噢，这是金声伯的，我们听一听，那时候，他们可以听录音了。嗨，他还不好，那个地方还不够，还得加，丰

---

① 当代苏州评话艺术家金声伯的话看似简单。在今天的中国，或许过去亦然，说书从来都不只是说书人的随口一说，但是金声伯对说书的定义直抵说书的本质。只有当我们追问什么是标准时，这种思考可以让我们深入一种特殊文化的审美的、社会的、政治的和经济的问题，这些早就在随口一说之前决定了说书的本质。

富，丰富，再丰富，再丰富，再丰富。

白：可是，最后的白玉堂是不是在他的个性上，还是书里面的那个白玉堂？

金：对呀，所以他跌到铜网阵里面以后，他没有想法在这个书本上，本子上没有交代。"哎呀"应该有很多想法的，想什么东西？哎呀是什么地方来的，我们就把这两个字推理、推理。第一个哎呀，"哎呀中了机关了；哎呀我上不去了，哎呀看起来我这回完了；哎呀我好后悔，我没有听智化的话，我没有听大哥的话；（哎呀）事情没有成功我先死了；还有个哎呀，死不瞑目，我这个印没有拿回去"。一般来说差不多了，如果说按照实际情况看，也就是了。但是，因为是艺术，可以夸张，还可以哎呀下去，对吗？还哎呀什么呢？"我跟您颜仁敏结拜兄弟啊，您对我这么好，今天我就不能跟您碰头了；大哥卢方，你对我这么好，我也不能跟你碰头了；夫人在家里，我好长时间没有回去；我的小孩子还小。"

白：我都不知道白玉堂结婚了。

金：有的，有的，有的。书里面没有，那是在《小五义》里。

白：在《三侠五义》里他没有讲。

金：这都可以畅想的。

白：不，我觉得，白玉堂结婚是很重要的一个不同。就是说，在他死的时候，他没有夫人，没有孩子。

金：不过，讲了，也是通的。因为按照我们中国人的习惯，十六岁就可以结婚了。

白：他们是侠义。

金：侠义又不是和尚。

白：侠义可能要晚一点结婚。

金：开玩笑，对吗！那么，如果这样想，也是可以的，也是合理的，应当是合理的。

白：我不希望他那个时候结婚，我不喜欢。

金：不喜欢，那就算了，下次你说，你就说不结婚，对吗？

白：我觉得他不应该结婚。

金：好的，这可以的，你讲不结婚就不结婚，这个反正都在我们嘴里。

话说到此，也正是结束我的故事的最佳时刻。

（辽宁师范大学刘思诚翻译）

Researching in China, Disseminating Results in the US

Susan Blader[*]

I have conducted folklore fieldwork and research for the past four decades even though I was trained as a sinologist, primarily working on translating classical Chinese texts as my future work.

In 1971, after completing my PhD courses and exams in the Oriental Studies Department of the University of Pennsylvania, off I went to Taiwan to begin research on my dissertation topic on two Tang poets, Li Bai and Du Fu. Had I stayed with that topic, I would probably still be trying to finish the thesis! After visiting bookstores in Taipei in search of a new topic, one that could be completed in my lifetime, I serendipitously happened upon an interesting-looking novel, *Sanxia wuyi* 三侠五义 (*Three Heroes and Five Gallants*, hereafter, *Three Heroes*), published in 1879.[②] The novel was "attributed to" Shi Yukun 石玉昆, a famous 19th century performer, most likely Manchu, of the alternating sung and spoken genre. Although completely ignorant about storytellers, storytelling, and the oral tradition, I providentially decided, on the spot, that a study of *Three Heroes* would be my new thesis topic. After reading several books about the oral tradition, suggested by a dissertation advisor, I gradually began to understand what it meant that *Three Heroes* was attributed to a storyteller, that its provenance was the oral tradition. I would never look at "literature" in the same way again. My research and my life were changed dramatically—and the

---

[*] Susan Blader is Associate Professor Emeritus of Chinese Language & Literature at Dartmouth College. With a doctorate degree in Chinese Literature from the University of Pennsylvania, Blader was one of a handful of US pioneers conducting field research on Chinese folk performances in the early 1980s. She has published on the relationship between oral narrative performance and literary text. From 1988 to 2000, she invited numerous Chinese storytelling artists and scholars to the US in order to introduce their brilliant artistry through lecture-performance visits to many colleges and universities. With the help of two ethnomusicologists from Beijing, she recently completed a documentary-style project of 30 hours of videotaped performances by some of China's greatest folk artists. She has demonstrated how folkloristics itself is interdisciplinary, how our field is strengthened by scholars who are not trained in Folkloristics, and how metafolklore is enriched through Sino-US communications.

② *Three Heroes and Five Gallants*, title from Hsien-Yi Yang and Gladys Yang's translation of Lu Xun's 中国小说史略 *A Brief History of Chinese Fiction*.

rest is history!

Included in the introduction to *Three Heroes* were three prefaces that were written by literary men to explain how they revised a song book manuscript version①: they removed the sung sections, which shortened the narrative enormously, and change some of the language to be less "vulgar," more literary, i. e., they removed most of the characteristics that demonstrated its oral provenance. It was Kate Stevens, Professor at the University of Toronto, who urged me to visit Academia Sinica, on the outskirts of Taipei, to search, among their huge collection of handwritten manuscripts brought from the mainland, for an early version of the narrative. Academia Sinica generously allowed me to view, in their Fu Sinian Rare Book Library, a handwritten manuscript titled *Longtu gongan* [Courtroom Cases of Magistrate Bao], a song-book (*changben*) designated a Shipai shu [Shi (Yukun) School Narrative] (To be distinguished from the Ming Dynasty collection of Magistrate Bao's Courtroom Cases). This manuscript was written down by scribes, hired by a "publishing house," to listen to and transcribe a storyteller's performance, what Albert Lord called a "command performance."

In 1977, I completed my dissertation, "A Critical Study of *San-hsia wu-yi* and (Its) Relationship to the *Lung-t'u kung-an* Song-Book," without ever having seen any performance by any storytelling artist!② It was not until the fall of 1981, under the auspices of the National Academy of Sciences' Committee for Scholarly Communication with the PRC, that I was finally able to visit China in search of any storytelling artists who still performed Magistrate Bao narratives. My host at Beijing University (Beida) was Prof. Jingshou Wang, who was a Visiting Professor at Stanford University when I arrived in October, 1981, and did not return until January, 1982. But, as soon as returned, doors that had previously been closed suddenly opened up. Prof. Wang was, I discovered, unique: even when it was quite dangerous to cooperate with foreigners, he was fearless in finding ways to help the scholars he hosted—while acting always within the bounds of correct behavior. He made everything possible for me and Kate Stevens, a passionate student of *Quyi* since the 1950s, who was already acquainted with some performing artists and ethnomusicologists. Thus, Prof. Wang and Kate, the best possible mentors and friends, smoothed my entry into the fascinating world of Chinese storytelling.

---

① Titled *Longtu erlu* 龙图耳录 (Aural Record of the Lord of the Imperial Sketch), i. e., a sketch of a man Song Emperor Renzong saw in a dream, a man who turned out to be Bao Gong (Magistrate Bao).

② It was in the Fu Sinian 傅斯年 Rare Book Library of Academia Sinica that I was generously given permission to examine a number of handwritten manuscripts from among the cases of items brought to Taiwan by those fleeing the communists in the 1940s. For my dissertation, the most important of these was the handwritten manuscript (in 50 *ce* 册, Chinese-style volumes of approximately 30 large size pages, sewn together), titled *Longtu gongan* 龙图公案 [Courtroom Cases of Magistrate Bao], a song-book (*changben* 唱本) attributed to the 石派书 [Shi (Yukun) School of Storytelling]. There were two other song-books attributed to the 石派书: *Fengbo Ting* 风波亭 [Fengbo Pavilion] and *Qingshi Shan* 青石山 [Black Rock Mountain], which were also of great interest.

My experiences working with Chinese performing artists over these 35 years have been the most meaningful and exciting times of my life. The storytelling artists I was privileged to meet and interview spoke sincerely and freely about their lives and their art. The most generous among them were: Sun Shujun and Zhong Yujie, Beijing Drumsong; Zhong Dehai and Bai Huiqian, *sanxian*; Chen Shaowu, *erhu*, Cao Baolu and Ma Zenghui, Tamborine Drumsong; Liu Sichang, Shandong Fast Clappertales; Li Jindou, Chen Yongquan, Li Boxiang, Du Guozhi, Comic Dialog; Among Southern artists: Jin Shengbo, Tang Gengliang, Suzhou Straight Narrative; Jiang Yunxian, *tanci* [sung and spoken]. They helped me understand what being a storyteller was all about.

The stories live in the minds/hearts of the tellers; it is their consummate skill that allows us to thrill to the stories—using only their mouths—they dramatize before us on stage. Most Chinese storytellers are unable to explain their art; they simply say "*kouchuan xinshou*" ([master's] mouth transmits, [their] heart/mind receives), then they transmit the stories "unchanged." However, we know that the greatest narrative artists have been able to work creatively within the tradition to keep their stories vital, relevant, and comprehensible to their ever-changing audiences in their ever-changing times and environments.

My first experience experiences in the field, from October, 1981 to August, 1982, were primarily in Beijing. Subsequently, I returned to China several times; my last visit, in November, 2000, was at the invitation of Prof. Wang to participate in an "International Storytelling Festival." There were presentations by international scholars and daily evening performances by storytellers as well as by "amateur" international performers. During the years before 2000, through generous funding from Dartmouth's Dickey Endowment for International Understanding, I hosted the visits of several Chinese storytelling artists and organized lecture/demonstration/performances for them at well-known American colleges and universities. Most recently, a large gift from David Martin, a Dartmouth alum, made possible a four-month visit—from March through end of June, 2016—of Cai Yuanli and Bao Chengjie, two Chinese ethnomusicologists from China's Academy of Theater and Performing Arts. They worked intensively with me to complete *Zhongguo shuochang yishu jilu* [中国说唱艺术记录, Documentary on the Art of Chinese Storytelling], a 30-hour-long repository of videotaped storyteller performances from 1981 to 2000. This Documentary will be available on line soon.

In the past, the main work of researchers/scholars of "folklore," the "oral tradition" or "oral narrative performance," was collecting texts, categorizing them, and, if in foreign languages, translating them. I readily admit guilt on that score. Of course, before going to China, meeting storytellers, and attending performances, there was no way that I could discuss anything but the texts. However, my interest in the "texts" of oral narrative has been to learn how cultural values are expressed by the characters, their actions, and the storyteller persona, commenting on the narrative's characters and actions—the *ping* of *pinghua* and *pingshu*; what kinds of changes, *bian*, in the story's events and characters—from era to era, from context to context—affect the story significantly; and at what point, because of *bian*, does the story become a different story, expressing different values.

Although I understood that, in the oral tradition, the concept of "original" or "authentic" version does not exist. But, in my many discussions with Jin Shengbo, the Suzhou *pinghua* artist who performed *Three Heroes*, I always came back to the issue of change, *bian*. In a discussion about *bian* in May 1982, Mr. Jin told me that he allows himself to make only two kinds of change in his narratives: 1) elaboration or enrichment (*fengfu*) of the story, and 2) making the story make sense, be logical, reasonable (*gaizao* 合理改造). However, when I then asked him whether or not these kinds of *bian* actually transform the story into a different one, he insisted, like many other documented storytellers, that he would never change the *shu* (the story itself; the events), that there are things that can be changed and those that cannot, that he makes his changes on the basis of Shi Yukun's story, and that none of his changes affect/change the story in a meaningful or significant way. Yet, in November, 1983, in an interview with Mr. Jin in the presence of his Performing Arts Troupe Leader (as though he needed her protection), he looked at me mischievously and said: "If you had to use only one word to characterize my storytelling, it would be *bian*!"

I conclude, therefore, with two excerpts from a discussion between a brilliant oral narrative artist and a very naive researcher. These two excerpts, I believe, capture what is at the very heart of the art of storytelling. At the very least, they will make you laugh![①]

Jin: I make changes on the basis of Shi Yukun's narrative (*shu*, here, book, i.e., the 19th Century published version that underwent three major revisions from a song-book). There must be changes. He didn't really say very much in [the book]. So, I feel that I must add things. That's not because I am very bold. But it's because there isn't much in the book; he left little for us. So, I must add to it. Adding is actually adding thoughts and small details. If he had one thing, I might consider it not enough, so I add the second and third things...

Bai: But, in terms of character, is the final Bai Yutang, still the same as the one in the Book?

Jin: Sure. So, after he fell into the Death Trap, there was nothing in the book about what was going on in his mind. None of the versions took care of that. There must be a lot of thought behind that "Aiya!" [what he cried out when he felt into the trap, a common expression when something goes wrong]. What was he thinking? Where did that "Aiya!" come from? What we do is take these two words and imagine, project. The first "Aiya": "Aiya, I've fallen into the

---

① This remark, made by the contemporary Suzhou storytelling artist Jin Shengbo, is deceptively simple. In China today, and perhaps in the past as well, storytelling has never been just stuff from the mouths of storytellers, and yet this definition by Jin goes right to the heart of the matter. It is only when we begin to ask what are the criteria, the considerations that determine the nature of this stuff before it is allowed out of the mouth that we run headlong into the aesthetic, social, political, and economic issues of a particular culture.

trap!"; "Aiya, I can't get out of here!"; "Aiya, from the way it looks, it's all over with me!"; "Aiya, I really regret having come. I didn't listen to Zhi Hua or Elder Bother!"; "Aiya, I will die before I have accomplished what I came to do." And there's another "Aiya": "Aiya, I will die with my eyes open [when one has unavenged grievance] because I haven't retrieved the [Magistrate's] official seal!" In general, you could say that this would be just about enough. If you consider the actual situation, then it would be just about right. But, because it's art, we can exaggerate, we can still go on "aiya" ing. Right? What can we "aiya" about now? "Since I became your sworn brother, Yan Renmin [Jin changed the name], you have been so good to me, but today I cannot see you one more time"; "Elder Brother Lu, you too have been so good to me, but I can't see you once more either"; "My wife is at home and I haven't been back to see her in such a long time"; "My children are still so young..."

It was at this point that my astonished reaction to the mention of a wife and children put a premature end to the "aiya"s:

Bai: I never knew that Bai Yutang was married.

Jin: He is. It's true. It's not in the book [Three Heroes]. It's in *Five Young Gallants* [the first continuation of *Three Heroes*].

Bai: It wasn't mentioned in *Three Heroes*.

Jin: But this can be imagined easily.

Bai: No! I think that Bai Yutang's being married is a very big difference. What I mean is that, when he dies, he has no wife and no children.

Jin: But, having told it that way, it makes sense, because, according to our Chinese customs, one could marry at 16.

Bai: They are gallants!

Jin: Gallants aren't monks, you know.

Bai: Gallants should, perhaps, marry later in life.

Jin: You must be joking! Right? When you think about it like this, then it's all right. It's reasonable, it *must be reasonable* [for him to be married].

Bai: I don't want him to be married then. I don't like it!

Jin: If you don't like it, then just forget it. Next time, when *you* tell the story, just say that he isn't married, right?

Bai: I don't think he should be married.

Jin: Fine. That's all right. If you say he's not married, then he's not married. After all, it's just stuff that comes out of our mouths.

And this is the perfect time to end my story.

合作研究中国民俗的一些往事

马克·本德尔[*]

我在 1980 年 8 月下旬的时候才开始对中国的民俗研究有所了解，此后不久我就到华中科技大学（华中工学院）任教，教授英语课程。此前两年，我曾到台湾进修学习，在台北、花莲、台中和台南地区参与了当地的各种民俗文化活动，包括庙会、巫术活动、赶集、乡村葬礼、婚礼、街头表演和说书、地方饮食，并游览了当地著名的小吃街及文化展馆。到武汉之后，我发现武汉跟台湾在传统文化和民俗文化方面完全不一样，可以说传统文化在武汉表现得并不明显。一次偶然的机会，我的学生带我到武昌区的一座桥下观看了一些民间小戏，那座桥就在长江边上的黄鹤楼左边不远处。

当时我还是一名刚从俄亥俄州立大学毕业的年轻教师。虽然也学过中文，并且上过一些人类学的课程，但我在那里讲授的是写作和美国文学。当时授课所用的教材是那种英文黄皮书，还有油印版的讲义。有一天在写作课上，我收到学生交上来的一篇关于广西壮族"对歌"（情歌）的小作文。这位姓吴的学生来自中国南部一个我从未听过的城市。读完以后，我立刻对文中所写的一些内容产生了浓厚的兴趣，并开始着手搜集关于中国少数民族文化的资料。最后，我在武汉市中心的一家新华书店里找到了几本有关史诗的书籍。由于我当时的中文不是很好，连简单的汉字都不大看得懂，所以就选了其中最薄的一本，并且找到一本字典（当时很难找到一本这样的字典），在业余时间开始一字一句地翻译这本书。那时的空闲时间比较多，因为很难接触到电视，也没有什么夜生活。

不久，我的这些行动受到了查汝强教授的关注。他已在北京的中国社会科学院工作，但当时也是一名进修英语的在校生。我每天晚上都和查教授一起散步，他会跟我讲一些中国过

---

[*] 编者注：马克·本德尔在获得俄亥俄州立大学的博士学位后，留校教授中国文学和民俗学课程已 20 余年。20 世纪 80 年代，他曾在中国生活了 7 年。与那时到中国的大多数美国人不同，本德尔通过在中国的生活经历使自己从一个寻找前途的大学毕业生转变成了一位严谨的民俗学家。换言之，他在中国积累的丰富的民俗生活经验，以及所得到的中国民俗学界的友好支持，在极大程度上促成了他今天的成就，成为一位卓有成就的研究中国民俗的专家。他在中国的广泛而持久的田野调查，也有助于他完成许多在中国口头文学和表演研究领域产生了重大影响的论文和译著。他与许多中国民俗学者的交流也为双方后来的进一步合作奠定了基础。作为一位受人尊敬的中国民俗专家，本德尔不仅培养了许多从事中国民俗研究的美国学生，同时也接收并帮助了很多来自中国的学生和学者。他以自己匠人一样的勤勉和智慧、诗人一般的浪漫和学者的严谨，继续为中美两国民俗文化的交流搭建着桥梁。

去的事情,以及未来的一些发展计划,并认为中国在 2020 年时有可能赶超美国。在当时那种情况下,这样乐观的心态真是令人印象深刻。查教授不论是在民俗研究方面还是民间文学的翻译方面都给了我很大的鼓励。最终,在他的帮助下,我于 1982 年在北京新世界出版社出版了一本关于彝族民间叙事长诗的书籍——《七妹与蛇郎》(Sai bo mo)。虽然我当时人在武汉,但我也帮助了两位分别来自广西桂林和湖南长沙的年轻学者翻译了一本讲述俄勒冈地区印第安人故事的书籍。一位叫史昆的学者后来又继续研究并发表了一些关于中国东北地区萨满教的文章,也和我继续合作翻译了一些其他作品。

1981 年上半年,我去了一趟北京,到查教授家里拜访,在他家住了几天。有一天,他把我介绍给中国最著名的民俗学家——北京师范大学的钟敬文教授。钟教授在中国民间文学研究方面给我提了一些建议,并建议我到中国西南地区教几年书。同年秋天,查教授把我介绍到广西大学任教了。我在夏天搬到了广西。很快,在那里我拜见了侯德彭教授,他是一位思想开放的校领导,也是查教授以前的同学。侯教授鼓励我在研究民俗学的同时教授美国文学、写作以及托福考试课程。我在广西大学的第一周就遇到了孙景尧教授。当时我们还没有分到学校住房(后来我被分到了学校一幢教职工公寓楼里),所以大家都住在学校宾馆里,于是便认识了对方。那个时候,孙教授刚刚从柳州铁道职业技术学院调过来。在那个年代,知识分子毕业以后都会被分配到偏远的农村,孙教授就是这样过去的(孙教授曾在复旦大学和贾植芳教授一起研究比较文学)。孙教授曾在贵州铜仁工作了几年,之后被调到柳州。21 世纪早期,他又被调到了上海大学,开始重返大学教师职业生涯。尽管我们之间有些语言障碍,但却一见如故,在相识短短数月内就一起合作创办了 Cowrie: A Chinese Journal of Comparative Literature,这个期刊里面的大多数文章都是我和孙教授的研究生一起翻译的。早期出版的刊物里还有很多中国民俗研究学者关于民族研究的文章,例如中央民族大学的马学良教授和云南大学李子贤教授的文章。我在空闲的时候,参加了柳州、南宁以及武鸣县当地的一些山歌节,还曾上过广西大学陈驹教授的中国民俗学课程。另外,我和当时的在校生苏花娜一起翻译了一本关于中国东北地区达斡尔族民间故事的书籍,这些故事都是孟志东收集的,最后由新世界出版社出版。当时由于项目需要,我 1982 年夏天还去到了内蒙古和黑龙江。在暑假和寒假期间,我废寝忘食地搜集民俗学和少数民族的书籍,获得了大量的珍贵资料并加以整理,其中有些甚至是几十年前的重印本(很遗憾,这些资料很大部分在一次柳州的洪灾中丢失了),这些书如今正在陆续出版。幸运的是,我搜集到了马学良和今旦 1983 年出版的《苗族史诗》。后来与今旦沟通之后,我翻译了这本书,这本书的质量在当时已经很高了,里面似乎还有一些苗语文章和注释。这本书出版几年后,我又出版了《蝴蝶妈妈:中国贵州苗族创世史诗》(2006)。

1982 年左右,我受到一部讲述两名苏州弹词年轻女演员的电影的影响,开始对中国传统说书感兴趣。由于孙景尧教授对此颇有些研究,于是我和孙教授以及他的两个研究生一起,开始翻译苏州弹词的故事文本。早期对弹词的浓厚兴趣,为我九十年代初研究弹词奠定了基础(孙教授于 1986 年调离苏州),我主要是在苏州和上海等地,对弹词表演艺术家及研究弹词的学者进行田野调查,如弹词表演艺术家龚华声和他的弟子,以及弹词评论家吴宗锡等。这项研究促成了我的学位论文——《梅竹：中国苏州弹词传统》，并于 2003 年以同名成书出版。

在 1985—1987 年间，我四次往返于中国西部、西南部的一些地区，包括云南楚雄、大理和西双版纳，贵州省黔东南，青海和西藏。当时我的未婚妻付卫经常陪我一起去。这些田野调查让我完成了几篇论文，并为我 21 世纪的研究项目奠定了基础，包括一部以中国民俗学家们提供的一些材料以及彝族、苗族的史诗和其他文章为主的著作——《哥伦比亚中国民间和通俗文学选集》[2011 年与梅维恒（Victor Mair）教授共同编写]。2012 年，我和今旦以及他的孩子吴一文和吴一方共同出版了一本名为《Hxak Hlieb / 苗族史诗 / Hmong Oral Epics》的共 711 页的著作。

21 世纪早期，由于我有中国民间文学的研究背景，于是我开始进行中国西南地区少数民族诗歌的翻译和研究，并将研究范围扩大到印度东北部、马来西亚、中国西南地区和内蒙古以及蒙古国等地区，关注以文化和环境的变迁为主题的诗歌。在过去的 30 多年里，我所有的研究几乎都是和中国的研究者们密切合作，为的是向世界各地的研究者们展现中国民间文学领域所取得的相关成果。这么多年来曾有许多人帮助我、鼓励我，并一直影响着我，我在这篇短文中所提到的只是其中的几个人。

（华中师范大学聂强、同济大学王安都翻译）

Some Recollections of Collaborative Works on Chinese Folklore Studies

Mark Bender*

I became aware of Chinese folklore studies in late August 1980, soon after I arrived to teach English at Huazhong Institute of Science and Technology (Huazhong gongxueyuan) in Wuhan. Two years earlier I had visited Taiwan on an extended study abroad and had experienced temple festivals, trance mediums, markets, a rural funeral, weddings, street opera and storytelling, foodways, and displays of indigenous culture in Taibei, Hualian, and central and southern parts of the island. I found the Wuhan area to be a much different place in almost every way, and the display of "traditional" culture was not as obvious. In time, however, I was taken by students to witness folk operas and storytelling performances on the Wuchang side of the Yangzi River right under the bridge and what was left of Yellow Crane Pavilion.

I was part of a small group of teachers who had just graduated from the Ohio State University. Although I had studied Chinese and took many courses in anthropology I was teaching composition and American literature, using the "yellow books" of essays in English and handouts prepared on stencil machines. One day in the composition class I received a short essay about antiphonal folksinging (qing ge) among the Zhuang ethnic minority group in Guangxi from a matriculating student named Miss Wu who was from the place in southern China—a place I had barely heard about. I became immediately interested in the subject matter of the essay and set out to find

---

* Mark Bender spent seven years in China before beginning his graduate study at the Ohio State University where he received his doctoral degree and has taught Chinese Literature and Folklore for over twenty years. Unlike most Americans going to China the 1980s, he transformed himself from a what-to-do-next wondering young man to a serious folklorist. In other words, it was the rich folklore in practice in China and the spirit of friendly collaboration of his Chinese folklore friends that nurtured him to be a scholar of Chinese folklore. His extensive and continuing fieldwork in China has resulted in a significant number of writings and translations well-known in the field of Chinese oral literature and performance. His collaboration with numerous Chinese folklorists has also spread the seed of future communication. A well-respected and popular friend to the Chinese folklorists, Bender has also turned many of his graduate students into China folklorists while receiving and hosting even more folklore students and scholars from China, building a wide bridge of Sino-US folkloristic communication with his own woodsman-poet-scholar hands.

materials on Chinese ethnic minority literature. I eventually found several thin volumes of epic poems in the Xinhua Bookstore in downtown Wuhan. As my reading of simplified characters was very poor I chose the thinnest volume and, after obtaining a dictionary (very hard to get at the time), I began translating it word by word in my spare time, of which there was a lot since there was little access to TV and no nightlife.

My activity soon came to the notice of Prof. Zha Ruqiang who was also a matriculating student brushing up on his English who worked at the Chinese Academy of Social Sciences in Beijing. I would take a walk with Prof. Zha each evening and he told me about China's recent past and plans to build a country that would rival and even surpass the US by the 2020's. I found this optimism impressive considering the circumstances at that time. Prof. Zha encouraged my study and translation of Chinese ethnic minority folklore and eventually helped me publish the volume entitled *Seventh Sister and the Serpent* (*Sai bo mo*) with New World Press, Beijing in 1982. While I was still in Wuhan, I also aided a couple young scholars from Guilin (a city in Guangxi) and Changsha (a city in Hunan) in the translation of Jerome Ramsey's *Coyote Was Going There*, which was a collection of Native American stories from Oregon. One of these scholars, Shi Kun, went on to write several important papers about shamanism in Northeast China and work with me on other translation projects.

During a trip to Beijing in early 1981, I visited Prof. Zha's home and spent several days with his family. One day he introduced me to Prof. Zhong Jingwen, China's best-known folklorist, at Beijing Normal University. Prof. Zhong gave me advice on studying ethnic literature in China and advised me to teach for a few years in southwest China. Soon afterwards, Prof. Zha arranged for me to begin teaching at Guangxi University in the fall of 1981. Moving to Guangxi during the summer, I quickly had an audience with Prof. Hou Depeng, an open-minded university leader who was Prof. Zha's former classmate. Prof. Hou encouraged my folklore studies as I taught American literature, composition, and TOEFL test preparation. The first week at Guangxi University in Nanning, I met Prof. Sun Jingyao who was staying in the university guest house before we were assigned housing on campus (I was assigned to a walk-up apartment building populated by other faculty and staff). Prof. Sun had just transferred from the Liuzhou Railway College in Guangxi. Like many other intellectuals of his era he had graduated from college (in his case, Fudan University, where he was a student of comparative literature with Prof. Jia Zhifang), and was sent to a rural area. After spending a number of years in Tongren, Guizhou province, Prof. Sun was assigned to the school in Liuzhou and was now making his way back into a professional university career, which ultimately led him to Shanghai University in the early 2000s. Prof. Sun and I hit it off immediately, despite the language barrier, and within a few months we had founded *Cowrie*: *A Chinese Journal of Comparative Literature*, which consisted mostly of articles translated from Chinese sources by Prof. Sun's graduate students and myself. Several of the early issues carried articles by

Chinese scholars of folklore or ethnic studies such as Ma Xueliang of Central University for Nationalities in Beijing and Li Zixian of Yunnan University. In my spare time I attended song festivals in Liuzhou, Nanning, and Wuming county and took a course on Chinese folklore from Prof. Chen Ju at Guangxi University. With a matriculating student named Su Huana I translated a book of folk stories of the Daur people of northeast China collected by Meng Zhidong (Mergendi) which was also published by New World Press. As a result of that project I travelled to Inner Mongolia and Heilongjiang in the summer of 1982. I was avidly collecting books on folklore and ethnic minorities during my summer and winter breaks, and was amassing a sizeable collection of books that were constantly being published during this time, some of it reprints from earlier decades (unfortunately most of this collection of hundreds of volumes was lost in a flood in Liuzhou). I eventually got hold of a copy of Ma Xueliang and Jin Dan's version of *Miaozu shishi* (Miao epics), published in 1983. I later translated this volume—which I felt was of exceptionally high-quality for its time, as if included some passages in Miao romanization and good notes—in consultation with Jin Dan, which years later resulted in *Butterfly Mother: Miao (Hmong) Creation Epics from Guizhou, China* (Hackett, 2006).

Around 1982, I was also becoming interested in Chinese professional storytelling traditions, stimulated by a film about two young female Suzhou *tanci* performers. As it happened, Prof. Sun Jingyao was very conversant with the tradition, so we and a couple of his graduate students began translating written versions of stories in the Suzhou *tanci* (chantefable) tradition. This early interest in the Suzhou *tanci* tradition lay the foundation for my later research in the early 1990s on site in Suzhou (where Prof. Sun had transferred in 1986), which included extensive fieldwork with a number of performers in Suzhou and Shanghai, including Gong Huasheng and his former student performers and interfaces with Suzhou storytelling researchers, including Wu Zongxi. This research resulted in my dissertation work and the 2003 book entitled *Plum and Bamboo: China's Suzhou Chantefable Tradition*.

During 1985-1987 I made 4 trips to other parts of southwest and western China, including the Chuxiong Yi Autonomous Prefecture, Dali, and Xishuangbanna in Yunnan province, Southeast Guizhou province, Qinghai province, and the Tibetan Autonomous Region, often accompanied by my fiancée Fu Wei. These trips resulted in several articles and formed the basis of further projects in the 2000s that included *the Columbia Anthology of Chinese Folk and Popular Literature* (edited with Prof. Victor Mair in 2011), which featured material from many folklorists in China, and further translations of Yi and Miao (Hmong) epic poetry, as well as a number of articles. For instance, in 2012, a tri-lingual 711 page volume entitled *Hxak Hlieb/Miaozu shishi/ Hmong Oral Epics* was published that was the result of cooperation between Jin Dan, his children Wu Yiwen and Wu Yifang, and myself.

In the early 2000s, my background in Chinese folk literature also led me into translation and research about Chinese ethnic minority poets from Southwest China and ultimately a poetry anthology including poetry on the themes of changing culture and environments in North East India, Myanmar, Southwest China, Inner Mongolia, and Mongolia. In almost every case of my work over the last 30-plus years I worked closely with Chinese counterparts in various parts of China to present research and items of folk literature to scholars and audiences in other parts of the world. In this recollection I have only named a few of the many people who have helped, encouraged, and influenced me over the years.

中国给我留下的最深刻印象是什么?

迈克尔·欧文·琼斯[*]

民俗学同仁们,我来给大家讲个故事。我在北京有过一次极其难以忘怀的经历!在中国,确实有像紫禁城、天坛之类的著名地标,金碧辉煌,历史悠久,威武雄壮。还有长城,直到现在我还为之叹为观止。但是,中国给我印象最深的是什么呢?不是那些人造的建筑艺术,而是中国的民众。我从未受到过这样热情、慷慨和温暖的体验。高丙中教授告诉我,他的学生(大多数学生都听了我周五的讲座,有几位还在那一周的时间里给我做向导)喜欢我说话时友好、慈祥、坦诚的风格。我和学生互有好感。我也很喜欢和他们在一起。他们睿智而且风度翩翩,乐于与我分享时间、关怀和知识。高丙中教授、巴莫曲布嫫教授、刘魁立教授,还有其他许多人,在各个方面都非常慷慨大方。我将永远无法报答他们,但我会经常回顾我们之间的友谊,将这次中国之行作为我生命中的一个亮点。

在街上、公园里和火车上的普通人也对我们展现了高度的热情。从长城到北京的火车里挤满了人,乘客数量是座位数量的几倍。人与人面对面,几乎没有空气流动的空间。一个大约三岁的小男孩坐在一张座位的桌子旁,他妈妈坐在他的旁边,另外两个人坐在那排座位的对面。他们把母亲和孩子座位的一角,让给和我们同行的一位女士(贝弗莉·斯道杰)。男孩偷看了我们几次,然后向我们挥手微笑。他一边磕着葵花籽,一边吃着妈妈给他的东西。贝弗莉和我微笑着向他挥手。然后我给了他一块口香糖,他也试着一起吹起来。过了一会儿,他妈妈告诉我的一个学生说,小男孩想要把座位让给我。男孩的妈妈把他抱在大腿上,坚持要我坐下。我看孩子在那位女士的膝盖上扭动,想着妈妈肯定会不舒服,很勉强地坐下。一段时间后,我站了起来,向母亲解释,通过翻译说明,因为我的右膝盖疼,不得不站起来(膝盖疼痛是去年的一次事故引起的,也和我的年纪日长有关)。当我站在过道的时候,在这个座位后面的一个男人站起来给我让座。我非常感谢他,但指了指我的膝盖让一个

---

[*] 编者注:迈克尔·欧文·琼斯最近从加利福尼亚大学洛杉矶分校退休为民俗学荣誉教授。2005年,受中国民俗学会的邀请,时任美国民俗学会会长的琼斯与理查德·鲍曼和贝弗莉·斯道杰一起来到中国,这是中美两国民俗学会建立官方联系的开端。旅程结束几周后,在美国民俗学会理事会的支持下,琼斯批准成立了东亚民俗分会。随后,他一直与中国许多民俗学者保持友谊,参加一些会议(如2006年的"中国人日常礼仪实践"会议等),通过美国民俗学会年会、西部民俗学年会与中国民俗学者保持互动,并为多名来自中国的年轻民俗学者提供帮助。他的部分关于民间艺术的文章已经被翻译成中文发表了。

学生解释说，我坐着膝盖就会更疼。

　　到了差不多第三站，许多人突然下车。过道对面有一个空座位，就在那个女人和男孩的后面。售票员指着我，用手猛敲着座位，坚持要我坐下。在车厢里还有另外五个人：两个三十多岁的夫妻和一个小女孩，后来我知道那女孩七岁。这个小女孩会一些英语单词和短语。大人们敦促她，要带着幽默感和我说话。然后，她说："新年快乐！"我也对她说"新年快乐"。她的父母又让她跟我说话，于是她说："爷爷，你高寿？"我告诉她我的年龄，然后拿出我总是随身携带的笔记本，写下"62"。那个女士原来不是她的母亲，也懂一点英语。我问女孩的年龄，她翻译说七岁。很长一段时间里，我们只是彼此微笑，女孩和我，大人们和我，女孩和她的家长们。她又一次祝我新年快乐。我给了她一个美国式竖起大拇指的手势（希望这没有冒犯到中国文化）。她笑了起来，也竖起大拇指。过了一会儿，她对旁边的女士耳语，然后女士对我说："她真的很喜欢你。"我说我也喜欢她，又给了她一个大拇指。在下一站，这对夫妻离开了。小女孩和我相视而笑。我想她可能会再次祝我新年快乐。然后她爸爸示意要我的笔记本和钢笔，写下字母"Dzara"，又指指女孩。我说："我的名字叫麦克。"Dzara听后微笑，点了两次头。后来，我画了四根长度递减的小棍子代表四个人，我在最长的那个代表我的"人"上头写上"62"，然后依次写上"37""7"和"11/2"。我从自己开始，给"每个人"写上名字。我想用这些数字代表我、我的儿子戴维和他的两个儿子塞巴斯蒂安和瑞。Dzara跑到椅子旁边，看着我的眼睛，说："爷爷，我爱你。"我回答说："Dzara，我也爱你！"她重复道："我也爱你！"

　　她的父亲问我："长城？"我点了点头。我用手指做了走路的手势。Dzara拿起钢笔，在笔记本上，她画了一段长城。我点了点头。她的父亲画了一个手杖，在手杖右边写上，"62 OK."，他对我竖起大拇指。我接过钢笔和笔记本。Dzara画的长城是水平的，好像我之前努力攀登的道路只是一条平坦小道。我在那段长城上，画了一个45度的角，这个角度看来与我疼痛的膝盖似乎更有关系。我把修改后的图给Dzara和她父亲，他们都笑了。

　　窗户旁边的桌子上有一个装着两瓶白色饮料的硬纸板箱。Dzara伸手拿了一瓶，在父亲的帮助下，往瓶子里插了一根塑料吸管，然后递给我。然后又往另外一个瓶子里插了一根吸管，她拿起瓶子说："新年快乐！"我举杯回敬。酸奶饮料为我解了渴，我非常感谢她。她的父亲示意借我的笔记本和笔。他粗略地勾勒出三个拱门的建筑，在中间一个大门上画了一个人，然后带有疑问地看着我。我说，是的，我去过故宫和天安门广场。

　　在北京郊区，我从隔了几个座位的行李架上，拿下了我的包。我翻遍了底部，发现一支老虎的牛奶糖棒（一种健康食品"能量棒"）以及一包口香糖，我把这些给了Dzara。她低声对父亲说了什么，父亲把手伸进包里，拿出一件报纸包起来的东西给了Dzara。然后，她打开报纸，把里面东西给我。那是一双绣了西瓜的鞋垫。这种慷慨的举动深深打动了我。我穿12码的男鞋，而这鞋垫可能更适合一个8码或9码的女鞋。我没打算用它们，但我把它们好好保管，以此缅怀当日那么多人对我的情意、温暖和热情。

　　中国民俗学会会长刘魁立教授、北京民俗博物馆馆长韩秀珍女士以及中国民俗学会秘书长高丙中教授，邀请我来参加这个关于传统节日和法定假日的会议。他们礼数周到地安排我参加会议，欢迎仪式无与伦比。我以前的学生、现在中山大学的巩郝崟教授，学生李荣蓉、陆静和张邵振带我参观，紧紧地扶着我的手，以防我在路面的冰上滑倒。他们还在购物时，帮我讨价还价、做翻译，让我准时吃午饭。在我到达之前，巴莫曲布嫫教授将我的论文翻译成英语（部分翻译成西班牙语）用在会议议程中；她的姐姐，巴莫石布嫫博士，在我到达之后，帮我阅读中文文件，还在我与杨利慧教授会面期间，充当我的个人翻译。少数民族文学研究所副所长朝戈金教授，在关于翻译介绍民俗学的英文著作的事情上，也耐心地向我征求意见。

帮助过我的人实在是太多了，他们的名字已经没有办法完全罗列出来。其实，我最感激的人就是高丙中教授和巴莫曲布嫫教授。因为没有赶上中国科技发展的步伐，我不会用PPT或者其他我不熟悉的电子器材，打算在会议上、北京大学的演讲上使用35mm 幻灯片。高教授为此找了很久，终于找到了幻灯机。得知我回去的时候想带一些有机茶，他就给了我一个二英尺长的袋子，塞满三个大容器。也正是他敦促我们乘地铁、坐火车去长城，以体验普通人所依赖的交通方式，从而让我有了之前提到的经历。巴嫫教授不仅翻译我的论文，还力求将论文出版。她还带我游览故宫、去购物、吃午饭。我向两位教授提到我对中国朋克摇滚的兴趣（我儿子小时候，我带他去洛杉矶；他在乐队弹奏电子贝斯，其中包括两个朋克摇滚乐队，他正在写一部关于加利福尼亚南部朋克摇滚的历史书，这本书将由加利福尼亚大学出版社出版）。他们不仅找到一家有几个乐队演奏的俱乐部，而且巴莫教授还给了我大量的中国最著名的朋克摇滚乐队光盘，送给我的儿子。

现在你明白了吧，为什么我说，虽然人造建筑也让人印象深刻，但最让我印象深刻的，还是"人"。所有人都彬彬有礼、慷慨大方、热情洋溢。我遗憾的是，我不知道他们中一些人的名字，例如，在火车上那个三岁的男孩和他的母亲。Dzara的父亲给了我他的名片，但我看不懂。我也没问到她妈妈的名字。但我会永远记得他们和我提到的其他人。

火车开进了北京车站，Dzara的父母准备离开。Dzara伸手握住我的手说："我爱你，爷爷。"我搂住她，她也抱着我。"我爱你，Dzara。"在人行道上，我们跟在他们后面走了几码，她两次转身挥手说："再见，再见。"我没有照相机拍下这个迷人的、宝贝的七岁小孩。但我保留着她给我的鞋垫。我还能清晰地记得她和我分享的酸奶饮料的清新味道。最后，我还保留了两页珍贵的图纸，是她和她的父亲试图与语言不通的外国人努力沟通的见证。

（湖南大学蒋海军翻译）

What Impressed Me Most in China?

Michael Owen Jones[*]

Folklore friends, let me tell you a story. I had an INCREDIBLE set of experiences in Beijing! Obviously, there are landmarks like the Forbidden City and the Temple of Heaven that are impressive for their massiveness, their history, their power. And the Great Wall; now that truly boggles the mind.

But what impressed me MOST? It's not the human-made artifacts, but the people themselves. I have never been shown so much hospitality, generosity, and warmth. Professor Gao told me that his students (to many of whom I lectured on Friday, and several others served as guides throughout the week) liked me for being friendly, fatherly, and candid in my remarks. The sentiment is mutual. I enjoyed being with them. I found them to be highly intelligent as well as personable, and unstinting in the time, attention, and knowledge they shared with me. Professors Gao, Bamo, Liu, and many others were incredibly generous in every way imaginable. I will never be able to repay them, but I will often reflect on their friendship and remember my trip to China as the highlight of my life.

Ordinary people on the street, in parks, and on trains likewise extended to us hospitality on a scale that I have never seen before. The train that we took from the Great Wall to Beijing was absolutely packed with people—several times as many standing as seated. There was scarcely enough space for air to slip between those facing one another. A little boy about three years old was sitting at a table with his mother on one side and two men on the other side of the booth. The woman in our party (Beverly Stoltje) had been offered the edge of a seat across from the mother and boy.

---

[*] Michael Owen Jones is Emeritus Professor of Folklore, recently retired from UCLA. As the President of the American Folklore Society, Jones, along with Richard Bauman and Beverly Stoeltje, was invited to a meeting in Beijing by the CFS in 2005, starting an official relationship between the AFS and CFS. Weeks after the trip, Jones supported and approved (with the AFS Board) the establishment of the East Asia Folklore Section under AFS. Subsequently, he has maintained friendship with many Chinese folklorists, attended a number of conferences (e. g. Chinese Daily Ritual Practice, 2006) and panels at AFS and WSFS meetings related to Chinese folklore studies, and lent a helping hand to a number of young folklorists from China. Several of his articles on folk arts have been translated and published in Chinese.

The boy peeked around at us several times. Finally he began waving and smiling. He was eating sunflower seeds and whatever else his mother would give him. Beverly and I smiled and waved at him. Then I gave him a stick of chewing gum. He tried to blow bubbles, and I did too. After a while his mother told one of the students with us that the little boy wanted me to have his seat. His mother lifted him onto her lap and insisted that I sit down. I did so reluctantly, thinking about how uncomfortable the woman would become with a squirming child in her lap. After a while I stood up, thanking the mother but explaining through the interpreter that I had to stand because my right knee ached (from an accident last year, not to mention just getting old). As I was standing in the aisle a man in the booth behind this one stood up and offered me his seat. I thanked him profusely but pointed at my knee; a student explained that the pain tended to increase when I was seated.

By about the third stop a number of people suddenly left the train. There was a vacant seat across the aisle and just behind the one that the woman and boy occupied. The conductor pointed at me and pounded her hand on the seat, insisting that I sit down. There were five other people in the booth: two couples in their 30s and a little girl who, I came to learn was seven years old. The little girl knew a few words and phrases in English. The adults were urging her—with good humor—to talk to me. Finally she said, "Happy New Year!" So I said happy new year to her. Then more urging from the adults for her to talk to me. Eventually she said, "Grandfather, how old are you?" I told her my age, then pulled out the notebook that I always carry and wrote down 62. One of the women, who it turned out was not her mother, also knew a bit of English. I asked the girl her age, which the woman translated. She was seven. We spent a lot of time smiling at one another, the girl and I, the adults and I, the girl and the other adults. She wished me happy new year again. I gave her the American thumbs up sign (hoping that it didn't mean something offensive in Chinese culture). She laughed and returned the thumbs up. After a while she whispered to the woman beside her who then said to me, "She really like you." I said that I liked her also, and gave her another thumbs up. At the next stop the couple left. The little girl and I smiled at one another. I think she might have wished me happy new year again. Then her father asked for my notebook and pen. He wrote in Chinese characters and then pinyin, "Dzara," pointing toward the girl. "My name is Mike," I said. Dzara nodded and smiled. She repeated it twice. Later I drew four stick figures of diminishing size, pointing to the tallest and then to me, writing "62" above the head. Then I wrote "37" above the next in size, and "7" and "11/2" above the others. I named each, beginning with me. I think I got across that these figures represented me, my son David, and his two sons Sebastian and Ray. At one point Dzara scooted to the edge of the bench, looked me in the eyes, and said, "Grandfather, I love you." I replied, "Dzara, I love you, too!" She repeated, "I love you, TOO!"

Her father said to me, "Great Wall?" I nodded. I made walking motions with my fingers. Dzara picked up the pen. In the notebook she drew a section of the Great Wall with one tower. I nodded. Her father drew a stick figure. To the right he wrote, "62 OK." He gave me thumbs up. I took the pen and notebook. Dzara's drawing of the wall was horizontal as if the path I had struggled to climb were simply a flat road. I drew the wall at a 45-degree angle, which to my aching knee seemed more accurate. I showed it to Dzara and her father both of whom laughed.

There was a cardboard container with two small bottles of white liquid on the table next to the window. Dzara reached for one and with her father's help stabbed a plastic drinking straw into it. She handed it to me. She put a straw in the other bottle. Then she held hers up and said, "Happy New Year!" I toasted her in return. The yogurt drink was quenched my thirst. I thanked her profusely. Her father gestured for my notebook and pen. He roughly sketched the front of a building with three arches and a picture of a figure above the center one, then looked at me quizzically. Yes, I said, I had been to the Forbidden City and Tian'an Men Square.

On the outskirts of Beijing I pulled down my tote bag from the luggage rack several booths behind us. I dug around in the bottom, found a Tiger's Milk candy bar (a kind of health food "power bar") as well as a package of chewing gum that I gave to Dzara. Soon after she whispered to her father. He reached into a bag at his feet and pulled out something wrapped in a piece of newsprint. He gave it to Dzara. She then unwrapped it and handed the contents to me. It was a pair of hand-embroidered inserts for shoes or slippers covered with a design of watermelons. This act of generosity touched me deeply. I wear a man's size 12 shoe and these inserts likely fit a woman's size 8 or 9 shoe. I have no intentions of walking on them, however. I have put them in a place of honor where they remind me daily of the cordiality, warmth, and welcome that so many people extended to us.

Professor Kuili Liu, President of the China Folklore Society; Ms. Xiuzhen Han, Curator of the Beijing Folklore Museum; and Professor Bingzhong Gao, General Secretary of the China Folklore Society, invited me to participate in this conference on traditional festivals and national holidays. The courtesies they extended to me, the financial arrangements they undertook to bring me to the event and keep me there, and the welcome they gave me were unsurpassed in my experience. Former student and now professor Haogun Gong at SUN Yat-sen University, along with students Rongrong Li, Jing Lu, and Shaozhen Zhang took me on tours—holding fast to my hand to make sure I didn't slip on the ice—as well as negotiated prices of items when we went shopping, translated, and made sure I had lunch. Professor Qubumo Bamo translated my paper in English (and partly in Spanish) to include in the conference proceedings before I arrived; her sister, Dr. Shibumo Bamo, read the Chinese version when I delivered the paper in English and served as my personal translator in one session along with Professor Lihui Yang. Professor Chao Gejin, Deputy Director of the Institute of Ethnic Literature, graciously sought my opinion regarding works on folklore in English that might be translated for a Chinese readership.

The list of people who helped me is nearly endless. Perhaps my greatest feelings of gratitude are toward Professors Bingzhong Gao and Qubumo Bamo. Not having caught up with the technological advances in China, I wanted to show 35mm slides at the conference and at my lecture at Peking University rather than use Power Point or other digital technology that I am unfamiliar with. Professor Gao searched long and hard, but finally located a slide projector. Having learned that I wanted to return with some organic tea, he handed me a two-foot-long bag of three large containers just before I left. It was also he who had urged us to take the subway and then the train to the Great Wall in order to experience the transportation relied by ordinary people, thereby making possible the experiences I described above. Professor Bamo not only translated my paper, but she is seeking publication for it. She guided my tour of the Forbidden City and she took me on a shopping trip and then to lunch. I mentioned to both professors my interest in Chinese punk rock. (When he was young I took my son to punk rock concerts in Los Angeles; he plays electric base in several bands, including two punk rock groups, and he is writing a book about the history of punk rock in southern California, to be published by the University of California Press.) Not only did they locate a club where several bands were playing, but also Professor Bamo gave me a large number of CDs with performances by China's best-known punk rock bands to share with my son.

Now you understand why I said that, as impressive as were the human-made edifices, the people I met impressed me the MOST. All were courteous, generous, and warm. I regret only that I do not know the names of some of them, for example, the three-year boy and his mother on the train. Dzara's father gave me his card, but I cannot read it. I failed to ask her mother's name. But I shall always remember them and the others I have mentioned.

Dzara's parents readied themselves to leave the train as it pulled into the station in Beijing. Dzara reached out to shake my hand. "I love you, Grandfather," she said. I put my arms around her and she reached up to hug me. "I love you, too, Dzara." As we followed along behind them on the sidewalk for a few yards, she turned around twice and waved. "Bye, bye," she said. I don't have a photograph of this charming, precocious seven-year old child. But I have the inserts for shoes that she gave me. I recall vividly the refreshing taste of the yogurt drink she shared with me. Finally, I have two pages of precious drawings she and her father made as they attempted to communicate with a foreigner who could not speak their language.

我与美国民俗学界的交流与译事

李 扬[*]

1982年，我考入辽宁大学中文系，后在乌丙安先生门下修读民俗学硕士课程。入学不久，就开始接触到美国民俗学的研究成果。那时在乌先生的主持下，董晓萍、孟慧英二位同门师姐，已经大致完成了著名美籍华人学者丁乃通教授的大作《中国民间故事类型索引》的翻译，我接着补译了部分篇例并校核了译稿。此书于1983年由春风文艺出版社出版，虽是简本，其工具书的重要作用未能充分体现，但毕竟让国内学界对丁先生以国际通行的AT体系对中国民间故事类型进行分类的研究有了进一步的认识和了解。后来，丁乃通先生访华时，我有幸在北京西苑饭店同丁先生晤面长谈，亲聆教诲，这位学识渊博、和蔼温良的老者，微笑道别、拄杖缓行而去的身影，从此深深印刻在我的记忆中。丁先生回国后，我们还保持通信往来，我至今保存着他的一封手书，密密麻麻写满五页信纸，介绍美国民俗学界和大学相关专业设置的情况，鼓励我学好英语，追求学业进步。我陆续又翻译了他惠寄的《答爱伯哈德先生》和《中国和印度支那的灰姑娘故事》等论文，将他的研究成果介绍给国内学界。翻开丁乃通先生当年寄给我的大作，为了省去我翻译时查阅资料的麻烦，他在英文原稿中的人名、书名、地名旁，仔细地一一标注中文。冬去春来，数十载转瞬而过，手迹犹在，丁先生已仙逝多年，每每忆及他的谆谆叮嘱，依然感念万端。

在辽宁大学读书期间，我们的英语课教师是来自美国的白开英（Kaye Bragg）女士。学了多年的哑巴英语，白开英女士是我碰到的第一个开始用英语交流的外国人。在她的帮助指导下，我的英语口语和听力有了明显的进步，为今后的学术交流打下了基础。更为重要的是，她是我与美国民俗学界发生联系的搭桥者。说来也巧，她的丈夫虽然在美国当律师，但硕士阶段修读的也是民俗学专业。白开英女士特意让他从美国寄来一本书，赠送给我，就是精装本的 The Study of American Folklore: An Introduction。在我的学术生涯中，这本书是至关

---

[*] 编者注：李扬在辽宁大学开始学习民俗学（民间文学），获得北京师范大学硕士学位，后在香港大学获得博士学位，目前是中国海洋大学中文系教授。他是1980年代初中国民俗学重建学科初期第一批新生力量的代表之一。他较早与"外界"的交往，译介大量新思想和成果，为中国的民俗学学科建设做出了极大贡献。通过译介丁乃通的故事类型研究、阿姆斯的母题研究、普洛普的"功能"论、布鲁范德的《美国民俗学》和"都市民俗"，以及本迪克斯的"本真论"，李扬不但构建了一座座沟通中外的学术桥梁，也同样维系着与外界学者的充满人情味的亚民俗桥梁（而且还一直是美国民俗学会的唯一来自中国的终身会员）。当然，他自己的有关民间故事和民俗理论的成果也影响着新一代年轻的民俗学者。

重要的。它不仅让我比较全面地了解了美国民俗研究的体系，而且由此建立了与作者、曾任美国民俗学会会长的著名民俗学家布鲁范德教授的长期交往和友谊。

当时国内民俗学界与西方学界的交流尚不多见，对于美国民俗学界的研究状况亦所知甚少。有鉴于此，我决定将此书翻译出来，介绍给国内同行。然而译事殊不易，学力不逮，加上毕业工作后冗务缠身，断断续续拖了数年。直到调到汕头大学任教后，稍有闲暇，得以倾力完稿。几经周折，1993年，中译本以《美国民俗学》之书名由汕头大学出版社出版，成为当时第一部较为系统全面地介绍当代美国民俗学研究的译著。中译本出版后，在学界引起了一定的反响，有不少学者荐介引用。钟敬文先生也曾予以关注，提出中肯的建议。

也是因了此书的翻译出版，我与作者布鲁范德教授取得了联系，书鸿往来频繁。他不但给予了译事和出版诸多指导和支持，还主动举荐我加入美国民俗学会，被学会批准接纳为终身会员（迄今仍是中国唯一的终身会员）。从那时至今，我得以免费定期收到跨洋过海寄来的《美国民俗学刊》。这份国际民俗学界的重要刊物，使我能够及时了解国外学界的最新研究成果和动态。1994年，布鲁范德教授提供了美国民俗学会召开年会的信息，我尝试给年会组委会寄去一篇英文论文，被年会录用。金秋十月，我第一次飞赴美国，和神交已久的布鲁范德教授终于在威斯康星州密尔沃基市会面，相谈甚欢。此次美国之行，既见到了民俗音乐学家洛马克斯这样世界闻名的老一辈大师级人物，也见到了利·哈林等正值盛年的学术中坚，以及印第安纳大学民俗学助教苏独玉等年轻一代学者。来自美国各地的数百位民俗学者们，按不同专题分组发言、热烈讨论，场下亦进行各种交流、书展活动，整个年会规模可观却组织有序，学术信息丰富，确实不虚此行，获益良多。旅途中在纽约机场转机时，在一家旧书店偶然购得一部厚厚的《人与兽：一部视觉的历史》，回国后将这部图文并茂、包含不少动物民俗资料的大部头译成中文，承蒙刘瑞琳女士支持，先后由山东画报出版社和台北大地出版社出版，这也是此次美国之行的一个额外的收获。

回国后，仍然不定期收到布鲁范德教授的新著。他的另一本重要著作、堪称美国都市传说开山之作的《消失的搭车客——美国都市传说及其意义》由我和王珏纯译出，同样是在刘瑞琳女士的支持下（此时她已转任广西师范大学出版社总编辑），2006年由广西师范大学出版社出版，这是国内第一部较为系统介绍研究美国都市传说的著作。2011年我去美国洛杉矶访学，布鲁范德教授听说后，立即联络他在洛杉矶的一位读者朋友弗莱德，帮助我联系租房等事宜。弗莱德是一位民间文学的爱好者，他尝试将民间故事传说运用于写作教学中，同时对中国民间故事传说也有着浓厚的兴趣。我们因布鲁范德教授而相识，结下了深厚的友谊。在洛杉矶期间，布鲁范德教授又专门寄赠了扩展版新著《都市传说百科全书》，煌煌精装两大卷，而且没有定价、市面无售，大概是专供各图书馆收藏之用，对于都市传说研究者来说，可谓是"无价之宝"，极具参考价值。后来，我和学生译出其中的重要章节《都市传说类型索引》，发表在《民间文化论坛》上。2011年，我根据布鲁范德教授寄赠的第四版，对1993年版《美国民俗学》（原著第二版）进行了补译，以《新编美国民俗学概论》之书名，由上海文艺出版社出版。新版在内容、体例等方面增补修订甚多，反映了美国民俗学界的研究新进展，新加入的"焦点"等环节也进一步增强了可读性和课堂教学的实用性。

今年已是83岁高龄的布鲁范德先生，已从犹他大学退休多年，目前正在享受孙辈绕膝的天伦之乐，享受滑雪、钓鱼的丰富多彩的退休生活，但他始终关心我这个万里之外的异国后学。就在写作本文时，布鲁范德教授又寄来新出的增订版都市传说集 Too Good To Be True 和它的有声读物版。

在与美国民俗学界学者的交流中，我与布鲁范德教授交往时间最长，成为忘年交的朋友，他给予我的帮助支持最多；对他著作文章的译介，也增进了国内学界对美国民俗学研究的了解。

另外一位我常常感念的美国学者，是世界著名的民俗学家、加州大学伯克利分校的阿兰·邓迪斯教授。上个世纪80年代末到90年代初，我在香港大学修读博士学位，博士学位论文选题是运用普罗普的形态学理论研究中国民间故事。在研究过程中，发现有学者提及，邓迪斯教授的一篇研究北美印第安人民间故事形态的论文《北美印第安故事的形态学研究》，对普氏理论有所修正，提出了一些新的概念，但当时在香港找不到其原文全文。无奈之下，我冒昧给邓迪斯教授写信求助，原本只想试一试，并没有抱太大希望。出乎意料的是，我很快收到了邓迪斯教授寄来的包裹，里面不仅有我需要的那篇论文，还有其他十多篇他发表的运用结构主义方法进行研究的论文复印件，这些材料对我的博士学位论文写作起到了重要的参考借鉴作用。在附信中，他对我的研究予以鼓励，并提到他和夫人卡洛琳即将访华的行程安排，希望在香港停留时，可以和我见面。非常遗憾的是，由于行程紧张，最终和邓迪斯教授缘悭一面，未能当面向他致谢和请教。邓迪斯教授于2005年遽然离世，他对我的慷慨相助，我会永铭五内。后来，我和王珏纯撰写发表了《略论邓迪斯源于语言学的"母题素"说》一文，评述了他有关母题素理论概念的阐释和意义。

此外，我还零星翻译了其他几位美国民俗学家的论文，如巴瑞·托尔肯关于民俗学科性质的论述、瑞吉娜·本迪克丝（后来她转赴德国任教）关于本真性的论述、丹·本-阿莫斯为《科技世界中的民间文化》所写的序言，等等，这些文章都收录在《西方民俗学译论集》（中国海洋大学出版社2003年版）。在此过程中，我也与上述学者建立了学术交流联系。今年与学生合作翻译了约翰·洛顿和乔纳森·古德温的论文《计算机民俗学研究：百年学术论文主题地图绘制》，发表于《文化遗产》2016年第5期，旨在向国内同行介绍美国学者运用计算机进行民俗学研究的最新进展成果。

2011至2012年，我有幸被遴选为富布赖特学者，承蒙加州大学洛杉矶分校人类学系阎云翔教授接待，在美国进行了为期一年的交流和考察。期间，结识了一些新的学者朋友，搜集了不少研究资料。更重要的是，得以亲身体验美国民众的日常生活，并自驾万里，考察美国各地的民风习俗，收获了许多书本上学不到的知识。特别值得庆幸的是，在美期间偶然发现，当年赠书引领我走进美国民俗学界的白开英女士，竟然也在洛杉矶的加州州立大学工作！阔别近30年，师生重相逢，虽然都已双鬓斑白，但真挚的友情没有丝毫改变。在她的邀请下，我专程赴加州州立大学，做了一场有关中国民间服饰习俗的讲座。

小儿李顿，目前正在美国密苏里大学新闻学院读本科。有一年感恩节，文学课老师安·玛莉教授邀请他去她位于郊外的家中一起过节、晚餐。安玛莉在书房里拿出一本中文书，是朝戈金翻译的《口头诗学：帕里—洛德理论》——原来，她丈夫就是已故的国际著名史诗学者、口头传统研究专家约翰·迈尔斯·弗里！世界真大，世界真小。希望中美民俗学者之间的交流对话，能在下一代继续传承进行下去。

因了各种机缘际会和师长相助，我在中美民俗学的交流和译介方面，略尽了微薄之力，但成绩确实微不足道。今遵张举文教授之嘱，草就此文，追溯回忆自己与美国民俗学者的交流和相关译事，感觉在这个方面，今后自己还应继续努力为之。我和举文亦是三十余年的老友，当年我在辽宁大学读研，他毕业留校任教，对民俗的共同兴趣使我们相识相知。现在他在美国大学任教，对中美两国民俗学界的交流往来多有贡献，主编此书，意义独具，殊应嘉赞。

1994年布鲁范德和李扬于美国民俗学年会。Jan Brunvand and Yang Li at AFS annual meeting in 1994. Photograph courtesy of Yang Li.

My Stories of Knowing American Folklorists and Translating their Works

Yang Li*

In 1982, I was admitted to the Chinese Department of Liaoning University, studying under Professor Bing'an Wu in the Folklore Master Program. Not long after my admission, I started coming in contact with American folklore research. At that time, Xiaoping Dong and Huiying Meng (my cohorts) had substantially completed a translation of the renowned Chinese American scholar Nai-tung Ting's (Ding Naitong) masterpiece, *The Type Index of Chinese Folktales*. I subsequently followed up and translated and proofread a portion of the book.

The book was published in 1983. Though it was an abridged version and was not fully taken advantage of by scholars in China, it introduced and furthered domestic scholars' understanding of Dr. Ting's contribution to the internationally recognized AT system for classifying Chinese folktales. Later on, when Dr. Ting came to visit, I had the privilege of having a long conversation with him at the Beijing Xiyuan Hotel. Experiencing his erudition and kindness, I still have the deep impression of the moment when he bid me goodbye with cane in hand and a braod smile.

After Dr. Ting returned home to the US, we maintained correspondence. To this day, I have still saved a handwritten, densely filled 5 page letter written by him that summarized the academic sphere of American folklore studies, encouraged me to learn English, and to further my academic progress. I have also translated essays that introduced his research works to Chinese folklorists, such as "Reply to Mr. Eberhard," "China and Indochina's Cinderella Story." In Dr. Ting's

---

* Yang Li is a Professor of Chinese, and also teaches folklore and literature. He began his folklore graduate studies in Liaoning University, and earned his Master's degree from Beijing Normal University and Doctorate degree from the University of Hong Kong. He is one of the first generation folklorists from the 1980s when Chinese folkloristics was restored. At that time, he also began his communication with American folklorists. He has introduced and translated parts of works by Nai-tung Ting on Chinese folktale types, Ben-Amos on motif, Propp on function, Bendix on authenticity, and Brunvand on urban legends and his complete book *The Study of American Folklore*. He has not only built academic bridges, but also maintained the "metafolklore bridge" with the folklorists outside of China (as the only Lifetime Member of AFS). Of course, his own research works and ideas on folktales and theories are also influencing the current young generation.

masterpiece that he sent to me that year, he had English names, book titles, and locations carefully translated into Chinese to save me from the laborious translating process. Dr. Ting is now no longer with us, but I often recall his earnest encouragement.

While at Liaoning University, my English professor was Kaye Bragg (Bai Kai Ying) from the United States. AfterI studied written English only for several years, I had my first experience in oral English communicating with Bai Kai Ying. Under her guidance, my English speaking and listening skills showed significant progress. More important, she was also the one who introduced me to the American folklore academic world. Coincidentally, though her husband was an American lawyer, it so happened that he also received a master's degree in folklore studies. Bai Kai Ying had him send a book from the States to me, which was the hardcover of *The Study of American Folklore: An Introduction* by J. H. Brunvand.

This book was essential to my academic career. It not only gave me a comprehensive introduction to the system of American folklore studies, but it also helped me foster a long term friendship with the author, who was also a former president of the AFS. At that time in the Chinese circle of folklore studies, academic exchanges with the West were very uncommon, and people knew little about the circumstance of the American folklore academic world. With this in mind, I decided to translate the book in order to introduce it to Chinese folklorists. Because translating this significant piece of work was difficult in itself, combined with my personal endeavors after graduation, this process dragged on for several years. It was not until 1993 when I became a professor at Shantou University that the translation was published.

This translation became the first book to introduce a more systematic and comprehensive study of contemporary American folklore. Publication of the Chinese version ignited intense folkloristic discourse. Because of the translation and publication of the book, I was able to contact the author, Professor Brunvand, and kept frequent correspondence with him. He not only assisted me in translating the book, but also took the initiative to recommend me to join the AAFS and become a Lifetime Member (and so far I am still the only Lifetime member from China).

From that time on, I was able to receive the *Journal of American Folklore* (JAF), which has kept me updated on the latest and most dynamic research results overseas. In 1994, Professor Brunvand invited me to participate in the AFS annual meeting. That October, I flew Milwaukee, Wisconsin and finally met and talked to my hero, Professor Brunvand.

During the US trip, I was able to meet other world-renowned masters such as A. Lomax, other folklorists like Lee Haring, and the younger generation of folklorists like Sue Tuohy from Indiana University. There were hundreds of folklorists from all over the United States at the meeting who provoked lively discussions, conducted various exchanges, and presented their works. The conference was of large scale but was well-organized and rich with information. It truly enriched and stimulated me.

While waiting for a flight transfer in a New York airport, I happened to stumble upon a thick book called *Man and Beast: A Visual History* in a secondhand bookstore. After returning home, I realized that this illustrated book contained a wealth of information about animals in folklore. I then translated it into Chinese with Ruilin Liu. It was first published by the Shandong Pictorial Publishing House and was then published by the Taipei Dadi Publishing House, which was a bonus to my trip.

After returning home, I would still occasionally receive new publications by Professor Brunvand. Another important book of his was about the urban legend, *The Vanishing Hitchhiker—American Urban Legends and Their Significance*, which was translated by Jue Wang and me. With the support of Ruilin Liu, it was published in 2006 by the Guangxi Normal University Press and was the first systematic presentation of American urban legend scholarship.

In 2011 I went to Los Angeles as a visiting scholar. As soon as Professor Brunvand heard the news, he immediately contacted his friend in Los Angeles, Fred, to help mearrange housing, rent, and other matters. Fred was a fan of American folk literature and often tried to apply it in his teaching and was additionally deeply interested in Chinese folktales. Because of Professor Brunvand, we were able to know each other and forge a profound friendship.

While I was in Los Angeles, Professor Brunvand sent me a special extended version of the new *Encyclopedia of Urban Legends* that was in two huge volumes. For urban legend researchers, this encyclopedia would be considered "priceless." Later on, my students and I translated one of the most important sections of "Urban Legend Index," which was later published in *Folk Culture Forum*. In 2011, I translated the 4th edition of the 1993 edition of Professor Brunvand's *American Folklore* (second Chinese edition) and entitled it *New Introduction to American Folklore*, which was published by the Shanghai Literature and Art Publishing House. This improved version included new studies of American folklore and provided better content for readers and teachers.

This year Professor Brunvand is 83 years old. Though he has been retired from the University of Utah for many years, and is currently enjoying his grandchildren, skiing, fishing, and a colorful retirement, he has always cared about me and my studies. As I write this essay, Professor Brunvand sent me an updated version of his set of urban legend books, *Too Good To be True*, as well as its audiobook version.

In regards to my communication with American folklorists, I have been in contact with Professor Brunvand for the longest time and have become his close friend. He provided me a great deal of assistance and encouragement, not only in the translation of his works, but also in enhancing the understanding of American folklore studies.

Another American scholar to whom I owe my gratitude is the world renowned folklorist from University of California, Berkeley, Professor Alan Dundes. During the late 80s and early 90s, I was pursuing a doctorate degree at the University of Hong Kong. My dissertation was about the use of Propp's morphological theory in the analysis of Chinese folktales. During the research process, I found out that researchers mentioned a paper by Professor Dundes, entitled "The Morphology of North American Indian Folktales." Propp's theory has some revisions that brought up some new concepts, but at the time in Hong Kong I was unable to find the entire original text.

In desperation, I took the chance of writing to Professor Dundes for help. I had planned on giving it a try originally, but I didn't count on him writing back. Surprisingly, I quickly received a package sent by Professor Dundes. Inside there was not only the article I needed for my dissertation, but also a dozen copies of his other articles based on the structuralist approach. These materials were crucial references for my dissertation. In his letter to me, he encouraged my research efforts and mentioned to me that he and his wife, Caroline, had an upcoming trip to Hong Kong and that he would like to meet up with me.

I very much regret that due to a tight schedule, I was unable to meet Professor Dundes and failed to thank him face to face and seek his advice. Professor Dundes passed away in 2005, but I will never forget his generosity to me. Later on, Jue Wang and I wrote and published an article, "On the Linguistic Origin of the Idea of Motifeme by Dundes," promoting his theoretical contribution on the concept of motifeme.

In addition, I also translated several other papers by American folklorists, such as Barre Toelken's on the disciplinary nature of folkloristics, Regina Bendix's on authenticity, Dan Ben-Amos's preface to Bausinger's *Science and Technology in the World of Popular Culture*, and so on. These translations are included in my *Translations of the Western Folklore Studies* (China Haiyang University Press, 2003).

In this process, I kept academic exchange with the scholars mentioned above. This year, in cooperation with my students, we translated John Laudun and Jonathan Goodwin's paper, "Computer Folklore Studies: 100 Years of Academic Papers Related to Mapping", which was published in *Cultural Heritage* (2016). This was aimed to introduce to Chinese folklorists their progressive US counterparts' use of the computer in the study of folklore.

From 2011 to 2012, I was honored to be selected as a Fulbright Scholar to study under Professor Yunxiang Yan at the Department of Anthropology, UCLA. During this period, I was able to make friends with many scholars, collect quite a bit of research information, but most important, I was able to experience the daily life of the American people, traveling thousands of miles by car to study folk customs around the nation, collect many books, and gain a great amount of new knowledge.

Fortunately while I was in the US, I discovered that the person who introduced me to the world of folklore studies, Bai Kai Ying, was teaching at the California State University in Los Angeles! After 30 years, we were able to reunite. Though both of us now have grey hair, our friendship had never changed. At her request, I made a special trip to California State University to give a lecture on Chinese folk dress customs.

My son, Dun Li, is currently an undergraduate student at the School of Journalism, University of Missouri. One year on Thanksgiving, his literature professor Ann Marie invited him to her home to celebrate the holiday and have dinner. Ann Marie took out a Chinese book from her study, which was *Oral Poetics: Parry-Lord Theory*, translated by Chao Gejin. It turned out that her husband was the internationally recognized scholar of oral tradition research, John Miles Foley! It is quite a small world. I hope that the exchanges and dialogue between Chinese and American folklorists will continue in the next generations.

Due to a variety of opportunities abroad and the help of many teachers, I have been able to contribute to the Chinese-US folkloristic exchanges through translations, but rather insignificantly. At the request of Professor Juwen Zhang, I reflected upon my experiences with American folklorists. Juwen and I have been good friends for over thirty years. During my graduate studies at Liaoning University, he graduated and began to teach there. Our mutual interest in folklore has kept us as friends. Now he is teaching in Willamette University, Oregon and has been making valuable contributions to the field of folklore and folkloristic exchanges between Chinese and American folklorists.

(Translation by Natalie Zhang)

中美民俗研究交流的记忆

萧　放[*]

2006年，首次参加在美国举办的学术会议

2006年6月2日至4日在美国俄勒冈州塞勒姆市崴涞大学举办了美国民俗学会东亚民俗研究分会召集的"中国人日常仪式实践研讨会"暨"第十届假日、仪礼、节日、庆祝与公共展示会议"。多数代表来自美国本土，他们共同关注中国民众的日常生活。有的代表是专门研究美国华人生活的专家，关注的是华人生活民俗，看他们在美国社会生活中如何与异民族共处，同时如何保存自己的文化传统。

在本次会议的组织者张举文教授的邀请下，经由北京大学高丙中教授的协助，中国民俗学会组派了以刘魁立会长、高丙中副会长、萧放副秘书长、理事陈泳超为代表的中国民俗学者进行了首次团体性的中美民俗学界的学术交流。刘老师讲的是邢台七夕，陈泳超讲的是一个葬礼，高丙中教授做了主旨发言，讲的是龙牌会的发展策略。本人在大会宣读的论文是《传统中国人的时间观念与节日形态》。会议期间中国民俗学者的系列发言引起美国学者的重视。这是中国民俗学者第一次在美国民俗学界的集体亮相，让美国学界直接感受到中国民俗学研究的实力。我们结识了一批美国民俗学者，为今后的学术交流打下了良好的基础。

为了利用本次会议的机会考察美国西部华人社会与印第安人民俗生活情况，我和另外几位中国代表一道，提前一周出发，沿途经历了洛杉矶、旧金山、波特兰等城市，从而对美国西部社会生活有了直接的感受。由于我们是第一次到美国，为了尽量多了解美国西部风情，会后，我们自费去了拉斯维加斯、大峡谷、旧金山，从洛杉矶返回。

在美国期间，最深的感触是社会处在一个放松的状态，从美国人的表情到行为，从言谈到举止，没有我们那样的紧张急切。美国旧金山有许多无家可归者，他们悠闲地在街道上散

---

[*] 编者注：萧放在北京师范大学获得民俗学博士学位，目前任该校社会学院人类学民俗学系主任。他是中国民俗学重建后的第一代民俗学者的代表之一，在历史民俗领域出版了大量著述。他不仅为中国民俗学会服务，从事民俗学研究，也通过媒体在节日传统方面为公众教育做了大量宣传工作。他还在"国际亚细亚民俗学会"发挥着重要作用。正如他的日志所载，与美国的交流不仅在学科方面，也在对美国人和社会的整体认识上使他有了更深刻和宽阔的视野，这也有助于他指导很多学生在学术交流中更注重历史和社会背景。这里是他四次来美国的部分日记，真实反映了他本人以及许多中国民俗学者在"走出去"的过程中的感受。

步。据说国家给他们每月零花钱，定期检查身体，每天一顿免费午餐。美国西部人口稀少，自然环境很好。美国是汽车轮子上的国家，没有汽车是寸步难行；城市交通通畅，道路很好，在路上极少见到交通事故。在美国很少见到警察，除非有事找他们。人们也很少为了琐事争吵。商场货物充足，物价便宜（就美国自己的收入比例看）。美国汽油比中国便宜。美国的汽车主动避让行人。我们在美国没有碰到一起治安事件，但听说洛杉矶黑人区抢劫事件经常发生。

我们还考察了俄勒冈州印第安人保留地。我们见到了该地政府的新闻负责人与印第安人报纸主编麦瑞尔先生。他热情地接待了我们，带我们参观了议会、法庭、老人公寓、教育中心、医疗中心、祭祀场所，给我们介绍了本部族的历史文化。这里住所共有，老人有免费午餐。老人在家作各种手工，十分自在悠闲。印第安人的事务完全由自己管理。其主要收入来源是政府特许他们开了一个赌场，周边的老人等都可来娱乐休闲。我在那里碰到了热情的爱尔兰人后裔的工作人员，说我的姓氏很像她们那里的。

在大会期间，主办者还邀请了曾获得美国国家级传统传承人奖的华裔艺人为大会代表表演了木偶戏，受到热烈欢迎。我们和美国学者一起参加了晚上的舞会。我们住在威涞大学的宿舍里，威涞大学有特别美丽的校园，虽然不大，但如同花园一样漂亮。记得年逾七旬的老者刘魁立教授，高兴起来在宿舍外草地上翻跟头。我们在张举文教授家吃饭，最后陈泳超将一盆螃蟹吃得干干净净。张教授自己开车带我们去森林公园观赏原始森林，到海边欣赏海景，在遥远的海边，居然见到了中餐馆"谭家菜"。

2007 年，参加美国民俗学会在加拿大举办美加两国联合年会，并访问美国

在美丽的秋季，应美国民俗学会与加拿大民俗协会邀请，中国民俗学会的刘魁立会长、高丙中秘书长、萧放副秘书长、张英敏与王霄冰会员作为代表团成员参加了 2007 年 10 月中旬在加拿大召开的"非物质文化遗产的政治与实践"两国民俗学会联合会议。会后应美国民俗学会之邀访问了美国纽约与华盛顿，与相关学术团体及官方基金会进行学术交流。

我们 14 日乘加航从北京到多伦多，16 日由多伦多乘火车到魁北克，沿途红叶，秋意正浓。魁北克的秋天色彩斑斓，美得醉人。我们参加了 17 日至 20 日的学术讨论会。在大会开幕式上，大会主席特地介绍了来自中国的民俗学者。我们在 20 日的专题论坛中发言，该论坛题目为："本土认同中的非物质文化遗产研究：中国的想象与事实"。我发表的论文题目是《全球化语境下中国民族节日的走向》。发言之后接受了听者关于非物质文化遗产与中国高等教育的提问，本人就此机会介绍了北京师范大学民俗学教育的传统及与建立文化遗产学硕士招生方向的情况，引起大家的兴趣。在四天会议中，我听取了多场发言，了解到非物质文化遗产在美加抢救保护情况，以及在与法国官员与东欧学者交谈中知道了欧洲同行的工作。他们对中国即将召开的民族学与人类学大会有相当的兴趣。美国民俗学会还在其下榻的希尔顿饭店开了专场欢迎中国民俗学会代表团的聚会，邀请了部分与会的对中国问题有兴趣的学者，大家共同交流。并就中美民俗学会学术交流的具体项目进行了商讨。

会后美国民俗学会邀请中国民俗学会代表团访问美国。21 日从魁北克经多伦多到达纽

约。在纽约期间，美国民俗学会长和执行秘书长全程陪同，参观了美国自然历史博物馆关于龙的特展；参加了与纽约市艺术管理局官员及纽约市民俗学家及专项基金会代表的座谈，就中美民俗文化交流的意向与具体问题交换了意见，其中有负责华人社区的人士急切需要中国民俗学会的指导，以便与华人建立良好的沟通，会后参观了美国纽约故老街区；考察了中国城，与华埠共同机构的特别顾问进行了座谈。

24日上午离开纽约前往华盛顿，在华盛顿期间仍然由美国民俗学会负责安排诸项活动。下午参观国立印第安人博物馆。25日上午与国会图书馆民俗生活中心负责人等座谈，我向该中心赠送了我的三本著作；《荆楚岁时记研究》《岁时——中国人的时间生活》和《春节》。民俗生活中心成立于1976年，是美国《民俗保护法案》通过之后的产物，它的主要职责是保存美国传统的民俗生活记录材料、档案、文件，包括民歌、口头表演、田野笔记、照片、图画等，主要针对移民美国的人与土著美国人的文化。下午与国会图书馆亚洲部进行学术交流，观看了他们的藏书情况及关于瑶族的文书资料。这里藏有三千多份纳西东巴资料，需要有人帮助整理研究。晚上到肯尼迪艺术中心观看例行演出的音乐会。

26日上午到史密森学会访问，会见民俗生活与文化遗产中心主任理查德·肯尼迪博士。他介绍了该中心的历史与概况。史密森学会是美国国立文化机构，它属下有几十家博物馆，从1965年开始，每年一度的民俗文化节就由该中心负责策划举办。民俗文化节已经连续举办了41届，每年有100万人参加。去年中国云南首次派人参加了湄公河民俗文化的展演，获得成功。这种民俗文化节成为美国人民了解世界文化的窗口，在美国影响很大。中国有56个民族，其实可以学习这种文化节的方式，让他们每年在固定时间展演自己的文化，这既有利于世界人民了解中国，也对社会的和谐稳定有重要作用。在这里我们参观了该中心收藏的历史唱片与电影资料档案，他们正在将唱片及幻灯片、录音带等转换成数码形式，并在网上公开了3000首以上的歌曲资料，供人访问下载。我送该中心一本《荆楚岁时记研究》，我说这是关于一千四百年前所记录的中国节日的研究著作，跟他们的民俗节日有对应关系。肯尼迪博士很高兴地接受了该书。

26日下午访问美国艺术基金会人文与保护部，与该部负责人等进行了学术交流，座谈中就中美感兴趣的学术问题进行了交流，并就民俗研究合作问题交换了意见，我结合北京师范大学重点学科的教学实践，介绍了中国民俗学教育中田野调查人才的培养问题。该部门重点是资助本国民俗艺术活动，对民俗艺术传承人进行认定、命名与奖励。

27日参观美国美术馆，下午考察美国华盛顿大教堂。28日早启程回国，结束在美国的学术访问行程。

在加拿大与美国期间感受到了西方世界整体发展水平与有机的社会秩序，我们真的还得学习，无论大处，还是小处，都值得借鉴。同时也感受到中国人在国际社会中的地位有了明显提升，美国同行对中国有相当高的评价，他们非常真诚地希望与中国进行学术交流合作。

同年12月，美国民俗学会代表团回访中国。艾伟会长和张举文教授在北京师范大学等校与同行们进行了学术交流。我觉得人与人的接触、思想与思想的碰撞是加深国际合作理解的重要途径，也是全球化时代的常态。

参加 2012 年美国民俗学会年会

2012 年 10 月 24—27 日，美国民俗学会年会在新奥尔良召开，我参会的论文题目是《关于非物质文化遗产与地方文化传统建设》。

这次参会经历说来饶有兴趣。原本没想参加，在举文兄的催促下提供了论文摘要。举文兄暑期来京又积极协助，让美国再寄邀请函来，原来说寄了纸质的，但一直没收到。后来补寄的纸质版依然没收到。直到 9 月开学我才去申请开会。由于 2012 年新规，出外学术交流要用公务护照，我就到指定照相馆照了相，到国际交流合作处办理护照申请与出国批件。等了十来天，批件很快下来了，但护照一直没动静，就去打听，结果办事人根本没有给我办理护照申请，她说没看到我的材料。而接我表格的人说给了。结果在一堆处理过的材料中发现我那申请材料。要不是我去催问，怕是永远不办了。这时离出国时间不长了，再等公务护照下来，怕是黄花菜都凉了。我赶紧跟陈处商量，就用我的私人护照签证。要是用私人签证，早就办了。因为我没时间，国际交流合作处帮我约了面签时间，是 10 月 11 日。11 日一早去了亮马桥美国大使馆，我不到 7 点就到了，那里已经排起了长队。等 7 点多上班。我是第三批进去的，接着按指纹，我因为湿疹手脱皮，好不容易才按合格，再排队面签。等到窗口，问了我的原因，知道我去过美国后，说你是博士？我说是。再无话，几分钟办好，签证官说祝你一路平安！然后去邮局办理护照邮寄手续。下午确定北京经芝加哥到新奥尔良，由奥兰多经芝加哥回北京的往返机票，共计 7900 元。十分便宜。三天后收到签证护照。

23 日从北京乘 AA186 航班到芝加哥，再转班机到新奥尔良。经历了 20 多个小时的长途飞行之后，当地时间下午七点终于到达目的地，有杜兰大学的教授与一中国留学生接机。住进了事先订好的宾馆。晚上儿子从佛罗里达来，到宾馆已经十二点了。24 日去了本市法语区、教堂、城市公园、密西西比河口、1 号公墓等看了。古老、欧洲风情，老城区馊水味浓郁，我说是生活气息。品尝了新奥尔良美味，水牛城鸡块沙拉、炸生蚝、意大利海鲜拼盘、新奥尔良炸鸡翅等。因为有翻译官，诸事顺利。万圣节快到了，一些家庭开始装扮怪异形象，商店也卖这些东西。还有巫术屋，吉卜赛人看手相的（教堂前）。晚上见市政厅前丰收节音乐节（连续六天，今天最后一天），许多人聚集那里，主持人鼓励大家参加下下周总统投票。我看到一群群的人聚谈甚欢。

25 日开会一天，上午 10 点，我与北京大学博士后韩成艳同场，来的人不少，有 30 人。我报告了自己的论文题目，讲中国非遗与地方文化传统复兴重建的关系。大家很关注，提了不少感兴趣的问题，如政府在非遗中的角色、人们如何利用非遗、个案如何。听众也帮助回答，形成讨论。会后，多位代表上来握手，说讲得好。中午我与本德尔、苏独玉、葛底斯堡学院李静、华盛顿艺术民俗学会的史威利、张举文、高丙中、游自荧等一起吃饭。下午听山东大学的刁统菊、新疆师范大学的南快莫德格、华东师范大学的田兆元等大会发言。与张举文商量未来合作办讲座和民俗影视班等事。

26 日早离开新奥尔良，前往佛罗里达大学，中间经迈阿密转机，晚上到，找三家旅馆，无住，回去睡儿子地铺。27 日早去佛大转转，学校漂亮，棒球馆／图书馆／鳄鱼池／餐厅。

图书馆自由出入,我找到有我的著作处,拍照留念。29日上飞机到芝加哥,转机飞回北京。

参加2015年美国民俗学会年会

2015年10月14日至17日,我以《人情与传统中国礼俗》为题,到加州长滩参加美国民俗学会的年会。在这里见到了老朋友张举文教授,他依然是我们的翻译人。他为中美民俗学会的学术交流奉献了心血,辛苦他了。这次我与中国传媒大学的王杰文教授、杭州师大的袁瑾博士同行,我们还见到了高丙中教授、周星教授等。中国民俗学会的会长朝戈金研究员率中国民俗学会代表团也参加了大会。

会后应张举文教授邀请,前往俄勒冈州的崴涞大学参加"东亚成人意义与成人礼研讨会"。这是时隔十年后重访崴涞大学,崴涞大学美丽依旧。研讨会前,我们重游森林公园,秋色美得不像真的。这次住在城中的宾馆,条件很好,早餐尤其美味。会议前的研讨特别有深度。会议由该校亚洲中心主任主持,开得正规有序。东亚学者与美国学者进行了较充分的交流,就成年仪式功能如何理解展开了讨论。未尽话题,大家12月回到北京,张举文也来了,在北京大学以"经典概念的当代实践"为题,借助"过渡礼仪"概念继续讨论。其实,至今我们还在继续着我们的讨论。

以上只是去美国的一部分记录。近年来,在北师大我们与美国和其他国家学者的交往和合作也越来越频繁和深入。相信我还有机会继续讲述与美国民俗学者交流的故事。

2006年6月中国民俗学会代表团访问俄勒冈的格兰特容德印第安联盟总部。高丙中、刘魁立、迈瑞尔(接待方)、萧放、陈泳超(自左向右)。The CFS delegation visiting the Confederated Tribes of Grand Ronde, Oregon, June 2006. Bingzhong Gao, Kuili Liu, Brent Merrill (host), Fang Xiao, Yongchao Chen (from left to right). Photograph by Juwen Zhang.

My Recollections of the China-US Folkloristic Exchange

Fang Xiao*

First time participating in a conference in the US in 2006

From June 2nd to June 4th 2006, the "Conference on Chinese Daily Ritual Practices", in conjunction with the 10th "Conference on Holidays, Ritual, Festival, Celebrations, and Public Display", was held at Willamette University, Salem, Oregon. Professor Juwen Zhang organized it on behalf of the Eastern Asia Folklore Section of the AFS, and the Center for Asian Studies at Willamette University. The majority of the representatives were from the United States and were mostly concerned with the daily lives of Chinese people in the US. Some attendees were experts who specialized in Chinese American studies and their papers focused on how Chinese and Chinese Americans lived in the American society and how they preserved their own culture at the same time.

Through the coordination between the conference organizer, Professor Juwen Zhang from Willamette University and Professor Bingzhong Gao from Beijing University, Dr. Kuili Liu, the President of China Folklore Society (CFS), led a delegation to participate in the first academic exchange taking place in the US. The delegates included CFS Secretary Bingzhong Gao, Yongchao Chen from Beijing University and me from Beijing Normal University (BNU).

Taking the advantage of coming to the US for the conference, we decided to leave China a week in advance and travel to Los Angeles, San Francisco, Portland and other cities to observe

---

* Fang Xiao earned his Ph. D. in Folklore from Beijing Normal University, where he is the Chair of the Department of Anthropology and Folklore. He is one of the first generation folklorists after the re-establishment of Chinese folkloristics. He has published a number of books and articles on history and folklore. He not only serves at the China Folklore Society and engages in research, but also promotes public education on folklore through public media. He also plays a key role in the International Association of Asian Folklore Studies. As he writes in his journals, communicating with American folklorists not only helps understand the discipline, but also broadens the understanding of the entire American society and people, and thus benefits him as he advices his students to pay attention to social and historical background. Here is a section of his diaries from his four visits to the US that truly reveal his feelings, as well as those of many other folklorists from China, about "going abroad."

Chinese American communities and Native American living situations in the US. During my stay in the States, I noticed that Americans were much more at ease than Chinese based on their expressions, manners and conversations. In San Francisco, I saw many homeless people taking leisure strolls around the city. I have been told that the local government gives them monthly paychecks, regular health checkups and one free meal a day. The western states also have beautiful natural scenery and large malls with affordable goods. Americans emphasize the priority of pedestrians, therefore there are few traffic accidents. We felt rather safe walking around the streets, though we have heard about robbery incidents in Los Angeles.

We visited a Native American Community in Oregon. At the Confederated Tribes of Grand Ronde, we met with the head of the local government and the chief editor of Native American Newspaper, Brent Merrill. He warmly welcomed us and introduced us to the history of their culture and community. He also gave us a tour of the community; we visited their senior center, educational center, medical center and worship center. The senior center provides shelter and free lunches for the elderly to live comfortably. The government allowed them to open a casino as a source of income to maintain the senior center. I met a very lovely Irish staff who told me my name sounded like hers.

At the conference, the organizer invited the NEA Awardees to perform Chinese rod puppet at the welcome banquet. Everyone participated and enjoyed the Irish square dance in the evening. We stayed on the campus of Willamette University. It was a like a garden. Dr. Kuili Liu was so happy that he even somersaulted on the lawn though he was over seventy years old. When we ate at Juwen's house, Yongchao Chen finished a whole basin of crabs and shrimps. Juwen took us to the forest park and other natural and cultural sites. We were surprised to see a Chinese restaurant even at the coast in Lincoln City, Oregon.

During the conference, American folklorists were very interested in the topics presented by Chinese folklorists. Since this was the first time a Chinese delegation participated and presented at a folklore conference in the US, American folklorists were very interested in conversing with us and we quickly became acquainted with each other.

First participation in the AFS annual meeting in 2007

In October 2007, the AFS and Canadian Folklore Society invited members of CFS including Kuili Liu, Bingzhong Gao, Yingmin Zhang and Xiaobing Wang to participate in the "International Conference on Politics and Practice of Intangible Culture" in Canada.

On October 14th, we flew from Beijing to Toronto. On the 16th, we took the train from Toronto to Quebec. We attended the seminar from the 17th to the 20th. During the opening ceremony, the president of General Assembly specially introduced folklorists from China. On October 20th, we presented our papers on "Intangible Cultural Heritage Studies in Localization in

China: Imagination and Reality." My topic was on the "The Effect of Globalization on Chinese National Festivals." After my presentation, many of them had questions about intangible cultural heritage in higher education in China. I took the liberty to introduce them to the folklore program in relation to cultural heritage studies in BNU. On the last day of the conference, I listened to a number of different presentations on the protection of intangible cultural heritage in the US and learned about the European plan from conversing with French officials and Eastern European scholars. The AFS held a special reception at the Hilton Hotel to welcome the representatives from the China Folklore Society and invited some Chinese folklorists to participate in an open discussion about China's problems.

After the conference, the AFS invited our delegation to the United States. On the 21st, we flew from Toronto to New York. The president and the executive director of the AFS accompanied us to a few public folklore institutions in New York. We visited the American Museum of Natural History and explored the dragon exhibition; we also participated in discussions with representatives of New York Arts Society and folklorists in New York. We also visited Chinatown where we had an informal discussion with special advisors of the Chinese community. On the 24th, we left for Washington D. C. and in the afternoon we visited the National Museum of the American Indian in Washington D. C.

On the morning of 25th, I chatted with the Director of American Folklife Center at the Library of Congress. I presented to him with three different books, *The Study of Jingchu Festivals*, *Time: Chinese Life* and *Chinese New Year*. The AFC was established in 1976 and their main duties are to preserve traditional American Folklore records and documents including folk songs, oral performances, field notes, photographs, drawings, etc. There are numbers of data collection, researchers and organizations in the AFC. In the afternoon, I interacted with the Asia Department at the Library of Congress. At the library, there are more than 3,000 copies of Naxi Dongba ritual texts. The library is fully managed and staffed. In the evening, I attended a concert at John F. Kennedy Center for the Performing Arts.

On the 26th, we went to the Smithsonian Institution and met with the Director of the Center for Folklife and Cultural Heritage, Dr. Kennedy. He introduced to me the history and overview of the center. The Smithsonian is a national cultural institution with a total of ninety museums. Some museums were established as early as 1965. Every year the center is responsible for planning the annual Folklife Festival. The center has held over 41 Folklife Festivals and every year millions of people attend. Last year, China's Yunnan Province sent people to participate in the Mekong River Folklife Festival. This type of events have become an opportunity for Americans to understand different cultures around the world. There are 56 ethnic groups in China, perhaps they should host a similar festival to showcase different ethnic group's culture. This could become an opportunity for everyone to better understand Chinese culture and potentially serve as an important role for social harmony. At the museum, we visited different collections of historical records and films. When I was at the museum, the staff were converting over three thousand old songs into digital files to upload onto the internet. I gave the museum my book on *The Study of Jingchu Festivals* and told them that this book is about the Chinese festivals with one thousand and four hundred years' history. In the afternoon, we visited NEA and chatted with the head of the department, Barry Bergey. We exchanged views on academic issues in China and the United States and gave each other advice. I also introduced to him teaching practices in Beijing Normal University.

On the 27th, we visited the Museum of Art and in the afternoon we visited the Washington Cathedral. On the 28th, we left the US, which marked the end of our academic trip for the year.

My trip to Canada and America opened my eyes to numerous new things. I have come to realize that we must strive to learn continuously and keep an open mind. After this trip, I noticed that the recognition of Chinese in the international community and the status of Chinese has improved significantly. At the same time, the United States has a more positive view toward China and therefore American folklorists now look forward to maintaining relationship with Chinese folklorists. In December, the AFS delegation visited China and had an academic exchange at BNU.

Participating in the AFS annual meeting in 2012

The annual meeting of AFS was held in New Orleans this year from October 24th to 27th. I presented a paper on "Intangible Heritage Culture and the Construction of Local Cultural Traditions."

Originally, I did not plan to attend this meeting. However, Professor Zhang persuaded me to attend. And there was dramatic experience in getting the visa, both with my university offices and with the visa interviewer. Nevertheless, I received the visa just about one week before the meeting. It turned out the plane ticket was still very cheap, only RMB 7900 (about US＄1,300).

On October 23rd, I took the flight from Beijing to Chicago then to New Orleans. I arrived at 7 pm and was picked up by a professor and a Chinese international student from Tulane University. I stayed in Queen and Crescent Hotel and in the evening, my son came to visit me. The next morning, we toured around the city and visited a church, a few parks and other places in New Orleans. The city is very breath-taking with beautiful European architecture and ancient buildings. Food in New Orleans is also very delicious. When we were there, it was almost Halloween. So some houses and stores had put up some weird decorations. I rested in the afternoon and in the evening, I attended a Harvest Festival in the city hall. Since it was the last day of the festival, there were many people there. There were also restaurants and other local shops at the festival.

On the 25th, I attended the conference for the entire day. There were about 30 scholars who attended my session. I presented my paper on the relationship between ICH and the reconstruction of local culture in China." There was strong interest in my topic, and attendees asked many questions. During lunch, I dined with Mark Bender from Ohio University, Sue Tuohy from Indiana University, Jing Li from Gettysburg College, Willie Smyth from Washington Institute of Arts and Folklore, Juwen Zhang and Bingzhong Gao. In the afternoon, Juwen Zhang and I talked about our future collaborations such as lecture and workshops. I attended a session in the afternoon by Tongju Diao from Shandong University, Namkamidog from Xinjiang Normal University, and Zhaoyuan Tian from East China Normal University. On the morning of the 26th, we left New Orleans and went to Gainesville. On the 29th, we flew to Chicago and then back to Beijing.

Participating inthe AFS annual meeting in 2015

On October 14th, 2015, I attended AFS annual meeting with a presentation on "Personal Relationship and Traditional Chinese Customs." At the meeting, I met my good friend, Juwen Zhang, who at the time also served as our translator. He has devoted a lot of his time and energy to the communication between the CFS and the AFS. This time, I attended the conference with Jiewen Wang from the University of Communication and Jin Yuan from Hangzhou Normal University. We also met Bingzhong Gao, Xing Zhou and other scholars. The president of the CFS also led a delegation to the meeting.

After the conference, Bingzhong Gao, Jiewen Wang and I went on to attend the International Seminar on "the Meaning of Becoming an Adult in East Asia" at Willamette University, with the invitation from the organizer, Juwen Zhang. I had visited Willamette University 10 years previously. During the seminar, there were invaluable conversations, and everyone wanted to continue the relationship. Indeed, in December, Juwen Zhang came to Beijing University and BNU and we continued to discuss this topic with "a seminar on the Modern Application of Classic Concept: The Rites of Passage." In fact, we are still continuing our conversations about it.

Above are only some of my notes involving Sino-US communication. In recent years, China has developed more and more collaborative projects with the US and other countries. I believe that I will have chance to continue experiencing new things and telling more stories.

(Translation by Emily Su)

美美与共：我们与美国民俗学界的交往

杨利慧　安德明[*]

从 2000 年第一次走出国门算起，我们已经共同参与了许多国际学术交流活动，但交往最多的无疑是美国民俗学界的同行。这些交往不仅形塑了我们个人的学术生涯，也在一定程度上推进了中国民俗学的发展。

我们与美国民俗学界的交往，同两次访学经历密切相关：第一次是 2000 年 8 月至 2001 年 8 月，前往美国印第安纳大学民俗学与音乐人类学系进行访问研究。这一年的访学为我们与美国民俗学界长期、深入的交流奠定了基础。第二次则是在 2006 年 8 月至 2007 年 8 月，前往哈佛燕京学社进行为期一年的访问研究，进一步提高了我们的理论认识和宣传中国民俗学的意识。

一、走出国门

2000 年春，我们确定去印第安纳大学，目的是学习民俗学的前沿理论和方法。当时国内学术界已比较开放，对新思想和新方法的渴望十分强烈，国外的理论著述被大量翻译引进。不过，民俗学界对新视角的介绍相对迟缓，同龄的同行中去国外民俗学重镇进行研修的尚寥寥无几。在这样的情形下，我们对出国访学、提升自己的国际视野充满了热切的渴望。

在印大，我们给自己的预期目标是深入、系统地了解当代西方的民俗学理论，特别是表演理论。所以，与理查德·鲍曼有过多次深入交谈和访谈，也与亨利·格拉西、琳达·戴格等人有过频繁深入的交流。

对表演理论的兴趣源于我们在实际科研工作中遇到的问题。1990 年代初，杨利慧在研究女娲神话时，已注意到民间流传的鲜活的女娲神话，并力图将女娲及其神话的理解置于特

---

[*] 编者注：杨利慧现任北京师范大学民俗学教授，民俗学博士。通过参与中美民俗学交流，她大量译介了美国民俗学的表演理论和公共民俗学等研究成果，也在国内首次开设了用英文教授的国际民俗学课程。而她自己的神话研究也突破了传统的文本研究，重视通过田野来关注活的神话信仰和讲述行为，提出了"神话主义"等观点。安德明是中国社会科学院研究员，民俗学博士。他在译介国外民俗学理论的同时，也通过自己的田野实践，提出了"家乡民俗学"等概念。目前，他还兼任《民间文化论坛》的主编。他们伉俪也都是中国民俗学在 1980 年代重建后的新一代民俗学者的代表。

定社区的民间信仰语境中加以探讨。当时国内对表演理论已有约略介绍，虽然不很详尽，但已经让我们感到，这一理论视角对现代口承神话研究将会有重大的启示意义。

我们旁听了鲍曼讲授的研究生课程"语言的社会符号学"，同时，拟订了翻译其代表性著述的计划，还对他进行了几次访谈。这些访谈后来整理出来，以《理查德·鲍曼及其表演理论》为题，发表于《民俗研究》2003年第1期。

格拉西教授是与我们接触最多、对我们帮助也最大的教授之一。说来惭愧：当2000年夏天他应北大王娟博士之邀来北京讲学时，我们对他一无所知，只被他讲课时明白浅显的语言、深邃的思想和富有感染力的激情所折服。到美国之后，我们才对他有了正确了解。在我们刚到印大的迎新会上，老师和研究生们都一一自我介绍，轮到我们时，我们心里有些紧张，英语又不够从心所欲，不免有些沮丧。没料想当我们介绍完后，格教授马上大声补充说："今年6月我在北师大民俗学所做了讲演，那里是中国民俗学的中心，和我们这里一样，是最老的民俗学所。所以，他们夫妇从中国最老的民俗学所来美国最老的民俗学所访问，是很有意义的。"他的补充无疑帮了我们大忙，以他的身份替我们做这番宣传，可以大大帮助别人了解我们和我们的工作单位。

我们听过他的"民俗学的理论与方法研讨课"。后来，第二个学期，为帮助我们迅速了解当代美国民俗学的理论和成就，格教授特意在百忙之中抽出宝贵的时间，为我们夫妇"开小灶"：由他精选出几本他认为好的书，让我们读了以后，每周一次去他的办公室里和他进行专门讨论。就是从这些阅读和讨论中，我们比较深入地了解了表演理论、民族志诗学以及公共民俗学等，觉得美国民俗学不再虚无缥缈，而是清晰生动了许多。

可以说，印大的每位教授都为我们打开了了解美国民俗学的一扇大门，也成了我们的好朋友。例如，戴格教授是民俗学系的另一位"杰出教授"，在民间叙事以及民间信仰领域卓有影响。我们访学的时候她已经退休，不过经由格雷戈里·施润普博士的介绍我们与她相识，以后还对她进行了几次访谈，内容涉及民俗学与大众传媒、研究个体表演者的意义、她的"以表演者为中心"的方法与表演理论的关联等等。2011年我们赴布鲁明顿参加美国民俗学会年会，再次见到了戴格教授，备感亲切。2014年10月，戴格教授去世，利慧曾在中国民俗学会的官网上发表了这样一段悼念文字："我一直认为：戴格教授的学术思想融合了美国和匈牙利民俗学研究的长处，独具一格。她的'以表演者为中心'的研究方法，是对鲍曼等人的表演理论的一大补充，至今值得我们认真学习实践。我十多年前从印大回来以后，曾经有很长时间在课堂上介绍戴格教授的民间故事研究成果，在我自己以及北师大部分博士生和硕士生的论文里，都可以见到戴格教授思想的影响。"

苏独玉是研究中国民歌和民间音乐的专家，尤其对西北花儿术有专攻，成就斐然。在印大期间，我们成了无话不谈的好朋友。2011年我们再赴印大，苏邀请我们住在她家里。会议结束后，她还专门召开了一个欢送所有参会的中国学者的招待会，亲手准备了丰富的食物，还拿出几瓶珍藏的茅台酒待客，让我们非常感动。

罗杰·哲奈里和任敦姬夫妇都是研究东亚民俗的专家，是民俗学系出了名的好老师。记得我们离开印大之前，他们把合著的《祖先崇拜与韩国社会》一书赠给我们，语重心长地说："这是我们70年代做的工作。我们当时调查的东西，今天在韩国社会已经找不到了，我们很高兴通过自己的工作把那些珍贵的历史记录了下来。希望你们从现在开始做这样的工作，因为中国也面临着巨大的转变，如果不尽快记录的话，许多东西就会转变或者消失了。这个工作具有历史意义。"一直到今天，我们双方都保持着密切的联系，每次见到他们，都感觉如同见到父母一般亲切。

系主任约翰·麦克道尔教授学识渊博，幽默风趣，自弹自唱墨西哥民谣的样子很酷，跟他交往让人感觉如沐春风。格雷戈里·施润普博士是神话学家，因此对我们特别关照，我们所有的提问他总是耐心作答。他还介绍了印大的另一位神话学家、古典学教授威廉·汉森与我们认识，这位教授对我们也有非常多的帮助（见下文）。此外，鲍曼夫人斯道杰教授、玛丽·爱莲·布朗教授，以及哈桑·爱尔-沙米教授，也给了我们许多帮助。

除了这些老师，我们同印大民俗学系的学生也有许多交往，其中不少人成了我们的好朋友，像杰西卡·安德森·特纳、约翰·冯和丽莎·戈尔曼夫妇、尹教任、凯西·罗伯特等等，他们目前都是美国高校或博物馆中民俗学专业的中坚力量。

二、美美与共

我们始终认为，中国民俗学的国际交流应该是双向的：一方面，中国民俗学者应该积极学习国外先进的理论和方法以及以开阔视野，拓展胸襟，同时也应结合中国本土的经验与问题进行自身的发展、创新；另一方面，还应该把中国民俗以及民俗学的成就尽力介绍出去，在国际舞台上发出中国学者的声音，从而实现平等交流、"美美与共"（费孝通先生语）的目的。

第一次访学期间，特别是归国以后，为了使更多的中国民俗学者和研究生能共同分享我们的留学收获和见闻，了解当代美国民俗学的学术成就和学科体系设置，我们在《民俗研究》杂志上开辟了"域外学术"专栏，连续发表文章，介绍印大民俗学系的总体状况、课程设置及学生培养，[①] 并针对中国民俗学界在建设和发展中的问题，有目的性地采访了多位当代美国民俗学界有影响的学者，请他们介绍自己的学术特点、使用的理论和方法以及当前美国民俗学关注的热点问题等，希望对中国民俗学界开阔视野、走向世界起到积极的作用。不过由于各种原因，这些访谈中仅有两篇被整理出来并在专栏上发表。[②]

表演理论的译介是我们第一次访学的重点。初见鲍曼教授，我们就提出了翻译的设想，并请他推荐合适的书目。他建议我们翻译1977年由纽博瑞出版公司出版的《作为表演的口

[①] 安德明、杨利慧：《印第安纳大学访学札记》，《民俗研究》2001年第2期；杨利慧、安德明：《美国印第安纳大学民俗学与音乐文化学系的学生培训与课程设置》，《民俗研究》2001年第3期。

[②] 杨利慧、安德明：《理查德·鲍曼及其表演理论》，《民俗研究》2003年第1期；《阿兰·邓迪斯：精神分析学说的执着追随者和民俗学领地的坚定捍卫者》，《民俗研究》2003年第3期，这一篇是我们访学结束前往加州大学伯克利分校访问邓迪斯教授的成果。

头艺术》单行本,认为这本书比较系统地介绍了他有关表演视角的观点。回国后,我们通过课堂教学、学术讲座和研究,一边继续学习、探索和介绍相关理论,① 一边翻译这本书。

随着对表演理论的了解日渐深入,我们发现,仅仅翻译该书,不能反映相关理论的新发展,而且也缺乏具体的实践案例,无法满足国内民俗学界的渴求。于是,我们与鲍教授再三商议,最终一同择定了中译本正文部分新的组成篇目。2008 年,我们翻译并编定的《作为表演的口头艺术》中译本由广西师范大学出版社出版。此后,2011 年及 2015 年,利慧又先后两次在《民俗研究》和《民间文化论坛》上组织表演理论的研讨专栏,邀请中国民俗学者进一步深化有关表演理论的反思。这些工作为国内同行比较深入、系统地了解表演理论提供了便利,对该理论的传播和发展起到了重要推动作用,也彰显了中国同行为丰富和修正该理论所做出的贡献。正是由于对表演理论的直接和间接推动,中国民俗学在近 30 年间,尤其是自 1990 年代中后期以来,逐渐发生了向注重语境、过程、表演者和当代社会的转型。②

除了表演理论以外,我们也积极梳理并介绍了民族志诗学和公共民俗学的理论和实践。2001 年春夏间,我们还听过茵塔·卡朋特博士开设的公共民俗学短期培训课程。她提出的民俗学者可以而且应该利用专业知识直接而有效地服务于社会的这一理念给了我们很大的触动。

2003 年底,周星教授约请我们为他编辑的《民俗学的历史、理论与方法》一书撰写一篇介绍当代美国民俗学理论与方法的文章。借此机会,我们写作了《美国当代民俗学的主要理论和方法》等文章③,系统介绍并评论了表演理论、民族志诗学和公共民俗学(我们当时译为"公众民俗学",主要是考虑到相关理论和实践均强调为民众服务、与社区合作)。这些文章为国内同行了解晚近的美国民俗学成就,提供了一些参考。

我们也同知名的公共民俗学家罗伯特·巴龙有过较多往来,并应他的邀请,参加了在波士顿近郊举办的洛尔民俗节,对公共民俗学者如何参与节日的组织、如何介绍或展示不同的民俗项目、如何与传承人及社区代表合作,有了更为切身的认识。这一次经验为德明 2014 年在华盛顿参加"史密森民间生活节"并顺利完成解说和主持工作,提供了重要的基础。

除了文章和著作,我们也通过授课和讲学等活动,向同行以及学生介绍美国民俗学的理

---

① 我们迄今发表的介绍、评论表演理论的论文包括:杨利慧:《表演理论与民间叙事研究》,《民俗研究》2004 年第 1 期;《民间叙事的传承与表演》,《文学评论》,2005 年第 2 期;《民间叙事的表演——以兄妹婚神话的口头表演为例,兼谈中国民间叙事研究的方法问题》(上、下),《励耘学刊》2005 年第 1、2 辑,第 186—199、238—255 页,后全文收入吕微、安德明主编:《民间叙事的多样性》,学苑出版社,2006 年,第 233—271 页;《表演理论及其对神话研究的启示——兼谈神话的综合研究法》,收入陈器文主编:《新世纪神话研究之反思》,《兴大中文学报》(台中)第 27 期增刊,2010 年,第 569—590 页;《表演理论》,《民间文化论坛》,2015 年第 1 期。

② 具体论述可参见杨利慧:《语境、过程、表演者与朝向当下的中国民俗学——表演理论与中国民俗学的当代转型》,《民俗研究》2011 年第 1 期。

③ 杨利慧、安德明:《美国当代民俗学的主要理论和方法》,见周星主编:《民俗学的历史、理论与方法》,商务印书馆,2006 年,第 595—638 页。其中有关民族志诗学和公共民俗学的成果,曾先期在一些刊物上发表,分别为:安德明:《美国公众民俗学的兴起、发展与实践》,《民间文化论坛》总第 127 期,2004 年 6 月;杨利慧:《美国公众民俗学的理论贡献与相关反思》,《广西民族学院学报》2004 年第 5 期;杨利慧:《民族志诗学的理论与实践》,《北京师范大学学报》2004 年第 6 期。

论与方法。自2001年迄今，杨利慧在北京师范大学民俗学专业研究生的课堂教学中，陆续介绍了诸多代表性学者的著述，包括鲍曼的《作为表演的口头艺术》，格拉西的《巴利玛林时光》，戴格的《民间故事与社会》以及《美国民俗与大众媒体》，麦克道尔的有关"反思民俗化"的文章，① 以及巴龙和尼克·斯皮泽合著的《公共民俗》，等等。这些著述中的学术思想，通过我们的教学和科研活动，渐渐为一些中国年轻学子所吸收，成为滋养中国民俗学建设的有益力量。

此外，自2001年起，我们还利用各种机会，邀请包括美国民俗学者在内的国际知名专家前来北师大和中国社科院举办学术讲座。近20年间，陆续来访的美国民俗学者包括：理查德·鲍曼、贝弗莉·斯道杰、张举文、苏独玉、杰西卡·安德森·特纳、约翰·范、罗伯特·拜伦、尼克·斯皮泽、罗杰·哲奈里、任敦姬、马克·本德尔、吕江、李靖、邝蓝岚、阿兰·伯德特等，还曾邀请麦克道尔、施润普、尹教任和威策尔到青海、云南等地参加神话学会议。

这里应该一提的是，如今我们培养的下一代学生也加入到与美国民俗学界的交流之中：王均霞、祝鹏程、张成福、张多，都曾分别前往印第安纳大学和俄亥俄州立大学进修民俗学，参加美国民俗学年会。完全可以相信，中美民俗学的交流将在下一代中谱写出新的篇章。

在印大期间，经由威廉·汉森教授的介绍，我们为美国ABC-CLIO出版公司撰写《中国神话手册》。此书是第一部由中国神话学者撰写的英文专著，反映了中国学者眼中的中国神话以及中国神话学百年来的成就，出版后得到了英语世界中一些同行的好评，后来被牛津大学出版社再版。好友杰西卡应我们的邀请，担任了全书的英文修订工作。

在印大访学的中后期，我们在系里举办了有关中国神话和民间信仰的学术讲座，利慧讲的是"女娲：当代中国的神话与信仰"，德明讲的是"中国农事禳灾习俗"。此外，应印大中国留学生会的约请，介绍"中国西北乡村的社火表演"；为东亚系主办的东亚文化短训班做"中国的民间剪纸艺术"专题讲座；还应布鲁明顿地方广播电台（WFHB）的约请，利用我们带去的几张光盘，在电台中介绍中国的民间音乐和传统音乐。记得在电台直播的过程中，不断有热心听众打电话来询问更多的细节。直播过后的第二天，有一位当地居民打听到我们的住址，在我们的公寓门口留下一大束自家菜园里收获的芦笋，感谢我们的解说打动了他的心。

总之，在印大一年里，我们和民俗学系的师生们结下了深厚的友谊。麦克道尔教授在我们举办的告别招待会上说：我们已被当作了民俗学系大家庭的一员，是中美文化交流的使者。

2006年，我们第二次到美国访问研究时，我们的专业研究有了更多进步，在国际交流上也更有自信，发出中国声音的底气也更足，也有了更多的讲学交流机会。哈佛大学尽管是

---

① John H. McDowell. "Rethinking Folklorization in Ecuador: Multivocality in the Expressive Contact Zone." In Western Folklore, Vol. 69, No. 2, Spring 2010, pp. 181–209.

世界一流的大学，然而民俗学专业却并不很强，仅有一个"民俗学与神话学研究项目"，开设有本科课程，负责人是斯蒂文·米切尔教授。但是，我们接触的每位教授都非常热情亲切。我们谈论中国和美国的民俗学教学和研究形势，也谈论以后的合作设想。我们曾积极联合几位民俗学、人类学专业的访问学者，发起了一个"亚洲文化讨论会"，并先后主讲了"当代中国神话的变迁"和"街子乡的社火表演"。

后来我们又在燕京学社的支持下，组织了一个"亚洲的宗教、大众文化与社会变迁"的研讨会，[①] 并分别发表论文《反全球化与中国民间传统的重建——以电视剧〈哪吒传奇〉为例》和《爷山上的庙宇与神灵：中国西北一个变迁中的村落中民间信仰的重建》。这些研讨活动的参与者来自世界多个国家和地区，有着不同的学科背景，因此举办这些活动不仅极大地拓展了我们的视野，也为我们在跨学科的国际交流平台上展示中国民俗学的成果提供了机会。

2006年10月，经张举文教授的帮助，我们获得美国民俗学会资助，参加了在威斯康星州密尔沃基举行的美国民俗学会年会，并分别在举文兄所组织的分会场发表论文《庙会的合法性与神话的解构与重构》和《街子乡的社火》。

2007年4月，又经举文兄的热心安排，我们应邀先后在威涞大学中国研究中心、俄勒冈大学民俗学中心、加州大学洛杉矶分校中国研究中心和加州大学伯克利分校民俗学中心，分别做了题为《中国的非物质文化遗产运动》《2008奥运会与中国民间传统的展示与变迁》《反全球化与当代中国民间传统的重建》《庙会的合法性与神话的解构与重构》等讲座，还参加了在加州大学洛杉矶分校举行的美国西部民俗学会年会，在会议上发表论文《神灵崇拜与社会变迁：衰落还是复兴——来自中国西北部一个变化中的村落的例子》《反全球化与当代中国民间传统的重建》。

这些活动，不仅进一步加强了我们同美国民俗学界的交流、强化了我们自身的国际学术交流能力，也为美国同行了解中国民俗文化、中国民俗学以及中国社会的历史与发展现状，发挥了积极的作用。

总体而言，与美国民俗学界近20年的交往，为我们在专业和人生经验两个方面都带来了丰厚收获。就专业而言，它打破了我们脑子里原有的一些僵化的条条框框，使视野变得更为开阔，对民俗学的学科特质以及美国民俗学的成就与不足都有了更为深入的认识；同时，也增进了对中国民俗学的自省和信心，并强化了自己的理论创新能力。我们近年来提出"家乡民俗学""神话主义""综合研究法"等新的观点，与我们的国际学术交流经历有着直接的关系。在人生的经验和境界上，美国民俗学者的友谊常常使我们感受到生活中的美好和温暖，许多民俗学者的学问和人品令我们不胜钦佩。仅就此两方面而言，与美国民俗学界的交往都已成为我们生命的滋养。

[①] 关于我们在哈佛大学访学期间的经历和见闻，可参见杨利慧的随笔《哈佛点滴》，http://www.chinesefolklore.org.cn/blog/?463/viewspace-11531。

II. 从面对文本到面对面——耕耘友情 153

亨利·格拉西与杨利慧,2000 年 10 月。Henry Glassie and Lihui Yang, Oct. 2000. Photograph courtesy of Lihui Yang.

亨利·格拉西与安德明,2000 年 10 月。Henry Glassie and Deming An, Oct. 2000. Photograph courtesy of Lihui Yang.

Sharing the Beauty: Our Exchanges with American Folklorists

Lihui Yang Deming An*

Since our first time going abroad, we have participated in numerous international academic activities. The most frequent contacts, however, were with American folklorists. These activities have not only reaffirmed our academic careers, but also, to a certain extent, helped advance Chinese folkloristics.

Our exchange with American folklorists is closely related to our two years of visits in the US. The first year was from August 2000 to August 2001 at Indiana University, and the second, from August 2006 to August 2007 at the Harvard-Yenching Institute. The first year laid the foundations for our long term relationships with many American folklorists, and the second elevated our theoretical understanding of the discipline and our conscious promotion of Chinese folklore to the world.

I. Going Abroad

In spring 2000, we chose Indiana University for our year as visiting scholars, with the purpose of learning the cutting-edge folkloristic theories and methods. While China was quite open at that time and had a great academic thirst for new ideas and methods, the folklore circle was relatively

---

* Lihui Yang is Professor of Folklore at BNU, where she earned her Ph. D. in Folklore. Through her involvement in the Sino-US communication, she has translated and introduced to the Chinese world a great deal of works on performance and public folklore by American folklorists. She was the first in China to offer a graduate course in English on world folklore. Her own works on myths demonstrate a breakthrough in connecting ancient texts and current telling of myths in everyday life through her extensive fieldwork in China, which has resulted in her concept of "mythism" (*shenhua zhuyi*). Deming An is Researcher at CASS and has a Ph. D. in Folklore from BNU. While introducing international folklore theories to China, he also developed his own theoretical concept of "hometown folklore." Currently he is also the editor of the journal, *Folk Culture Forum*. Both Yang and An are representatives of the first-generation folklorists after the restoration of Chinese folkloristics in the 1980s.

slow to respond. Few folklorists of our age went aboard. For this reason, we were hoping that our trip abroad would broaden our vision.

At Indiana University, we set a goal for ourselves: to thoroughly and systematically understand Western folklore theories, especially the performance theory. For this reason, we had a number of long conversations and interviews with Professor Richard Bauman. We also had frequent exchanges with Professors Henry Glassie and Linda Dégh, and some others.

Our interest in the performance theory originated from our practical work. In the early 1990s, Lihui Yang, in studying the myth of Nu Wa (a creator in Chinese myths), noticed the vivid tellings of the myth among the common people. She tried to understand this myth by putting it into the context of folk belief in particular communities. At that time, there were brief introductions of the performance theory to China, but nothing detailed. We felt that this theory could shed great light upon the studies of the oral transmission of myths in modern times.

We audited Professor Bauman's graduate course, Social Semiotics of Language. At the same time, we made plans to translate his representative works and conducted several interviews with him. These interviews were eventually organized into one piece titled "Richard Bauman and His Performance Theory", published in the journal, *Folklore Studies* [2003 (1)].

Professor Henry Glassie was one of those who helped us most, and with whom we interacted most while we were in IU. It was a shame that we had known almost nothing about him when he was invited to lecture in Beijing University by Juan Wang in the summer of 2000, except that we were impressed by his passionate lecture with clear language and deep thoughts. It was only after we arrived at IU that we began truly to know and understand him. When we first appeared at the welcome party for all the newcomers in IU, each person made a self-introduction. We felt nervous and ashamed of our English. Before we struggled to the end of our self-introduction, Professor Glassie rescued with his loud voice, "I went to BNU to give a lecture this June. That is the center of Chinese Folklore Studies, the oldest folklore program in China, like ours in the US. So this couple from the oldest folklore program in China are now visiting us, the oldest folklore studies center in the US. It is significant!" That was a great help not only for that occasion, but also for others to know more about us and our own institutions in the time to come.

He also allowed us to audit his class, Proseminar in Folklore Theories and Methods. During the second semester, he shared his precious time with us by selecting a few books and then asking us to discuss them with him each week in his office. It was through these discussions that we began to grasp the deep meaning of performance theory, ethnopoetics, and public folklore, and that we gained a vivid picture of "American folklore studies."

Obviously, each professor in the department at IU opened a door for us to understand American folklore studies, and became our good friend. Linda was retired when we were there, but she gave several interviews to us, and helped us understand "performance-centered" approach with her own studies. We were so happy to have the chance to revisit her during the AFS meeting in 2011. When she passed away in 2014, Lihui Yang wrote a memorial essay for the CFS website: "I believe that Professor Dégh integrated American and Hungarian folklore studies and made a great complementary contribution to the performance-centered approach, and that is worthy of further study. I have been introducing her achievement in my classes since I came back from IU over ten years ago. Her influence is easily discernable in many people's works in BNU, including mine."

Sue Tuohy is a China expert with particular interest in the *huaer* performance in Northwest China. We became good friends and discussed many topics together. When we revisited IU in 2011, she hosted us in her own house, and held a party all the scholars from China. She cooked all the dishes and opened a few bottles of *maotai* liquor that she preserved for years, which truly moved us.

Roger Janelli and Dawnhee Yim are experts on East Asian folklore, well respected in the department. When we left IU, they presented us their collaborative book, *Ancestor Worship and Korean Society*, and said, "This is what we did in the 1970s. What we recorded is no longer practiced in Korea. We are glad that we preserved part of precious history in this book. We hope you can begin to do this kind of work because China is changing rapidly. If things are not recorded, they will disappear quickly. It has great historical significance." We still keep in touch, and revere them as deeply as parents.

John McDowell is such a learned and humorous scholar. His cool style of singing Mexican folk songs while playing his own guitar makes people feel rejuvenated. Gregory Schrempp is an expert of myths. He patiently answered all the questions we asked, and introduced us to another great expert, William Hansen, who gave us some unusual help (see the story below). Professors Beverly Stoeltje, Mary Ellen Brown, and Hasan El-Shamy also helped us in many ways.

In addition, we also made friends with many students at the time, including Jessica Anderson Turner, John Fenn, Lisa Gilman, Kyoim Yun, Kathy Roberts, and some others, who are now the leading folklore scholars in many universities, museums, or organizations.

II. Sharing the Beauty

We have always believed that the exchange of Chinese folkloristics with the rest of the world should be a two-way exchange. On the one hand, Chinese folklorists should actively learn the advanced theories and methods from other countries and broaden our vision, while, at the same time, developing Chinese originality based on the local experience. On the other hand, however, Chinese folklorists should also present their voices and achievements on the international stage so as to realize equal exchange, and "share the beauty" from each culture (in Xiaotong Fei's sense).

During our first year abroad, especially after our return to China, we created a column in the journal, *Folklore Studies* (2001, No. 2; No. 3), with the hope of systematically introducing the overall situation of curriculum and program training in the Department of Folklore and Ethnology of IU with a series of articles in order to share our experience abroad as well as help other Chinese folklorists to know more about American folkloristic studies. Further, we interviewed a number of established scholars for the purpose of introducing their scholarship, theories, and other cutting edge issues in the field to help Chinese folklorists broaden their vision. For various reasons, we only published two interviews: one on Richard Bauman, and the other on Alan Dundes.

Because the performance theory was our focus during our first year in the US, we asked Professor Bauman to suggest his works for translations. He recommended his *Verbal Arts as Performance* (1977). We then began to translate it while we also organized our notes to develop articles. As a result, we have published a series of seven articles on "performance theory."

As we learned more about the theory and related practices and ideas, we thought it would not be enough simply to translate the book. We then, with Professor Bauman's suggestions and approval, developed a reader on performance theory along with his original book, which was published in 2008. Furthermore, Lihui Yang organized two seminars on the theory by inviting interested scholars and publishing their reflections in 2011 and 2015. These efforts clearly helped Chinese folklorists correctly and thoroughly to understand the theory. As a result, Chinese folkloristic studies began, especially from the mid-1990s, to shift the paradigm from text-centered approach to pay more attention to context, process, performer, as well as the modern society.

In addition, we also systematically introduced the theory of ethnopoetics and public folklore. During spring semester 2001, we audited Inta Carpenter's training course on public folklore. We were deeply touched by her idea that folklorists should and must serve the society, directly and effectively, by applying their specialties.

Toward the end of 2003, Professor Xing Zhou invited us to contribute one chapter of American folklore theories and methods to the reader that he was editing, *History, Theory, and Methods of Folkloristics*, which was published by Shangwu Yingshuguan in 2006. Thus we provided a long chapter covering the above-mentioned theories with updated information and ideas.

We also had many chances to work with the public folklorist Robert Baron. He once invited us to the Lowell Folk Festival near Boston, explained to us how public folklorists got involved in the organization of various folklife projects, and how they work with tradition bearers. This experience certainly helped Deming An play his role well as an interpreter and commentator during the 2014 Smithsonian Folklife Festival.

We also have tried our best to introduce American folklore studies to our students through teaching. Since 2001, Lihui Yang has systematically introduced her students in BNU to Bauman's *Verbal Art as Performance*, Glassis's *Passing Time in Ballianmaline*, Dégh's *Folktales and Society*;

Story-telling in a Hungarian Peasant Community, and *American Folklore and Mass Media*, McDowell's "Rethinking Folklorization in Ecuador: Multivocality in the Expressive Contact Zone," as well as Baron and Spitzer's *Public Folklore*. These ideas have been deeply absorbed by the new generation of folklorists in China, who are fast becoming the main force of Chinese folkloristics.

We have also invited a number of American folklorists to lecture at BNU and CASS since 2001. Among these visitors are Richard Bauman, Beverly Stoeltje, Juwen Zhang, Sue Tuohy, Jessica Turner, John Fenn, Robert Baron, Nick Spitzer, Roger Janelli, Dawnhee Yim, Mark Bender, Jiang Lv, Jing Li, Lanlan Kwan, Alan Burdette. We also invited John McDowell, Gregory Schrempp, and Kyoim Yun to Qinghai, Yunnan and other places to attending meetings.

What is worth mentioning here is that our students have begun to join the Sino-US communication. For example, Junxia Wang (see her story in this volume), Pengcheng Zhu, Chengfu Zhang, Duo Zhang have either studied at IU or OSU, and participated in the AFS annual meetings. There is no doubt that the new generation will write a new chapter in this history of exchange.

While we were at IU, Professor Hansen introduced us to the ABC-CLIO press, where we eventually published *Handbook of Chinese Mythology*. It remains the first comprehensive book on Chinese mythology by Chinese folklorists, and reflects the achievements of Chinese scholarship. It was well received, and was reprinted by Oxford University Press. Our friend Jessica Turner took the task of proofreading the English at our request.

Later in our year at IU, we held lectures to introduce Chinese culture and folklore studies. Lihui gave a talk on the contemporary belief in the myth of Nu Wa, and Deming on the agricultural rituals in China. In addition, we presented at different meetings and classes on the northwestern ritual performances and paper-cutting in China. When we were invited to introduce Chinese traditional and folk music at a local broadcast station (WFHB), we played some CDs brought from China. There were quite a few phone callers who asked questions. The next morning, we found a bouquet at our door with a basket of squash. It turned out that one listener found out our address and wanted to thank us with his own garden vegetable.

Overall, our year at IU was filled with wonderful memories and friendships. As Professor McDowell said at the farewell party, we were now seem as members of the Department "family" and ambassadors of Sino-US cultural communication.

In 2006, we spent a year at Harvard University. By then we had gained more confidence in international communication while our own theoretical understanding improved, and there were more opportunities to exchange ideas with others. The folklore program at Harvard was not very strong at the time, with only the Program in Folklore and Mythology. There were few undergraduate level courses on folklore. Professor Stephen Michell was in charge of the Program. Every professor we had contact with was extremely warm and friendly. We worked with some other visiting scholars and started the Asian Cultures Seminar, and presented on "Transformations of Myths in Contemporary China" and "*Shehuo* Performance in Jiezi villages in Gansu, Northwest China." We also organized a symposium on the Religion, Popular Culture, and Social Changes in Asia, and, respectively, presented on "Anti-Globalization and the Reconstruction of Chinese Folk Tradition: A Study of the TV Series *The Legend of Nezha*" and "Temples and Gods on Ye Mountain: Reconstruction and Readaptation of Popular Religion in a Changing Village in Northwest China." These opportunities broadened our vision, and extended the Chinese folklorists' communication with the rest of the world. We also published our experience on the CFS website.

In October 2006, the AFS funded our trip attend its annual meeting. We presented on the "Legitimacy of Temple Festival and Deconstruction and Reconstruction of Myth" at the panel sponsored by the newly established Eastern Asia Folklore Section that Juwen Zhang initiated.

In April 2007, Juwen invited us and helped arrange a series of talks at Willamette University, University of Oregon, and UC Berkeley, and we presented on the topics such as the ICH in China, 2008 Olympic Games in China and the change of traditions, anti-globalism and the reconstruction of Chinese folkloristics. We also attended the WSFS annual meeting with a paper on the "Gods Worship and Social Changes: Decline or Reviving? Example from a Changing Village in Northwest China." Again, these activities enriched us and also promoted Chinese folklore studies.

All in all, we have benefited both personally and professionally in the past twenty years through various exchanges with the American folklore academia. In terms of our professional lives, these visits broke the rigid boxes we were confined to and broadened our views. We were able to gain a deeper understanding of the academic characteristics of folkloristics and the achievements and flaws of American folklore studies. At the same time, it increased my introspection and confidence in Chinese folklore studies, and strengthened my innovative capabilities in terms of theories. The new concepts we have brought up in recent years such as "hometown folklore studies," "mythism," "integrated studies methods," etc. are directly related to our international academic interactions. In terms of our personal lives, our friendships with American folklorists often reminded us of the beauty and kindness of this world. Many folklorists have incredibly deep knowledge and admirable personal character. From just those two aspects, our exchanges with the American folklore academia have contributed greatly to our lives.

(Translation by Juwen Zhang)

安德明（抱女儿安昕）、杨利慧、弗莉·斯道杰、理查德·鲍曼（自左向右），2007 年 7 月。Deming An (carrying Xin), Lihui Yang, Beverly Stoeltje, and Richard Bauman (from left to right), July 2007. Photograph courtesy of Lihui Yang.

Ⅲ. 从书本民俗回到生活民俗——共拓新途

民俗学在中国兴起和发展的轨迹与欧洲和美国的是相同的：出于民族主义思潮，由文学精英对"民间文学"的关注发展到对民间歌谣的搜集，后来再转到对物质生活和信仰行为的研究，直至今天对民众日常生活的探究。但是，对不同国家来说，这个历程中所经历的不同阶段的长短和领域的宽窄则各有特点。

从中美的民俗研究交流可以看出，在1980年代，中国的民俗学基本还是民间文学的代名词。例如，对故事类型、神话、母题等概念的深究。到了1990年代，新一代（即那时获得民俗学博士学位）的民俗学者开始对民间生活有了关注。而美国是在1970年代出现了"公共民俗"（或应用民俗）部门，使民俗研究从学院派扩延到公共生活。那时兴起的"表演论"依然是以"口头艺术"为核心。1980年代后才开始出现越来越多的对物质文化的研究。在中国，近几年来以非物质文化遗产为中心的中国民俗学研究似乎极大地影响了学科的走向。而在2015—2016年的几次有关日常生活的研讨会似乎表面是要寻找更广阔的学科发展新方向。而在美国，因为没有"非遗"的政治影响，学科相对及时地反映了社会的发展，但对日常生活的关注似乎越来越多，例如，族群问题、散居民认同以及当今的有关互联网为媒介的民俗活动，都体现了学科关注点的变化。

无疑，学科关注点的发展变化体现其国家的不同政治和社会背景，以及对传统价值观的态度。从这个意义上说，中国民俗学者的实践似乎正在呈现出一条他们自己的路，无论是研究领域还是研究角度。这将有益于未来的交流，因为未来的世界民俗学发展将会是更多文化的、多国民俗学者之间更平等的、更日常的交流互动。

公共民俗学科发展的扩延，也是美国社会特定时代的产物。这也是民俗研究"回到民间"的必然，是具有"美国特色"的民俗学组成部分。经过几十年的努力，美国的公共民俗部分已经在全国形成了一个自上到下（从国家人文基金会到每个州的"公共民俗学者"专门职位，再到每个市镇的民间文化保护机构）的网络，利用国家和地方政府资助以及民间资源，从"文化保护"开始，一直在做着现在所谓的"文化遗产"的工作。以每年在首都举办的"民间生活节"为代表，推动了全国各地的类似的民间生活节庆活动。同时，利用各级各类博物馆展现民俗传统、建立各级"历史区"（Historic District）突出当地历史和文化、举办各级多元文化节强调地方民俗传统，以及成立各种非政府机构或项目（包括以互联网为平台的项目）推动当地多元文化互动和记录民俗文化传统。

在中国，一方面可以说"公共民俗"是一个新概念；另一方面也可以说中国的（即使是从新中国算起）各级文化部门，从国家的文化部到乡镇的文化馆站，已经是一个完整的公共民俗网络，一直在从事类似"公共民俗"的工作。特别是在过去的十多年里，通过"非遗"运动，具有"中国特色"的公共民俗得到了空前的发展。但是，中国的公共民俗更多的是在政策的实践层面，还有待足够的学术理性和地方社区的支持。这也许是今后中国民俗学需要特别关注的方面。当然，以中国民俗学会为代表的中国民俗学者利用 2005 年的学术会议，使得中国政府对国家的节日体制做出新的改变，这无疑是学术和公共民俗的巨大成就的例证。而目前数千个不同级别的非遗项目无一不包含着民俗学者的努力。

这部分的故事集中反映了民俗学走出"文本"研究，对"民众"生活的关注，体现了三个方面：1）通过对民俗文化和公共民俗的概念的交流和实践，双方都有收获。罗伯特·巴伦的故事更是在感受中进行了理论升华，体现了只有在交流后才有的深刻认识和客观态度，以及对互相学习、取长补短的渴望。道格拉斯·布兰迪的故事便是将民间故事运用于跨文化交流的极佳例证。是否让狼死掉所隐含的问题绝不是故事母题的改变问题，而是一个文化价值观和世界观的问题。他的故事也让我们学会如何在面对面的协商中达到和谐。陈泳超的感受不仅是关于从文学到民俗的跨越，也涉及跨文化交流中的全球化与本土化的问题本质。杨利慧和安德明以自身的经历展示了中国民俗学在对外交流中的成长，以及在走向世界的过程中的角色转换。2）以合作方式利用博物馆进行传统文化的教育和跨文化传播。杜赫斯特、麦克多维尔、谢沐华、杜韵红、张丽君分别从他们个人角度讲述了在博物馆交流项目的感受，展示了在中国公共民俗的发展空间。3）通过民俗影视工作坊培养民俗学者对日常生活的记录。莎伦·谢尔曼和孙正国以举办民俗影视工作坊的经验讲述了另外的将学术民俗与公共民俗结合的事例，同时也讲述了个人在交流互访中所经历的观念的改变。

III. From Folklore in Books back to Folklore in Practice—Opening Up New Paths

Chinese folkloristics originated from and developed along the same path as that of the West (Europe and the US): driven by an upsurge of nationalism, the literary elite began to pay attention to "folk literature"; they first began to collect ballads, then turned to material culture and behavioral studies, and, finally, to today's exploration of everyday life. The depth and breadth of investigations into folklife at each stage in this process, however, showed different characteristics in different countries.

As seen in Sino-US folklore communication, by the 1980s, folk literature (*minjian wenxue*) was the term used generally for folklore in China; it focused on tales, myths, and motifs. By the 1990s, however, the new generation of folklorists (those who received doctorates in folklore and some in folk literature), turned their attention to folklife.

A similar interest in folklife, or "public folklore," in the US had emerged in the 1970s, as an expansion of folklore studies which had begun to use the performance-centered approach that was still focusing on "verbal art." This new interest emerged from that particular society in that particular historical period. American public folklore has its own "American characteristics": it has become a sector with a national network from top to bottom: from non-governmental resources and federally funded NEH and NEA to the state and town funded "folklorists." Its "culture conservation" work has been engaged in what in other places is called "cultural heritage" projects. Meanwhile, the annual national folklife festival has stimulated similar festivals all over the country at different levels. For example, the US has been defining and building various folklife museums and "historic districts" across the country, in order to recognize and protectlocal cultures and traditions and to enrich the diversity of "American culture." These investigations and events are very much like those in other countries with the ICH label.

It was after the 1980s that interest in material culture, as well as "ethnic/immigrant folklore" grew in the US. In China, the attention to safeguarding "Intangible Cultural Heritage" (ICH) since 2003 seems to have greatly influenced the direction and scope of folkloristic studies. However, a series of seminars on everyday life in Beijing and Guangzhou in 2015 and 2016 were designed to seek new directions for the discipline. In contrast, American folklore studies, probably because the US has not ratified the UNESCO's ICH Convention, seem not to have been affected by the political aspect of the Convention. Thus, folklore studies in the US appear to have been growing robustly, but with more focus on its own ethnic issues, diaspora identity, and current Internet groups. Academic foci reveal the political and social development in a county, as well as its change of attitude toward traditional values. Chinese folklorists seem to have found a path for enhancing the scope and perspective of their discipline by recognizing their cultural roots. Future discourse in the realm of world folkloristics will benefit from China's new perspective and will move toward more diverse and regularized cross-cultural exchanges and, most importantly, toward communication on a basis of equality.

In China today, public folklore, on the one hand, is a new concept; on the other hand, since the 1950s China has been equipped with a national public folklore network through culture departments at all levels from the Ministry of Culture to Culture Stations in remote villages. The nationwide ICH movement in the past ten years or so has boosted a "public culture/cultural industry" sector with "Chinese characteristics." However, China's ICH practice is largely at the policy level, and needs to be supported with more academic theories and local communities. This is an aspect of Chinese folkloristics that needs to be strengthened. Of course, that theCentral Government changed the festival system because of the effort of folklorists (e. g., the AFS and CFS conference in 2005) is certainly a great example of the achievement of academic and public folklorists. Thousands of ICH items, currently recognized at all levels, are inseparable from the hard work of Chinese folklorists.

Stories in this section also reflect Sino-US communication on the issue of the "folk" through folklife studies, which have moved away from the "text-centered" approach, as demonstrated in the following: 1) Mutual benefit advances through communication on the concept and practice of folk culture and public folklore. Robert Baron, in writing about his experiences, reveals a deep understanding and objective attitude, which could only have been achieved through sincere and equal exchanges with his Chinese colleagues. Douglas Blandy's story best illustrates how a folktale can be used to reach the very goal of cross-cultural understanding. Whether or not to kill the wolf is never simply a question of a motif in a tale; it is, rather, a question of cultural values and worldview. His story teaches us how to achieve harmony through face-to-face interaction. Yongchao Chen's experience not only is a crossing from literature to folklore, but also involves the core issue of globalization and localization in cross-cultural communication. 2) Engagement in public education through collaborative museum projects. Kurt Dewhurst, Marsha MacDowell, Mohua Xie, Yunhong Du, and Lijun Zhang tell their stories about the museum exchange projects, pointing out the direction for future development in Chinese public folklore. 3) Training folklorists to document everyday life through video camera. Sharon Sherman and Zhengguo Sun tell their stories about holding workshops in China and the US, connecting academic and public folklore interests, as well as how their personal views have changed.

初识的印象，持久的记忆

罗伯特·巴龙*

2007年，当我第一次被邀请到中国参加系列讲座时，我并不知道会发生什么。那次同行的还有尼克·斯皮泽。中国起初并不在我的访问清单上，但是当我被邀请时，我感到欢欣雀跃。我想象着那会是怎样迅猛发展和高度现代化的国家，揣测着其传统文化能否适应这种快速的发展进程。关于中国，生长于五六十年代的我被灌输的是妖魔化、异类化和作为敌对方的"红色中国"。从90年代开始，通过接触来自中国的访问学者，我心底存留的误会被修正了。但是中国对我来说还是充满异域的神秘感，我知道要想真正了解中国，亲自去一趟是必要的。我对中国的公众民俗学实践和研究知之甚少。鉴于民俗学这一学科在许多国家日渐衰落，我并没有奢望在中国的民俗学界看到多么蓬勃繁荣的学术氛围。见到中国民俗学者高丙中、安德明让我联想到，在美国民俗学会的国际文化交流组织计划执行伊始的2007年年会时，我注意的民俗学在中国是一个备受尊敬的学科，承载着众多有识之士的重要学术贡献。虽然许多年前我就到过南亚和东南亚地区，但是我知道中国是不同的，我有些焦虑，不知道学术交流和人际沟通的礼仪是什么。我阅读了有关外来旅华者应该如何表现的文献。我的老朋友安德鲁·科利尔是一位驻香港记者，他给了我很好的建议。他中肯地指出，我作为一个美国人到中国作讲座要保持谦逊。我不能想当然地认为美国人对中国的民俗学科了如指掌，甚至认为对中国的一切了如指掌。当提起美国对中国历史认识和文化史认识时，我需要承认我们犯了错误，并且试着指出和修正它们。

朋友们，2008年1月初，在一个寒冷的早晨，当我终于抵达北京时，我惊讶极了。从落地的那一刻起，我就明白这是一次需要每时每刻保持清醒、张开每一个毛孔去感知的充满新奇、令人兴奋的旅程。这个国家蕴藏的活力和能量比我想象中的还要巨大。它处在极快速

---

* 编者注：罗伯特·巴龙现任纽约州艺术委员会民间艺术项目和音乐项目的负责人，同时任教于古彻学院文化可持续性方向硕士项目。他在宾夕法尼亚大学获得博士学位。作为一个公众民俗学者，他不仅领导开展了许多公众民俗学项目，还出版了很多理论著作，例如合编的《公众民俗学》（2007）和《克里奥尔杂糅化：文化的创造力》（2013）。他的访问、讲座和翻译过来的文章在中国很受欢迎；同时他在中国致力于推广公众民俗学的概念，这一工作极大地鼓舞了同样躬耕于这一领域的中国民俗学者。《中美民俗学现状》一文是他与中国民俗学者康保成、王敦合作的成果之一，于2014年发表于《美国民俗学刊》上。他深刻的反思和建议代表了美国民俗学者的看法，某种程度上也反映了在亚民俗交流中受益良多的中国民俗学者的心声。

的发展节奏中,高楼林立,后现代建筑灯光闪耀,在新设计的高速公路、同心环路上,在城市街道间,在新建的地铁里,繁忙的交通随处可见。但是,相比于纽约,我惊叹于这里相对平静的生活节奏,我非常高兴能够看到古老的庙宇、街上的商贩,体会充满文化活力的传统饮食民俗。尼克和我在中央民族大学住了一个星期,中央民族大学有很多来自全国各地的少数民族的学生。我从前听说在中国文化里,汉族在方方面面都是权力持有者,但是在这个充满多元文化的大学里,少数民族是权力持有者,我的误解又一次被消除了。在民大里,民俗学和人类学这两个学科都建设得很好,其中人类学所是由马林诺夫斯基的一个学生创建的。我看到这里开展了大量的少数民族对本民族文化的研究。

从开始访问,中国主办方就极尽地主之谊,热情友善地招待我们。我们在参观当地历史古迹、文化名胜和宗教场所的过程中,与许多学生建立了友谊,他们全程陪着我们参观。和其他来华参观者一样,我们享受这种同行们经常聚在一起吃一大桌子菜、觥筹交错的饭局。我们在民大周边的少数民族小饭馆喝酒喝到凌晨。我们收到了很多小礼物,有些是同学们做的非常朴实的小礼物。

我们在民大作了讲座,第二周又到北京的其他高校作了讲座。这些学生对美国的民俗学研究和生活都展现出了极大的兴趣。访问期间,他们也围绕北京这座城市,围绕长城,为我们介绍了中国的文化。我们惊异于中国的年轻一代和他们的上一代有那么大的不同。在上一代里,除了那些在美国做过访问学者的教师,其他教师都不会说英语。与之不同的是,这一代学生虽然也都没去过美国,但是他们能够用英语交流,对美国流行文化的熟悉程度更是惊人。那天我在北京大学的讲座结束了,中午吃饭时,中央党校的一名学生拿来一份他英译的中共中央五年规划建议给我看。几天后,尼克和我叫他一起吃饭。他告诉我们他最近很焦虑,因为他即将参加国家公务员考试,竞争非常激烈。我问他那是怎样的考试,他说就像GRE那样。我太吃惊了。和我们遇到的许多中国年轻人一样,他也喜欢《绝望主妇》和《越狱》这类电视剧。

我们在讲座上讨论了自经济大萧条以来的美国公众民俗学理论和实践的整体发展情况。在我的记者朋友安德鲁·科利尔的建议下,我们对美国解决自身难题的方式有所认识,我们认识到公众民俗学实践能够创造一个尊重多元文化的平等社会,进而解除这些难题。我们从中国同行那里了解到中国民俗学在学科建设方面的困境和成绩。北京师范大学是繁荣兴盛的民俗学中心,这里已经培养出了一百多名民俗学专业的研究生。但我们了解到这一中心被分割为两个民俗学研究所:一个侧重从民间文学的视角开展教学与科研活动,另一个侧重民族志的研究方法。后者是我们受邀开展讲座的研究所。在北京大学,民俗学研究是在人类学系开展的。两位来自中国社会科学院的学者热烈地讨论了我的报告,他们受到胡塞尔的影响,从现象学层面对民俗进行了分析。这里的民俗学者正在把高深的理论推向实践,投身于重要的民俗学工作。但这些美国都不知道;不幸的是,这些到现在也没有翻译到美国。鉴于近年来缺少新的民俗学理论,美国应该关注中国学者在界定概念方面的成果。

能够在中国社会科学院设有以民俗为研究对象的研究所,足见民俗学在中国的地位和对民俗学研究、对民俗的重视。在中国同类研究机构中,社科院是最重要的智库和研究中心。

读罢那名学生给我的中共中央五年规划建议译文，发现这个在中国起关键作用的政策制定机构，能够把保护那些有价值的濒危传统文化放在优先地位，我感到又惊又喜。我还震惊地发现在中国，民俗学比人类学拥有更大的学术园地，有30多个研究生项目。放眼全球，民俗学的学科地位在许多国家都已衰落，在中国却正在攀升。

通过到中国演讲，把我的想法传播给非美国听众，我关于公众民俗学的思想逐渐结晶。我在中国演讲的部分内容，见于随后发表的两篇文章中：一是《美国公众民俗学：历史、问题和挑战》，中文译文发表于中山大学主办的《文化遗产》期刊，英文发表于印度的《印度民俗研究期刊》；二是《异化之罪？——公众民俗学和文化旅游项目中的机构、媒介和社区的文化自决》，发表于《美国民俗学刊》。

自2008年初次访问中国后，我又四次前往中国做讲座和参加会议。最近的一次是在2015年，我在华东师范大学、上海美国文化交流中心（北达科他大学／上海理工大学）和南京美国文化交流中心（纽约科学技术研究所／南京邮电大学）做了讲座。我分别于2010年和2011年两次前往广东。其中一次是为了参加由美国民俗学会中美计划和中山大学组织的"首届中美非物质文化遗产论坛：政策比较"研讨会。在中山大学访问期间，我接受了王敦的访谈，介绍了纽约州的民俗和我作为纽约州艺术委员会民间艺术项目负责人的工作情况。这次访谈发表在《文化遗产》上（《他山之石：对话纽约州艺术委员会民俗部罗伯特·巴龙》，2012年第4期，第110—115页）。几个月后，我和王敦、康保成在网上进行了一次三人谈。康保成是中山大学的资深教授。这次访谈和先前关于纽约民俗的访谈内容一起发表于《美国民俗学刊》（127：264—284，2014），题为《中美民俗学现状：三人谈》（与康、王）。康对中国民俗学研究范畴的论述，加深了我对中国民俗学学科的敬意。它有与亚洲、欧洲、美国对话的学术视野，进而形成了自己独特的学科发展路径。作为公众民俗学者，当我听说中国现在可以授予非物质文化遗产（非遗）方向的博士学位，我很嫉妒。非遗博士学位相当于公众民俗学博士学位。中国斥资数千万美元扶持制定非遗政策和保护非遗项目，资金投入令美国在公众民俗学政策和项目上的投资相形见绌，在这一背景下推进非遗保护的前沿性研究意义重大。

通过中国之行，我们和中国同行们建立了长期的工作关系和友谊。几年过去了，尼克和我总算于2013年和2014年，在美国组织了学术交流和文化体验活动作为答谢。2013年，尼克和我在圣塔菲高级研究院组织了一次主题为"非物质文化遗产政策与实践对传统文化的保护：中美比较"的高级研讨会，中国民俗学者安德明、杨利慧、高丙中、张巧云和非物质文化遗产相关领导马盛德，与美国民俗学者伊丽莎白·彼得森和杰茜卡·特纳一道参加了会议。新墨西哥是一个展现美国传统文化活力的绝佳地点。前往西班牙裔社区和普韦布洛社区的旅程让我们的中国同行感到难以置信的惊喜，就像我们在中国体验到的那种惊喜。我们邀请我们的朋友安德明、高丙中和云南民俗学者黄龙光观摩和出席2014年以中国为主题的史密森民俗节。他们对美国公众民俗学运行模式的亲身体验和向美国民众展示中国民俗的经历，能够帮助他们理解我们在中国做讲座时所讨论的内容，并为他们在中国的学术研究和顾问工作提供思路。为了回应圣塔菲高级研究院的会议，云南大学、红河学院和尼克、我联合组织了一次题为"从东亚和美国的视角看传统艺术作为非物质文化遗产的传承与保护"的会议。会议集聚了来自中国、日本、韩国、菲律宾、越南,以及美国史密森尼民俗与文化传统中心和美国国会图书馆的美国民俗中心的民俗学同行们。把学术对话的范围扩展到东亚其他国家,我们看到他们保护非物质文化遗产的长期经验为美国提供了重要的范式。这包括由当地利益驱动的创意文化旅游规划和为表彰杰出传统文化传承人(包括支持传统文化传播)而设置的项目。他们对非遗保护实践的成绩和困境的分析也具有指导意义。中国学者通过多次的民族志调研,观察当地对在日常生活中展示宗教性实践项目的反响,进而对政府非遗保护计划对当地社区的影响进行了极为深入的评估。

美国民俗学者将维持这种互惠互利的学术交往,这对所有参与者来说都将带来转变,收获满满。对我而言,这在我的人生经历和职业生涯中具有重要的奠基意义。它们改变了我作为一名实践者和学者的思维方式和实践方式。我很珍视这些经历,常常忆起这些经历。

(辽宁师范大学刘思诚翻译)

First Impressions, Enduring Memories

Robert Baron*

I didn't know what to expect when, in 2007, I was first invited to visit China for a lecture series with Nick Spitzer. China wasn't on my bucket list of places to visit, but when invited I leapt at the opportunity. I imagined rampant development and hypermodernity and wondered about the resilience of traditional culture in a rapidly changing nation. Growing up in the fifties and sixties I was exposed to the demonization and othering of "Red China" as an antithesis of the United States. My interactions from time to time since the 1990s with visitors from China corrected residual distortions I'd internalized, but China remained exotic and mysterious and I knew that a firsth and experience would be indispensable to begin to truly understand it. I knew little about the public practice and study of folklore in China. Since folklore has declined as an academic discipline in many countries, I didn't expect to find a thriving academic field in China. Meeting Chinese folklorists like Bingzhong Gao and Deming An brought to the 2007 annual AFS meeting at the onset of the AFS initiative, I saw that Folklore is a respected discipline possessing intellectually adventurous scholars producing important scholarship. Although I had travelled to South Asia and Southeast Asia many years before, I knew China would be quite different and I was uncertain and anxious encountering its protocols of professional and interpersonal behavior. I read up on how travelers should behave in China. And my old friend Andrew Collier, a Hong Kong based journalist, gave me great advice. He counselled me to be humble as an American when lecturing in China. I should not assume that Americans know it all about their discipline—or anything else.

---

* Robert Baron currently directs the Folk Arts Program and the Music Program at the New York State Council on the Arts and teaches in the Masters in Cultural Sustainability Program at Goucher College. He received a Ph. D. in Folklore and Folklife from the University of Pennsylvania. As a public folklorist, he has not only conducted many public folklore projects, but also published many theoretical studies, including co-edited *Public Folklore* (2007) and *Creolization as Cultural Creativity* (2013). His visits, lectures, and translated articles in China have been well received, and his work in promoting the concept of public folklore in China has greatly stimulated Chinese folklorists who are struggling to define such a field. One of his collaborative work with Chinese folklorists, Baocheng Kang and Dun Wang, resulted in the article on the States of the Folklore Profession in China and the United States in the *Journal of American Folklore* (2014). His sincere reflections and suggestions here are representative of all American folklorists, and Chinese counterparts as well in this sense, who have been involved in such mutually beneficial communication.

When discussing the American historical and cultural experience, I should acknowledge that we made mistakes and have tried to address and correct them.

Oh man, how I was surprised when we finally arrived in Beijing on a chilly morning in early January 2008. From the moment I landed it was clear that this was the kind of trip where I would be highly conscious every waking hour, with my pores way open to novel and exciting experiences. The dynamism and expansive energy of the country pulsed even more that I expected. It was developing at an extremely rapid pace with forests of very tall apartment buildings, postmodern architecture with dazzling lighting and loads of traffic everywhere on newly designed superhighways and concentric loop roads as well as along city streets and in freshly built subways. Yet, coming from New York City, I was struck by the relatively unfrenzied pace of life, and delighted to see old temples and street vendors and experience the traditional dining customs and foodways of a resilient ancient culture. Settling into our lodgings for a week at the Chinese University of Nationalities (CUN, now known as Minzu University of China), Nick and I were immersed in a university community made up of minorities from all over China. I'd heard of Han domination of all spheres of Chinese culture, but here again misperceptions were dispelled in experiencing a remarkably diverse university, with ethnic minorities holding positions of authority. Folklore and Anthropology are well established disciplines at Minzu University, with the anthropology department founded by a student of Malinowski. I saw that the study of minority cultures is extensively undertaken by the members of these cultures themselves.

The fellowship, friendship and warm hospitality of our Chinese hosts was nearly overwhelming from the outset of our visit. Students accompanied us everywhere, and we became friendly with many of them as we visited local cultural, historical and religious sites. Like other visitors to China hosted by colleagues, we enjoyed frequent meals with a large variety of dishes shared among us, and boisterous mutual toasting over drinks. The drinking continued to the wee hours at small ethnic restaurants in CUN's neighborhood. We received many little gifts, even from students of very modest means.

Students expressed great interest in American folklore studies and about life in the United States at Minzu and the other Beijing universities, where we lectured the second week. And they, in turn, introduced us to Chinese culture in our journeys around the city and to the Great Wall. We were struck by the vast generational differences between young people and their elders. With the exception of those who had been visiting scholars in the US, no faculty members spoke English. In contrast, students, none of whom had been to the US, spoke English colloquially and were startlingly familiar with American popular culture. At a lunch following my lecture at Peking University, a student at Party School of the Central Committee of CPC asked me to look at an English translation he made of the Central Committee's five year plan for the nation. Nick and I took him to dinner a couple of days later. He told us he was anxious because he was among those chosen in a highly competitive selection process to take the examination for the civil service of the Central Committee which would occur soon. I was taken aback by his response to my question about what the test is like: "It's like the GRE's." Like many other Chinese youth we met, his favorite television programs included *Desperate Housewives*, and *Prison Break*.

Our lectures discussed American public folklore theory and practice, providing an overview of its development since the Great Depression. Following the advice of my journalist friend Andrew Collier about recognizing how the US tries to work through its problems, we considered how applied and public folklore addressed the challenges of the US in creating an egalitarian society that respected cultural pluralism. From our Chinese colleagues we learned about the disciplinary challenges and advances of their folklore discipline. At Beijing Normal University, a thriving center for folklore studies with well over a hundred graduate students, we learned that there are two separate folklore programs. One teaches and researches folklore from a literary perspective, the other, where we lectured, has an ethnographic approach. At Peking University, folklore is studied within an anthropology department. Scholars at the Chinese Academy of Social Sciences (CASS) who critically discussed my lecture included two who approach folklore phenomenologically, influenced by their study of Husserl. Here were folklorists practicing high theory, engaged in a critical folkloristics unknown and, unfortunately, as yet untranslated in the United States. Given the dearth of folklore theory in recent years, the conceptual work of Chinese scholars needs to be known in our country.

The presence of a department of the CASS devoted to folklore demonstrates the respected status and importance of folklore studies, and folklore, in China. CASS is the most important think tank and research center of its kind in China. Reading the translation of the five year plan of the Central Committee that the student gave me, I was surprised and delighted to see that safeguarding of valued, endangered traditions was viewed as a priority for this key policy making body. I was also astonished to learn that Folklore is a bigger field than Anthropology in China, with more than 30 graduate programs. In a world where Folklore's disciplinary status has diminished in many countries, in China the discipline is on an upswing.

My talks in China proved invaluable as opportunities to crystallize my ideas about public folklore in communicating them to a non-American audience. Two subsequent publications included portions of my talks in China: "American Public Folklore: History, Issues, Challenges," published in Chinese in *Cultural Heritage*, a journal of Sun Yat-sen University and in English in India in *Indian Folklore Research Journal*, and "Sins of Objectification? —Agency, Mediation and Community Cultural Self-Determination in Public Folklore and Cultural Tourism Programming," published in the *Journal of American Folklore*.

I returned to China four more times for lectures and conferences since my initial visit in 2008. Most recently, in 2015, I lectured at East China Normal University and the American Centers for

Cultural Exchange in Shanghai (University of North Dakota/University of Shanghai for Science and Technology) and Nanjing (New York Institute for Science and Technology/Nanjing University of Posts and Telecommunications). I made two trips to Guangdong, in 2010 and 2011, one of which was for the First China-US Forum on Intangible Cultural Heritage: Comparative Policies, organized by AFS's China-US initiative and Sun Yat-sen University. While visiting Sun Yat-sen University I was interviewed by Dun Wang about folklore in New York State and my work as Folk Arts Director at the New York State Council on the Arts. This interview was published in *Cultural Heritage*. I subsequently engaged in a trialogue, carried out in cyberspace over a number of months, with Dun Wang and Baocheng Kang, a senior faculty member at Sun Yat-sen University. It was published along with the previous interview with me about New York folklore in the *JAF* as "States of the Folklore Profession in China and the United States: A Trialogue" (with Kang and Wang) (127: 264 - 284, 2014). Kang's account of the range and scope of Chinese folklore studies reinforced and expanded my esteem for the discipline in China. It spoke to the breadth of scholarship from Asia, Europe and the US that has influenced Chinese folklore scholarship as it has forged its distinctive, developing approach to the discipline. As a public folklorist, I was envious when I heard that it is now possible to earn a doctorate in Intangible Cultural Heritage (ICH), which could be compared to a Ph. D. in public folklore. Advanced study in ICH is of great importance now that China is investing tens of millions of dollars for programs to document and safeguard ICH, an investment which dwarfs American funding for public folklore documentation and programming.

Our experiences in China created enduring professional relationships and friendships with Chinese colleagues. It took several years, but Nick and I were able in 2013 and 2014 to reciprocate with academic exchanges and cultural experiences in the US. Nick and I organized an advanced seminar in 2013 at the School for Advanced Research (SAR) in Santa Fe, "Intangible Cultural Heritage Policies and Practices for Safeguarding Traditional Culture—Comparing China and the United States" that included the Chinese folklorists Deming An, Lihui Yang, Bingzhong Gao and Qiaoyun Zhang and intangible cultural heritage leaders Shengde Ma along with American folklorists Elizabeth Peterson and Jessica Turner. New Mexico was a perfect place to introduce resilient American traditional cultures. Tours to Hispano and Pueblo communities provided an experience of the United States that was wholly unexpected to our Chinese colleagues, providing pleasant surprises to them that paralleled the surprises we experienced in China. Our friends Deming An, Bingzhong Gao and the Yunnan folklorist Longguang Huang were invited to observe and present at the Chinese program of the 2014 Smithsonian Folklife Festival. Their firsthand experience of public folklore methods in the US and presentations of Chinese folklore to American audiences illustrated what we had discussed in our lectures in China and provided ideas for their own scholarship and advisory work in China. Reciprocating for the SAR conference, Yunnan University and Honghe University collaborated with Nick and me to organize a conference, "Safeguarding and Representing Traditional

Arts as Intangible Cultural Heritage: East Asian and American Perspectives." The conference brought together folklorists from China, Japan, South Korea, Philippines, Vietnam, along with American colleagues from the Smithsonian Center for Folklife and Cultural Heritage and the American Folklife Center of the Library Congress. Broadening our dialogue to include other East Asian countries, we saw that their long experience of safeguarding intangible culture heritage provides important models for Americans. These include innovative cultural tourism initiatives driven by local interests and programs for honoring outstanding tradition bearers that include support for transmission of their traditions. Their critical analysis of both successful practices and pitfalls of safeguarding ICH was also instructive. Chinese scholars have developed especially trenchant analyses of the impact of government ICH initiatives upon local communities, with many conducting ethnographic research local responses on efforts to present religious practices as secular, display events.

American folklorists continue to engage in reciprocal, mutually beneficial relationships that are immensely fruitful and personally transformative for all involved. For me, they have been keystone personal and professional experiences of lifelong value. They have changed the way I think and act in my work as both a practitioner and scholar. I treasure these experiences and think of them often.

让不让狼死掉

道格拉斯·布兰迪[*]

"中国藤"网页的使命在于教育英语世界的儿童、青年和成人了解中国文化的遗产。这项任务的推广主要借由中国藤的门户网站及社交媒体，如脸书、图享、网络相簿、推特、风云、视频播客网站、新浪和土豆等来实现的。中国藤还有公开的文档资料，可通过俄勒冈大学图书馆获得（网址 https://oregondigital.org/sets/chinavine）。中国藤相关的公开可用资料是免费的，在知识共享许可的授权下用于非商业性的教育目的。

中国藤起源于2007年，是由中佛罗里达大学的克里斯汀·康登、山东艺术设计职业学院的潘鲁生，还有我本人的合作项目而开始的。自成立以来，来自中国的更多的民俗学者，包括北京师范大学的杨利慧、华东师范大学的陈勤建和中央民族大学的苏日娜都参与到了该项目的合作或咨询中。

中国藤的核心在于它是来自中美两国的不同师生团队的田野合作。此前的田野合作在北京、上海、济南和山东的农村、云南、贵州、内蒙古以及四川省甘孜藏族自治州已经陆陆续续展开了。被调查的对象包括藏族、蒙古族、苗族、白族和汉族。田野工作者记录了传统手工艺人、音乐家、当代艺术家的作品以及一些节日和表演。田野团队作为学习社团而工作，参与到由围绕中国文化遗产的民俗问题所引导的知识获取与建构中，同时也向公众解释和传递这一遗产。

过去十多年的项目工作带来了无数难忘的回忆。诸如，我们了解到一个制作传统风筝的家庭在"文革"期间如何保护风筝的模型；采访到所剩不多的其中一位中国戏曲鬃人制作者；看到一本具有数世纪历史的西藏唐卡绘画比例的书；记录了内蒙古屠羊的仪式并确定如何以最佳方式将其呈现在儿童和青少年可以看到的网站上；还包括受邀去参加云南白族人的绕三灵节，苗族的姐妹节和内蒙古巴戎寺的敖包节。

然而，我所关注的一次难忘的经验是克里斯汀·康登和我的学生们如何充分地与中国的师生互动，并以此获取知识。对于很多参与田野工作的美国学生，以及由此所产生的文化解

---

[*] 编者注：道格拉斯·布兰迪现任俄勒冈大学艺术与行政教授，副教务长。布兰迪在俄亥俄州立大学获得艺术教育博士学位，发表许多有关艺术、文化和教育方面的著述，并以独特的途径参与了有关中国民俗的项目：通过互联网的视频和文字方式传播中国村落生活以便教育英语受众。布兰迪与中国民俗学者合作的经历具有典范性意义，扩延了传统的学科界限。而他在此所讲述的故事触及了跨文化交流的核心，也揭示了我们记录亚民俗的目的。

释，中国藤提供了初次的经验。中国藤上的内容都是与中国合作伙伴商议的结果。对于美国学生而言，初次形成的解释材料没有完全符合中国观点这并不罕见。中国藤的重点在于解释方法产生碰撞时的调解过程。

神话和民间故事植根于文化价值内，往往会产生这样的碰撞。想象一下，正在进行的就迪斯尼公司将民间故事和神话挪用作商业和娱乐目的的讨论。有时，这也被称作"迪斯尼化"，这样的解释过程往往会导致与特定文化群体或传统有关的对故事的重大改变，以使故事对于受众来说易于理解。

以狼为例。狼的形象出现在包括北美、欧洲、亚洲等跨文化的神话和民间故事中。在中国，孤立的狼故事渗透在文化中，一个众所周知的故事是关于中山狼的，他所讲述的是软心肠面对邪恶而带来的危险。另一个与狼有关的故事与山东省冠县狼村相关。这个故事是中国藤田野工作队所收集到的，故事与讲给儿童青少年听的狼的故事就有出入。它们都被提议放到中国藤网站上。

狼村的得名，与附近地区的一则民间故事有关，这则民间故事为当地人所熟知。在中国历史上的战国时期，狼这种动物折磨着狼村，它们攻击并咬死儿童。为了挽救孩子们，村人将烹制面团制成儿童的样子，内装毒药，然后投喂给狼，以此杀死狼群。

制作面人在狼村一度是普遍的，狼秀才是仅存不多的几个仍在持续此传统的村民之一。他将制作好的面人在市场上当作玩具出售，并解释说他所制作的面人代表着对于中国文化很重要的美德以及狼村的历史。山东艺术设计职业学院民间艺术研究院的学者估计，经狼秀才所制作的面人有超过两千多不同的造型。

动画书《狼和面人儿童》被放在中国藤网站上（http://chinavine.org/2011/06/16/wolf-and-dough-children/），作为解释狼村和由狼秀才所制作的面人的一个部分。这本动画书的学生开发者起初修改了这个故事的结尾，狼并没有因为吃到投喂的有毒面团而致死，而是生病逃走了。故事结尾改变的动机在于，书籍的开发者出于对保护美国濒危物种狼群的敏感，以及对于杀死狼可能会过度引起恐慌的担忧，因为儿童会看这本书。

在与中国藤的合作过程中，康登、几个美国学生和我就在《狼和面人儿童》中所出现的狼应不应该被杀死的问题与民俗学者杨利慧及她的几个研究生展开了讨论。在杨看来，狼应该被杀死似乎是没有疑问的，不杀死狼会影响到故事的本真性。她的研究生在这一问题上更加坚决，并且激烈地辩论（应该杀死狼），否则就会成为被西方人所持有的帝国主义观点所左右的又一个例子。就此反应，我和克里斯汀并不感到惊讶，或许早已经预感到了这种结果，但仍想教育我们的学生去认识世界文化遗产背景中的复杂性和情感问题。

关于杀死狼的交谈极其丰富、细致入微并且富含知识。对于中国藤不可或缺的是中国当前正在发生的快速变化以及这些变化对中国传统文化遗产的影响。我所遇到的中国的民俗学家、艺术家和其他学者，他们都表达了保护传统的愿望，同时也承认传统正在发生演化。《狼和面人儿童》，如同任何一个跨地域和跨语境的物质文化的例子，需要就与其相关的不同的思想意识及世界观而受到完全和公开的质询，因为它跨越时间、文化和语境。然而，考虑到中国藤的使命，与此项目相关的民俗研究方法，以及这个故事对于狼村集体认同的中心性地位，学生们开始理解尊重狼村受访者们所讲述的故事本身的重要性。在此书的结尾，狼被毒死了。

　　与《狼和面人儿童》相关的解释过程证明了中国藤田野工作团队的真实的学习历程，之所以真实是因为对与项目相关的解释所进行的质询包含有中美两国师生的价值观、态度和信仰；之所以真实是因为通过阐释所获得的知识是经过商讨的，商议的过程是通过与具体田野经历相关的有意义的社会互动，通过对产生首次解释以及随后对这一解释的审议并由此在中美两国参与者之间就做出最终结论而达成相互共识的经验进行深思而实现的。解释《狼和面人儿童》的这次经历之所以难忘，是因为这一经验在传统大学课堂教学环境中很难得以实践。

（北京师范大学张丽翻译）

狼秀才 Láng Xiucai. Photograph by Douglas Blandy

狼秀才做的面人 Dough figures by Láng Xiucai. Photograph by Douglas Blandy

Killing the Wolf

Douglas Blandy[*]

ChinaVine's mission is to educate children, youth, and adults about China's cultural heritage. This mission is primarily realized through the online portal *ChinaVine.org* along with social media such as *Facebook*, *Instagram*, *Flickr*, *Twitter*, *Soundcloud*, *Vimeo*, *Sina*, and *Todou*. *ChinaVine* also consists of an open archive available through the University of Oregon (UO) Library at https://oregondigital.org/sets/chinavine. The publicly available materials associated with *ChinaVine* are freely available for use for educational non-commercial purposes under a Creative Commons license.

ChinaVine originated in 2007 as a collaboration between Kristin Congdon at the University of Central Florida, Pan Lusheng at Shandong Vocational College of Art and Design, and me, Doug Blandy, at the UO. Since its inception, additional folklorists in China have collaborated or consulted on the project including Lihui Yang at Beijing Normal University, Qinjian Chen at East China Normal University, and Surna at Minzu University of China.

Core to *ChinaVine* is collaborative fieldwork by teams of scholars and students from China and the United States. Fieldwork has been conducted in, and around, Beijing, Shanghai, and Jinan as well is in rural Shandong, Yunnan, Guizhou, Inner Mongolia, and the Kandźe Tibetan Autonomous Prefecture in Sichuan Province. Interviewees have included members of the Tibetan, Mongolian, Miao, Bai, and Han ethnic groups. Fieldworkers have documented the work of traditional craftspeople, musicians, contemporary artists as well as festivals and performances. Fieldwork teams operate as learning communities engaged in knowledge acquisition and construction guided by folkloristic questions around China's cultural heritage along with the interpretation and

---

[*] Douglas Blandy is Professor Arts and Administration and holds the position of Senior Vice Provost for Academic Affairs at the University of Oregon. With his doctorate in Art Education from Ohio State University, Blandy has published extensively on art, culture and education, and engaged in projects on Chinese folklore through a unique revue-educating English speakers on Chinese culture by audio-visual-text showing Chinese village life via the Internet. Blandy's exemplary work in China and collaboration with Chinese folklorists has extended the traditional disciplinary boundary, and his story here touches the very core of cross-cultural communication, as well as the very purpose of documenting our metafolklore.

communication of this heritage to others.

Over the ten-year history of the project there have been numerous memorable experiences. These have included learning about how a traditional kite making family preserved kite patterns during the Cultural Revolution; meeting one of the few remaining Chinese opera bristle doll makers; being shown a centuries old Tibetan Thangka painting book of proportion; documenting the ritual slaughter of a sheep in Inner Mongolia and determining how best to represent on a website accessed by children and youth; and being invited to attend the Bai people's Rao Song Ling Festival (Yunnan), the Miao people's Sister Meal Festival, and the Mongolian people's Bayon Oboo Festival (Inner Mongolia).

However, my focus here is on a memorable experience that exemplifies how Kristin Congdon and my students have learned from their interactions with Chinese scholars and students. For many of the US students participating in field work, and the resulting cultural interpretation, *ChinaVine* provides a first experience. Nothing is posted on *ChinaVine* that is not the result of deliberations with the project's Chinese partners. It is not unusual for US students to initially develop interpretive materials that are not fully congruent with a Chinese perspective. Key to *ChinaVine* is the process of mediation that occurs when interpretive approaches collide.

Myths and folktales, inherently grounded in cultural values, are often sites of such collisions. Consider, for example, the ongoing debates associated with the Walt Disney Corporation's appropriation of folktales and myths for commercial and entertainment purposes. Sometimes referred to as "disneyfication," this process of interpretation often results in significant changes made to stories associated with particular cultural groups or traditions in order to make stories palpable for a mass audience.

Wolves, given a territorial range that includes North America, Europe, and Asia, figure prominently in myths and folktales across an abundance of cultures. In China isolated pockets of wolves exist throughout the country. A well-known story in China is the story of the Wolf of Zhongshan—a tale with a lesson about the dangers of soft heartedness in the presence of evil.

Another story about the wolf in China is associated with Láng Village in Guan County in Shandong Province. It is this story that exemplifies a collision between the story as it was told to a *ChinaVine* fieldwork team and an interpretation of that story for children and youth that was proposed to be posted on *ChinaVine. org*.

Láng Village, is named after a folktale associated with the surrounding region and which is well known among locals. During the warring states period of Chinese history, wolves were tormenting Láng Village by attacking and killing children. To save the children, the villagers made representations of children out of cooking dough, laced them with poison, fed them to the wolves, thus killing the wolves.

While the making of dough figures in Láng Village was once common, Láng Xiucai is one of the few remaining villagers continuing the tradition. He now sells the figures as toys at local markets. Láng Xiucai describes the figures that he makes as representing virtues important to Chinese culture and Láng Village history. Scholars at the Folk Art Research Institute at Shandong Vocational College of Art and Design estimate that there are over two thousand different dough figure shapes produced by Láng Xiucai.

Posted to *ChinaVine. org* is an animated book *The Wolf and the Dough Children* (http://chinavine. org/2011/06/16/wolf-and-dough-children/) as a part of the interpretation of Láng Village and the dough figures created by Láng Xiucai. The student developers of this animated book initially modified the story's ending in such a way that the wolf did not die from eating the poisoned dough figures, but instead was sickened and ran away. The motivation for changing the story's ending was that the developers of the book wanted to be sensitive to the preservation of wolves as an endangered species in the US and a concern that, because children might access the book, killing the wolf might be too disturbing.

In keeping with *ChinaVine's* collaborative approach, Kristin, several of our students and I met with folklorist Lihui Yang and several of her graduate students to discuss the issue of whether or not the wolf should be killed in *The Wolf and the Dough Children*. In the view of Yang, there was no question that the wolf should be killed. To not kill the wolf would render the tale in-authentic. Her graduate students were much more emphatic on this issue and argued vehemently that to do otherwise would be one more example of an imperialist point of view by westerners. Kristin and I were not surprised by this reaction, could have predicted this response, but wanted to introduce our students to the complexities and passion associated with global cultural heritage.

The conversation about killing the wolf was rich, nuanced, and informative. Integral to *ChinaVine* is the rapid change currently taking place in China and the effect of these changes on China's traditional cultural heritage. Among the folklorists, artists, and other scholars that I meet in China there is the expressed desire to both protect while simultaneously acknowledging that traditions are evolving. *The Wolf and the Dough Children*, like any example of material cultural that is crossing boundaries and contexts, needs to be interrogated fully and openly about the different ideologies and world views associated with it as it moves across time, cultures and contexts. However, given *ChinaVine's* mission, the folkloristic research method associated with the project, and the centrality of the tale to the collective identity of Láng Village, the students came to understand the importance of honoring the story as it was recounted by those interviewed in Láng Village. In the book's conclusion the wolf is poisoned to death.

The interpretive process associated with *The Wolf and the Dough Children* demonstrates the authentic learning associated with *ChinaVine* fieldwork teams. Authentic because the interrogation of interpretation associated with the project involves the values, attitudes, and beliefs of Chinese and US scholars and students. Authentic because the interpretation leading to knowledge is negotiated through meaningful social interactions associated with concrete experience in the field, reflection upon that experience leading to a first interpretation followed by a vetting of that interpretation among Chinese and US participants leading to a mutually agreed upon finalization. Contributing to the memorability of this experience in interpreting *The Wolf and the Dough Children* is that it is an experience rarely achieved in the traditional university classroom environment.

世界平台与本土命题：
我与美国民俗学界交往之管见

陈泳超[*]

我一向以为学者应该虚怀面对整个世界，而不必规于专业的拘囿。我是从外专业跨入民间文学、民俗学行列的，在民俗学界空无依傍，古今中外来者不拒，只看是否跟自己的学术理念和当下趣味相合。

2003 年我主持召开了"民间文化青年论坛"第一次学术会议，在国内民俗学界引起了较大反响。紧接着，素昧平生的张举文先生不耻下问，主动在美国通过网络传唤我，后又在 2005 年回国之时屈尊枉顾，与刘魁立先生以及高丙中、萧放等一起商量去美国开会事宜。当时我对美国学界所知不多，也不知道该提交什么论文。经过高丙中和张举文的耳提面命，我决定用"传统的发明"作为理论背景，来讨论家乡常州的一种丧葬习俗及其变异情况。具体的调查写作不必分说，反正最后是努力完成并到张举文所在的俄勒冈州崴涞大学参会并宣读了论文。

行前丙中兄知道我一向邋遢，特意关照要穿西服正装。我自从婚礼上沐猴而冠地穿过一回西装，之后就再没碰过，临行前拿起新郎装一试，竟然已经不合身了，连夜又去当代商城买了一套，在会议上人模狗样地好生别扭。后来看见美国学者也不是个个正装，像本德尔先生就穿了一件 T 恤，看上去似乎并不比我的本来面目正经多少。而会前会后与美国一些学者交流，感觉大家都有强烈的沟通意愿，许多话题值得深入探讨甚至可以进行某种程度的合作。当时最深刻的印象之一是自己英语太差，不能透彻地自由交流；之二是有点像命题作文，似乎尚未发挥自己的所思所想。

之后几年分别认识了本德尔、苏独玉、罗仪德等美国民俗学界热心于中美交往的同行，与他们有过深浅不等的交流，颇有收获。苏独玉的这个中文名字很是好听，与她结识最是巧

---

[*] 编者注：陈泳超现任北京大学中文系教授，主要讲授民间文学和民俗学。他对神话和民间叙事的研究代表了中国民俗学中民间文学的基础，但同时又以他提出的民俗动力学拓宽了传统民间文学和民俗学的研究领域。他不仅关注传统的神话研究，也关注校园的涂鸦；不仅参与古文献研究，也参与民间歌谣的搜集。在过去的十多年里，他积极推动的"民间文化青年论坛"（而且还在继续，尽管在形式上融为中国民俗学会网络的一部分），通过年度会议和网络平台，在吸引民俗学新生力量的同时，也在社会上普及宣传了民俗学知识，为中国民俗学学科建设做出了极大贡献。

然。记得是在北师大开一个什么学术会议,期间我们两个总是不期而遇地跑到会场外抽烟,于是就聊成了朋友。后来我到她供职的印第安纳大学演讲时,校园全部禁烟,她那辆只剩一个反光镜的破车,成了我们抽烟者的俱乐部,我能感觉到她内心的欢笑与自嘲。她的烟瘾比我大多了,眼里却依然闪烁着孩童般清澈的光芒。

2010年,游自荧君(我的硕士生,当时在俄亥俄州立大学本德尔名下攻读博士学位)跟白幕唐君(我名下的高级进修生,时为芝加哥大学东亚系博士候选人)在我的饭局上认识并商量要在当年度美国民俗学大会上组成一个小组,邀我前去呐喊掠阵。当时我刚完成关于白茆民歌的调查项目,便在2010年10月11—22日,赴美国田纳西州纳什维尔市参加美国民俗学会第122届年会,宣读了一篇有关山歌的论文。这一程为时甚长,除了参会外,期间我还在芝加哥大学东亚语言与文明系作题为《一个民歌乡在国家思潮变动中走过的60年》的演讲,在俄亥俄州立大学东亚系作题为《当代中国学者的民俗学田野作业:我们怎样做》《中国上古神话传说的民间传承》两场演讲,在印第安纳大学东亚系作题为《华北的民间庙会和信仰》的演讲、在该校民俗学与音乐人类学系作题为《一个民歌乡在国家思潮变动中走过的60年》的演讲。上述最后一场演讲尤其热闹,来了许多据说颇有名望的人物,尊敬的前辈学者鲍曼先生、格拉西先生(前此均只在北大有过一面之缘)也自始至终枉驾捧场。可惜我的英语依然蹩脚,讲演完后又被一些热心听众问这问那,未能与他们款曲襟抱。

这一次的交流很充分,我的感受也非常强烈。一个有趣的现象是,我发现我可以用英语让美国人发笑了,当然只是偶一为之,并且要配合一些肢体语言。我相信不是我的英语有多大进步,是我的心态放松了,我能明确感知在美国不只是单方面学习,而是互通有无、平等交流。

当我看到所参加的美国民俗学年会竟然已经是第122次,很感吃惊,就悄悄推算了一下,应该是从1888年计数的。这一年,美国民俗学会宣告成立,它是继1878年英国民俗学会成立后的第二个民俗学国家学会。这让我无比惊讶和钦敬。我们通常总爱自诩历史悠久,对美国这样缺乏古老性的国家便天然有些轻慢。其实,人家一旦有了历史,便有着更强烈的历史感,能自成立之年开始持续100多年不间断,可见其自觉与发达。此后我在每学期的民俗学课上,都要跟同学们分享这一认知,让他们明白历史不能只是一种遥远的光荣,需要更多人有接续与传承的自觉意识和具体实践。如今的美国民俗学年会,几乎就是世界民俗学大会,来自世界各大洲的学者哜哜嘈嘈盈盈一堂,每个人都可以根据自己的爱好满载而归,这也让我由衷感喟,深表服膺。通过交流,我断言当今中国是全球民俗学者的天堂,因为中国的社会正在进行着史无前例的大变动,它不像"文革"那样来自政治(影响相对较小),而是来自经济模式的转变,这使得千百年稳定的生活方式发生了轰然巨变,将以前需要很长时间(甚至超过个人的生命长度)才能观察到的民俗变化浓缩在很短时间内放大了演示,为民俗学者提供了施展身手的绝大场域。我在美国到处宣扬我的这一论调,似乎也得到了一些人的呼应。正是基于这一认知,我相信中国民俗学者当然还要继续虚心向欧美学习,尤其是他们的理论方法和问题意识;但更重要的是,我们必须从自己脚下大地正在发生的变化中提炼出更有生命力的本土命题,并且通过自己的思考,将之证明、提升为世界性话题,真正对全球民俗学的进步做出独具特色的贡献。此后我不断教育学生要至少精通一门外语,将来的学者必然是世界性的,大家在同一平台上各自发声,优胜劣汰,不能再像我们这一代因为语言而出现这么大的学术进出口逆差了。

当然,这次参会也有一事让我警醒:美国民俗学年会一面说是世界民俗学的盛会,另一面也可以说是世界民俗学的庙会,琳琅满目大于精深专攻,外行看热闹的成分多了些,似乎更适宜于学术圈的建构而非学术深度的推进。这次回来,我坚定了弱水三千只取一瓢的信念,从此更愿意参加小型的主题会议。

这几年我的学术趣味日益转向中国传统民间信仰,便与美国新泽西州立大学哲学与宗教系赵昕毅教授共同主持了一个"中国北方农村的社区与宗教"工作坊,先于 2012 年 6 月 23—26 日在山东青岛召开了一次小型国际学术讨论会,到会的有海峡两岸知名专家以及欧美的库伯、周越和刘迅等先生。在此基础上,我们才在 2013 年 5 月 3—5 日,于美国新泽西州立大学召开了"Community and Religion in Rural North China: Searching for a New Paradigm"国际学术会议,题目很小,参会人数也不多,但都有共同的兴趣和针对性,每人有半小时的发言和 1 小时的讨论,关键是,英语和汉语两种语言同时作为会议正式用语,像我就可以用汉语尽情发抒自己在洪洞调查的最新心得。会上虽然也有像韩书瑞先生、于君方先生这样的学术大腕,但发言的主要还是中青年学者。会议允许放言无忌,形成了开放的氛围,大家都感觉受益良多。

我一共就在美国参加过三次学术会议,每次都有不同的感受和心态,希望今后仍然对此抱有饱满的热情,继续在世界舞台上展示自己的命题和对人类文化的共同思考。

World Stage and Local Tasks: A Glimpse of the China-US Folkloristic Exchanges

Yongchao Chen*

    I have always thought that scholars should be courageous enough to face the whole world, rather than be restricted to one professional domain. I came to folk literature and folklore from a different discipline, with no connection to the field of folkloristics. Therefore I accept anything ancient or modern, domestic or foreign, so long as it fits my academic interests.

    In 2003, I presided over the first "Youth Forum on Folk Culture" conference, which had a big impact the domestic folklore field. Shortly afterwards, Dr. Juwen Zhang, whom I did not know before, approached me from the US, and paid a visit to me in 2005, when he talked with Mr. Kuili Liu, Bingzhong Gao, Fang Xiao and me about attending a folklore meeting in the US. I did not know much about the American folklore circle, and I did not know what topic to present. With Bingzhong Gao and Juwen Zhang's help, I decided to use the "invention of tradition" as the theoretical background to discuss a funeral custom and its variation in my hometown of Changzhou. Needless to mention the details, I finally managed to present it at the meeting in Willamette University, where Juwen Zhang teaches.

    Bingzhong knew that I had always been careless about my attire, and specifically told me to prepare a suit of formal dress. I had worn a suit only once—at my wedding. Now it could no longer fit my grown body. I had to buy a suit the night before I left for the US. However, at the meeting, I saw that American scholars were all in casual clothes, like Mr. Mark Bender who was in a T-shirt, and they did not look more serious than I was. Nevertheless, before and after the meeting, I felt

---

    * Yongchao Chen is Professor of Chinese at Beijing University, teaching folk literature and folklore. His research on myth and folk narration is the foundational work of Chinese folkloristics, but at the same time he has broadened the traditional folk literature and folklore studies with his ideas on folklore dynamics. He not only studies myths, but also pays attention to campus graffiti; not only participates in ancient text research, but also in the collection of folk songs. In the past ten years, he has actively promoted the "Youth Forum on Folk Culture" through an annual meeting and online forums, which continues as part of CFS online platform, to attract new folklorists and to popularize folklore knowledge in the public, and thus has made great contributions to the construction of Chinese folkloristics.

that American folklorists had a very strong desire to communicate with us on many topics, and even discuss in-depth about possible cooperation. One of the deepest impressions of the time was that my English was so bad that I could not communicate freely; another was that my presentation was like a given topic for a composition, which seemed to have not fully played out my own thoughts.

In the following years, I got to know some American folklorists who were enthusiastic about Sino-US communication, like Mark Bender, Sue Tuohy, Tim Lloyd and some others, and I learned quite a lot from them. Sue Tuohy, with her unique Chinese name, is a most direct and candid person. Once we were both at a meeting in Beijing Normal University, and we simultaneously went out to smoke, and then chatted, and then became friends. When I later visited her at Indiana University, where the whole campus was smoke-free, she and I had to get into her old car which had only one mirror, where it became a club for smokers. I could feel her inner joy and self-mocking. Her cravings for cigarettes were much more than mine, and her eyes were still shining with a childlike clarity.

At a dinner in 2010, Ziying You, who was my former M. A. student, then a graduate student at the Ohio State University studying under Mark Bender, met Max Bohnenkampk, who was a graduate student from the University of Chicago and was studying under me then. They decided to present together at the AFS that year, and invited me join their panel. At that time, I had just completed a project about the folk songs in Baimao, Jiangsu, so I agreed. It was in Nashville, Tennessee. The meeting was the 122nd annual meeting of the AFS. I read my paper, "Trading Mountain Songs across the River: Folksongs Revolutionary and Not." In addition to attending the meeting, I gave a lecture titled "The 60 Years of a Folk Song Village in the Changing Trend of National Thought" at the Department of East Asian Languages and Civilizations at the University of Chicago. And at the Ohio State University, I gave two talks, "Contemporary Chinese Folklorists' Fieldwork: How We Do That and Chinese Ancient Myths and Legends Continued among the Folk." At the Indiana University, I gave a talk on "North China Folk Temple Fair and Belief." At Department of Folklore and Ethnomusicology, I gave a talk on "The 60 Years of a Folksong Village in the Changing China." The last talk was particularly lively, some distinguished scholars like Richard Bauman and Henry Glassie were present as well. Unfortunately, my English was still bad, but there were many good questions asked by the enthusiastic audience.

This time the exchange was quite extensive, and it left a deep impression on me. One interesting phenomenon was that I found that I could make Americans laugh in English, of course, only occasionally with some body language. I believe that it was not because my English was improved, but that I was relaxed. I could clearly sense that my time in the United States was not just unilateral learning, but it was an extensive and equal exchange.

I was very impressed when I learned that the AFS had been meeting annually for 122 years since 1888. It made me feel surprised and appreciating of such a long history. In China we usually love to boast our long history. In fact, if a people has a history, the strong sense of history matters more to them. A meeting lasting over 100 years shows the awareness of history, and the maturity of this awareness. Since then, I always share this story in my folklore class so that the students can understand that history is not just a distant glory, but also requires more people to have a sense of continuity and inheritance. Today, the AFS annual meeting is almost the world folklore conference, a fact I sincerely admire. Through communication, I believe that today China is a paradise for world folklorists because China is undergoing unprecedented social changes. It does not come from politics (relatively small impact) such as the "Cultural Revolution" but from a change in the economic development. This change provides the best platform for folklorists. I spread this idea everywhere I went in the United States, and it seemed there were people echoing this thought. It is based on the understanding that Chinese folklorists, on the one hand, of course, should continue to learn from Europe and the United States, especially their theoretical methods and awareness of the problem; on the other hand, more important, we must change to refine theories and methods through local practices, and through local propositions to make them part of world discourse. That will be our true and unique contribution to the world. Since then I have encouraged my students to at least be proficient in one foreign language because the future of scholarship is bound to be worldwide.

Of course, I was also shocked by another fact: the AFS meeting was also like a world's folklore "temple fair" with most people doing window-shopping business. For this reason, I decided to attend more small meetings rather than big ones.

In recent years, my academic interest has turned to Chinese traditional folk beliefs. I co-chaired a meeting with Professor Zhao Xinyi at Rutgers University. It was held in Qingdao, Shandong from June 23 to 26, 2012, attended by some well-known experts from both sides of the Taiwan Strait, as well as some from Europe and the United States such as Eugene Cooper, Adam Chau and Xun Liu. On this basis, we held another international symposium on "Community and Religion in Rural North China: Searching for a New Paradigm" from May 3–5, 2013 at Rutgers University. Some important attendees include Susan Naquin and Junfang Yu, but the majority were young scholars. The meeting allowed each person to fully express themselves, and reached the goal of building a community and harvesting new thoughts.

I have so far participated in three academic conferences in the United States, and each time had different experiences and feelings. I hope I will continue my enthusiasm for these meetings in the future, and continue to present my thought on the world stage and share my thinking about human culture.

(Translation by Juwen Zhang)

建立关系：中美民间生活与合作

科特·杜赫斯特*

  1992 年，我和同事玛莎·麦克多维尔有幸获得福布莱特项目的资助，前往泰国从事大学博物馆的改造工作，主要是深入宗教文化类的博物馆，以应对泰国日益突出的种族多样性问题。具体而言，要对曼谷新建的国家文化中心提出发展建议，其中包括一家展现本土多重文化的国家博物馆。这项工作让我们有机会继续追寻对汉文化族群的兴趣，他们历经几个世纪迁徙至泰国北部，在某些情况下，晚近更多是越南战争后沦为难民逃到泰国北部。在密歇根我们开展了一次关于苗族难民群体的田野调查和展览，主要研究名为"pajntaub"（字面意思为花布，准确地说是刺绣花布）的纺织传统的传承与变化。① 这个老挝的纺织传统根在中国，许多东南亚民族传统布艺的设计、主题、工艺、色彩选择等方面以及其他纺织品的文化表征都存在类似情况。

  上述工作使我十年来对亚洲纺织品传统的兴趣更为浓厚，这体现在博物馆所举办的各种节日项目、藏品征集、展览和出版物各个方面。2007 年，在担任史密森民俗与文化遗产中心咨询委员会主席期间，我有机会结识中国昆明的云南民族博物馆馆长谢沫华，他当时正参与筹备名为"湄公河：汇通文化"的史密森民俗节项目。② 2012 年，《化零为整：美国 21 世纪的 25 位拼布艺术家》在云南民族博物馆展出期间我们再次碰面（这次联合展览由我馆与中西艺术和南方艺术联合举办，并得到美国驻华大使馆协助）。③ 展览期间，我们开始与谢沫华及其团队探讨如何对接中国的民族博物馆和美国的民间及传统艺术项目，尤其是那些

---

  * 编者注：科特·杜赫斯特既是英语教授、学院派民俗学者，也是公共民俗学者，指导参与了从地方到国际的各种民俗活动，为此赢得多项殊荣，也发表了许多作品。他不仅是密歇根州立大学"艺术文化行动倡议"的负责人，也是密歇根州立大学博物馆的名誉馆长与文化遗产与民俗部门负责人。在担任美国民俗学会会长期间（2010—2011），他通过促成美中民俗学会联合项目（2011—2016），使中美民俗学界的交流得到推进和扩展，使双方的交流走向常态。这一联合项目囊括了合作展览、学术交流、影视工作坊以及本文集中提到的其他合作项目。他为中美两国的民俗学者树立了融合学术研究和博物馆展览等公共民俗研究的样板。他是美国民俗学会的资深会员。他的中国同事们习惯用他的中文名字——胡世德。

 ① 参见科特·杜赫斯特，玛莎·麦克多维尔编《密歇根苗族艺术：变迁中的纺织品》，东兰辛：密歇根州立大学博物馆，1983 年。
 ② 参见《汇通文化：湄公河》，史密森民俗节项目手册，华盛顿特区：史密森民俗节，2007 年。
 ③ 参见《化零为整：美国 21 世纪 25 位拼布艺术家》，中西艺术，南方艺术和密歇根州立大学博物馆，2012 年。

基于博物馆的项目,例如密歇根州立大学博物馆的密歇根传统艺术项目。由此吸引到亚洲文化协会的资金支持,开启了两家博物馆的合作。这包括专业技术交流、美方中国传统艺术藏品的"数字化归还"、初步的培训计划和展览项目的合作计划。

大概同时,美国民俗学会得到路思基金的资助,开始着手中美民俗学会非物质文化遗产论坛。那时我担任美国民俗学会会长,因此能够参与路思基金赞助的一系列中美民俗学会非物质文化遗产论坛。过去几年中,其中两个论坛集中关注非物质文化遗产和博物馆这两个议题,参与论坛的博物馆主要是多次举办民俗项目的三家中国民族博物馆和三家美国博物馆。[①] 项目成果颇丰,主要包括《中国西南拼布》国际巡回展览,及其具有开创性的出版物[②](详见本书玛莎·麦克多维尔关于此次展览的文章),但可能最重要的是,参与其中的田野工作者、展览组织者、教育者、策展人、藏品主管和其他博物馆工作人员,既有资深人士,更有不断涌现出的年轻人——正是他们的合作,让中美双方在学术研究和专业技能方面都得到不断的交流。

过去几年,我们相互合作,不断增进感情,其中有许多令人难忘的故事。对我而言,有一件事情记忆犹新,就是领略到了几家博物馆相互分享的那些记录着中国传统文化的大量藏品。我们很早就发现民俗学同仁们普遍对田野工作和保护文化传统与传承人兴趣盎然。我们的博物馆分享任务始终关注对不同民族的记录、保存和展示,尤其是再现那些被边缘化的族群,同时,也服务于那些过去未被重视的观众。

我还记得我们密歇根州立大学博物馆筹展和藏品部门的工作人员在云南民族博物馆文物收藏区查看一些纺织品藏品时那种真正的兴奋。云南民族博物馆的同事一边激动地展示着这些藏品,一边告诉我们征集这些藏品的故事,告诉我们它们如何制作以及它们原本在生活中如何使用。很快,人员互访交流也使我们的馆藏品得到交流。学到的东西扩展了我们对于自家许多藏品的理解,这些藏品既有我们的大学同事在中国搜集而来的,也有其他收藏家捐赠的,除此之外,还有具有针对性的田野调查的学术成果。在这些跨国的"藏品巡展"过程中,我们深入了解了各家的藏品情况,厘清了未来田野调查中的重点问题,而且这一过程实际上也以某种方式让美国的藏品和他们的家乡相互联系。使用数字技术,我们能够轻松地分享藏品的照片,对比文献与片段。这些体验在很多层面上得到升华。虽然不能叫作"收藏之旅",但我们发现只要与中国博物馆筹展同仁建立联系,就能极大扩展我们对自家藏品的了解,他们所拥有的本土知识,反过来进一步丰富我们的收藏品知识。这使我们对藏品有更加精准的认识和定位,无论在展览上,还是相关的教育体验上,都能对我们的观众有的放矢,对于那些使用这些藏品来保持他们文化知识的传统社区的成员,也有助于他们传承他们的文化知识。

---

① 更多有关中美民俗和非物质文化遗产工程的信息,请参见美国民俗学会主页:http://www.afsnet.org/default.asp?page = FICH(accessed 9/24/16)。

② 玛莎·麦克多维尔,张丽君编:《中国西南拼布艺术》,云南民族博物馆 / 贵州民族博物馆 / 广西民族博物馆 / 密歇根州立大学博物馆 / 印第安纳大学马斯瑟世界文化博物馆 / 圣塔菲国际民间艺术博物馆 / 内布拉斯加—林肯国际拼布艺术研究中心博物馆联合出版,2016 年。

在密歇根州立大学和云南民族博物馆具有开拓性质的工作之后，六家主要博物馆之间日渐熟稔，我们又给六家博物馆的参与员工创造了新的学习机会。除了欣赏我们的藏品，员工们还有机会去拜访他们社区中的传统艺术家和传统艺术传承人。美方员工的体会更深，根据安排，他们在中国游览了中方正在创建和经营的生态博物馆。这样的经历让我们更加理解在尊重当地文化价值和当下传统社区生活经济现状的前提下，博物馆所发挥的保存、维护、展现文化传统的作用。我们相互分享了一些值得瞩目的项目，例如国家与地方遗产保护项目、技艺传承项目和非遗大师认证项目。我们还在双方国家安排了其他的博物馆专业类游览。在今天看来，这些游览项目都颇有建树并取得了不俗的成绩。

中美民俗学者之间的交流轶事层出不穷。我们也都学到很多，例如彼此如何开展工作，怎样学到新的理论知识和实践技能，还有就是如何在诸多因素影响下坚持跨国工作的挑战性。

我们相互学习到的东西很多，其中之一就是建立彼此信任是需要有长期打算的。利用通信设备沟通当然很有必要，但只有在博物馆中一同工作，一起研究藏品，才能培养一种真正的和谐关系，从而推进深层的合作和分享。中美博物馆工作人员都承认两国文化和语言的差异显著，需要不断沟通。我们也已经认识到，成功的伙伴关系无论是在计划阶段还是实施阶段，都要保持诚实、坦率、公开和有效的沟通。幸运的是，我们的沟通行之有效，我们的行动心诚意满，因此无论是个人层面还是体制层面，我们的关系都合理而健康。过去几年，双方的体制架构和管理流程都需要我们去努力了解，因为这些不仅需要尊重，也是成功合作所必需的。最后，可能也是最重要的，我们一致认为：合作虽然辛苦，但回报绝对不菲。再加上对相互的收藏品和博物馆活动的全新理解，合作关系又得到升华。

由于职业发展的因素，我总是能找到机会把中国非遗和博物馆方面的工作与我自己的职业角色结合起来，例如在担任密歇根州立大学"大学校园艺术与文化拓展项目"总监的时候就是如此。我和同事们共同提议下一个大学主题年围绕中国展开。我与项目委员会（一个由我主持的主要由人文艺术领域的院长与主任组成的团体）成员们一起为密歇根州立大学起草了一个为期18个月的《体验中国》的计划。① 这个计划包括有关中国的展览、演出、节日项目、厨师交流、艺术实习、座谈会、讲座和研讨。我们学校大概有五万名学生，中国学生超过四千五百名，我们与他们一道见证了这个项目的成果：无论对于中国籍学生，还是非中国籍学生，抑或是学校所在的社区，跨文化的意识和体验都得到了促进。

组织这场大规模的项目可能是让人印象最深的故事。这次挑战将美国密歇根推上一个更大的舞台，甚至影响在美国之外。经过激烈讨论，我们决定和斯巴达人仪仗队组织一次橄榄球中场表演项目来彰显中国文化。我们担任创意顾问，曾经参与北京奥运开幕式和闭幕式的詹尼佛·温·马也参与进来。② "大学校园艺术与文化拓展项目"、大学的同事们（其中不乏民俗学家和人类音乐学家）与我们共同策划了一次乐队游行项目，这个项目在斯巴达人仪

---

① 参见密歇根州立大学艺术与文化主页上的《体验中国》：http://artsandculture.msu.edu/ （accessed 9/24/16）。
② 詹尼佛·温·马的更多信息请参见：http://www.littlemeat.net/words/words_CV.htm （accessed 9/24/16）。

仗队创意组的指挥下，将中国民间音乐和流行音乐相结合。我们利用大屏幕播放中国、美国及密歇根州立大学的影像，甚至还用观众方阵举牌展示。2015年10月14日，斯巴达体育场内七万五千名观众观看了演出，他们为三百名声乐演员鼓掌，为传统中国大鼓叫好，也为绚烂的烟雾而喝彩。这段视频现在被密歇根州立大学在中国招生和培训时使用。其他大学的仪仗乐队也纷纷效仿，尤其是中国学生规模庞大的高校。

最后，中美民俗学界的关系始终不断向前发展。我相信，中美博物馆将会迎来更多的合作与交流，而博物馆正是民俗学家的靓丽舞台。根据中国文化部的数据，中国平均每天都有一个博物馆开放。随着民俗学者不断在博物馆就职或从事与博物馆相关的工作，中美博物馆之间将有更多的机会扩大和探索新的专业合作。再考虑到美国民俗学会将要成立民俗与博物馆这一新的部门，我们有理由期待两国博物馆的民俗学家将就中国问题有更多的合作。因此，"故事"必将继续讲下去。

（内蒙古科技大学苗露翻译）

Ⅲ. 从书本民俗回到生活民俗——共拓新途   193

密歇根大学博物馆和云南民族博物馆工作人员分享文化藏品数据库。MSUM and YNM staff share their collection data base systems of their cultural collections. Photograph by C. Kurt Dewhurst.

云南民族博物馆工作人员向密歇根大学博物馆人员展示一件纺织品。YNM curators carefully describe a textile for MSUM staff. Photograph by C. Kurt Dewhurst.

云南民族博物馆安排到传统的民族地区参观生态博物馆情况，为玛莎·麦克多维尔等密歇根大学博物馆人员提供结识当地传承者的计划。YNM staff arranged field expeditions to traditional ethnic communities and ecomuseums that they are developing. This provided MSUM staff members, such as curator Marsha MacDowell, the opportunity to meet local textile artists/tradition-bearers in their homes and communities. Photograph by C. Kurt Dewhurst.

Building Connectivity: China-US Folklife and Collaborations

Kurt Dewhurst[*]

In 1992, my colleague Marsha MacDowell and I had the good fortune to receive a Fulbright grant to support work on the transformation of university museums in Thailand into regional cultural museums with a focus on the growing ethnic diversity of Thailand. This included advising on the development of a new national cultural center in Bangkok that included a national museum that would feature multicultural nature of the nation. During this work we were able to pursue our interest in the ethnic Chinese cultural groups that had migrated overcenturies and settled in northern Thailand, in some cases, more recently as refugees following the Viet Nam War. We had conducted fieldwork and mounted an exhibition on Hmong refugee communities in Michigan to especially to examine the continuity and change in the textile tradition called *pajntaub* (literal translated as flower cloth but more accurately meaning embroidered or decorated cloth).[①] This tribal Lao textile tradition has its roots in China, as do many of the ethnic tribal traditions in Southeast Asia and the designs, motifs, techniques, color selections, etc. that appear in traditional clothing as well as other cultural expressions in textiles.

This early work fostered a continued interest for the next decades in the textile traditions of Asia and it was manifested in museum-based festival programs, collection development, exhibitions,

---

* Kurt Dewhurst is both an academic folklorist, being Professor of English, and a public folklorist, directing and curating various folklife events at local and international levels, with many publications on and awards for his public folklore efforts. He is also Director of Arts and Cultural Initiatives at Michigan State University as well as Director Emeritus and Curator of Folklife and Cultural Heritage at the Michigan State University Museum. During his tenure as the President of AFS (2010–11), Dewhurst accelerated, broadened, and institutionalized the Sino-US folkloristic communication by enabling the first AFS-CFS joint project (2011–16) which engaged multiple aspects including the joint exhibitions, scholar exchanges, workshops, and other collaborative projects mentioned by several others in this volume. He has exemplified the fruitful blending of academic research, museum exhibitions and public festivals for both Chinese and American folklorists. He is a Fellow of the American Folklore Society. His Chinese colleagues are used to his Chinese name: Hu Shide.

① See Dewhurst, C. Kurt and Marsha MacDowell (eds.), *Michigan Hmong Arts: Textiles in Transition*. East Lansing: Michigan State University Museum. 1983.

and publications. In 2007, I had the opportunity to meet Director Mohua Xie, Director of the Yunnan Nationalities Museum in Kunming, China in my capacity as Chair of the Advisory Council of the Smithsonian Center for Folklife and Cultural Heritage. He was part of the planning team for the Smithsonian Folklife Festival program entitled, *Mekong River: Connecting Cultures.*[①] In 2012, we reconnected when the exhibition, *The Sum of Many Parts: 25 Quiltmakers in 21st Century America*, traveled to the Yunnan Nationalities Museum (our museum played a coordinating role with Arts Midwest and South Arts with support by the U. S. Embassy in China and the U. S. partners).[②] During this exhibition tour, we began a dialogue with Director Xie and his staff about the commonalities between the role of the nationalities museums in China and the folk and traditional arts programs in the U. S. —and especially those based at museums—such as the Michigan Traditional Arts Program at the Michigan State University Museum. This led to the crafting of a successful grant proposal from the Asian Cultural Council to begin a partnership between the MSU Museum and Yunnan Nationalities Museum that would focus on professional staff exchanges, "digital repatriation" of Chinese traditional arts in our collections, informal training initiatives, and planning for collaborative exhibitions/projects.

Around the same time, the American Folklore Society had formally commenced the AFS/China Folklore Society Forum on Intangible Cultural Heritage that was funded by the Henry Luce Foundation. At that time I was serving as President of the American Folklore Society and I was able to participate on the programs for what became a series of Luce Foundation sponsored *AFS/CFS Forums on Intangible Cultural Heritage*. In the past few years, two of these forums have been developed to focus on ICH and Museums—and the number of lead participating museums has grown to three Chinese Nationalities Museums and three American museums with strong folklife programs.[③] While there have been many notable outcomes, including a major international touring exhibition, *the Quilts of Southwest China*, with a groundbreaking publication[④] (see article on the exhibition by Marsha MacDowell in this volume), what is perhaps most significant is the growing scholarly and professional relationships that have been established by both senior and, more importantly, emerging young fieldworkers, curators, educators exhibition designers, and collections managers, and other museum staff.

---

① See "Mekong River: *Connecting Cultures*. Smithsonian Folklife Festival Program Book. Washington, DC: Smithsonian Folklife Festival. 2007.

② See *The Sum of Many Parts: 25 Quiltmakers in 21st Century America*. Arts Midwest, South Arts, and Michigan State University Museum. 2012.

③ To learn more about the China/US Folklore and Intangible Heritage Project, go to the American Folklore Society website: http://www.afsnet.org/default.asp?page = FICH (accessed 9/24/16).

④ MacDowell, Marsha and Lijun Zhang (eds). *Quilts of Southwest China*. A collaborative publication of YNM, GZNM, GXNM, MSUM, Mathers Museum of World Cultures at Indiana University, Museum of International Folk Art in Santa Fe, International Quilt Study Center & Museum of Nebraska-Lincoln. 2016.

While there are many remarkable stories that have emerged from the growing partnerships from these past few years, one of the most lasting images for me has been learning about the rich collections that our museums share that document the traditional culture of China. We discovered early on that our folklife staff members have a common passion for fieldwork and safeguarding cultural traditions and tradition-bearers. Our shared museum missions with a focus on the documentation, preservation, and presentation of diverse ethnic, often marginalized cultural groups, and reaching underserved audiences.

I can still recall the genuine excitement when members of our Michigan State University Museum curatorial and collections staff examined examples from the textile collections of the Yunnan Nationalities Museum in their Cultural Relics collections storage area. Our YNM colleagues were thrilled to show-off their collections and tell the stories of how they were collected, how they were made, and how they were used in the communities of origin. Immediately, the staff exchange brought to life our own similar collections back home at our museum—as well. The knowledge we were gaining enriched our understanding of many of the objects in our collections that were collected by university faculty who spent time in China, as well as other collectors who donated their work—in addition to some of our objects that did come to our museum as a result of targeted scholarly fieldwork. During these kinds of bi-national staff "collection journeys" we learned a great deal about our respective collections, identified key questions we need to address in future fieldwork, and, in a way, virtually reconnected the U.S. held collections with their home communities. Using digital technology, we were able to readily share images of our collections and compare/contrast pieces and documentation. The experience has been enlightening on many levels. While not "crowd sourcing" we began to realize we can dramatically expand our understanding of our own collections by calling on our Chinese curatorial colleagues and they in turn can draw in local community knowledge to further enrich our knowledge of our collection holdings. This has enabled us to more accurately identify and contextualize these items when featured in exhibitions and for related educational experience for our visitors and the visiting traditional community members that use these collections to sustain their cultural knowledge.

As the partnership developed between our six primary museums after the pilot work between the MSU Museum and the Yunnan Nationalities Museum, we created new learning opportunities for our participating staff members from the six museums. In addition to visits to our collections areas, we structured experiences for our respective staff members to visit traditional artists and tradition-bearers in their communities. This was further enhanced by arranged visits for our U.S. staff members (when in China) to travel to ecomuseums that are being developed and managed by the Chinese partner museums. Such experiences allowed for deep exploration of the role of museums in the preservation, safeguarding, and presenting cultural traditions that honors local cultural values and the economic realities of traditional community life in the twenty-first century. We shared strategies of both honorific programs such as national and state heritage programs, apprenticeship programs, and intangible heritage masters recognition programs. We also arranged for other professional visits to museums in both countries that are known today for their innovative work and "best practices."

The stories continue to flow from the communications between Chinese and American folklorists. We have collectively learned a great deal too about how we each do our work and how we are learning not only new theory and practice but we are also learning how challenging it is to sustain international work due to a variety of factors.

Among the many things that we have learned from one another is that it takes time to build trust over distance. While electronic communication is valuable, spending time together at one another's museums and in collections has forged a strong sense of comfort and ease that enables deeper sharing and collaboration. The museum staff members from China and the U.S. have acknowledged there are significant national cultural differences and language differences need to be constantly addressed. We also have realized that successful collaborative partnerships require honest, direct, open, and transparent communication for planning as well as implementation of our partnerships. Fortunately, we were able to develop effective strategies for communication and a sincere commitment for sustained equitable individual and institutional relationships. Over the past few years, we had to learn a great deal about our respective institutional hierarchies and administrative processes that need to be respected and followed to be successful. In the end, probably what was most important was our strong collective view that, while collaborative work is demanding, the rewards are worth it and partnerships can be transformative in terms of understanding our collections and museum practices in our respective nations.

In terms of professional development, I had the timely opportunity to create synergies with my China ICH and museum work and my role as Director of Arts and Culture for University Outreach & Engagement at Michigan State University. Along with some of my colleagues, we proposed that our next university thematic year should focus on China. Together with my colleagues on the MSU Cultural Engagement Council (comprised of Deans and Directors primarily in the arts and humanities—a group I chair), we produced an eighteen-month *China Experience* initiative for MSU.① This included exhibitions, performances, festival programs, chef exchanges, artist residencies, symposia, lectures, and seminars on China. With over 4500 Chinese national students on our campus of approximately 50,000 students, the programming proved to help build cross-cultural awareness and experience that benefitted both our Chinese students, other MSU students, and the communities we serve.

Perhaps the most memorable story that emerged was a response to the challenge to create a

---

① See *the China Experience* at the Michigan State University Arts and Culture website. http://artsandculture.msu.edu/ (accessed 9/24/16).

large-scale event that would connect on a larger stage to the state of Michigan, U. S., and beyond. After some lively discussion, we decided to develop a football halftime program with the Spartan Marching Band featuring Chinese culture. We engaged as a creative consultant, Jennifer Wen Mah, one of the creative team for the opening and closing ceremony for the Beijing Olympics.① Working with the CEC and campus faculty, including folklorists and ethnomusicologists, we developed a marching band program that featured a combination of Chinese folk music and popular music under the leadership of the creative team of the Spartan Marching Band. We utilized the jumbo screens for video images of China, US, and MSU and even developed a card section. This was featured on October 14, 2015 at Spartan Stadium in front of 75,000 fans who cheered the dramatic choreographed program with over 300 vocal performers, traditional Chinese drums, and, of course colorful smoke. A video of this program was posted on YouTube and was a sensation: https://youtu. be/lZ-mcdOIZ9w. The video is now used in MSU student recruitment and orientation programs in China-and now other university marching bands are interested in replicating something like this—especially those universities with large Chinese student populations.

In closing, it has been a remarkable evolving relationship between our Chinese and American folklore community. I feel confident that we will see a growing number of connections and partnerships between Chinese and American museums where folklorists are active in the years ahead. According to the Chinese Ministry of Culture, an average of one museum opens every day in China. With the growing number of folklorists finding work as museum staff or with museums, there will only be more opportunities for expanding current and initiating newfolklore museum partnerships between American and Chinese museums. Given, too, the creation of a new *Folklore and Museums* section within the American Folklore Society, we anticipate that overtime we will have more Chinese presentations and collaborative work between museum-based folklorists in both countries. So, the "stories" will only continue to unfold in the years ahead.

---

① To learn more about Jennifer Wen Ma go to: http://www. littlemeat. net/words/words_ CV. htm (accessed 9/24/16).

反思合作：中国西南拼布展项目

玛莎·麦克多维尔*

我如何开始关注中国拼布

2008 年，我开始与中国学者就传统艺术进行跨文化交流，当时是以美国民俗学会的执行理事和传统艺术专家的身份开始这一工作的。我来到一个中美民俗学者的会议桌前，他们正在讨论如何加强国际合作以更好地保护非物质文化遗产。当时我的研究对象很广，从传统文化的基本内容到生活应用的调查研究都有涉猎，但我最关注的还是妇女纺织传统中的产品及其用途和意义，尤其是拼布工艺。

2010 年，罗仪德（美国民俗学会执行会长）、艾伟（美国民俗学会前会长）、杜赫斯特（美国民俗学会现任会长）和我受邀参加广东中山大学民俗学系在南昆山举办的"美学与文化生态建设"国际论坛并宣读论文。我的论文《美国民俗生活藏品创新和使用的新方向》介绍了三个文化资源数据库，分别是：密歇根彩色玻璃统计，密歇根谷仓和农舍调查，拼布索引。这些数据库都是我任密歇根州立大学博物馆（美国密歇根东兰辛）馆长时或指导或参与的项目。② 会后，我们四人与中山大学博士生陈熙一同前往昆明参观了云南民族博物馆。这是一个集中国 56 个民族的传统物质文化为一体的宝库。馆长谢沫华与主任杜韵红带我们看了展览，我们也因此有机会看到未曾展出的藏品。我很快就注意到那些纺织品，无论是展出的还是馆藏的，都跟拼布有关。我们坐下来商量怎样合作，我于是建议云南民族博物馆和密歇根州大学博物馆联合举办一次拼布及床罩的调研。

2012 年，我参与的一次展览让我有机会推进两家博物馆的合作。这次展览名叫《化零为整：21 世纪美国的 25 位拼布艺术家》，该展览由"中西艺术"和"南方艺术"（美国的两家区域艺术机构）共同主办，美国驻中国大使馆协办。作为本次展览的高级顾问，我参

---

* 编者注：玛莎·麦克多维尔一直以来都是活跃的民俗学者，同时也在公共民俗学项目上投入大量精力——又一个跨越和扩展学科领域的例证。麦克多维尔在艺术和教育领域训练多年，也活跃于美国民俗学会，在学会的委员会就职。自 1980 年代中期以来，她一直参与和领导了密歇根传统艺术节项目。她对各种民间手工艺品兴趣盎然，所以她的工作足迹也遍布各地。她参与的中美民俗学会的合作项目已经成为业界典范，对中国民俗学和博物馆学产生了深远影响。

② 玛莎·麦克多维尔：《美国民俗生活藏品创新和使用的新方向》，会议论文，美学与文化生态建设国际论坛，中山大学主办，南昆山原始森林度假村，广东，2010 年 9 月 1 日—3 日。

与编目，撰写其中主要段落，并为展览推荐"中西艺术"的拼布艺术家，也将此次展览推荐给云南民族博物馆及中国其他博物馆做全国性的巡回展出。展览在昆明开幕，而且得益于亚洲文化协会的额外支持，我和密歇根州立大学博物馆的三位同事也一同前往昆明参与展览相关的教育项目。

那时我们交流的重点是中国民族博物馆和美国民俗与传统艺术项目如何对接，尤其是那些依托于博物馆的项目，例如依托于密歇根州立大学博物馆的密歇根传统艺术项目。由此得到了亚洲文化协会的全力资助，开启了两家博物馆的真正合作。这些合作包括专业技术人员交流、美方中国传统艺术藏品的"数字化归还"、初步的民间培训以及关于展览或项目的合作计划等。

为与中国民俗学会进一步交流，路思基金出资支持美国民俗学会。路思基金主要资助基于博物馆的项目活动。作为先行者的密歇根州立大学博物馆和云南民族博物馆，开始着手计划关于中国的拼布项目。双方决定再各自邀请两家博物馆参与，但这些博物馆不仅要对民族纺织品富有见地，富于藏品，还要在教育和（或）展览项目上富有经验。因此甄选了印第安纳大学马瑟斯世界文化博物馆（美国印第安纳布卢明顿）、国际民间艺术博物馆（美国新墨西哥州圣塔菲）、广西民族博物馆、贵州民族博物馆共襄盛举。内布拉斯加林肯大学的国际拼布研究中心博物馆（美国内布拉斯加州林肯市）由于拼布藏品丰富，随后也参与进来。

路思基金的资助加上所有项目参与博物馆的努力，中国西南拼布展项目终于问世。作为来自密歇根州立大学的民俗学者，我成为美国方面的项目理事；中国广西民族博物馆的民俗学者张丽君成为中国方面的项目理事。这次项目包括学术和专业技术交流合作的方方面面，从拼布历史的研究到展品的开发和设计，从营销、募资、多媒体项目到评估和教育事宜，连衍生的出版物也囊括其中。[①] 2015 年 9 月，展览在密歇根州立大学博物馆开幕，2016 年 6 月开始在美国的合作博物馆间巡回展览。

我学到了什么

中国学者早已开始研究并搜集中国各民族的布艺形式，但很少有学者关注家用纺织品的制作和使用，包括各民族的拼布及床罩。在美国，对于拼布及其应用的研究吸引了来自各学科的学者，研究这一物质文化传统积累了大量的文字成果。中国西南拼布所做的研究和搜集工作为学界提供了不少一手文献，这些文献展现出这种物质和非物质的文化遗产如何用小块织物拼接成兼具美观和实用的纺织品。

在美国，"quilt"这个词语对于一部分人来说，专指床上使用的一种纺织品，这种纺织品共有三层：装饰层，保温的夹层和背面一层。但如今"quilt"被很多人用来描述多种纺织品，包括那些挂在墙上的饰品和那些仅有一层或两层的纺织品。在中国，床上纺织品有很多

[①] 玛莎·麦克多维尔，张丽君编：《中国西南拼布》，广西民族博物馆，2016 年。参见 a) 密歇根州立大学博物馆的拼布图片与装置：https://www.flickr.com/photos/msumuseum/albums/72157658499870573；b) 马林·汉森采访玛莎·麦克多维尔的视频：https://www.youtube.com/watch?v=Wv8oD2z6xMA；c) 国际拼布研究中心博物馆的网上展览：http://www.quiltstudy.org/exhibitions/online_exhibitions/swchina/main.html。

名字，包括被译作"quilt"的各种产品。被子，实际上是带着被面的盖被，通常用很大块的布料做成。拼布被面，是缝合了很多层布料的纺织品。在中国，两到三层的拼布不算大，通常作为床上用品、布艺和褯褓。中国的床上用品有时候只用一层碎布或花布拼成，而拼缝的技术往往跟西方的拼布工艺类似。陈熙在她的文章《中国西南拼布》中指出汉英词典中"quilt"给出的是多种的因此也是令人困惑的定义。文章提到汉语对"quilt"的不同解释给这次项目提出挑战。"这也是当初合办展览前中国主办方一头雾水的原因。的确，根据当时中国同事的反映，他们不知道博物馆里什么是'quilts'，因为这个概念不仅太过陌生，而且这个东西也太不起眼。作为一名参与者与旁观者，我在双方交流中担任翻译和协调人，因此可以说我很了解中国同事的想法。让他们困惑的大概是一个婴儿包布竟也会是拼布艺术品，而且这个东西还让美国人那么痴迷。"①

当只有一个双语编辑的时候，合作撰写和编辑双语出版物就是一项极具挑战的事情。中国西南拼布项目需要翻译的内容更加繁复。例如，原本是汉语起草的展览目录中的标签或说明，只能由张丽君一人翻译，然后再由只通英文的我整理，最后再由张丽君与汉语对照。对于双方来说，这都是一项耗费时间和耐心的事情。但我们都认同举办一次双语展览并编目出版是这次项目的重要环节。只有这样，双方观众才都能领会这些专业性的知识。

项目成员一起到各国旅行以及专业技术人员间的交流，对于双方快速建立信任、快速熟悉对方文化习俗和体制结构是非常关键的，而这些文化实践和体制结构对项目的计划和顺利实施至关重要。想象一下，中美两国的博物馆专家在中国西南山地间协同工作几天之后便可以同车高唱"she will be coming round the mountain"；想象一下，当我们怂恿并见证了一位中国同事为品尝美国早餐而点了双份之后大家的笑声。

中国西南拼布展项目使我坚信合作务必要建立在项目基础之上。联合计划并执行一个项目，尤其是这次这样多方合作的项目，使个人不再仅仅满足于讨论，而是付诸行动和展示。结果往往达到连学者自己都未曾意想到的深度、广度和全新的理解。他们也非常愿意和更多的观众共鸣。

总　结

纺织品是历史和文化的物质证明，可以告诉我们很多关于贸易、宗教、传统、族群迁徙、社区和个人的信息。那些纺织品的非物质特性，包括应用、意义、故事、技术和产品的知识通常会反映出社区和个人的文化遗产和身份认同。中国西南难以计数的少数民族的传统服饰是民族文化身份的重要标记，对其进行研究和搜集也已经蔚为大观，而这个项目则扩展到床上用品这一尚未进入公众视野但却很重要的西南少数民族文化表征。这次的基础调研为未来研究画下标线，希望这次展览和出版物会吸引更多学者转向这类调查。

如何理解和沟通不同体制和文化习俗，如何在不同时区用不同语言进行工作，对于这次

---

① 陈熙：《名字的定义：不同的文化，不同的语言，不同的术语》，载玛莎·麦克多维尔、张丽君编《中国西南拼布》，广西民族博物馆，2016年。

拼布工艺的跨国研究非常重要。通过这次活动，我扩展了自己对纺织物传统的理解，这些纺织物传统和我在美国长期研究的物质文化形式既有差异也有相似之处。同时它也加深了我对中国文化历史、当代文化习俗与体制规范以及学科视角的理解。最后，它促进了我与美国同事的关系和友谊，并且让我结交了很多中国朋友，这都预示着未来我们将会有更加愉快的合作。

（内蒙古科技大学苗露翻译）

Reflections on Collaborations:
The Quilts of Southwest China Project

Marsha MacDowell[*]

How I got engaged in research on Chinese quilts

My engagement in cross-cultural exchanges with Chinese scholars of traditional arts began in 2008 when, as an elected member of the executive board of the American Folklore Society and as a specialist in traditional arts, I was brought into an emerging circle of Chinese and American folklorists to discuss strategies to facilitate stronger international relationships pertaining to the study and preservation of forms of intangible cultural heritage. While my research has covered a wide range of basic and applied investigations of traditional culture, my deepest inquiries have been into the production, use, and meaning of women's textile traditionsand, particularly in realm of the quiltmaking.

In 2010, Tim Lloyd (executive director of AFS), Bill Ivey (past president of AFS), Kurt Dewhurst (president of AFS) and I were invited to give papers at the International Forum on Aesthetics and Cultural Ecology Construction coordinated by the folklore department at Sun Yat-sen University in Guangzhou and held in Nankunshan. My paper, "New Directions in Creating and Using Folklife Collections in the United States" focused on three digital repositories of cultural data—the Michigan Stained Glass Census, the Michigan Barn and Farmstead Survey, and the Quilt Index—all of which I had served as either a director of or consultant to as part of my work as a

---

[*] Marsha MacDowell has been an active academic folklorist who is also heavily engaged in public folklore projects, another example of crossing the boundaries and expanding the field. Trained in arts and education, she has long been active in the American Folklore Society where she has served on the society's Board and is a Folklore Fellow. Since the mid-1980s she has served as the director of the Michigan Traditional Arts Program (a museum-based, statewide program to document, present, and preserve the state of Michigan's intangible cultural heritage). She has connected her research interests in local traditional culture with national and international activities. Her involvement in AFS-CFS joint project has yielded exemplary results that will have lasting impact on folklore and museum studies in China.

curator at the Michigan State University Museum (East Lansing, Michigan, USA).① Following the conference, the four of us journeyed with Xi Chen, a doctoral student at Sun Yat-sen University to Kunming where we visited the Yunnan Nationalities Museum (YNM, Kunming, Yunnan, China), a major repository of traditional material culture of members of China's 56 nationalities. Museum director Mohua Xie and curator Yunhong Du showed us the exhibitions and gave a behind-the-scenes tour of collections. Immediately I notice textile items, both on view and in storage, that were referred to as quilts. When we all sat down to discuss possible collaborations, I suggested a mutual investigation of quilts and bedcovers by the YNM and the Michigan State University Museum.

In 2012, I had a chance to advance work between the YNM and the MSU Museum through an exhibition, *The Sum of Many Parts*: 25 *Quiltmakers in 21st Century America* that was produced by Arts Midwest and South Arts (two regional U. S. arts agencies) with support from the U. S. Embassy in China. As the senior content specialist for the exhibition, I co-wrote the major essay for the catalogue, made the recommendations for quilts artists from the Midwest to be included in the exhibition, and made the recommendation that the exhibition travel to the YNM on its national tour to other museum venues in China. When the exhibition opened in Kunming and with additional support from the Asian Council, three colleagues from the MSU Museum and I travelled to Kunming and participate in related educational programs.②

In our dialogues during that time we discussed the commonalities between the role of the nationalities museums in China and the folk and traditional arts programs in the U. S. —and especially those based at museums—such as the Michigan Traditional Arts Program at the Michigan State University Museum. This led to the crafting of a successful grant proposal from the Asian Cultural Council to begin a partnership between the MSU Museum and YNM that would focus on professional staff exchanges, "digital repatriation" of Chinese traditional arts in our collections, informal training initiatives, and planning for collaborative exhibitions/projects.

When the AFS received a Luce Foundation grant to facilitate deeper relationships with the Chinese Folklore Society, one of the strategic components of the grant was to support a project-based activity with museums. Michigan State University Museum and the YNM, serving as leads, were able to commence planning for a project focused on Chinese quilts. Each museum brought in two other additional museums from their respective countries that had strong ethnographic textile

---

① MacDowell, Marsha. "New Directions in Creating and Using Folklife Collections in the United States." Invited paper. International Forum on Aesthetics and Cultural Ecology Construction, sponsored by Sun Yat-sen University, held in Nankunshan Primeval Forest Resort, Guangdong Province, China, September 1-3, 2010.

② MacDowell, Marsha and Mary Worrall. 2012. "The Sum of Many Parts: 25 Quiltmakers from 21st-Century America" in Teresa Hollingsworth and Katy Malone, eds. The Sum of Many Parts: 25 Quiltmakers from 21st-Century America. Minnesota, Minneapolis: Arts Midwest, pp. 13-34. For more about this project see: http://www.southarts.org/touring-arts/the-sum-of-many-parts/.

research, collections, education and/or exhibition programs: Mathers Museum of World Cultures, Indiana University (Bloomington, Indiana, USA), Museum of International Folk Art (Santa Fe, New Mexico, USA), Guangxi Nationalities Museum (GXNM, Nanning, Guangxi, China), and Guizhou Nationalities Museum (GZNM, Guiyang, Guizhou, China). Later, because of the strength of its quilt collections, The International Quilt Study Center and Museum, University of Nebraska-Lincoln (Lincoln, Nebraska, USA) joined the project.

With an additional grant from the Luce Foundation and in-kind support provided by all participating museums, *the Quilts of Southwest China* became a reality and I, an American folklorist based at Michigan State University Museum served as project manager for the U.S. side and Lijun Zhang, a Chinese folklorist based at the GXNM, was project manager for the Chinese side. The project has included scholarly and professional exchanges and collaboration on all aspects of this endeavor, including researching the quilt traditions, developing and designing the exhibition content, related marketing, fundraising, multi-media projects, evaluation, educational activities, and the production of an accompanying publication.[①] The exhibition opened at the Michigan State University Museum in September 2015 and in June 2016 began touring to the partner U.S. museums.

What I have learned

• While Chinese scholars had long been investigating and collecting the clothing arts of Chinese nationalities, little attention had been given to the making and use of other domestic textiles, including quilts or bedcovers, of the nationalities. In the United States, the study of the production and use of quilts is one in which scholars from many disciplines have been engaged and there is a rich body of literature about this material culture tradition. The research and collecting done for the *Quilts of Southwest China* project provides some of the first documentation of the intangible and tangible cultural heritage associated with the traditions of using small pieces of fabric pieced and appliquéd together to form artistic and functional textiles.

• In the United States, the word quilt is understood by some to only describe a textile that is made for the purpose of serving as a bedcover and is constructed with three layers—a decorative top, a backing and a middle section that serves as insulation. The word "quilt," however, is used by many today to describe a variety of textiles including those made as art for walls and those that have only one or two layers. In China, textiles used on beds are known by a number of different names,

---

① MacDowell, Marsha and Lijun Zhang (eds). 2016. *Quilts of Southwest China*. Nanning, China: Guangxi Nationalities Museum. See also: a) images of quilts and of installation at the MSU Museum: https://www.flickr.com/photos/msumuseum/albums/72157658499870573; b) interview with Marsha MacDowell conducted by Marin Hanson, https://www.youtube.com/watch?v=Wv8oD2z6xMA; and c) an online version of the exhibition as installed at the International Quilt Study Center and Museum http://www.quiltstudy.org/exhibitions/online_exhibitions/swchina/main.html

including terms that translate as "quilt" in English. *Beizi*（被子）are comforters with covers often made of large pieces of cloth. *Pinbu beimian*（拼布被面）are textiles that incorporate layers of cloth quilted together. Two-or three-layer quilts in China are usually smaller pieces of textiles made as bedcovers, clothes, and to hold and carry a baby or small child on a person's back. Chinese bedcovers also sometimes are made with single layers of blocks of pieced patchwork and appliqué, textile construction techniques commonly associated with Western quilts. Xi Chen, in her essay in *Quilts of Southwest China*, noted that Chinese-English dictionaries also gave differing and thus confusing definitions for the word. She observed that the various linguistic understandings by Chinese of the word quilt posed a challenge for this bi-national project, "It is the partial reason why the communication about quilt exhibition between the Michigan State University Museum and the YNM became kind of blurred at China side at the very beginning. Indeed, at that time, according to our Chinese colleagues, they recognized very few "quilts" in their museum, because of the conceptual recognition and the little importance in their eyes. As an insider and outsider, when I was working as an interpreter and coordinator for the China-America museum communication, I had access, at certain extent, to know what the Chinese colleagues thought. What confused them were like why a collection of a backpack for carrying a baby is regarded as a quilt and, why quilt interests American curator."[①]

· Co-writing and co-editing a bi-lingual publication when only one of the editors is bi-lingual is a challenging endeavor. *The Quilts of Southwest China* project required multiple instances of translation. For instances, exhibition labels or essays for the catalogue which were originally written in Chinese had to be translated into English by the bilingual co-editor (Zhang), then edited by the English-only editor (MacDowell), then the edits incorporated back into the original Chinese by the bi-lingual editor. This process took an incredible amount of time and patience on the part of both editors. However, we feel that having a completely bi-lingual exhibition and publication was an important goal for this project as the scholarship would be immediately more accessible to audiences in both countries.

· The traveling that project members did together in each other's countries and the staff-to-staff professional exchanges were critical to more quickly building trust in each other and in becoming familiarized with cultural practices and institutional structures that were interconnected to planning and implementing this project. Imagine a busload of Chinese and American museum professionals singing "She'll Be Coming Round the Mountain" after spending a couple of days traveling together through the mountains of Southwest China. Imagine the laughter as we encouraged and then witnessed a Chinese colleague order two American breakfasts in order to sample our morning cuisine.

[①] Xi Chen, "What Is in A Name: Different Cultures, Different Languages, Different Nomenclature", in MacDowell, Marsha and Lijun Zhang (eds). 2016. *Quilts of Southwest China*. Nanning, China: Guangxi Nationalities Museum.

· *The Quilts of Southwest China* project confirmed my commitment to collaborations that are, indeed, project-based. The joint planning and execution of a project, especially with so many dimensions as this one had, forces individuals to move beyond just discussions to actions and outputs. The resulting products often reflect a breadth and depth of content and interpretation that are not evidenced in outputs realized by individual scholars; they also have tend to have resonance for broader audiences.

Summary

Textiles are material evidence of history and culture and can tell us much about trade, religion, traditions, migration, communities, and individuals. The intangible characteristics—the uses, meanings, stories, skills and knowledge about production—associated with these textiles are often integral to the identity and cultural heritage of individuals and communities. The traditional clothing of the millions of minorities living in Southwest China are considered important public cultural markers of ethnic cultural identity and have been extensively studied and collected. This project explored bedcovers—a far less public but nonetheless important cultural expression of Southwest Chinese minorities. This foundational investigation identified many lines of research for future study and it is hoped that the exhibition and publication will spur more scholars towards those investigations.

The understanding of and then navigation of differing institutional and cultural practices as well as learning how to work across time zones and in different languages was critical to conducting this bi-national study of quiltmaking. I know that through participation in this project I broadened my understanding of a textile tradition that had similarities and differences to a form of material culture that I had long studied in the United States and, equally as important, it facilitated my broader understanding of Chinese cultural histories and contemporary cultural and institutional practices and protocols, and disciplinary perspectives. Lastly, it fostered deeper relationships and friendships with U.S. colleagues and created new friendships with Chinese colleagues all of which augurs well for working together on new projects in the years to come.

我的两个故事

谢沫华*

我与美国民俗学界的交往始于 2007 年。当时的美国民俗学会会长艾伟和美国威涞大学教授张举文以及一位学会秘书访问了云南民族博物馆。从此,双方展开了一系列合作项目,硕果累累。其中有趣有意义的故事真是难以完全用几页文字讲述出来,姑且就提两件事吧。

第一件是有关《中国西南拼布》展览。2010 年 9 月美国民俗学会执行会长罗仪德博士一行五人到访云南民族博物馆,我有幸认识了玛莎·麦克多维尔博士和科特·杜赫斯特博士,密歇根州立大学博物馆的两位民俗学家。两年后,《化零为整:21 世纪美国的 25 位拼布制作者》展览由美国驻华大使馆介绍引进云南民族博物馆,第一次向云南观众展示了美国拼布艺术的魅力。不同的元素被重新调动、组合、拼接在一副拼布作品上,展现着艺术家的才华、创意和想象力,而他们的故事、生活和情感也通过这些拼布传达给我们,感染着我们,吸引了我们。

这种艺术形式是如此地具有异域风情,但有时却又让人感到非常熟悉。作为中国唯一的民族类国家一级博物馆,我馆长期致力于收藏、研究、展示少数民族传统文化,我们很快就注意到了美国的这项文化传统与我们中国民族民间生活中的审美和创造有异曲同工之妙。在我们博物馆的藏品中,也不乏美丽的被面、背被(拼布)等。精美的造物也凝聚着各少数民族人民的审美、才华、情感和故事。

美国人对于拼布传统的珍重和对于拼布艺术的热情,启发我们开始以一种新的角度重新审视我们的拼布收藏。麦克多维尔博士正巧也是《化零为整》展览的资深学者,作为项目的一部分,在展览期间她和杜赫斯特博士回到中国昆明进行讲座和参加展览。我们成为好朋友,也建立起了云南民族博物馆和密歇根州立大学博物馆两馆之间的友谊。这些友谊促成了两馆在拼布收藏、资源共享、数字化、员工交流和其他领域的合作。密歇根州立大学博物馆

---

* 编者注:谢沫华在担任现职之前曾任云南民族博物馆馆长十多年,期间,也是较早并较广泛地与国内外民俗学者交流的博物馆界人士之一。他的贡献不仅在于开拓了云南民族博物馆的视野(另见杜韵红和张丽君文),也使得国内民俗学对民族博物馆有了新的学科认知,特别是与美国密歇根大学博物馆的合作,为国内民族博物馆树立了一个典范。虽然博物馆方面的研究还是中国民俗学界较薄弱的环节,但良好的开端已经展现。2016 年初,谢沫华转任云南省少数民族古籍整理出版规划办公室、云南少数民族记忆遗产研究中心主任,无疑也将会从"少数民族记忆"方面丰富民俗学的研究。他的故事的一些细节可见本文集中杜韵红的记述。

和云南民族博物馆共同策划了中美民族博物馆交流项目，杜赫斯特和我作为协调人。我们还共同引入了其他四家博物馆作为合作伙伴：广西民族博物馆、贵州省民族博物馆、马瑟斯世界文化博物馆和圣塔菲国际民间艺术博物馆。我们相继在中美两地召开多次协调会议，并得到了美国路思基金会和美国民俗学会的支持。作为这一合作项目的第一个成果，《中国西南的拼布》展览于 2015 年 9 月在密歇根州立大学博物馆开幕，并将在其他至少三家美国的博物馆进行巡展至 2017 年。

我个人要感谢杜赫斯特会长、麦克多维尔、杰森·杰克逊馆长、玛莎·波尔馆长、高聪馆长、王颀馆长，和他们相识、相交、相知是一件愉快的事，也要感谢中美六个合作博物馆的团队为此付出的辛劳。杜赫斯特教授曾经提倡用"协作"代替合作，在中美博物馆之间创造一种紧密无间的战略合作伙伴关系，我赞同他的意见。我们中国人用"同舟共济扬帆起，乘风破浪万里航"来形容有共同理想的合作伙伴齐心协力所能展开的前景。两国的民族博物馆专家如今已经在同一条船上扬帆起航，让我们期待一次成功的远航！

第二件是有关"云南民族竹乐器展示活动"。2013 年 10 月 26 日，由云南民族博物馆和美国威涞大学张举文教授联袂策划的"云南民族竹乐器展示活动"在该校图书馆拉开序幕。该活动是学校及整个社区的一次大型活动，持续到 11 月 3 日。期间推出了系列活动，包括"云南民族竹乐器展览"，展示云南民族代表性竹乐器 49 套（件）；举办中国民乐主题音乐会，与玉溪聂耳竹乐团进行在线交流互动；举办专题讲座及中美音乐专题研讨会，并进行在线展示，扩大受众面。活动对于促进中美两国文化的交流与合作，增进两国人民的了解与友谊，宣传弘扬云南民族传统文化产生了积极影响。

这次活动也说明，很多有意义的活动不一定需要很大的规模和很多经费。小型的小专题的展览、展示、讨论，以及互动也会达到深度的交流。为此，我要感谢张举文教授的牵线搭桥，及其为此次中美文化交流展览活动付出的辛劳。

中美博物馆合作项目馆长策划会，昆明，2013 年。前排坐者从左向右：印第安纳大学马瑟斯世界文化博物馆馆长杰森·杰克逊、圣塔菲国际民间艺术博物馆馆长玛莎·波尔、密歇根州立大学博物馆馆长科特·杜赫斯特、玛莎·麦克多维尔、云南民族博物馆馆长谢沫华、广西民族博物馆王頠馆长、贵州民族博物馆高聪馆长。Sino-US Museum Partnership Program-Director's Planning Meeting, Kunming, 2013. Sitting from left to right: Jason Jackson of Mathers Museum of World Cultures, Masha Bol of Museum of International Folk Art, Kurt Dewhurst of MSUM, Marsha MacDowell of MSUM, Mohua Xie of YNM, Wei Wang of GXNM, and Cong Gao of GZNM.

My Two Stories

Mohua Xie*

My entrance into the world of Sino-US folkloristic communication started in 2007. At that time, AFS President Bill Ivey, Willamette University Professor Juwen Zhang, and an AFS assistant director visited Yunnan Nationalities Museum. From that point on, both sides began a series of notable collaborative projects. It is truly difficult to provide a full account of all of the stories and experiences. For the time being, I will bring up just two of these stories.

The first relates to the "Quilts of Southwest China" exhibition. In September 2010, AFS's delegation led by President Dewhurst, Executive Director Tim Lloyd, and three other members visited YNM. I had the pleasure of meeting Michigan State University Museum's folklore specialists, Marsha MacDowell and Kurt Dewhurst. Two years later, thanks to the U. S. Embassy in China, *The Sum of Many Parts*: 25 *Quiltmakers in* 21st *Century America* was displayed at the YNM. For the first time an audience saw the charm of an American quilt display in Yunnan. The display brought different elements into play combining cloth into a quilted work of art displaying the artists' talents, creativity, imagination, and stories. The artists' lives and feelings greatly touched us and influenced us as the audience.

This type of art has a foreign grace, but leaves some people feeling very comforted. As China's only first class nationalities museum, we have been engaged in collection, research, and the display of minority traditional cultures for a long time. We have taken note of the differences in production and esthetics of America's cultural tradition and how it affected the lives of the unofficial

---

* Mohua Xie served as the Director of Yunnan Nationalities Museum during the years when AFS-CFS collaborations developed. Xie has engaged in extensive exchanges with domestic and foreign scholars of folklore museums. Not only has he opened new horizons for the Yunnan Nationalities Museum (see also Yunhong Du and Lijun Zhang's stories in this volume), but he has extended China's folklore studies to recognize minority nationalities museums as new branches of the field. Through his collaborative work with Michigan State University Museum, he set an example for other Chinese nationalities museums to work with folklorists at home and abroad. Although museum research is still low on China's priorities there have been favorable emergences. At the start of 2016, Mohua Xie took his current position as the director of the Research Center for Minority Nationalities Memory Heritage in charge of classification and publication of minority texts in Yunnan Province. He will undoubtedly contribute to historical folklore studies from the perspective of "the memory of the minority nationalities."

Chinese ethnic groups leading to equally wonderful pieces. Our museum has numerous beautiful quilts and many other works. The delicate pieces highlight every minority ethnic group's aesthetics, ability, puzzlement, and stories.

With American's value and passion towards traditional quilts, Americans enlightened us starting with a new point of view by reexamining the collection of our quilts. Dr. MacDowell happened to be a veteran scholar of *the Sum of Mary Parts* and acted in part on the project. During the exhibition, Dr. MacDowell and Dr. Dewhurst returned to Kunming to present a few lectures and attend an exhibition. We became good friends and established the partnership between the YNM and the Michigan State University Museum. Such a partnership facilitated the collection, digitization, and exchange of quilts, staff, and other methods of cooperation. Both institutions have recently been planning a US-China ethnic museum exchange project coordinated by Dr. Dewhurst and me. We have successfully collaborated with four other museums: Guangxi Museum of Nationalities, Guizhou Museum of Nationalities, Indiana University's Mathers Museum of World Cultures, and the Museum of International Folk Art in New Mexico. We have made steady progress with meetings on both sides, with support from the AFS and the Henry Luce Foundation. The first result of this cooperation is *the Quilts of Southwest China* exhibit that first opened September 2015 at Michigan State University Museum. Needless to say, the exhibition is in the progress of making rounds to at least three other American universities until 2017.

I would like to thank Marsha MacDowell, Kurt Dewhurst, Jason Jackson, Martha Bol, Gao Cong, Wang Wei, and all the acquaintances I made along the way; meeting them was a delightful experience. I also would like to thank the teams at all six museums that invested much time and energy into this collaboration. Dr. Dewhurst once advocated the use of "coordination" in place of cooperation. Such a strategy brought about this inseparable relationship between American and Chinese museums as cooperative partners, and I fully value his opinion. We Chinese say, "Crossing a river in the same boat to set sail, braving the wind and the billows to travel a thousand miles," to describe a partner with similar dreams, both using our own abilities to work toward the future. Nowadays the specialists of both countries are already on a joint boat to set sail, letting us watch their successful voyage!

The second story is about "The Exhibition of Bamboo Musical Instruments and Performances from Yunnan." On October 26th, 2013, thanks to YNM and Willamette University Professor Juwen Zhang's collaboration, the exhibition opened in the library and the performance raised the curtain at the concert hall. It was the school and community's first large activity. The series of events included an exhibition of 49 pieces representative of the bamboo musical instruments from various ethnic groups in Yunnan, a Chinese traditional music concert, online interaction with the Yuxi Nieer Bamboo Orchestra, special lectures on Chinese and US music, and a seminar on traditional music and healing in the modern world. The performance was meant to promote cultural exchanges and cooperation between China and the US, to further the understanding and friendship among people of the two cultures, to publically promote Yunnan traditional culture and have a positive influence to the community.

These activities show that it is not necessary to have a large scale and expensive activity to make an event meaningful. Small scale activities using specific topics, exhibitions, discussions and interactions, all build a deep understanding. For this reason I want to thank Professor Juwen Zhang's hard work at building a bridge behind the scenes between Chinese and US cultures for this exchange.

(Translation by Euchari Majors)

十年：中美博物馆合作项目记述

杜韵红[*]

2015年9月28日，"中国西南拼布展"在美丽的大洋彼岸美国密歇根州立大学博物馆开展了，消息传来，参与合作的中方——云南民族博物馆、广西民族博物馆、贵州民族博物馆无不欣喜振奋，历经八年的辛苦与周折，交流项目终于结出了硕果。这是中美民俗学会博物馆项目合作的第一期成果，凝聚了中美双方同行的心血。

中美两国博物馆间的合作肇始于2007年。彼时，中国民俗学会与美国民俗学会刚刚开启了中美学会间的专家学者的对等互访交流，时任美国民俗学会会长艾伟、美国崴涞大学教授张举文博士等一行在中国民俗学会秘书长叶涛先生的陪同下到访云南民族博物馆，单位派我陪同他们一行赴古城丽江考察。艾伟先生是美国克林顿政府时期的首席文化顾问，此行是他本人第二次到访云南。上一次来访云南时，他陪同克林顿总统访问了丽江。再次回到丽江，艾伟对于当时紧张有趣的行程仍然津津有味，一路上我们共同分享了他愉快的记忆之旅。记得在穿城而过的河边就餐时，清风抚柳，暖暖的阳光透过树枝洒在身上，我们不由得一起轻轻吟唱了"County Road"，一同感怀着当下美好时光。怀着对纳西洞经音乐的美好记忆，在我们陪同下，艾伟再次聆听了宣科先生的洞经音乐会。短暂的丽江之行结束时，双方认为中美在非遗保护与传承、文化多样性研究、博物馆进入社区等方面找到了契合点，促成了合作的意愿。

在双方民俗学会的推动下，2010年9月5—6日，美国民俗学会代表团再次来访云南民族博物馆。代表团有时任美国民俗学会会长科特·杜赫斯特、执行会长罗仪德、博物馆合作项目负责人玛莎·麦克多维尔以及前任会长的艾伟。当时陪同到来的中山大学的陈熙女士担任了翻译。此时云南民族博物馆谢沫华馆长与代表团就未来中美博物馆之间的合作进行了商谈，双方确定在博物馆数字化建设、青年学者的交流互访、开展非遗保护、举办交流展览等方面达成合作意愿。在会谈结束的晚宴上，一个惊喜是当天正是艾伟先生的生日，在温暖浓

---

[*] 编者注：杜韵红现任云南民族博物馆办公室主任，研究员，从业20余年，一直致力于陈列展览策划推介工作，推出和引进展览百余次。主要关注民族文化的人类学和民俗学研究工作，研究专著《物微补志——茶马古道记忆与变迁》获得业内奖项。研究成果发表于国内核心期刊及韩国、越南等国家专业学术期刊。多年来参与与美国民俗学会和密歇根大学博物馆的合作。她这里所记述的体现了中国的民族博物馆在与民俗学融合中所取得的成就，也展示了近年来与外界合作的历程。

情的烛光蛋糕中又迎来了他新的一年，似乎预示了中美两国博物馆间合作交流的新起点。

玛莎·麦克多维尔在密歇根州立大学博物馆有多年的累积。她策划的《化零为整：21世纪美国的25位拼布制作者》展览由美国驻华大使馆推出，在中国的部分博物馆中展出。鉴于两馆间将要展开的合作，大使馆把展览推荐给了云南民族博物馆，我馆欣然接受了该展。展览第一次向云南观众展示了美国拼布艺术的魅力。考虑到合作的需要，接下来我馆根据麦克多维尔教授的建议，开始了有计划的筹备，就拼布进行了补充征集工作，将征集工作扩大至不同民族、不同区域的拼布艺术收藏。几年时间里，我馆在拼布艺术的收藏数量与品相方面有了突破与进展。

2013年12月8—14日在昆明召开了"中美博物馆合作项目馆长策划会"，会议由云南民族博物馆主办，邀请了合作方美国民俗学会代表团一行10多人的团队，其中包括罗仪德、马瑟斯世界文化博物馆馆长杰森·杰克逊、新墨西哥圣塔菲国际民间艺术博物馆馆长玛莎·波尔等，确定中美双方由中国云南民族博物馆、美国密歇根州立大学博物馆馆长作为项目发起人，代表中美双方各自选定3家博物馆，一共6家博物馆开启合作，举办"中美拼布艺术展"，在美国巡展。经过多方努力，该项目在2014年顺利获得了资助。

同时，基于已经搭建起的良好合作基础，经由美国威涞大学教授张举文博士引荐，我馆与张教授所在的学校联袂策划了"云南民族竹乐器展示活动"，由我馆杨莉副研究馆员代表云南民族博物馆远赴美国参加了此次活动。2013年10月26日展示活动如期在美国威涞大学图书馆拉开序幕，这是学校及整个社区的一次大型活动，时间一直持续到11月3日（另见谢沐华文）。

2014年，中方在中国民俗学会会长朝戈金先生带领下一行20多人赴美国。作为该次合作的联络人，我也参加了此次人员的交流访问，其他人员还有我馆学术交流部的罗文宏馆员，贵州民族博物馆高聪馆长、社交部李姝爱主任，广西民族博物馆王颀馆长、研究部龚世扬主任三馆共六人。我们前往美国新墨西哥州圣塔菲市、密歇根州立大学、印第安纳大学的博物馆开展了学术论坛、田野考察、交流培训，就非遗保护、非遗数字化、策划展览等方面开展交流，为2015年联合展览做好前期准备。

我们一行还参加了2014年美国民俗学会年会，其中博物馆专场召开了"第五届中美民俗和非物质文化遗产论坛：在民族志博物馆和遗产地桥接物质的与非物质的文化遗产"专题会议。会议期间，代表们一同考察了印第安人保护区，特别对他们的纺织工艺、陶器制作、金属器加工等传统工艺流程进行了观摩考察，使得代表们对于美国开展原住民的非遗保护、保护策略，有了直观的认识，可以看出各自国家在保护理念方法上的异同。

在圣塔菲国际民间艺术博物馆，我们有幸深入到了该馆的库房，参观了他们的收藏，该馆的策展人向我们专题介绍了他们近年来的策展情况。当时他们正在策划一个传统工艺染色展。该展览已经准备了五年，计划于2015年展出。

我国博物馆在1949年以后长期以来受到苏联以及欧洲办馆模式的影响，加之自身传统文化背景因素影响，精品意识强，皇权贵族、庙堂之上的文物才是重点，注重文物的历史价值、艺术性，强调的是精英意识。文物珍贵，有历史感是重要的，却忽略了民间普通民众的真实生活，传递的思想、价值观相对单一，与普罗大众的现实生活距离甚远。自然而然，民众除了对知名度较高的展品或遗址遗物有较高的兴趣外，对于知名度一般、大历史背景事件关联甚少的文物自然兴趣大减。从专业的角度去分析问题，原因虽然多种多样，但与未能深入挖掘文物的文化内涵、使文物与现实关联度较低不无一定关系。

接下来，我们又到访了马瑟斯世界文化博物馆，该馆开展的志愿者工作、陈列展览给我留下了极为深刻的印象。博物馆的工作人员同时兼职该系教授，时任博物馆馆长杰森·杰克逊也是该系的教授。博物馆为在校的大学生、研究生提供了实践学习的机会，教学课程设置是博物馆的相关学科，博物馆的实践条件为在校学生提供从理论回到应用的机会。

我们的第三站是密歇根州立大学博物馆，也是玛莎、杜赫斯特就职的博物馆。由玛莎创办的大学节日历经20多年的运作积淀，如今已经成为他们所在城市的兰辛市的年度民俗节，已然成为密歇根州兰辛市的品牌。每当节日来临，来自美国不同区域的民俗工艺技艺项目就会汇聚至此，如同美国史密森尼学会举办的民俗节一样，只是这里的规模没有他们的盛大。

2015年9月在美国密歇根州立大学博物馆首站推出"中国西南拼布展"，展品由中美两国六家博物馆提供，每一家博物馆提供3—5床最具民族特色工艺、图案的拼布被子，涉及的拼布被子都为当地传统工艺制作而成，配合展出同期播放一部拼布艺人的影视视频作品。而此前，围绕拼布工艺各馆已经进行了田野调查，围绕拼布专题开展了研究，六家博物馆研究成果汇集成册，专题出版（另见玛莎·麦克多维尔和张丽君文）。

笔者全程参与了该合作，对于项目有着深刻的感受。客观地评价，此次合作展览规模并不大，较之国内的合作，展品数量极少、制作简单、展厅面积不大等，展览"硬件"条件并不好。但通过比较会发现，双方从策展开始就显现了区别。首先选题切入点小，但策展时间长，围绕展览的相关调查、研究及出版成果缺一不可。一般来说，国内举办规模如此之小的展览时，基本只做简单的展陈，后续研究成果鲜有呈现。其次，就非遗展来说，国内目前一般呈现出场面大，制作大，投入不少，长期以来宏大的叙事风格导致展览总是"高大上"。近些年来中国博物馆的发展势头迅猛强劲，展览经费颇为充足（也不乏经费仍然紧缺的博物馆），馆际间的合作交流步伐加快，各馆就非遗联合展出先后举办了形式多样的各种展览活动。仅以刚过去的2016年遗产日各馆举办活动来看，国内博物馆对于非遗保护是有积极性的，但有时缺乏对于小项目的运作热情，缺乏后续的研究拓展。

2016年3月，凝聚了中美博物馆的专家学者的研究成果的《中国西南拼布》在中国出版，中国民俗学会会长朝戈金博士在序言中写到："中美民俗学会在过去八年一直致力于创建一个连接专家、学者和机构的网络以共享两国的学术专业志趣。其中的活动以非物质文化遗产政策和博物馆实践为主题，包括在两国举办论坛以及进行两个学会中的研究生、年轻学者和资深会员间的交流和互访。"朝戈金会长的总结完全诠释了博物馆项目的核心，馆际间的交流将继续朝着这个方向发展，合作交流将会迎来更美好的未来。

阿果兹诺、谢沫华、艾伟、起国庆、杜韵红（自左向右），2007年12月于昆明。Mable Agozzino, Mohua Xie, Bill Ivey, Guoqing Qi, Yunhong Du (from left to right), Kunming, Dec. 2007. Photograph by Juwen Zhang.

Ten Years: China-US Museum Collaborations in Retrospect

Yunhong Du*

The Exhibition of *the Quilts of Southwest China* opened in the US on Sept. 28, 2015. When the news came to the three museums involved, everyone felt so pleased and excited. It was the fruit of eight years' hard work, the result of the first phase of AFS-CFS joint project, and embodied the efforts of both Chinese and American counterparts.

Collaborations between the museums in China and the United States began in 2007. At that time, the CFS and AFS had just initiated mutual visits. The AFS President Bill Ivey led a delegation, including Dr. Juwen Zhang and others, accompanied by the CFS Secretary General Tao Ye, and visited YNM. I was assigned to host the guests to Lijiang. Mr. Ivey had visited Lijiang as the NEA Chair during Clinton Administration. This was his second visit to Lijiang. He shared his fond memories along the way. When we had meals along the river, with gentle wind and sunshine, we could not help but sing together the song, "Country Road". We also experienced the traditional Naxi music. It was a short visit, but the common interest and desire to preserve and protect diverse cultures enabled future collaborations.

With the support of AFS and CFS, an AFS delegation led by the then AFS President Kurt Dewhurst and Executive Director Tim Lloyd, the Museum Program Director Marsha MacDowell, the former AFS President Ivey, and Xi Chen of Sun Yat-sen University, visited us again on Sept. 5 – 6, 2010. As a result, the two sides discussed and agreed to engage in the construction of digital museum, exchange of young curators, and other exchange programs. It was a surprise to us that it happened to be Bill Ivey's birthday. The candle-lit cake seemed to have shed light upon the future

---

* Yunhong Du is Office Director and Researcher at the Yunnan Nationalities Museum, having curated more than 100 exhibitions in over 20 years. Her research focuses on the minority nationalities in Southwest China, and has been published in journals at home and abroad. Through AFS-CFS projects, she has been involved with University of Michigan Museum and other US museums. Her story here reflects how the nationalities museum in China became integrated into the larger national network in China through folklore projects, and became involved in international collaboration in recent years.

collaborations between the museums on the two sides.

Marsha MacDowell has rich experience in curating exhibitions in the Michigan State University Museum. The exhibition she curated, *The Sum of Many Parts*: *25 Quiltmakers in 21st—Century America*, was sponsored by the US Embassy in China. It toured in a few museums in China, and the embassy recommended us to host one. We were happy to do so and were able to show the charming art of quiltmaking in the US to the people in Yunnan for the first time. Under her advice, our museum began to systematically collect quilts from different ethnic groups in different regions, which enriched our collection.

From Dec. 8 to 14, 2013, the Sino-US Museum Partnership Program-Director's Planning Meeting was held in Kunming, Yunnan. A delegation of more than ten people came from the US, including Jason Jackson of Mathers Museum of World Cultures, Masha Bol of Museum of International Folk Art, Kurt Dewhurst of MSUM, Marsha MacDowell of MSUM, Mohua Xie of YNM, Wei Wang of GXNM, and Cong Gao of GZNM. The six museums then began a collaboration to hold the exhibition of *the Quilts of Southwest China*, which was successfully funded in 2014.

At the same time, based on the previous good relations, Dr. Juwen Zhang initiated the "Yunnan National Bamboo Musical Instrument Exhibition" in Willamette University, Salem, Oregon from Oct. 26-Nov. 3, 2013. On behalf of our YNM, Li Yang of YNM Researcher took dozens of bamboo musical instruments and participated in a series of events there. It was a major event related to Chinese culture in the university community. (See also Mohua Xie's story in this volume.)

In 2014, the CFS President Chao Gejin led a delegation of over 20 members to the US. I was happy to be one of the members. We visited the Museum of International Folk Art in New Mexico, the Michigan State University Museum, and the Mathers Museum of World Cultures of Indiana University. The conversations and discussions covered a wide range of issues related to staff exchange, ICH protection, ICH digitalization, and other aspects, and prepared us well for the joint exhibition in 2015. Our delegation also joined the 2014 AFS annual meeting, and visited the Indian Reservations in New Mexico, which greatly improved our understanding of the conservation of the Native American culture. We learned many new ideas.

At the Museum of International Folk Arts, we had the privilege of going deep into the storage facility and visiting their collections. The curators of the museum gave us a special tour of their collections and recent exhibitions. At that time they were planning an exhibition of the traditional dyeing process.

In China after 1949, museums were influenced by the Soviet Union and the European models. Besides, with the traditional cultural concepts, our museums have paid attention to the fine quality of the collected objects and their imperial symbolism, and emphasized the historical, artistic, and elite values. Therefore we ignored the real life of the common people, their ideas and values, and kept a great distance from everyday life. As a result, people are educated only to have interests in the famous exhibitions and cultural relics, and have little interest in those objects without "grand" history. There are many reasons for this reality, but not exploring the inner meaning of cultural objects and relating them to realities is certainly one of the reasons.

We later visited the Mathers Museum of World Cultures. It had the system of using volunteers for exhibitions, which impressed me greatly. Some staff were also professors, such as the then Director Jason Jackson. The museum was also used for teaching and student research, providing opportunities for the students to apply theories.

At the Michigan State University Museum, we learned that Marsha MacDowell had created a University Festival for over 20 years. It then became an annual folklife festival for the city as well. It is like the Smithsonian Folklife Festival, but only smaller in scale.

The Quilts of Southwest China began its tour exhibition with the MSUM in September 2015. The exhibition contains the objects from the six museums. Each museum provided 3 – 5 quilts that are most distinctive of the local traditions. During the exhibition, there were also video demonstrations of the quilts being made. Also, a catalogue was published.

I have been involved in all of these events in the past years, and have strong feelings about the differences between the museums in the two countries. Honestly speaking, the scale of these exhibitions are not as big as those within China in terms of the number of objects, and other "hardware" of the museums. However, the ways of curating an exhibition shows the difference. The first is in choosing a theme. In the US, the theme is often small, but the planning stage is long. In China, our regular exhibitions are often too simple and small, and without follow-up research. In terms of the ICH exhibitions in China, we tend to present huge size and big investment seeking to be the "most or best" in all aspects. In recent years, Chinese museums have been developing quickly with sufficient financial resources (though not always the case). Exchanges between museums are increasingly frequent. There are various great exhibitions on the ICH items. Simply by looking at the exhibitions in 2016, one can easily see that there is strong interest in the ICH protection, but there is lack of small scale exhibitions and related research work.

In March 2016, *The Quilts of Southwest China* was published in China. It is the fruit of the Sino-US collaboration. In the Preface, CFS President Chao Gejin writes, "The CFS-AFS have been engaged in the past eight years in creating a network of experts, scholars, and institutions that can be shared by the people from both countries. One of the themes is the ICH policies and museum practices, including the forum and young scholar exchange programs." This statement well illustrates the core concerns of our museum program. By continuing to move in this direction, our collaboration will have an even brighter future.

(Translation by Juwen Zhang)

我所参与的博物馆交流项目

张丽君*

  我很高兴分享我参与中国西南拼布展的经验，这也许可以代表在一次合作项目中的中方视角。从2013年到2016年，我担任双方合作的博物馆项目的中方联系人。所以我有机会深入参与项目，并协调参与合作的三家中国博物馆的工作。

  我要感谢中国民俗学会和美国民俗学会，为我这样的年轻学者提供了一次难得的学习机会。我从中国和美国的同事那里学到了很多东西。作为一个年轻的民俗学者和博物馆研究员，能够目睹和体验中美两国民俗学会之间的交流和合作，我感到很幸运。罗仪德在2008年访问中国时，我担任他和中国民俗学会会长刘魁立的翻译。他们那时在北京讨论了两国学会之间未来可能的合作。我仍然保留着他们的会谈笔记。在讨论的许多事情中，一个关键点是联合举办展览和一起出版。我当时是北京师范大学的研究生，现在我则参加了中美民俗学会推广的一个重要的合作项目，即西南地区的拼布展和相关出版物。这些年来，中美合作取得了长足进展，涉及民间艺术和博物馆等多种形式的不同领域。

  对于这个由中国和美国的六个博物馆合作的特别项目（本文集中其他同事也提到了），我们专注的问题是，作为无形和有形遗产的拼布的纺织形式，其如何吸引两国研究人员和观众的共同兴趣。通过拼布，我们不仅了解了西南地区的纺织品传统，而且还研究了传统的社会和文化情况以及该地区健在的拼布艺术家的状况。

  虽然中美双方有很多共同点，但在与两个国家的不同机构的联系过程中，两国的文化、制度、专业实践和政策都存在差异，需要的是相互理解、调整、协商和灵活性。参加中美非物质文化遗产和民族博物馆合作项目的三家中国博物馆是云南民族博物馆，广西民族博物馆和贵州民族博物馆。这三家博物馆在许多方面具有共同性。首先，它们都是在文化丰富多样的西南地区，彼此相邻。云南有26个民族，广西有12个民族，贵州有18个民族。博物馆都致力于保护和促进民族文化，它们属于所谓的"民族博物馆"。这里的民族一词是指"少

---

  * 编者注：张丽君现任广西民族博物馆的研究员，从事生态博物馆和其他文化遗产实践的研究。她参与策划了两个展览：密歇根州立大学博物馆的"中国西南拼布展"；"中国西南篮筐编制"。她在印第安纳大学获得了民俗学和音乐民族学博士学位。她是从美国获得博士学位，然后回到中国的年轻民俗学者的代表之一。她所参与的合作项目为中国同仁们展示了学术与公共民俗之间的联系。正如她在此所说，通过与美国民俗学者的合作，中国民俗界学者和机构也加深了他们之间的联系和合作。

数民族",也许是个不好翻译的词。从本质上看,中国的民族博物馆更像是美国的民族学或人类学博物馆。其次,博物馆的藏品都多是纺织品,着重于该地区的少数民族的纺织品。纺织品的类别包括民族服装、织锦和绣花日用品、宗教服装、锦缎和绣花装饰品和装饰品、被套和床罩以及婴儿吊带等。最后,这三个博物馆都积极地与当地社区互动,并与其他博物馆互动。例如,云南民族博物馆为移民民族社区举办传统节日,广西民族博物馆邀请传统艺术家定期在展厅做示范。

此外,这三家博物馆一直积极探索与国内外其他博物馆和文化机构进行交流和合作。他们都强调在博物馆培训年轻学者和工作人员,并为他们提供更多的机会学习和参与合作项目。这三家博物馆在参加"中国西南拼布展"项目之前已经有着在其他项目上的合作关系。他们的共同点为中美合作展览和出版项目奠定了基础。

然而,我也看到了各个博物馆之间的一些差异。三个中国博物馆不是各自独立的,不是独立于国家体系。由于某些原因,虽然他们都是民族博物馆,但它们属于不同的国家行政系统。云南民族博物馆和贵州民族博物馆隶属于国家民族事务委员会。广西民族博物馆隶属于国家文化事业部门。不同的行政从属关系为这些博物馆和其他博物馆在实践和政策方面带来不同的资金来源。例如,如果博物馆将注册商品借给国外展出,他们需要分别向不同的政府部门报告。国家民族事务委员会和国家文化部对这些项目制定了不同的政策和法规。

中国的博物馆的管理、结构和实践不同于美国的博物馆。通常,中国博物馆由办公室、研究部、收藏部、展览部、公共教育部以及安全和服务部门组成。办公室是行政中心,协调博物馆不同部门的活动,以及与其他机构的互动。一个小型的美国博物馆的工作,如收购和收藏、管理、文献、研究、展览和出版等一个人做的工作,在中国被分发到不同部门。

对于"中国西南拼布展"项目,我们在每个博物馆有一个联系人,负责博物馆内部的项目协调,并与其他博物馆联系。我来自广西民族博物馆的研究部,也是中国方面的总联系人。由于三个博物馆的结构安排不同,我们有不同程度的协调工作和协作。首先,三个博物馆需要在内部不同部门之间进行协调。其次,三个博物馆之间也要有协作。同时,我们还与美国博物馆进行着双边合作。

我认为该项目是一个相互沟通、相互理解、相互学习和分享的过程,并且是互利的。三家中国博物馆各自从他们的藏品中为展览贡献了四床被子。为此,我们准备了描述和解释文字与相关照片。基于民族学实地调查,我们制作了三个视频,展示艺术家在实际创造中的情况,作为展览的背景,并通过解说介绍这些艺术家。我们还提供了地图和高清图像。

该项目也为三家中国博物馆的相关人员的学术交流提供了平台。我们有两名馆长和四名馆员参加了2015年在美国圣塔菲举办的美国民俗学会年会,以及同时举办的中美博物馆和非物质文化遗产论坛。四名年轻的工作人员也有机会参观三家合作的美国博物馆,并与他们交流。在美国期间,中方的工作人员也参观了美国其他一些博物馆。该合作项目有助于促进学者和公众对拼布被面这一中国纺织传统的独特形式的认识和了解。被邀请参加"中国西南拼布展"的拼布被面艺术家黄碧玉在展厅展示并与参观者交流。黄不仅专门为"中国西南拼布展"做了一床被子,而且这个过程也通过视频被展示在美国的展览中。

作为一个跨文化的项目,语言和术语的使用对我们的合作工作提出了挑战。例如,在西方意义上,很难找到一个相等的词表达中国的拼布。由拼接和装饰在一起的小件织物制成的物品在中文是叫拼布。它不一定是床上使用的物品。它可以是挂在墙上的衣服或装饰纺织品。此外,还有中文使用的其他名称,如百家衣或百衲衣,以及拼布被面,它们也不同于英语术语 quilt。正如麦克多维尔在她的文章中所描述的,这是一个令人着迷的学习过程,但我们最终找到了应对这个概念的方法。因为在美国的展览的观众是美国人,被子展览需要借出的物品是在床上使用的被子。起初,我们中方的一些同事不明白为什么必须要是床上使用的棉被。我们不得不处理对术语的不同理解,这也是文化翻译的问题。

这个合作项目是一个渠道,沟通了参与的各个机构和个人,使大家对各自的文化、制度、专业实践和政策增进了解。这些合作还建立了关系,有助于开拓进一步的研究和打开未来的合作之门。在 2016 年底,广西民族博物馆和马瑟斯世界文化博物馆已经开始讨论广西文物遗产民族志的合作研究项目。我期待着参与这样的项目。

(张举文翻译)

My Involvement in the Museum Exchange Projects

Lijun Zhang*

  I am glad to share my experience in curating *the Quilts of Southwest China* as a collaborative learning project from the perspective of one who works at a Chinese museum. From 2013 to 2016, I was the curator and main contact for the exhibition on the Chinese side. I got the chance to be deeply engaged in the project and coordinated the work among all the three Chinese museums participating.

  I would like to express my gratitude to the China Folklore Society and the American Folklore Society for providing junior scholars like me this great opportunity and precious learning experience. I personally learned much from Marsha MacDowell and other co-workers from both China and the United States. Marsha is a wonderful and extremely experienced and knowledgeable mentor for me. And the Michigan State University Museum has done some marvelous work.

  As a junior folklorist and museum curator, I feel fortunate to witness and experience the fast development of communication and collaboration between CFS and AFS. I served as the interpreter for Tim Lloyd and Kuili Liu, the President of China Folklore Society, at their meeting in Beijing during the spring of 2008 to discuss possible future collaboration between CFS and AFS.

  I still keep the notes from their dialogue. Among the many things discussed, one key point was the goal to hold collaborative exhibitions and present a publication together. I was a folklore graduate student at Beijing Normal University at that time and now I am participating in one of those major collaborative projects promoted by AFS and CFS, that is, *the Quilts of Southwest China*

---

  * Lijun Zhang is a researcher at the Guangxi Nationalities Museum, where she focuses on the study of ecomuseums and other cultural heritage practices. She has co-curated two recent exhibitions: "Quilts of Southwest China" at the Michigan State University Museum, and "Putting Baskets to Work in Southwest China" at the Mathers Museum of World Cultures, Indiana University. She earned her Ph. D. in Folklore and Ethnology at Indiana University as part of a generation of young folklorists receiving doctorate degrees in the United States before returning to China. Her involvement in the collaborative projects show the connection between academic and public folklore. As she emphasizes below, through the help of with American folklorists, her Chinese colleagues and institutions reaffirmed their connections and collaborations.

exhibition and related publication. For these years, the China-US collaboration has gone a long way and covered different areas like folklore and museum work in various forms.

For the quilt project, a partnership between three museums from China and three from the United States was formed. We focused on the tangible and intangible heritage in the form of quilts that draw common interests from researchers and audience alike in both countries. From these quilts we not only learned about textile tradition in Southwest China, but also studied the social and cultural situations in practice and the conditions of the living quilt artists in the region.

While we share a lot of things in common, there are challenges in the process of conducting the project within institutes in both countries regarding cultural, institutional, professional, and policy practices that require coordination, mutual understanding, adjustment, negotiation, and flexibility between both parties.

The Chinese museums partnering in the China and US "Intangible Cultural Heritage and Ethnographic Museum Project" are Yunnan Nationalities Museum (YNM), Guangxi Nationalities Museum (GXNM), and Guizhou Nationalities Museum (GZNM). The three museums share many common aspects.

First, they are geographically adjacent to each other in the culturally rich and diverse southwest China. There are 26 ethnic groups in Yunnan, 12 ethnic groups in Guangxi, and 18 ethnic groups in Guizhou. The museums are all committed to the preservation and promotion of ethnic cultures falling into the "nationalities museum" category. While the literal translation for the Chinese word *minzu* is "ethnicity" there are wider translations. In essence, these kind of Chinese museums are more like the ethnographic or anthropological museums in the United States.

Secondly, the collections are rich in fabric, with emphasis on ethnic textiles from the region. The textile categories include ethnic costumes, brocades, embroidered items for daily use, religious costumes, embroidered ornaments and decorations, quilts and bed covers, and baby slings.

Thirdly, all three museums actively interact with and engage the local communities in their museum activities. For example, YNM holds traditional festivals for migrant ethnic communities while GXNM invites traditional artists to do demonstrations in exhibition rooms on a regular basis.

Last but not least, the three museums have all been actively exploring opportunities of cultural exchanges and collaborative projects with other museums and institutions both at home and abroad. They all emphasize training junior scholars and museum staff providing them with more opportunities to learn and to participate in collaborative projects. The three museums have already established collaborative relationships on other projects prior to their participation in the "Quilts of Southwest China" project.

On the China side, many of the commonalities among the three museums set the foundation for the current China-US exhibition and publication projects. However, I also perceived some of the differences among the museums involved. The three Chinese museums are not autonomous and independent from the national institutionalized system. For example, although they are all ethnic or ethnographic museums, they belong to different national administrative systems. YNM and GZNM are under the State Ethnic Affairs Commission which is in charge of affairs relating to ethnic groups. And GXNM is under the State Cultural Administration which focuses on national cultural affairs. The different administrative institution affiliations result in different funding, resources, practices, and museum policies. For instance, if the museums lend registered items abroad, they need to report to different governmental units because the State Ethnic Affairs Commission and the State Cultural Administration will have different policies and regulations regarding the items.

In China, museum management, structure, and practice are somewhat different from the museums in the United States. Usually a Chinese museum consists of an office, research department, collection department, exhibition department, public education department, and a security and service department. The office serves as the administrative center and coordinates activities in the other departments as well as the museum's interaction with other institutions. While a traditional curator's work in a smaller American museum dealing with acquisitions and collections care, documentation, collection research, conducting exhibition and publication are instead distributed to separate departments in Chinese museums.

For the project of *the Quilts of Southwest China*, we appointed a contact person in each museum in charge of the coordination of the project within their and other museums. I am from the research department at GXNM and I was the general contact person for the China side. Due to the structural arrangement of the three museums, we have various levels of coordination and collaboration. First, there is collaboration among the different departments within each of the three museums. Second, there is coordination and collaboration between the three museums. And we also have the international collaboration with the American museums.

I perceive the project as a process of communication, mutual understanding, sharing, and mutual learning that ultimately results in mutual benefits. The three Chinese museums each contributed four quilts from their museums for the exhibition. With the quilts we prepared descriptions and interpretations as well as ethnographic photos. Based on ethnographic fieldwork, three videos of the featured quilt artists in action were produced providing context for the exhibition and additional written introductions of the quilt artists. We also provided maps and high-resolution images.

The project also is a platform for scholarly exchanges and communications for museum professionals from these three Chinese museums. We have two directors and four staff who attended the China-US Museum and Intangible Cultural Heritage Forum at AFS in Santa Fe in 2015. The four younger staff also had the chance to visit the three partnering American museums and have in-depth communication with their American colleagues. During the travel exhibitionin the US, the

Chinese museums sent staff to each of the three collaborating museums and other museums in the US.

The collaborative project contributes to the promotion of scholarly and public awareness of quilts as a distinctive form of textile tradition in China. A featured quilt artist Biyu Huang, who made a quilt for *the Quilts of Southwest China*, was invited to demonstrate and to communicate with the visitors in our exhibition hall. Huang not only made a quilt for *the Quilts of Southwest China*, but was also featured in one of the videos shown in the US exhibition.

As a cross-cultural project, language and terminology presented some challenges in our collaborative work. For example, it is hard to find an equivalent Chinese word for the term quilt in the western meanings. Items made of small pieces of fabric pieced and appliqued together are referred to as *pinbu* in Chinese. It does not necessarily mean items used on the bed. It could be clothes or decorative textiles hanging on wall. Further, there are other names used in Chinese such as, *baijiayi* or *bainayi*, and *pinbu beimian*, which are also different from the English term, quilt. As Marsha described in her essay, it was a fascinating learning process to find ways to cope with this concept.

Since the majority of the audience was American, the quilt exhibition required the lent items to be quilts used on a bed. At first, some of our Chinese colleagues couldn't understand why it had to be quilts used on the bed and we had to deal not only with different terminology, but also with different cultural understandings.

The project was a channel for the participants to learn about the cultural, institutional, and professional practices and policies of other institutions, and to learn to work together. It also built relationships that helped open doors for further research and future collaborations. As of the end of 2016, GXNM and Mathers Museum of World Cultures have already started to talk about collaborative ethnographic research collaborations concerning cultural heritage in Guangxi. I look forward to being involved in such future projects.

我的中国之行

萨伦·谢尔曼[*]

2006年,我第一次来到中国,受邀在武汉参加一次非物质文化遗产保护的国际会议。从那以来,我已经去过中国三次,也在好几个会议和大学做了报告。因为我跟中国的民俗学家建立了交流关系,我对中国的理论观点有了更多的了解。

从中国视角发展起来的民俗理论打开了我的视野,让我看到非物质文化遗产研究的重要,并对中国所模仿的美国民俗理论也有了新的认识。2006年之前,我跟中国学术界的交往很有限,我的认识还停留在中国是一个共产主义社会,所以要非常注意自己的言行举止。我曾一直以为中国人没足够的饭吃;小时候我的父母总是以"中国人都在饿肚子"这种理由让我把饭吃完。当然,中国现在已经相当现代化了。很多中国的食物和产品都输出到美国和世界各地,这证明了中国在世界经济上的地位,以及其接近资本主义的制度。温饱已不是问题。我在中国经常被邀请吃饭,旋转餐桌上总是有很多道大家共享的菜肴。我发现很多人喜欢出去吃饭,因为准备中餐需要很多配料,也很费时间。大家想品尝的都是在家做会特别耗时间的菜。

这次中国之行使我有机会再次与中国同仁相聚,例如,刘魁立博士,还有高丙中和萧放。他们在2006年6月来到美国俄勒冈参加会议,我们得以相识。由此,我们成为朋友,进一步交流我们作为民俗学者的感受。

民俗学在中国一直被认为是很重要的。相反,一些美国民俗学家认为他们的学科是被边缘化了。而在中国,这个学科受到欢迎。政府的兴趣和对非物质遗产的重视肯定是一个推动力。刘魁立博士跟我解释说,"许多年前,民俗文化被忽略。现在政府开始突出民俗文化的重要性"。将遥远的小村庄浪漫化的态度导致许多地方都力争被列入被保护名录。问题是如何做出选择,保护什么样的村庄、民间故事、信仰、歌曲或物质文化。假如一个群体被选出来,相邻的群体就会被轻视,虽然他们有类似或几乎相同的民俗。遗产名录这个问题在全世界普遍存在。当谈论一个特定的群体或地点时,大家都会先指出其是否被选定为世界文化遗

---

[*] 编者注:莎伦·谢尔曼是俄勒冈大学荣退民俗学教授。从1970年代开始,她通过民俗影视教学和自己拍摄的作品,开启了结合影视的民俗学研究领域。她强调利用影片来理解传统,扩展了传统的文本中心的民俗研究思想和方法。她的《记录我们自己》(1998)仍然是少数几本关于民俗和影视的民俗学研究著作之一,现在已有中文版。她通过在美国和中国参与民俗影视记录工作坊,进一步推动了利用影视记录民俗和非物质文化遗产的思想和实践。

产地。

2006年,我在中国的前几天在北京第一次见到游自荧。不久,她到俄勒冈大学成为我的学生。张举文和游自荧带我去了几个旅游景点,也去了长城。一路上,有许许多多民间艺术家在不断创作或制作他们的作品。我看到一位妇女在一个小瓶子内壁画美丽的场景,一面是花,另一面是山。两个场景有一点像,但也有不同。在小瓶子里的画如民间艺术的魔术。我站在旁边很好奇地看了很久。画家在长城上做生意(画画)肯定很成功。我自己就买了两个小瓶子带回美国给学生和朋友看。刻版画、草编筐、剪纸等都是长城边销售的手工艺术品。

有一个小孩子的爷爷问我可不可以让他的孙女给我讲个故事练习她的英语。这个故事很长,显然是背下来的,但是我发现孩子觉得学英文是很自豪的事情。大部分的八岁以下的孩子都能说一点英语。那时中国在准备奥运会,所以有些人有动力学第二语言。这个爷爷很高兴,把他孙女给我讲故事的场面都拍摄下来了。

有一件小事让我认识到了作为一个"老外"是什么感觉。一个年轻人站在离我几米的位置盯着我。我等了等,以为他有什么要跟我说。我终于忍不住问他是不是想知道什么,他还是一句话不说地盯着我瞧。举文解释给我说,那个年轻人很有可能"像我一样"是从一个偏远的农村来旅游的。对于他来说,我就是个"景观"。举文觉得他可能从来也没有见过像我这样的金发女郎,而这样的情况几十年前都很正常。通过亲身体会作为一个"老外"的感觉后,我更清楚地意识到那些民俗学家与人类学家身处异地研究"他者"时的假想会是什么。

到武汉之前,我受邀到北京讲学。在北京师范大学,我有幸结识了杨利慧。她曾与其丈夫安德明到印第安纳大学访学一年,后来出版了一部有关中国神话的作品。我们互相交流了在印第安纳的经历并很快成为挚友。我的第一次讲座是关于美国的案例:"民俗与民族纪录片:以摄影保护美国之根"。第二次讲座是在中国社会科学院,题目是"俄勒冈民俗案例分析之22部影视作品"。讲座开始于讨论学生们提供的样本和我自己的实地考察的经历,再到其他中国民俗学者们提供的样本,最后是对比样本的讨论。利慧和德明都参加了2006年的美国民俗学会年会,并受到会议的资助,这是因为美国民俗学会在推动中美民俗学会的交流。2007年,他们夫妻二人来到俄勒冈州的威涞大学和俄勒冈大学讲学,我们几个老朋友得以重聚叙旧。

当时,游自荧也加入了2006年的武汉会议。三周之前,她刚刚成家。为了汲取更多的知识,她承担了我在大会发言的翻译。我报告的课题是《谁拥有文化,谁来决定?伦理、电影与非物质文化遗产保护》(这篇文章2008年发表在《西部民俗》)。许多民俗学家参加了那次会议。我渐渐发现原来口头程式理论在中国是非常有名的,并且口头艺术论也是大受欢迎。部分原因是因为访问哈佛大学的中国学者们将在那里发展并采用的口头程式理论带了回来。另一部分原因则是中国出版了一些有关口头程式和表演理论的译本。有些基础理论,如邓迪斯的《世界民俗学》已经有了中文译本。我在中国期间就有许多人迫切地与我谈论邓迪斯,对他非常敬仰,因为邓迪斯曾访问过中国,与很多人有接触,也因为他的(被翻译的）书给大家留下深刻印象。

在2006年的会议上，以口头艺术和非物质文化遗产为要点，我讲解了我用影视采集资料的方法，希望能通过这种形式，更加完整地记录非遗，达到文字所达不到的目的。我提倡以故事的讲述或叙述过程作为重点，而不是将从此过程中抽出的故事内容为重点。我展示的一些样片是我的和我的学生的作品，记录了物质文化的不同方面，如叙事、仪式、歌唱，以及其他非物质表达行为。

界定和保护物质和非物质文化遗产是个有争议的问题，也引出许多伦理问题。研究仪式、故事、歌曲和其他传统表现行为的学者该如何记录这些呢？进行录音或录像的民俗学者经常面对道德困惑，这涉及民俗学学科的核心问题。选择记录哪些社区，为什么？如果他们愿意展示自己的身份，我们该如何在影视中介绍人物？材料归谁？该如何储藏？影片会被编成一个"真实"的例子吗？因为政府鼓励记录，所以当地不同群体得到资助。这种情况是否有助于强化"表演"的动机？

鼓励使用影像并没有导致民俗学者的全面接受。出席会议的人一个个都在用手机拍摄演讲者和提问者；他们拍了很多团体照。拍的大多数是照片，加上少数的视频。对于年轻人来说，视觉上的吸引力往往比其他感官要大，这点与美国的情况没有区别。我的报告结束后，引出了很多有关如何掌握这些方法的问题。很多人，特别是学生，产生了很大的兴趣。我们讨论了许多有趣的话题。

接下来的一周，会议集中讨论的是理论与方法论方面的问题。后来，我们也去了些小村子，在一个很漂亮的树林里参加了一次土家族的宴会。在长阳县，我和游自荧出去逛商店。她是穿着西方的白色婚纱结婚的，当她看到红色的嫁衣，就解释说它们是传统的婚礼服。我过去经常在课上提到类似的文化差异的例子，现在亲眼看到了。店里面的裁缝也慷慨大方地与我们谈论婚礼的传统。

我和中国同仁们到现在还保持着联系。我与张举文在武汉（2014）和美国（2015）举办的民俗影视记录工作坊让我结识了许多参与的学生和学者。第一届工作坊的主题是"龙舟节：拍摄与剪辑"。在短短的两个星期内，学生们就拍摄了四段不同的视频。2014年，我访华的最后一站是上海的华东师范大学。我受邀在那里讲了我最新在厄瓜多尔拍摄的影视作品：《珠莱怎么样了？全球化、跨国主义、女权主义和反思性问题》。有关中国、厄瓜多尔和美国的态度和习俗之间的比较引起了一场漫长又有趣的关于女权的讨论。

第一届工作坊如此成功，以至于有几位又参加了2015年的第二届工作坊，其主题是"民俗与非物质文化遗产影像记录：（美国）崴涞河谷的圣诞节"。这届工作坊由华中师范大学主办，中美民俗学会的路思项目部分资助。学员分为四个小组从四个主题分别拍摄和编辑了四个样片。他们在俄勒冈州的尤金、塞勒姆和波特兰分别采访拍摄，其样片结果好得令人惊讶。对学员来说，俄勒冈的圣诞节就是"他者"文化。犹如"陌生人价值"所示，当地的人愿意与我们的学员交谈。我非常高兴又见到一些以前认识的朋友，也相信我们一定还有机会再见的。

2009年，因为不同的一个项目，我参与了俄勒冈大学的"中国藤"团队（参见道格拉斯·布兰迪的故事），到山东工艺美术学院参加了一次国际论坛会议，"手工创造财富：传统手工艺的保护和发展"。我做了学术报告：《从铅笔和笔记本到录像：数字民俗研究》，并受到电台采访。我们也在北京走访了一些民间艺术家。无疑，是因为我参与了中美民俗交流活动才受到邀请参加这次中国之行。

这些交往扩大了我们的了解，也为未来的交流打下基础。我们现在与中国同行建立了非常密切的关系，主要是因为中美两国民俗学会的努力。这些中国之行不但对我们很有教育意义，而且也对学科建设有益。此外，也充满情趣。我在湖北长阳学了跳"撒叶儿嗬"舞，在武汉唱了卡拉OK。总而言之，每次中国之行都是无比美好的经历。

（陈妍、苏慧中、毛丹婷、李清源、张举文翻译）

My Journeys to China

Sharon Sherman*

I first arrived in China in 2006 as an invited lecturer for the International Intangible Cultural Heritage Protection Conference in Wuhan. Since that initial visit, I have traveled to China three times and given lectures at various conferences and universities. Because of my visits to China and the subsequent visits of Chinese folklorists to the United States, I have learned much about Chinese theoretical perspectives and have become friends with several Chinese colleagues.

Folklore theory from a Chinese perspective opened my eyes to significant studies of intangible cultural heritage and a host of theoretical approaches that often mirrored the work of folklorists in the United States. Prior to the 2006 trip, my experience with Chinese scholarship was quite limited as was my vision of China as a Communist society where I assumed one had to be careful about behavior and what one might say. I also thought people were hungry; as a child, I was told to eat my food "because people in China are starving." Of course, China was quite modernized. Its food and the production of many objects shipped to America, and elsewhere, demonstrates China's emergent standing in the world and its strong economy that verges on capitalism. Food was never an issue, as large meals, ordered by our hosts, appeared at every turn, in sizable rotating turntables containing many dishes shared by the group. I learned that quite a few people enjoyed eating out of the house because Chinese dishes, which had a multitude of ingredients, took a lot of preparation. Most wanted to savor various dishes that would take too long to make at home.

This trip gave me the opportunity to reconnect with Chinese folklorists whom I had met at a conference on ritual at Willamette University, Oregon, among them, Dr. Kuili Liu (then President of the Chinese Folklore Society) who then led a delegation to the US, Bingzhong Gao, and Fang

---

* Sharon Sherman is Professor Emerita of Folklore at the University of Oregon. She pioneered the field of folklore and film beginning in the 1970s, through teaching, shooting and editing films. Her emphasis of using film to document and understand traditions expanded the traditional text-centered studies of folklore. Her book, *Documenting Ourselves* (1998), remains to be one of few folkloristic studies on folklore and film, and is now available in Chinese. Her involvement in the workshops of video recording folklore held in China and the US has further promoted the idea and practice of documenting folklore and intangible cultural heritage through video.

Xiao. Despite language difficulties (on my part) we became friends and talked about our experiences as folklorists.

Studying folklore was considered essential in China. Whereas some American folklorists thought their discipline was marginalized, in China it was celebrated. Government interest and the focus on intangible heritage was surely a driving force. As Dr. Liu explained to me, "Many years ago, folk culture was being ignored. Now the government is showing how important it is." The attitude of romanticizing people in small villages led to lists upon which groups strove to be included. The problem was how groups were chosen or what folktales, beliefs, songs, material culture would be selected. If one village stood out, other nearby villages were slighted although they had similar or practically identical folklore. This problem with heritage listing is pervasive throughout the world. Everyone, when talking about a specific site, will point out if it has been chosen as an international heritage site.

My first few days in China in 2006 were spent in Beijing where I met Ziying You, who later became my student at the University of Oregon (see her story in this volume). Juwen Zhang and Ziying took me to several tourist places, including the Great Wall. Along the way, numerous folk artists plied their wares. A woman painted beautiful scenes, one side of flowers and the other of a mountain, inside a tiny bottle. Both scenes were similar yet different. Painting inside the bottle seemed like a folk art magic trick. I stood in wonder and watched. Being on the wall certainly made her business successful. I bought two bottles to show to classes and to friends who would most likely not have believed the process otherwise. Etched paintings, baskets, and paper-cut art were some of the many arts along the wall.

A small child and her grandfather approached me and the grandfather asked me if the girl could tell me a story to practice her English. This story, a common folktale, was long and obviously rehearsed and memorized, but nevertheless demonstrated to me that young children were proud to be learning English. Most children under eight-years-old could speak some English. The Olympics were coming soon which gave people another reason to attempt a second language. The grandfather was pleased, and took pictures of this storytelling session.

One incident made me recognize what it is like to be "the other." A young man stood a few feet from me and stared. I waited for him to talk to me. When I finally asked him what he wanted to know, he continued to stand silently. Juwen explained that he was probably a tourist from a remote village and was visiting the city, like me. I was a spectacle to him. He had never seen a white woman with blond hair, and that was a common scene a few decades earlier, Juwen suggested. Putting my sense of otherness into a personalized framework expanded my awareness of assumptions folklorists and anthropologists make when in the field studying those who are "different."

Before traveling to Wuhan, I was invited to give two presentations in Beijing. At Beijing

Normal University, I met Lihui Yang. She had published work on Chinese mythology and had been at Indiana with her husband, Deming An, for a year. We compared our Indiana experiences and became fast friends. My first talk focused on American materials: "Folklore and Ethno documentary: Protecting America's Roots Through Video." The second talk, "A Case Study of Folklore from Oregon with Examples from 22 Films," was presented at the Institute of Ethnic Literatures, China Academy of Social Sciences. Providing examples from students and my own fieldwork experiences, as requested, led to other examples from the Chinese folklorists, and to comparative discussion. Both Lihui and Deming attended the 2006 Annual AFS meeting at the onset of the AFS initiative to encourage exchanges between the Chinese Folklore Society and the American Folklore Society, and came to Oregon, gave talks in 2007. Thus, we met up again and continued our relationship.

Ziying joined the group of scholars traveling to Wuhan in 2006. She had married only three weeks earlier but wanted to learn more and she served as my translator at the Conference. My talk was entitled "Who Owns Culture and Who Decides? Ethics, Film, and Intangible Cultural Heritage Protection" (a version of which I published in *Western Folklore* (2008). Many folklorists attended and it became obvious to me that oral formulaic theory was well-known in China and the verbal arts were favored, in part, because of visits by Chinese scholars to Harvard where this theory was developed and adopted. Translations of publications on that topic and on performance theory played a role as well. Basic works, such as Alan Dundes' *The Study of Folklore* (1965), were translated some time ago and Dundes also had visited China. Indeed, people wanted to talk to me about their interactions with Dundes, whom they held in high regard.

At the 2006 conference, with the highlight on verbal arts and Intangible Cultural Heritage, I spoke about my own area of filmmaking as a methodology for gathering the intangible in a holistic manner by documenting events rather than texts. I advocated that storytelling or narrating was the focal point rather than the story abstracted from the narrating process. Some video examples from my own and student films addressed tangible material culture, while others examined narrating, ritual, singing, and other intangible expressive behaviors.

Defining and protecting tangible and intangible cultural heritage is controversial and raises ethical questions. How might scholars of ritual practices, stories, songs, and other traditional expressive behaviors document them? The folklorist who conducts audio or video recording often faces ethical dilemmas that reach to the very heart of the development of folkloristics. Which community is selected and why? How do we identify people in the films, if they wish to be identified? Who owns the material? How is it to be stored? Will a film be codified as the one "true" example? Because the central government encourages documentation, money becomes available to local groups. Does that situation provide an incentive to "perform"?

Encouraging film and video has not led to wholesale adoption of film (now video) by folklorists. Attendees sat around us clicking their mobile phones at speakers and questioners; they took many photos of groups of people. They shot still images, and occasional videos. The desire for the visual predominates for certain people who are young ("Millennials"), just as it does in the United States. Questions about how to learn this approach followed the talk and the end of the first day. Many people, especially students, wanted more information and were enthused. We spoke about what might serve as good topics.

The conference continued through the week in seminars about theory and methodology. We later traveled to small villages, attended an astonishingly beautiful banquet in the trees. Visiting Changyang, Ziying and I wandered out to window shop. Having been married in a western style white dress, Ziying looked at red wedding dresses and explained that they were traditional. I had often mentioned this cultural difference in class, but now actually saw these dresses. The dressmaker generously gave us her time and talked with us about wedding traditions.

My contact with colleagues has been kept alive. And I met many new students and scholars who attended video workshops that Juwen Zhang and I led in Wuhan in 2014 and in the United States in 2015. The first workshop was about *The Dragon Boat Festival*: *What to Shoot and How to Edit*. Within two weeks, students had created four different videos. I ended my 2014 journey to China at East China Normal University, Shanghai where I was invited to talk about my latest film project, shot in Ecuador, and its implications: "*Whatever Happened to Zulay*? Issues of Globalization, Transnationalism, Feminism, and Reflexivity" at East China Normal University. Questions and comparisons between Chinese, Ecuadorian, and American attitudes and practices led to a lengthy and engaging discussion of feminism.

The first film workshop became so significant that many of the same students came to a follow-up workshop: "Second Workshop on Video Documentation of Folklore and Intangible Cultural Heritage: Christmas in the Willamette Valley," funded by the AFS-CFS Luce Project and organized by CCNU, 2015. Students formed groups to shoot and edit four separate Christmas themes. We met in Eugene to shoot some of the materials and then later in Salem, Oregon, to see the results. Amazing materials emerged. For some students, Oregon and Christmas were "other." Like "stranger value," people were willing to talk to the crews. I was delighted to reconnect with the people we had worked together earlier, and am certain we will meet again.

In 2009, for a different project, I joined with folklorists from the University of Oregon and *ChinaVine* (see the story by Douglas Blandy) to speak at the International Forum: "Handicraft Creates Wealth—The Protection and Development of Traditional Handicraft" at Shandong University of Art and Design. I gave a talk, "From Pencils and Paper to Video: Digital Folklore Studies," and was interviewed for a radio piece. We also visited folk artists while there and in Beijing. My attendance at the AFS-CFS meetings undoubtedly led to this invitation.

These connections have led to an expansion of knowledge and plans for future activities. We are now establishing very close ties with our counterparts in China, largely due to the joint efforts of AFS and CFS. The trips were educational and beneficial to the discipline of folklore. They also were fun—to top it off, I learned the *basang* dance and sang Karaoke with the group in Wuhan. All in all, amazing experiences.

我在中美民俗学交流中的两件事

孙正国*

在近年的中美民俗学交流中，我很高兴以不同的角色多次参与合作交流项目。在此，仅讲述两件事中的感受：一是合作创办民俗影像田野记录工作坊，一是我首次参加美国民俗学会议。

2014年夏天，作为中美民俗学会的合作项目之一，我校与美国崴涞大学联合创办了"中美民俗影像记录田野工作坊"。此前，我与美国崴涞大学亚洲研究中心张举文教授已有学术联系。这次，我受中方主办人陈建宪教授的委托，与美方的主办人张举文一起联合组织了工作坊，得到了华中师范大学的刘守华教授和黄永林教授的支持，以及我的同事和研究生的帮助。我们邀请到代表不同学术观点的学者，如美国的谢尔曼教授，中国的陈建宪、邓启耀、熊讯教授，以及代表电视台纪录片制作者的王光艳导演。有8名来自不同高校的博士生和青年教师参与了此次工作坊。通过对中国端午节四个世界遗产申报地——湖北宜昌和黄石、湖南岳阳、江苏苏州进行端午民俗的实地调研与影像记录，讲员与学员都从中体会到国际学术交流的重要性。

2015年冬，我们举办了第二期工作坊。首先在武汉对学员进行理论培训，随后19名学员对美国西北地区的圣诞节进行影像田野记录。张举文教授热情周到地负责工作坊所有学员在美国部分的食、宿、行，十分辛苦。他还精心设计了对商场、教堂、街区和家庭的四个层面的影像记录与调查。期间，在美访学的熊讯教授作为导师全程参与，另外，谢尔曼教授、在美访问的周星教授和张霞博士也积极参与。经过两周的调查，学员们收获巨大。工作坊也在理论上做出了一些总结，《民间文化论坛》《民族艺术》《广西民族大学学报》发表了学员和导师的专题论文。同时，张举文教授也正在组织力量编写教材，计划主编《民俗影视记录手册》（与谢尔曼合作出版英文版《民俗影视记录手册》）。

受到前两期的成功的鼓舞，2016年夏天，由于中美合作项目的结束，我们便完全依靠中方资助，举办了第三期工作坊。此次是华中师范大学与广西民族大学合作。除了在广西的

---

* 编者注：孙正国现任华中师范大学教授，文学博士。近年来，他在国内特别推动了民俗影视记录的人才培养，通过工作坊的形式，使得许多年轻的民俗学者具有了影视记录的意识和能力，为民俗学学科建设做出了贡献。目前，民俗影视记录工作坊已经成为年度活动，连接了国内几十个民俗学学位点。同时，他不仅自己积极参与国际交流，也鼓励和帮助学生走向世界民俗学的交流平台。

实践外，还到日本名古屋、大阪、东京等地进行了夏日祭的影像调查实践。目前，正计划第四期工作坊。无疑，中美合作的种子已经结出越来越多的果实。

三年的国际合作与交流，多校研究生和青年教师的共同努力，比较清晰地建构起基于民俗影像工作坊的国际学术交流模式，为今后的交流打下基础。这也呈现出全球化互动的当代文化特征。通过互动，一些有意思的故事被创造出来，永久地成为美好记忆了。

我第一次出国学术交流是2015年4月参加美国西部民俗学会年会。会议邀请方是美国华裔学者张举文教授。他热情周到地安排了与会的食宿与交通。

会议在加州大学洛杉矶分校举行。与我同一组的还有两位中国学者与会，一是任职日本爱知大学的周星教授，一是武汉大学蔡琴教授。此前他们都在美国作访问交流，参加会议很方便。我第一次出国，又独自从上海飞洛杉矶，心里有些紧张。原计划约好与举文教授在机场出口会合。由于手机断电，加之语言较弱，对美国机场也不熟悉，到处找地方充电。直到两小时以后，好不容易发现了电源插座，急忙充电，终于联系上举文教授，总算化解了一场失联危机。

两天的会议，学者完全自助自费，只有两三名志愿者负责会费收缴、会议手册发放和相关资料出售。会议以小专题展开，五六十位学者自由发言，涉及军队、战争、工业记忆等新领域的民俗研究，启人思考。我们中国学者组成一个小组，分别汇报了华北面花、手工艺和被中国承袭的圣诞习俗，也引来了几位美国学者对于民俗的区域化和全球化现象的关注和讨论。

会议结束后，我预留了三天体验生活。主要观察洛杉矶市的社区生活空间、大学图书馆与城市购物中心。印象最深的是社区大型洗衣中心和古旧用品市场。洗衣中心如同一个洗衣工厂，两间大房：一间沿三面墙放置了几十台自助洗衣机，可供社区使用；另一间提供餐饮服务。洗衣中心可以看作一个社区的日常生活场所，社区的服务设施良好，但自助理念非常明显。自助是我体验美国生活的重要收获。首先是服务设施都注重自助功能的开发，其次是每个人在接受自助服务时接受了自助的观念。后者更为重要。因为自助不是简单的技术使用问题，它所隐含的是每个人所承担的社会责任意识与自我实现精神。每个人力所能及地完成一项任务，每个人义务接受一项社会任务，都与自助有关。它不再只是志愿者的奉献，而是多了一份自我在内的社会义务。它还包括一种可贵的自我实现精神，在自助的过程中，发现了自我的价值，实现了自我面向社会的存在感。这种自我实现，是对自我义务的升华，是从社会化压力转向自我个性化的动力，日复一日地从自助机上获得技术之外的人文精神，取消了简单的付出疲劳，而增加了个人的自律品格和自强能力。

洛杉矶的古旧用品市场好似废品收购站，但是前者没有垃圾场的外观，而与其他城市商铺一样，有着正规的区位、门楣和购物服务。更重要的是，古旧用品十分驳杂，除了有西班牙运来的13世纪的石雕艺术品，也有本地传统的日常用品的瓷器碎片，还有上世纪七八十年代留下来的破损的通信和交通设施用品，如红绿灯支架、小半截电线杆，以及五六十年前家庭用的各类物品，从门楣、窗格，到门把手、锈迹斑斑的锁和钥匙，各种布艺、灯具、电话、桌椅。这些物品非常杂乱，以至于无法像正规商店那样作出归类和摆放设计。店里的物品价格从几美分到数万美元,从一般日用供给到古玩收藏,让人觉得古旧市场的定位有点模棱两可。

　　令人惊奇的现象在大学里。去洛杉矶分校的东亚图书馆,发现他们收藏了一套上海木版年画,以十分醒目的位置悬挂在二层楼梯间旁的一整面墙上,耀眼而古雅。图书馆主要收藏的是中国、日本和韩国的图书与期刊。虽然不尽全面,但也有一些珍贵文献。我花了两天时间在图书馆里体会美国大学的味道,开放、自由,不需要任何证件,而且设立若干类型的图书馆。一层靠右设有西餐吧台,提供面包、蛋糕和各类饮料,方便整天在图书馆学习的人。开放的图书馆也是开放大学的特点。行走在这样的图书馆里,有一种自由自在的轻松感。

　　晚上的校园里有许多不同肤色的人群在举办不同的活动,让人感受到世界性的多元文化魅力。真是幸运,我在23:00走出图书馆时,竟然在校园里邂逅了中国狮舞的表演训练。我静静地坐在石阶上,非常惊讶地看着七八个大学生表演中国狮舞,他们组成了红、蓝、黄三只狮队,狮子道具精美,看得出他们不是随便凑成的临时队伍。表演开始,红狮出场,它先是前后左右地奔走、跑动,前面的学生一会儿高举狮头,一会儿低垂徘徊。后面的学生则如影随形,宛如一体。突然,狮头冲天而起,径直地立起身,竟至2米多高。原来,前面的学生跃上了后面学生的肩上,稳稳地矗立着,还缓缓地前行呢。旁边击鼓的学生也使足劲儿地敲击起来,急促的鼓点密集地渲染着紧张而精彩的表演,令人叫绝。直立表演结束,又表演攀登技艺,几张长凳叠架而起,雄狮灵巧地绕凳而上,稳健地作出各种高难度动作。大约10分钟后,红狮安全着陆,表演训练结束。另外两只雄狮以红狮同样的程式进行有条不紊的训练。整个过程约2个小时。等到训练结束,我怀着急切的亲近感跑过去,发现他们大多都是洛杉矶和附近城市的华裔二代,不懂中文,但都知道自己的父辈来自中国。还有一位是中国台湾刚刚移民的留学生。我与她的闽南语方言作了简单而艰难的沟通,知道这次舞狮训练是洛杉矶地区最大的一个舞狮协会的常规计划,每周三的21:00至23:00固定在加州大学洛杉矶分校博物馆前面的广场进行训练,学员来自洛杉矶地区和附近地区的多所大学的学生。有的学生乘飞机来参加每周一次的训练。他们有专门的网站和社团组织,每年参加各种层次的舞狮大赛,前几年夺得过全美国冠军,在美国的舞狮社团中占有重要地位。

　　狮舞邂逅,极大地震动了我。这是不是此次国际学术交流意料之中的必然收获呢?可能是吧。因为它不是发生在普通社区的小街上,也不是简单的中国文化巡演的一次展示。它发生在大学里,它是由一些华裔大学生自发组织的狮舞社团,这就构成了文化交流的两个必要条件:一是文化交流的主要场所,一是文化交流的重要群体。中国人移居美国之后,他们必然要将自己文化的核心符号随身带到异文化地区,因此也必然要将自己的文化作为基因传承给自己的后代。于是,我见到了他们,见到了我和他们共有的文化核心符号,他们是那样的热爱这些符号,而且已经将其融入到了异文化的整体之中,成为这个原来并不属于他们的文化之一部分了。尽管语言已遗忘,尽管故里已渺远,可是他们实践着的狮舞艺术却将他们融合在一起,形成鲜明的文化胎记,闪耀着中华文化的光辉。

My Stories about the China-US Folkloristic Communication

Zhengguo Sun*

I am happy that I have been involved in the Sino-US folkloristic exchange in recent years through different roles, but I will limit my stories to two: one is about holding the workshop on video-documenting folklore, and the other is the first time I attended a folklore meeting in the US.

In summer 2014, as part of the AFS-CFS joint project, CCNU and Willamette University jointly held the first Workshop on Video-Documenting Folklore. Prior to the workshop, I already had academic exchanges with Dr. Juwen Zhang. Then I was asked by Professor Jianxian Chen to work with Dr. Zhang. With the support from Professors Shouhua Liu and Dr. Yonglin Huang, and my colleagues and students, we were able to invite several distinguished scholars to be the instructors for the workshop, who represented different school of thoughts—for example, the US folklorist Sharon Sherman, the folklorist Jianxian Chen, the visual anthropologists Qiyao Deng and Xun Xiong, and the TV station director Guangyan Wang. There were eight doctoral students and young teachers, as well as some MA students, who participated in the first workshop. They were divided into groups to document the celebration of the Dragon Boat Festival in four locations that were listed as Intangible Cultural Heritage sites by the UNESCO. It was a great experience learning the importance of international exchange.

In winter 2015, we held the second workshop. Over fifty graduate students from more than twenty universities participated in the training in the first week. During the following two weeks, nineteen participants went to Oregon to document the celebration of Christmas throughout the Willamette Valley while the rest of the participants documented the celebration of Christmas in

---

* Zhengguo Sun is Professor of Chinese at the CCNU with a Ph. D. in Literature. In recent years, he has promoted video-documenting folklore by holding workshops to train young folklorists in this method which, when combined with traditional pen and pencil methods, has greatly contributed to the development Chinese folkloristics. The workshop of video-documenting folklore has become an annual event involving several countries and many folklore programs in China. At the same time, he also actively involves himself in international communication and encourages his students to do the same.

Wuhan, China. Dr. Zhang took the trouble to make all the arrangements and designed the program by assigning the participants to document the festival from four aspects: the commercial site of shopping malls, religious site of two churches, neighborhoods, and families. Professors Sherman and Xiong were with the students at various sites. Dr. Xing Zhou, who was visiting the US, and Dr. Xia Zhang who was teaching at Portland State University, also joined the workshop. As a result, four ten-minute sample films were made, and over ten articles were published in three journals. Professors Juwen Zhang and Sharon Sherman are also editing a handbook of video-documenting folklore.

Encouraged by these two successful workshops, we put together our own resources to hold the third annual workshop in summer 2016, even though the AFS-CFS joint project was completed. This time we worked with Guangxi Minzu University. There were over forty participants from about twenty universities. After the first week of training, one group went to Japan (Nagoya, Osaka and Tokyo) to documents the summer sacrificial rituals, and the rest in the workshop went to Pingguo County, near Nanning, Guangxi to document the folksong fair. Clearly, the seeds from the initial AFS-CFS collaboration had already yielded much fruit.

The three years' collaboration and exchange involved the efforts of many students and young teachers, as well as the instructor, and built a pattern of international exchange, paving the way for future communication. This is also characteristic of current global cultural interaction. Through these interactions, some interesting stories were created, and they became beautiful memories forever.

My first time going abroad for an academic meeting was to the WSFS annual meeting in April 2015. I was invited by Dr. Juwen Zhang who also helped arrange my room and board and transportation.

It was on the campus of UCLA. There were two other Chinese scholars in my session, Dr. Xing Zhou and Dr. Qin Cai, who were both in the US as visiting scholars. It was my first time going abroad, and I flew from Shanghai to Los Angeles. I was quite nervous. Originally we planned for Dr. Zhang to meet me at the exit, but, at that moment, my cellphone ran out of power. I had no confidence in my English, and was not familiar with the airport. I looked for places to charge my phone. It took me two hours finally to find an outlet, and I rushed to charge my phone. I finally got connected with Dr. Zhang, solving a potential crisis of lost connection.

For the two-day meeting, attendees paid for their own room and board as well as transportation. There were only two or three volunteers helping with registration and book sales. The meeting had a number of small subjects covering new research areas such as military, warfare, and industrial memories. They were quite inspiring. There were about fifty to sixty presenters. The presenters in our panel reported on the traditions of making steamed-buns in Northwest China, handicrafts, and Christmas celebration in Chinese cities, which attracted some attention to the issues of regionalism and globalization in China.

I reserved three days after the meeting to experience the life in Los Angeles, mostly to observe LA's use of urban space, university library, and commercial shopping centers. What left the deepest impressions were the large laundromats and the antiques market. The laundromat was like a big factory with dozens of washing machines for the community members. There was also food service nearby. The laundromat could also be a space of daily community life. The notion of self-service was very obvious, which was an important experience I had in the US. It was not only at these facilities; the concept was well-accepted by everyone. This is important because self-service is not a technological issue, but it implies the awareness of social responsibility and the spirit of self-realization, which is also a process of discovering the values of self in a society.

The antiques market was like a recycling center, but looked like a shopping mall. There were things like a sculpture from 13th-century Spain, broken pieces of ceramics from local production, and household objects from the 1950s. Things could be as cheap as a few cents or as expensive and thousands of dollars. It was hard to categorize such a market in terms of cultural space or market space.

What was surprising to me was the phenomenon on the campus. In the East Asian Library of UCLA, I found that they had a set of woodblock prints of Chinese New Year celebrations in Shanghai, which were hung on the entire wall between the first and second floor. They were attractive and elegant. There were books and journals in Chinese, Japanese and Korean. I spent two days in the libraries and experienced their openness and freedom. There was no need of any identification to enter different libraries. There were also food services nearby providing convenient services to the people studying there. The openness was a unique characteristic. Walking in such libraries, one would have a sense of carefree relaxation.

There were many activities involving people of different colors on campus even in the evening, which made me feel the charm of diverse human cultures. I was lucky to even see a lion dance practice when I walked out of the library at 11 pm. I sat on the stone steps and watched a group of seven or eight students practicing. They showed very high skills of jumping and moving along with the exciting drumming. It was excellent. The practice took about two hours. I walked up to them as they cleaned up, and tried to talk to them. I was excited to see they were Chinese, but it turned out that they were the second-generation Chinese who did not speak Chinese. Fortunately there was one student who recently came from Taiwan speaking the Minnan dialect. We had a hard time using gestures and a few words to communicate and I learned that they were in a lion dance association which regularly practiced there on Wednesdays. The students were from different places nearby. There were even students taking the plane to join the weekly practice. A few years earlier they even won the championship in a national competition and were quite influential among lion dance teams in the US.

The surprising encounter of the lion dance shocked me. Was it asort of reward I was "deserved" from this international academic exchange? Perhaps so. This did not take place on a common street, nor in a special street demonstration of Chinese culture. It was on a university campus, spontaneously by a group of students of Chinese heritage. This formed the two necessary conditions for cultural communication: the public space and people for cultural exchange. When the Chinese migrate to the US, they naturally bring with them their cultural symbols, and then pass them on to their children. Although their descendants may no longer maintain the skill of speaking their ancestral language, their common practice of the lion dance brings them together in demonstrating their shared Chinese cultural heritage. They love their cultural heritage and make it integral to the larger society. Thus I saw the cultural symbols that they and I commonly share.

(Translation by Juwen Zhang)

Ⅳ. 从单向离散的到双向机制化的交流——学术交流的新常态

至此，可以清晰地看出，中美（中外）民俗学交流已经从过去的个别交往走向机制化，并是多方位、多层次的。这其中体现的是中国民俗学在趋于成熟，展现出特色，从模仿者到思想者，从跟随者到引领者。例如，在中国召开的国际会议越来越多，中国参与的国际项目也越来越多（见朝戈金的故事）。当然，中国民俗学会在整个过程中的角色至关重要。越来越多的中国民俗学者走向世界，或是通过到国外学习然后回到中国工作（或是留在国外工作），他们都在为中国民俗学的发展与对外交流发挥着重要作用。反过来看，美国民俗学会也起了关键性作用。美国民俗学者对中国的兴趣也越来越大，越来越多的人到中国考察或做研究。美国的刊物也在发表越来越多来自或有关中国民俗的文章。显然，双方的交流愈加频繁、广泛和深入。有理由相信，如此趋于成熟的交流将为双方带来更健康的学科发展，这不仅体现在形式上的多样和丰富，更重要的是体现在观念上的自信和平等。这将是世界民俗学交流的新日常。

这些都可以清楚地从这部分的故事中看出来。周星和王霄冰不仅有着中国经历，也有着跨文化的独特的经历，他们的参与更开阔了交流的视野。宋俊华和安东尼·布切泰利侧重个人参与的两国民俗学会的交流活动。游自荧代表了从中国走出去并在国外工作的新一代民俗学者。南快莫德格以在中国边疆地区的少数民族学者的眼光比较了学者队伍建设中的问题。王均霞和程鹏也代表了即将承担起中国民俗学建设和对外交流的新一代。也许我们常听的故事结尾同样适于此时：从此，（中美民俗交流）快乐地延续着。

IV. From One-way and Scattershot to Two-way and Institutionalized Communication—A New Norm of Academic Communication

In summary, Sino-US folkloristic communication has progressed from the stage of individual exchange to the current stage of institutionalized communication on a large scale. This process reveals that Chinese folkloristics is maturing with its own characteristics: from mimicking to independent thinking, and from following to leading. Both the CFS and the AFS have played key roles in increasing communication in this historical period and mutual understanding and appreciation has deepened and become truly equal. This benefits everyone and will be (has already become) the new norm of world folkloristic communication. Stories in this section are evidences of this new norm-widening in scale and deepening in meaning. Perhaps we can end our stories just like fairy tales do: Sino-US folkloristic communication will continue "happily ever after."

我的一年美国访学

周 星[*]

2015年4月2日至2016年3月29日,我受惠于日本爱知大学的教员海外研修制度和张举文教授的帮助,有机会前往美国崴涞大学东亚系访学一年。我在美国非常有限的经验,虽然基本上和中美民俗学及日美民俗学的官方交流没有关系,但是对我个人而言,收获还是挺大的。

我的外语教育背景和能力不足以支持我在美国做自如的学术交流,之所以选择去美国研修,主要是因为与美国崴涞大学的张举文教授有着共同的研究兴趣。张举文教授在2014年末至2015年初,曾应爱知大学国际中国学研究中心(ICCS)的聘请,给爱知大学的博士生们讲了一门主题为"仪式研究"的课程,我和我的学生们均从中受益良多。张举文教授曾将法国民俗学家阿诺尔德·范热内普的《过渡礼仪》译成中文,在国内民俗学和人类学界产生了广泛而又深远的影响。长期以来,我一直想把中日两国有关成人历程和"成人式"的社会文化设计做一番比较民俗学的研究。此前,在2009年3月,我和他在德国布莱菲尔德(Bielefeld)参加一个国际学术会议时相识。在相互的交流中,他也认为有关人生过渡仪式中"成人式"的中、美、日跨国比较研究会有较大的学术可能性。于是,我的此次访学,主要就是想在自己整理的有关中国和日本"成人式"资料的基础之上,能够获得张举文教授在相关学术理论方面的启示,以及在他的帮助下,通过"在美"的视角而多少能够将中日比较研究之局限于东亚的思路稍微有所转变。

归纳起来,我一年访学的收获有以下几点:

---

[*] 编者注:作为中国本土培养的第一位民族学博士,周星的研究不是狭隘的民族学,而是联通了人类学、社会学、民俗学和民族学的文化研究。周星也是中国在1980年代相关学科的重建中最年轻的学者,将老一辈学者(如杨堃、费孝通)与新一代连接起来,因此,他也是当前最活跃的一代学者中的"长辈"之一。他的学术影响也不仅局限于中国,更是在日本和韩国等地受到学者的敬重。他对成人过程中的"夹生与催熟"论、对彝族的"死给"习俗的理论概述、对桥俗的理论化、对民族政治学学科的建立,以及有关中国的宗教、文化政策等方面的论述,都在国内产生很大影响。他的研究特点是不拘于西方的理论体系,而是从中国特有的实践中发现和构建理论话语。他在北京大学教学和研究十多年后,继续到日本爱知大学讲授中国民俗文化,至今已经又十多年了。当越来越多地受西方理论训练的学者回到中国时,周星这位从中国本土成长起来的学者在一步一步走向更远的外界。他对东亚之外的亲身经历也反映在他的学术思想中。随着他的著作的英文翻译的出版,如《西部民俗》(2017)有关中国非遗的专题,周星的理论观点会更多地得到外界的认知。

1. 张举文新译的《祈颂姑：赞比亚本巴人的一次女孩成人礼仪》一书，我有幸成为译稿的第一读者。这本由英国女性人类学家理查兹撰写的经典民族志作品，堪称女性成人礼研究的力作，故对我的课题有很大参考。在张举文的鼓励下，我还写了一篇"读后感"，忝列译本之后（该译本于 2017 年由商务印书馆出版，列入高丙中主编的《汉译人类学名著》丛书）。

2. 我初步完成了《现代民俗学的视野与方向》一书的编辑工作。其中涉及美国"公共民俗学"的第五部分，得到了张举文的指导，他还为此专门翻译了美国民俗学家黛布拉·科迪斯的"想像公共民俗"一文。该书将于近期在商务印书馆出版。

3. 我初步完成了题为《现代东亚社会的成人礼与成人问题》的书稿。作为一项跨文化的比较民俗学研究，多少是在意识到美国青少年的"成人"过程及相关问题的前提之下，对于东亚的中国和日本有关"人"的成长、预期及文化设计等方面展开了细致的比较分析。东亚的"成人"伴随着国家的强力介入，中国是要把青少年培养成"接班人"，日本则是要育成合格的"国民"。相比之下，美国青少年的"成人"过程则可能是较多地受到基督教文化或其相关意识形态的影响。

在美国期间，我有机会参加了美国民俗学界的几次学会活动。2015 年 4 月 18 日，出席了美国西部民俗学会在加州洛杉矶分校举办的 2015 年度学术年会，并在其专设的"中国民俗"分组会上，发表了有关黄河流域"花馍文化"的调查成果，强调了"花馍"在乡民人生通过礼仪中的作用。由于有张举文的翻译，这场发表引起了在座的美国和中国同行的兴趣，美国学者对女性和花馍文化的关系感兴趣，这对我也是很好的刺激。在这次会议上，经张举文介绍，见到了美国民俗学家艾略特·奥林，他的《反反"民俗"》一文很有影响，在我主编的《民俗学的历史、理论与方法》中曾经收录了由宋颖博士翻译的该文的中文版。

2015 年 10 月 16 日，又出席了在加州长滩召开的美国民俗学会 2015 年度年会，也是在以"中国日常生活的仪式实践"为主题的中国民俗学专场，我以《汉文化中"人"的生涩、夹生与成熟》为题目作了口头发表，论述了汉文化对于"人"的成长和成熟的高度期许。同样，也是因为有张举文的鼎力翻译，这个看起来稍难的话题才得以和在座的中美两国民俗学家有所交流。值得一提的是，在这次年会上，我见到了美国印第安纳大学的民俗学家苏独玉教授，我们一起回顾了 20 年前她到北京大学社会学人类学研究所访问时的情形，皆有恍若隔世之感。

对我来说，访学期间最为重要的收获是，由崴涞大学亚洲研究中心资助，于 2015 年 10 月 22 日在俄勒冈首府瑟勒姆举办了一次以我的研究方向（东亚的成人与成人式）为主题的小型国际会议。来自美国（主要是崴涞大学亚洲研究中心的学者）、中国和日本的十多位学者出席。我在这次会议上，分别以《成人的"生"与"熟"》和《现代社会的成人礼》为题目，做了两次发言。北京大学高丙中教授、北京师范大学萧放教授、中国传媒大学王杰文教授、日本爱知大学铃木规夫教授，也都分别就研讨会的主题发表了各自的论文。

从美国通过 Skype 视频方式，参与北京大学高丙中教授于 2015 年 12 月 11 日组织的学术会议（主题为"经典概念的当代阐释：过渡仪礼的理论与经验研究"），也是一个极好的经验。中美之间的学会交流通常总会伴随着"时差"的困扰,但通过电脑视频,却可以和远在北京的学界同行轻易交流,此类方式其实不妨推广。

此外,在张霞博士的安排下,我还于2016年3月4日,在波特兰州立大学的孔子学院作了一次讲演,主题为"中国北方的花馍:从礼馍到文化遗产"。张霞博士担任翻译的此次讲座,虽然也有当地的美国市民前来,但听众更多的却是波特兰州立大学孔子学院的中国老师们。讲座引起了孔子学院中国老师们的兴趣,令我备感亲切。

尤其有意义的是我与张举文共同主持编辑了《西部民俗》(*Western Folklore*)学刊的一期特刊[2017,76(2)期],主题是"非遗在中国的实践"。四篇文章(另外有高丙中和萧放的)都在理论层面探讨中国的非遗现象和核心问题。这似乎是第一次将中国的非遗理论讨论以英文形式与国外同行对话。

除上述那些写作、学会发表和讲演活动之外,我还有机会去纽约、洛杉矶、旧金山、西雅图以及波特兰等多个城市里的"唐人街"旅行。这些旅行很难说是像样的考察,却也通过观察获得了一些重要的印象。例如,对于那些中国元素的符号(在西雅图和洛杉矶,同时还有若干日本元素的符号)究竟是如何作为城市"公共文化"的一部分而被表象的问题,经由走马观花获得的印象也是非常重要的。在张举文的安排和介绍下,我有机会接触到塞勒姆和波特兰的一些美国普通居民和华侨、华人居民,其中美国华人社会的"多重认同"成为我和他反复讨论的话题,当然还包括华人二世、三世的"成人"困扰,以及他们的"美国化"趋势等。塞勒姆和波特兰的华人、华侨,通过与中国传统音乐相关的艺术活动,以及以"吃喝"("吃喝团"成为其重要的标识)为媒介的社交活动等,积极地致力于维系和建构独特的华裔亚文化认同的努力,令人印象深刻。

在美国逗留期间,我和张举文曾就中国民俗学的相关问题展开了一些对话。我们分别对美国民俗学和日本民俗学有所了解,也都分别参与了美中民俗学和日中民俗学的一些学术交流活动,我们身在海外但都关心中国民俗学。希望我们的对话今后仍能够继续深入下去。

王杰文、高丙中、萧放、铃木规夫、周星、张举文（自左向右）在美国崴涞大学参与"东亚成人意义研讨会"，2015 年 10 月。Jiewen Wang, Bingzhong Gao, Fang Xiao, Norio Suzuki, Xing Zhou, Juwen Zhang (from left to right) during the Seminar on the Meaning of Becoming an Adult in East Asia, Willamette University, Salem, Oregon, Oct. 2015. Photograph courtesy of Juwen Zhang.

My Year in the US

Xing Zhou[*]

With the help of Professor Juwen Zhang, I spent my sabbatical year from Aichi University as a visiting scholar at Willamette University from 2015-2016. Although this visit was not directly related to Sino-US and Japan-US folklore communications, I became involved in them through this experience and benefited tremendously.

The main reason why I chose to go to Willamette University is because I have common research interests with Professor Juwen Zhang. Earlier, in March 2009, I met Professor Zhang at an international conference in Bielefeld, Germany. From the end of 2014 to the beginning of 2015, Professor Zhang was invited by the International Center for Chinese Studies (ICCS) at Aichi University to teach a class on Ritual Studies for our Ph. D. program. Professor Zhang translated the book "Les Rites de Passage" by the French folklorist Arnold van Gennep into Chinese. The students from the folklore and anthropology departments had the opportunity to broaden their views.

The main purpose for my visit to Willamette Universitywas to organize research on "adulthood" in China and Japan and to exchange views on the topic of adulthood with Professor Zhang. With his assistance, I have gained much on the following areas:

1. I was the first reader of Professor Zhang's new book translation, *Chisungu: a girl's initiation ceremony among the Bemba of Northern Rhodesia*. This book is by a British anthropologist, Audrey I. Richards, and is a masterpiece on the study of female rites of initiation. The book helped me as I was working on the topic in East Asia. Eventually, I wrote a reflective commentary on it.

---

[*] As the holder of the first doctorate of ethnology from a Chinese university in the 1980s, Xing Zhou studies not only ethnology, but also anthropology, sociology and folklore. He has been one of the most active scholars of the current generation. His academic influence is not limited to China, but also well-known in Japan and South Korea. Regarding his theoretical ideas on the transformation of adulthood, he has developed such ideas as, "half-cooked" (*jiasheng*) "inducing" (*cuishu*) in describing the process of becoming an adult, and "die-for" (*sigei*) in women's role in maintaining community traditions. These ideas contribute to ethnology and politics of ethnology, as well as the policies of religion and culture in China. After more than ten years of teaching and researching in Beijing University, Xing Zhou has been teaching in Aichi University in Japan since 2000. As more scholars are being trained in Western theories and are returning to China, Xing Zhou has begun to explore beyond China. With his works being translated into English (e. g., the 2017 *Western Folklore* special issue), his ideas will be better known by the outside world.

2. I finished compiling a collection, *Modern Folklore Vision and Direction*. Juwen Zhang translated an article by the American folklorist, Debora Kodish, "Imagine Public Folk." The collection will soon be published by Shangwu Yinshuguan (Commercial Press) in Beijing.

3. I completed a manuscript, *The Rites of Initiation and Problems of Becoming Adults in Modern East Asia*. In this cross-cultural comparative research, I focused on American adolescents' awareness and problems regarding the rites of initiation.

I had the opportunities to participate in several folklore events. On April 18th 2015, I attended the Western States Folklore Society annual meeting in Los Angeles, California. My presentation on the relationship between women and the flour steamed buns (*mantou*; *huamo*) interested both American and Chinese colleagues. At the meeting, Professor Zhang introduced me to Professor Elliott Oring, whose influential article, "Anti Anti-folklore," was included in the collection that I edited in Chinese, *History, Theory and Method of Folklore Studies*.

On October 16, 2015, I attended the AFS annual meeting in Long Beach, California. The main focus of the panel I participated in was "Chinese Everyday Ritual Practices: The Meaning of Becoming an Adult." I presented on the topic "the raw, half-cooked, and cooked persons in Chinese culture." At the meeting, I coincidentally met Professor Sue Tuohy from Indiana University. We reminisced over the time when she was in Beijing University in the 1990s.

For me, the most important achievement I've accomplished during my visit is the organization of "An International Seminar on the Meaning of Becoming an Adult in East Asia." I am thankful for the support I received from Willamette University's Center for Asian Studies. More than a dozen scholars from the United States, China and Japan attended the seminar. I presented on two topics: "The raw and cooked in becoming an adult" and "The rites of initiation in modern societies."

In addition, with the help of Dr. Xia Zhang, I gave a lecture at the Confucius Institute at Portland State University on March 4th, 2016. My topic was on "Steamed Bread [*mantou*]: From a ritual offering to an intangible cultural heritage in North China." There were some American locals who attended my lecture, but most of them were Chinese teachers of the Confucius Institute at Portland State University. The majority of them were very interested in my lecture, which made me feel at home.

Furthermore, in collaboration with Juwen Zhang, we edited a special volume for the journal of *Western Folklore* (forthcoming in 2017) on the topic of the Intangible Cultural Heritage and Chinese Practices. This special issue deals with the core issues in understanding the ICH phenomenon in China, which seems to be the first collective effort from scholars of China and of Chinese background to engage in a discussion on the topic in English.

In addition to these events, I visited the Chinatowns in New York, Los Angeles, San Francisco, Seattle, Portland and a few other cities. Although I did not do extensive fieldwork in the US, I did make some meaningful observations, for example, the use of traditional Chinese symbols in public spaces. In Los Angeles and Seattle, I also paid close attention to the use of Japanese cultural symbols.

Furthermore, I had the opportunity to meet with some local residents in Oregon. This experience helped me better understand the concept "multiple identities" in the Chinese American community, which was also a common interest for me and Professor Zhang. Chinese and Chinese Americans from Salem and Portland are becoming more engaged in activities and events related to traditional Chinese music. Moreover, there is the "eat-and-drink group" that reveals many issues in Chinese identity; their active efforts on building and maintaining a Chinese identity are very impressive.

During my short stay in the US, Professor Zhang and I had multiple conversations about the problems of Chinese folklore. We share many common perspectives on the folklore studies in the US, Japan, and China, though both of us happen to be living and working outside of China. I am sure that our dialogue will continue.

(Translation by Emily Su)

我与美国民俗学的邂逅

王霄冰[*]

民俗学虽然是一门国际性的学科，但每个国家根据自己的历史文化和国情，都发展起了各自不同的"一国民俗学"。我平时在上《民俗学概论》课时，说到"世界民俗学"这个概念时，总不免含糊其辞。日本民俗学家柳田国男是"一国民俗学"的早期倡导者。他在《民间传承论》中写下了"迈向世界民俗学之路"一节，其中提到"跨国比较研究"的方法，但他更多地把这看成一种努力的方向，认为实现起来比较困难。美国民俗学家阿兰·邓迪斯在《世界民俗学》中曾尝试使用来自世界各国和各民族的资料，阐释民俗的概念、功能、传播等问题。近年来，我在和日本民俗学者交流的过程中，发现他们也逐渐地把研究视野从日本本土扩展到了东亚乃至东南亚，像福田亚细男等学者推动的中日民俗联合调查项目。我自己在最近几年中，也应邀参加了日本国立历史民俗博物馆的松尾恒一教授主持的一项题为"东亚宗教的交流与变异"的研究课题，有幸借机前往日本的东京、奈良、长崎和韩国的首尔等地考察。这些"世界民俗学"的研究尝试，可以说都是建立在使用比较方法的基础上的。

然而即便不以建立"世界民俗学"为目的，中国民俗学者对于世界各国的民俗学一直都非常关注。有很多英国、美国、德国、日本、俄罗斯等的民俗学名著，都已被翻译成了中文，成为我们高校民俗学课程的重要参考资料。由于民俗学是一门起源于欧洲的现代学科，在引入中国的过程中也不免受到了近邻日本的影响，所以中国民俗学者总是自觉不自觉地以欧美和日本为师。我对这一点感触之所以非常深刻，是因为自己曾长期在日本和德国两个国家留学，我的博士学位就是在德国的波恩大学取得的，直到 2010 年底才从国外回到中国的大学（中山大学）工作。在国外期间，每次回国参加学术活动，我都会被要求"多介绍些

---

[*] 编者注：王霄冰现任中山大学非物质文化遗产研究中心教授。她在中国受到文学、民族学和民俗学的培训，在日本生活工作五年，在德国获得博士学位并生活工作十多年。凭着她非凡的学识和多语言能力，她不仅向中国翻译介绍了大量的欧洲民俗学研究成果，也与国内诸多民俗学者和机构在多个研究领域合作。她的主要研究兴趣是文字、仪式和记忆。近年来，她与美国民俗学者的交流，代表了当今有着国际视野的中国民俗学者的风范。王霄冰对民俗学，特别是中国的民俗学，有着独特的体会和认知。正如她在本文所说，对中国民俗学者渴望了解外界的解读可以是传统的——向外界学习，因为自己落后；也可以是从局内人的角度——为了更好与外界平等交流。而后者正是只有王霄冰这样的经历的人才能看到的。

德国民俗学的理论和方法"。这一开始给我的印象，好像是国内的同仁对于自己的理论创新能力尚缺乏自信，总是想借用国外现成的理论与方法，用以解决目前中国民俗学研究实践中遭遇的各类问题。但后来自己回国工作后，才明白情况并不是我当初想的那样。中国民俗学经过近百年的历史，已经形成了自己的一套相对比较成熟的研究范式。国内学者之所以如此渴望看到更多的对于西方同行论著的介绍，恰恰是为了与国际学界展开平等、开放的交流，在互通有无中推动本学科不断向前发展。

我所在的中山大学也是中国民俗学发展史上的一座重镇，在 20 世纪 20—30 年代这里曾经集聚了一批国内著名的民俗学家和人类学家。改革开放以后，中山大学是最早恢复人类学和民俗学学科的大学之一。进入 21 世纪后，中大又率先参与了由联合国教科文组织倡导和中国政府主导的非物质文化遗产保护运动，在我所在的中文系成立了中国非物质文化遗产研究中心。这也是目前中国唯一的一个与非遗有关的教育部重点研究基地，其运行经费得到教育部的直接资助。从 2011 年开始，我们同中国民俗学会、美国民俗学会以及其他一些中美高校和机构合作，连续共同举办了四期中美非物质文化遗产论坛，分别在广州、那什维尔、武汉和华盛顿特区举行。我有幸参加了全部四届研讨会并作发言，从和美国同行的交流中学习到了不少东西。

之前虽然在德国留学，但我对美国民俗学其实了解不多。唯一一次的交流，就是应张举文博士之邀，和中国民俗学会的刘魁立会长、高丙中教授、萧放教授一起，参加了 2007 年在加拿大魁北克举办的美国民俗学会年会。当时的印象，就是到会的人非常之多，会议专题也比较分散。在会议期间，时任美国民俗学会会长的艾伟先生高规格地招待了我们中国代表团，他与他的同仁们的亲切友好给我留下了极深的印象。

通过参加四届中美非遗论坛，并且两次前往美国，我对美国民俗学有了更多的了解。有一个比较深的感触，就是女性主义对美国民俗学界的影响显然比对中国民俗学的影响更大。我们在交流的过程中，就先后有两位女性学者登上了美国民俗学会会长的宝座：Diane Goldstein 和 Michael Ann Williams（另外，没见过面的现任会长，Kate Turner，也是女性，而且正在选举的下届会长也将在两名女性候选人中产生）。而且在和她们的交谈之中，我发现她们往往显示出较强的女性意识，而不像我们中国的女学者那样，常常会刻意地隐去自己的女性身份，在公共场合尽量给人一种中性化的或无性别差异的形象。我觉得这是特别值得我们反思和学习的地方。

美国民俗学者的公共服务意识也是令我深为钦佩的一个方面。虽然在美国也有所谓的"学院派"，但我在美国期间，确实也接触到了很多从事公共民俗学的学者。他们中有很多人都在没有长期正式职位的情况下，通过申请国家课题，推广民俗知识，帮助社区民众构建自己多样化的文化生活。中国目前也正处于社会改革的时代，公共的文化领域和民众的日常生活都非常需要民俗学方面的知识，但很多民俗学者对于学者是否可以干预生活、是否应该积极地投入非遗保护运动，都持怀疑态度。美国虽然至今尚未加入联合国教科文组织的非遗保护公约，但他们在公共民俗学方面做出的努力，尤其是其中所蕴含的学术服务社会的理念，为广大乐于参与社会文化建设的中国民俗学者提供了榜样和理论依据。

尽管中美民俗学相互接触的时间还不算很长,但已经显示出了有效的成果。希望今后两国的民俗学继续加强交流。如有机会,我本人很愿意为此贡献微薄之力。

My Encounters with American Folkloristics

Xiaobing Wang[*]

Folkloristics is an international discipline, but each country has its own history and culture, and thus has its own "one nation's folklore studies." There is, however, a concept "world folkloristics" which is often used ambiguously. Japanese folklorist Yanagita Kunio was an early advocate of "one nation's folklore studies." In his *Theory of Folklore Transmission*, he devoted a chapter on "The Road toward World Folkloristics," which introduced the transnational comparative research approach. He took it as a goal, knowing that it would be difficult to realize it. In *The Study of Folklore*, Alan Dundes also tried to explain folkloristic concepts, functions, and transmissions by integrating studies of various peoples in different places around the world. Recently, I noticed that Japanese folklorists have extended their research from Japan to East and Southeast Asia, and even promoted Sino-Japanese joint research projects. I was also invited to participate in a project on "Exchange and Variation of Religion in East Asia," led by Matsuo Kochi from the National Museum of History and Folklore of Japan. These "world folkloristic" research projects are based on the application of comparative methods.

Even though Chinese folklorists never had the desire to establish "world folkloristics," they have always had strong interest in learning about other country's folklore studies. There are many folklore studies from other countries that have been translated into Chinese and become reference materials for university-level courses. Folklore is a modern subject originating in Europe. However, the Japanese exerted great influences on the Chinese understanding of folklore when folklore study

---

[*] Xiaobing Wang is Professor of Folklore at Sun Yat-sen University. She has studied literature, ethnology, and folklore in China, worked in Japan for five years, and received her Ph. D. in Germany, where she lived for over a decade. With her extensive knowledge and multilingual abilities, she has not only translated a large number of works by European folklorists, but also collaborated with many Chinese and oversea Chinese folklorists on a number of topics. Her main research interests are ancient inscriptions, rituals, and cultural memory. She represents the Chinese folklorists who have international experiences and perspectives. As she says in this story, the Chinese folklorists' desire to understand the outside world can be perceived from an "outsider's view," that is, to learn from the outside because they are behind; this desire, however, can also be understood from an "insider's view," that is, to learn from the outside so as to equally communicate with the outside. This nuance can only be "discovered" by people like her with extensive international experiences.

was introduced into China at the turn of the 20th century. This fact had a deep impact on me since I studied in Japan and Germany. I got my Ph. D. in Germany at the University of Bonn, and only returned to China in 2010 to work at Sun Yat-sen University. Every time I returned to China while I was studying abroad, I would be asked to introduce some German folklore theories and research methods. In the beginning, I had the impression that Chinese folklorists lacked self-confidence regarding their own theoretical innovations and always wanted to borrow foreign theories and methods to solve the problems they encountered in their folklore research. Only after I returned to China to work did I realize that the situation was not what I had thought before. With a history of nearly one century, Chinese folkloristics has already formed its own relatively mature research paradigms. As a result, Chinese scholars are very eager to learn more about their Western counterparts simply because they have the desire to contribute to the development of the discipline by engaging in the international academic discourse in an equal and open way.

Sun Yat-sen University is a center for the development of Chinese folkloristics. During the 1920s-30s, it attracted a number of important folklorists and anthropologists. It was also one of the first folklore programs when Chinese folkloristics was restored in the 1980s. Entering the 21st century, SYSU established the only center for ICH research in China, as a response to the ICH movement launched by the UNESCO. From 2011 to 2013, our Center and the AFS held four forums on the ICH practice in China. I was lucky enough to have attended and presented each time, and thus learned very much from American colleagues.

Although I studied in Germany, I did not know much about American folklore studies. The only exchange I had was at the 2007 AFS annual meeting in Quebec, Canada, along with the CFS colleagues. What impressed me was that there were so many participants and so many topics. During the meeting, AFS president, Bill Ivey, held a special reception for the CFS delegation. I left with a great impression of American colleagues for their friendship and hospitality.

By attending the four Sino-US forums and travelling to the United States twice, I now have a better understanding of American folklore studies. I noticed an obvious phenomenon, that is, feminism seemed to have a greater impact on American folklore studies than on Chinese folklore studies. In the course of our communication, two female folklorists were elected to be the AFS President: Diane Goldstein and Michael Ann Williams (the current president Kate Turner is a female, and the two candidates for next term are also females). Through our conversations, I discovered that they had a strong sense of being female, in comparison to Chinese female scholars who often deliberately conceal their female identity in the public sphere. I think Chinese women should learn from the Americans and embrace gender differences, instead of trying to neutralize the issues and direct attention away from them.

Another admirable aspect of American folklorists is their consciousness of public service. Although there is also "academism" in the United States, I have come into contact with a lot of

American folklorists engaged in public folklore. Many of them promote folk knowledge and help the community to build up their own diverse culture, even though many of them do not have stable jobs or positions. China is now in the era of social reform, so people need to use folklore knowledge in their daily activities. However, many folklorists are skeptical about whether or not they can intervene in people's lives and actively engage them in intangible cultural heritage protection campaigns. Although the United States has not yet joined the UNESCO ICH Convention, its public folklorists' efforts have set an example for Chinese folklorists in terms of integrating theories and social services.

The history of Sino-US folklore communication is still short, but the achievements are already obvious. I hope that it will not only continue and strengthen, but also flourish. I am ready to contribute my own modest share.

(Translation by Erica Mao)

从碰撞到共享：中美民俗学者的交流

宋俊华[*]

我们与美国民俗、非遗学界新的学术结缘是从"干杯"开始的。

2007年12月，中国民俗学会副理事长叶涛教授陪同美国民俗学会会长艾伟和美国崴涞大学亚洲研究中心教授张举文等来到广州访问，晚上我们在海印桥附近的炳胜餐厅设宴招待。我们与来访美国学者是第一次吃饭，相互之间有点客气、拘谨。于是，有人建议大家喝一些白酒，一者可以让客人们解解乏，二者让美国学者感受一下中国酒文化。喝酒时，大家聊到中文"干杯"的英译问题，说用"cheers"一词似乎无法准确译出中文"干杯"那种味道。张举文教授灵机一动，说"干杯"的"干"有碰撞、进攻的意思，他解释说，他注意到"干杯"已改变为起身主动向"客体"发起"碰撞"，不再是在座位上的象征行为，就译为"attack"吧，相当于主人或客人"出击敬酒"！大家一边说好，一边现学现卖地用起来，你"attack"我"attack"，气氛一下子就活跃了起来。这次关于"干杯"与"attack"的讨论，是我第一次与美国民俗学者面对面的"民俗"交流，也算是中美民俗、非遗学术交流的一个趣事吧。在此后的学术交流中，"attack"竟然成为我们这些中美民俗、非遗学者一听就心领神会的特殊用语。"干杯"，让我们拉开了与美国民俗、非遗学界新的交流序幕。

"干杯"一词的来源，有多种说法。许多人认为源于16世纪爱尔兰的"toast"一词，原意是烤面包。当时爱尔兰人有个习惯，在喝酒时要把一片烤面包放入一杯威士忌酒或啤酒中，以改善酒味及去除酒的不纯性。到了18世纪，"干杯"才发展为祝酒礼仪。至于为什么喝酒要相互碰杯，也有各种说法。有的说人们互相碰杯就像在教堂敲钟一样，是为了表达驱除恶魔的意思。"干杯"在英语中除了用"toast"表达外，还经常用"cheers"表达。如果说前者意思与喝酒的习惯有关，后者则与喝酒的功能有关。

"干杯"一词，在中国原本是喝干杯中酒的意思，后来也发展为祝酒礼仪，如金代元好

---

[*] 编者注：宋俊华现任中山大学中国非物质文化遗产研究中心主任、教授。作为中国非物质文化研究和学术出版（如《文化遗产》双月刊）的重要基地之一，他所领导的中心在学术界和政府的文化政策制定等方面都发挥了积极而重要的作用。他的研究领域是古典文学和戏剧，特别是戏剧服饰。近年来，他在非遗研究方面发表了许多文章，特别是组织编辑出版《中国非物质文化遗产保护发展报告》（2014, 2015, 2016），对非遗的文化政策和学术反思有着重大意义。他在此所讲述的不仅是他个人的感受，而且体现了他所在的中心在中美交流中的重要作用，特别是在主持几次有关非遗的论坛会议中发挥的作用。

问《续夷坚志·梁梅》中就有"梅素妆而至，坐久干杯，唱《梅花·水龙吟》"。把中文"干杯"译成英文的"attack"，虽然是一个玩笑，但在中国当代的劝酒文化中还是有一点道理的。在中国，"干杯"除了喝干杯中酒、碰杯等字面意义外，还带有一种斗酒、拼酒的意思，与"attack"的"攻击"意思有相似之处。当然，中国式"干杯"与美国的"cheers"有一点是相同的，那就是祝福客人快乐、自己也快乐的意思。

从中国与美国在"干杯"文化上的异同，我想到了这样一个问题：来自不同文化背景的人就像中美民俗、非遗学者，是如何实现交流的呢？"干杯"和"cheers"这两个词不就是一个很好的比喻吗？中国的"干杯"强调的"干"的动作、过程，即"碰撞"，美国的"cheers"强调的则是结果，即"共享"，但二者都是以祝福快乐为目的。所以，从"干杯"到"cheers"，从"碰撞"到"共享"，不正形象比喻了中美民俗、非遗学术交流的路径？

在过去十年里，我们与美国民俗、非遗学者的学术交流，是通过一次次的"碰撞"、不断的"共享"来实现的。如2009年爱达荷州博伊西的美国民俗学会年会，2010年田纳西州纳什维尔的美国民俗学会年会，2011年广东佛山的首届中美非物质文化遗产论坛，2012年田纳西州纳什维尔的第二届中美非物质文化遗产论坛和湖北武汉的第三届中美非物质文化遗产论坛，2013年华盛顿特区的第四届中美非物质文化遗产论坛和北京的第五届中美非物质文化遗产论坛，2014年新墨西哥州圣达菲的美国民俗学会年会和中国民族博物馆合作研讨会，2015年贵州贵阳的中美民族博物馆合作研讨会和加州长滩的美国民俗学年会，2016年佛罗里达州迈阿密的美国民俗学会年会（详见美国民俗学会网页，中美民俗与非遗项目：https://afsnet.site-ym.com/?page=FICH），通过这些会议、论坛以及穿插期间的中美民俗学会工作会议、人员互访等，我们彼此在不断碰撞、共享中加深了了解，收获了学术，增强了友谊。

我们每一次去美国开会，都能感受到一次新的文化碰撞和共享。2010年我们在田纳西州纳什维尔开会，艾伟教授为了让我们感受美国不同阶层的餐饮文化，亲自带我们去美国蓝领阶层、白领阶层、金领阶层常去的餐厅各用了一次餐。这种细心的安排，不只是让我们体验了美国餐饮，了解了美国餐饮民俗，更重要的是让我明白了民俗、非遗学者之间交流的一些"窍门"：让大家对彼此的文化和研究多一些接触、体验，在接触和体验中增强相互理解，实现共享。此外，在我们去美国交流期间，艾伟教授举办的家庭聚会、听歌剧，罗伊德教授安排的庭院聚餐，以及美国民俗学会安排的纳什维尔的乡村音乐体验、俄亥俄州的农场生活体验和阿米什人生活考察、新墨西哥州圣达菲的印第安文化考察，一次次零距离的文化"碰撞"，不断加深了我们对美国文化及其美国研究者的理解。当然，美国学者来到中国，也会有类似的文化体验安排。

正是上述以合作举办会议、论坛等项目为主，以民俗、非遗体验为辅的一系列交流安排，使参与交流的中美学者彼此间有时会形成一种超越语言的心灵默契。2010年我和欧阳光、蒋明智教授到纽约拜访罗伯特·巴龙教授时，与纽约州艺术委员会的学者们举行了一次座谈会。在交流中我们得知，那天正好是一位在场美国女学者的父亲的生日。为了向她表示感谢和祝贺，蒋明智教授现场特地为她父亲写了幅字——"福如东海，寿比南山"。由于当时没有专门翻译，我只好硬着头皮，一边说着蹩脚的英语，一边用手势比画，没想到竟然被那位女学者听懂了。她感动得直抹眼泪，一边双手握着蒋明智教授的手，一边不停地说谢谢。在那一瞬间，我似乎突然明白了一个道理：人与人之间的交流，只要真心、用心，语言其实不是障碍。中美民俗、非遗学者之间的学术碰撞、共享之所以顺利、成功，其实也是同样的道理。

事实上，对于我们这些民俗、非遗学者来说，每一次田野工作，都是一次从"碰撞"到"共享"的交流历程。当我们以"他者"身份进入一个陌生的社区，面对陌生的调查对象，我们和调查对象必然会有一系列"碰撞"，即彼此接触、彼此展示、彼此了解的过程，由此产生彼此认可、彼此分享，即信息、文化、情感的"共享"。这种碰撞、共享，以及贯穿其中的理解、尊重，是民俗、非遗田野工作的基本方法和伦理原则，也是中美民俗、非遗学术交流的基本方法和伦理原则。

从"干杯"到"cheers"，从"碰撞"到"共享"，中美异曲同工的"干杯"文化，让中美民俗、非遗学者为文化、学术交流，为相互理解、友谊走到了一起。让我们为中美民俗、非遗学术交流更上一层楼而"干杯"吧。

中山大学宋俊华（站立者）在欢迎晚宴上唱西北民歌，北京，2011年7月（坐者：朝戈金、杜赫斯特，自左向右）。Junhua Song of SYSU (standing; Chao Gejin and Kurt Dewhurst sitting from left to right) singing a Northern Shaanxi folk song at a welcome dinner in Beijing, July 2011. Photograph by Juwen Zhang.

From "Attacking" to "Sharing":
Exchanges between the Sino-US Folklorists

Junhua Song*

It was through "*ganbei*" that we began our connection with American folklorists.

In December 2007, AFS President Bill Ivey led a delegation to visit us in Guangzhou. They were accompanied by the CFS Secretary General Tao Ye. We held a welcome dinner. It was our first time dining with the American visitors, and it appeared that everyone was polite but somewhat restrained. Someone at the table suggested having some Chinese liquor to let our guests relax a little, and have an experience of Chinese liquor culture. One question came out as we began drinking: how to translate "*ganbei*." It seemed that "cheers" could not bring out the flavor of *ganbei*. Professor Juwen Zhang had an idea. He said that *gan* was originally a verb meant clash or attack. Then it began to have the meaning of active movement toward guests to offer toasts by clinking glasses with them, as if "attacking" others. Upon hearing his explanation, everyone began to use it, and the atmosphere came alive. This exchange between *ganbei* and *attack* was my first face-to-face contact with American scholars. Though only from an anecdote, our use of the word "attack" has become an insider's cue in the subsequent gatherings between Chinese and American folklorists. It was *ganbei* that lifted the curtain of our Sino-US exchanges.

There are many explanations about the origin of the word *ganbei*. Many think that it originated in the 16th century from the Irish word "toast," which was the word for toasted bread. Back then Irish people had a habit of putting a piece of toast into a glass of whiskey or beer, in order to improve the taste. By the 18th century, "toasting" became a drinking etiquette. As for why we

---

* Junhua Song is Director of the Institute of Chinese Intangible Cultural Heritage, Sun Yat-sen University, and Professor of Chinese and Folklore. The Institute in an important base of Intangbile Cutlrual Heritage studies in China and publishes the bimonthly journal, *Cultural Heritage*, playing a leading role in academic research and in influencing government culture policies. Song's own reseach interests are in classic literature and drama, particularly in theatracal dress. In recent years, he has published many articles on ICH, and edited the series *Report of China's Intangible Cultural Heritage Protection and Development* (2014, 2015, 2016), which encourages the academic reflections on cutlural policies regarding the ICH. What he tells here is not only his own perosnal experiences, but also the importancce of his Institute in the Sino-US exchanges, especially through the forums on ICH.

clink cups, there are many explanations for that too. Some people say clinking glasses is like ringing the church bell—it symbolizes an exorcism. The word *ganbei* is often translated as "toast" or "cheers" in English. The former is connected to the practice of drinking, while the latter represents the function of drinking.

The word *ganbei* in Chinese initially meant to drain the wine in one's cup, and later developed to be a toasting etiquette. In the *Supplementary Records of Foreign Customs* (Xu Yi Jian Zhi) by the poet Yuan Haowen (1190-1257), there's a line describing a scene of *ganbei*. Although translating *ganbei* into "attack" is a humorous way of looking at it, it reflects contemporary Chinese drinking culture. In China, *ganbei* has its literal meanings of draining the cup and clinking glasses, but also carries a provocative tone. It is similar in meaning to the word "attack" used as an imperative. Of course, the Chinese *ganbei* is similar to "cheers" in that it wishes happiness to the guest and oneself.

By comparing and contrasting Chinese and American *ganbei* culture, I came to wonder: How do people from different cultural backgrounds, such as Chinese and American folklorists, communicate with each other? Aren't *ganbei* and "cheers" a great analogy? Chinese *ganbei* stresses the action and process of *gan*, the clash. American "cheers" emphasizes the result of sharing. But both words have the goal of wishing happiness. So from *ganbei* to "cheers," from "clashing" to "sharing," doesn't that represent the path of Sino-US folklore and intangible heritage academic exchanges?

In the past ten years, we have interacted with American folklorists and intangible heritage scholars through a series of "clashing" and "sharing." The AFS Conference in Boise, Idaho (2009), ASF Conference in Nashville, Tennessee (2010), the first Sino-US Intangible Heritage Forum in Foshan, Guangdong (2011), the second Sino-US Intangible Heritage Forum in Nashville, Tennessee, the third in Wuhan, Hubei (2012), the fourth Sino-US Intangible Heritage Forum in Washington, DC, and the fifth in Beijing (2013), the collaborative conference between AFS and China National Museum in Santa Fe, New Mexico (2014), the joint Museum Project Planning meeting in Guizhou, China and the AFS meeting in Long Beach, California (2015), the AFS meeting in Miami (2016); all these conferences, forums, meetings and mutual visits (see some details: https://afsnet.site-ym.com/?page=FICH) let us develop a deeper understanding and connection with each other through endless clashing and sharing.

Each time we go to the US for conferences, we can feel a clashing and sharing of cultures. In 2010 when we were at a conference in Nashville, Tennessee, Dr. Ivey took us to restaurants that catered to different income levels so that we could experience the dining culture of each class. Not only were we able to experience American dining, understand American dining culture, I learned some "tricks" of communication between folklorists and intangible heritage scholars. We should all enhance our understandings of each other's culture through personal contact and immersion. During our visit to America, we also attended Dr. Ivey's house parties and concert invitations, Dr. Lloyd's courtyard meals, Nashville's country music fests arranged by the AFS, Ohio's farm life and lifestyle investigations of the Amish, and Santa Fe's Indian cultural research. All of these cultural "clashes" deepened our understandings of American culture and American scholars. Of course, when American scholars visit China, there would be similar arrangements for cultural immersion.

The conferences, forums, and folklife experiences allow Chinese and American scholars to form bonds that transcend language. In 2010 when Dr. Guang Ouyang, Dr. Mingzhi Jiang and I visited Dr. Robert Baron in New York, we held a seminar with New York Art Committee scholars. That very day was the birthday of the father of one female scholars in attendance. In order to show our appreciation and well-wishes, Dr. Jiang calligraphed "May your fortune be as boundless as the East Sea and your life as long as the South Mountain" for the woman's father. Since there wasn't an interpreter present, I had to convey the meaning with my poor English and hand motions. To my surprise, she understood! She was moved to tears and kept thanking Dr. Jiang while holding his hands. At that moment, I came to a revelation: language is no barrier in sincere communications. The success of Sino-US scholars' clashing and sharing work by the same principle.

As a matter of fact, to us folklorists and intangible inheritance scholars, every field study is a process of "clashing" to "sharing." When we enter a strange community as an "outsider," with strangers as our research subjects, we are bound to have a series of "clashes" with them. It is the process of us contacting, demonstrating, and understanding each other. Through this we can reach mutual recognition and sharing, that is, the sharing of information, cultures, and emotions. This clashing and sharing, and the understanding and respect throughout the process, is the moral principle of field studies in folklore and intangible heritage studies. It is also the basic code of exchange for Sino-US folkloristic interactions.

From *ganbei* to "cheers," from "clashing" to "sharing," the communication, understanding, and friendship of Chinese and American folklorists lead us to the same end through different means. Let us *ganbei* to a brighter future of Sino-US folkloristic exchanges!

(Translation by Eurydice Chen)

我经历的中国故事

安东尼·布切泰利[*]

就我而言，有机会和我的中国同事们一起从事民俗学研究，不仅在专业上和知识储备上是一种收获，而且也是一种诗意般的人生回溯。那是 2002 年，我住在昆明，作为云南大学的英语老师，我第一次踏入学术领域的民俗学。如今作为一个专业的民俗学者，作为美国民俗学会和中国民俗学会专业交换项目的一部分，我尤其感到高兴！同时，我也很激动能有这样一个机会，和我的朋友兼同事艾米·斯基尔曼一起访问内蒙古。这是一个我在云南的时候就一直想去但始终未能如愿前往的地方。也许这就是为什么尽管我们每到访一处都能遇到很棒的同仁，但是当张举文提议收集关于中国和美国民俗学家交流的故事时，我和艾米第一时间就想到了内蒙古。特别是一次出乎意料的有关蒙古传统音乐和运动的知识收获，令我们记忆犹新。

2013 年 6 月 14 日中午，我们到达内蒙古自治区省会呼和浩特市，内蒙古师范大学社会学民俗学学院的讲师、内蒙古民俗学会的执行委员会委员额尔德木图来机场接我们，他把我们带到酒店。我们在这里和敖其会面，她是社会学民俗学学院的教授，同时也是内蒙古民俗学会会长，乌仁毕力格担任我们的翻译。我们在酒店吃了便餐，然后他们陪同我们参观了离酒店不远的内蒙古师范大学主校区的民俗学项目中的民间艺术画廊和蒙古历史画廊。

在民间艺术画廊，额尔德木图负责收集和展示大部分用于展览的物品。他亲自带领我们参观，还向我们描述了每一个展品的大量细节，讲述了一些展品是生活在草原上的人民捐赠的。他还向我们简要介绍了蒙古族乡民民俗生活的概况。作为这次信息量极大的谈话的一部分，额尔德木图还告诉我们三种传统的蒙古族运动——骑马、射箭和摔跤——在蒙古族人民民俗生活中的重要性和实践性的一些细节。

参观完这些之后，我们被带到一个正式的欢迎晚宴，并被正式介绍给内蒙古师范大学云国宏校长、陈副校长，还有一些人文和社会科学领域的高级研究人员。精心准备的晚宴节目

---

[*] 编者注：安东尼·布切泰利现任美国学教授，获得"美国学和新英格兰地区研究"方向博士，民俗学硕士。他的出版物主题涵盖了有关人种、种族与记忆等领域。除了他对中国的兴趣和经历，布切泰利还致力于研究旧金山美籍华人的亚民俗，这一研究体现在他对 Jon Lee 的研究中（《讲述唐人街》，2017；以及 2014 年发表于《美国民俗学刊》的一篇论文）。他是又一个因为"中国经历"而转变为民俗学家的例子。在这个转变过程中，一个学者的个人生活和学术生涯是不断交融、并肩前行的。

中包括有音乐伴奏和声乐合唱的传统蒙古族欢迎仪式,还有马头琴表演。晚宴尾声是云校长赠送给我们绘有蒙古马的一幅皮革卷轴画,我们也向他们赠送了一些个人小礼物以感谢他们的热情招待。

第二天早上,学校为我们安排了去位于鄂尔多斯市伊金霍洛旗草原上的成吉思汗陵参观,还要听一场马头琴音乐会。一早,我们就和敖其、额尔德木图、乌仁毕力格乘着校方给我们提供的汽车出发了,但是我们抵达的比预期的午餐时间晚了些。到达后,先和鄂尔多斯旅游局的局长和副局长会面,一行的还有敖其以前的学生,现在也在鄂尔多斯工作。他们带我们在一家家庭经营的蒙古包餐厅里进餐,菜肴很精致,这种经营方式已经成为当地旅游业的常见特色。这次宴饮和昨天的晚宴相似,但相比而言不那么正式,也包含了种类繁多的食物(尤其是无处不在的蒙古奶茶)、一个欢迎仪式以及由雇佣的表演者进行的音乐表演。但是,和前一天晚上更正式的场合不同的是,在表演者唱完之后,还会鼓励用餐者自己唱歌。

这是我们在访问期间一系列表演中的第一次,也是仅有的一次。老实说,我已经记不起我们中的每一个人那天唱了什么,也许彼得、保罗和玛丽的《魔术龙普夫》是其中之一。午餐结束的时候,由于时间太晚所以去参观成吉思汗陵已经来不及,所以,敖其教授便安排我们去一个附近的赛马场参观蒙古骑马特技和骑马射箭。

骑手们都非常棒。作为一个美国人,我觉得这种骑马活动可以和美国的牧人马术表演做一个很有意思的比较。美国人往往更注重于应对家养动物的技巧,如套马、放牧和骑乘野马,而蒙古族人的马术主要集中在骑马特技和在马背上射中靶心的运动。活动结束后,东道主把我们带去和骑手们见面。我们还没反应过来,就已经被带领着骑在了马上(对我而言,他们让马行走得太慢,太小心了,因为我曾经在马术跳杆上花的时间和在马背上一样多)绕着赛马场骑行。

短暂的骑行过后,我们被带到了赛马场附近的一个小场地,这里树立了一个箭靶,他们还给我们弓和箭。艾米和我以及东道主们轮流射箭,一直到车来接我们。相比之下,我们的大部分箭是射在草地上而不是箭靶上。我想得更多的是,在这次内蒙古之旅中,我们经常会被请去"体验"而不仅仅是观看事物。对我来说,这一系列学术交流最难忘的瞬间,就是我们的同仁以一种很直接的方式邀请我们去体验他们想让我们理解的文化实践。我认为这是专业交流项目里,对于促进国际学术交流和合作来说至关重要和不可替代的一个方面。

(天津大学史静翻译)

My Narratives of China Experience

Anthony Buccitelli*

For me, the opportunity to engage as a folklorist with my colleagues in China has been not only professionally and intellectually rewarding, but also a kind of poetic return. It was while I was living in Kunming in 2002, as a young English teacher at Yunnan University, that I first encountered folklore as a scholarly field. So coming back to China in my now capacity as a professional folklorist as part of the American Folklore Society and China Folklore Society's Professional Exchange was especially pleasurable! Similarly, I was excited to have had the opportunity, along with my friend and colleague Amy Skillman, to visit Inner Mongolia province. I had wanted to visit the province my time in the Yunnan had never been able to get there. Perhaps this is why, though Amy and I met wonderful colleagues in every place we visited, it's the time in Inner Mongolia that came immediately to mind when Juwen Zhang proposed collecting stories about communications between Chinese and American folklorists. In particular I remember an unexpected lesson we received on traditional Mongolian music and sports.

We arrived in Hohhot, the capital city of the Inner Mongolia Autonomous Region, at about mid-day on June 14, 2013. We were met at the airport by Erdemtu, lecturer in the Folklore Department at Inner Mongolia Normal University and an Executive Committee member of the Inner Mongolian Folklore Society. He took us to our hotel, where we were met by Ao Qi, professor in the Folklore Department and President of the Inner Mongolian Folklore Society, and our translator Wurubilige. They took us for a casual lunch in our hotel, before escorting us to tour the folklore program's folk arts and Mongolian history galleries on the main campus of IMNU, which was close by our hotel.

In the folk arts gallery, Erdemtu, who had been responsible for collecting and displaying most

---

* Anthony Buccitelli holds a Ph. D. in American and New England studies and an M. A. in folklore, and now teaches American Studies and Communications. His publications cover such topics as race, ethnicity, and memory. Besides his China interests and experiences, Buccitelli also recovered the metafolklore of Chinese Americans in San Francisco, as seen in his work on Jon Lee (*Telling Chinatown*, 2017; and an article in *JAF* 2014). He is another example of being transformed into a folklorist through China experience, where a scholar's personal life and academic career get intertwined and strengthened.

of the items on exhibit, gave us a personal tour. He described each piece in great detail, talked about some of the people in the grasslands who donated the items, and gave a brief overview of rural Mongolian folklife. As part of his extremely informative talk, Erdemtu instructed us on "the three traditional Mongolian sports": horseback riding, archery, and wrestling, describing each in some detail in terms of practice and importance in Mongolian folklife.

After the tour of these facilities, we were taken to a large reception dinner where we were formally introduced to the University President Guohong Yun, Vice-President Chen, and a group of senior faculty in the humanities and social sciences. The elaborate dinner included a traditional Mongolian welcoming ceremony with musical accompaniment, as well as vocal performances, and performances on the Mongolian horse-headed fiddle. At the end of the evening, President Yun presented us with leather scroll paintings of Mongolian horses. We also offered the president some personal gifts as a thank you for the hospitality of the university.

The next morning, the university arranged for us to visit Ordos in Ejin Horo Banner to see the Mausoleum of Genghis Khan and to hear a concert of horse-head fiddle music. We set off early with Ao Qi, Erdemtu, Wurubilige, and the driver of the university-provided van, but arrived later than expected around lunchtime. When we arrived, we were met by the Director and Assistant Director of the Ordos Tourism Bureau, along with a group of Ao Qi's former students who now worked in the area. They took us for an elaborate meal at a family-run restaurant housed in a yurt, a business operation that has become a commonplace feature of the local tourist industry. Similar in form, but far less formal than the previous evening, this meal also included a vast and diverse array of foods, most especially the ubiquitous *suutei tsai* or Mongolian milk tea, a welcoming ceremony, and musical performances by hired performers. However, after the hired performers had sung, the diners were also encouraged to sing their own songs, which had not been the case in the more formal setting of the previous night.

And so we sang what would be only the first in a series of performance during our visit! To be honest, I can't recall what either of us sang that day, although I think Peter, Paul, and Mary's "Puff the Magic Dragon" may have been one of the selections. By the time that the lunch concluded, it was too late for us to reach Genghis Khan's mausoleum in time to see the exhibit, so instead Ao Qi made arrangements for us to visit a nearby horse track to see an exhibition of Mongolian stunt riding and mounted archery.

The riders were excellent. As an Americanist, this riding event was an interesting contrast to riding events I have seen at American rodeos. While the US emphasis tends to be on skills for the dealing with domestic animals, such as roping, herding, or bronco riding, the Mongolian horsemanship in this event focused on stunt riding and hitting targets from horseback. Little did we know that just as we were asked to sing after the professional singers displayed their skills, we would also be called on to display our riding skills! After the event ended, our hosts brought us down to the track area to meet the riders, and before we knew it, we were on horseback ourselves being led (very slowly and carefully in my case, since I've probably spent just as much time on a pogo stick as on horseback) around the track.

After a short ride, we were led to a small field next to the track where a target was set up and given a bow and arrows. Amy and I, and our hosts each took turns shooting at the target until the van arrived. I think more of our arrows ended up in the grass than the target, but the experience of being asked at each point in our trip in Mongolia to "do" instead of just watch was, for me, a memorable moment in this series scholarly communications, a time when our colleagues invited us to experience in a more direct way the cultural practices they wanted us to understand. This is the one aspect of the professional exchange program that I believe is vital and irreplaceable as a way of promoting international scholarly exchange and collaboration.

中美民俗学交流对我个人的影响

游自荧*

  我是 2002 年 9 月进入北京大学中文系攻读民间文学专业的硕士研究生，当时我的导师陈泳超教授正在主持"民间文化青年论坛"网络论坛，并在 2003 年 7 月召开了主题为"中国现代学术史上的民间文化"的第一届论坛学术会议。会议是在网上召开，大家先后讨论了吕微、陈连山、陈建宪、鹿忆鹿、钟宗宪、萧放、施爱东、刘晓春、安德明、陈泳超、巴莫曲布嫫、秦燕春和朝戈金的会议论文，并且针对中国民俗学学科很多重要的基本理论问题（诸如田野和文本的问题、神话研究的最终目标等）展开了热烈讨论（陈泳超 2004）。时隔十二年之后再去看这段网上唇枪舌剑热烈讨论的时光，真的是我学术启蒙最重要的阶段。当时受朝戈金、巴莫曲布嫫、杨利慧、安德明和王娟的影响，我对于西方的民俗学理论产生了浓厚的兴趣，更在同门的影响下决定申请出国读书。因为准备不充分，自我定位不清晰，我第一次申请失利了。

  在 2005 年夏天硕士毕业前夕，崴涞大学的张举文教授到北大讲学。经过他的介绍，我对美国民俗学的研究现状有了更加清晰的认识。毕业之后，我去学苑出版社任职，担任学术期刊《民间文化论坛》的助理编辑。后来，该期刊面临停刊的危险。在面对何去何从的两难困境下，我最终选择出国读书。因为张举文的牵线搭桥，我认识了美国俄勒冈大学的莎伦·谢尔曼教授，并在 2007 年 8 月投入她的门下学习影视民俗学，开始尝试自己拍摄民俗学纪录片。因为俄勒冈大学的民俗学项目是在英文系下，我本科和硕士都是在中文系，攻读博士学位专业不是很对口。在 2009 年 6 月我以民俗学专业硕士毕业后，便到俄亥俄州立大学东亚语言文学系跟随马克·本德尔教授攻读中国民俗学方向的博士学位。

  到美国之后，我从 2008 年开始参加美国民俗学会的年会，至今从未间断。美国民俗学会的年会吸引了来自世界各地的民俗学家，会上学者们积极交流自己最新的研究成果，与听众之间有特别积极的互动，每每让我受益良多。也是自 2007 年起，中国民俗学会和美国民俗学会互派代表团参加很多学术交流活动。每次开美国民俗学会年会，我都可以看到中国民

---

* 编者注：游自荧在美国俄亥俄州立大学获得博士学位，目前任教于美国伍斯特学院。她代表了那些在中国获得良好的学科知识培训，然后在国外获得学位并继续工作，同时关注中国民俗学建设，并为中外交往不断做出贡献的新一代民俗学者。他们将使今后中美的交流更趋于日常化，更具有理论深度。她的学术经历也体现了中国（也包括美国）民俗学近些年的发展壮大，不断吸引着一些有知识、有理论、有见识的年轻人加入民俗学队伍。

俗学家的身影。他们向美国听众展示中国民俗学的研究成果，让我备受鼓舞。中间跟他们有很多交流，对我自己的研究也有很多帮助。2011 年"中美非遗论坛"在美国路思基金会的资助下启动之后，我有幸地参与了很多活动。

　　2012 年 4 月 29 日到 5 月 1 日，我在美国田纳西州纳什维尔市的范德堡大学参加了"第二届中美非物质文化遗产论坛：个案研究"，现场与其他几位同仁合作做同声传译。在阔别五年之后，我在会上见到了朝戈金和施爱东。我们会下聊了很多，谈学术，聊人生。两位老师给了我莫大的鼓励，让我在学术的马拉松上坚持不懈地奔跑下去。会上，我也听到有关传统传承和非遗保护的精彩个案研究，激发了我研究中国非遗保护个案的兴趣。休斯顿大学的卡尔·林达尔和帕特·加斯帕做了题为《"卡特里娜"和"丽塔"飓风之下的幸存者：以休斯顿幸存者为核心的灾难应对研究》的会议报告，让我了解到美国最新的有关灾难传说和灾难救助的研究与实践。谁曾想，会上的收获会决定我之后几年的研究方向。

　　我的博士学位论文选择的个案研究是山西洪洞的"接姑姑迎娘娘"走亲活动。2007 年我跟随陈泳超教授一行去当地做调查，2012 年夏天和 2013 年春夏我返回当地做博士学位论文的田野调查。陈泳超的研究重当地的传说动力学，而我侧重研究传统的传承、变迁、冲撞、协商与再生产。洪洞走亲习俗在 2008 年被列入第二批国家级非物质文化遗产名录，我在考察了非遗申报前后当地各种冲突之后，写出了《变迁中的主体和权力关系：当代中国有关非遗保护的地方争议与冲突》的文章。这篇文章于 2015 年发表在美国民俗学期刊《民俗研究杂志》第 2 至 3 期的特刊上。该特刊由美国民俗学家迈克尔·迪伦·福斯特和丽莎·吉尔曼编辑，特刊题目是《民众眼中的联合国教科文组织：非物质文化遗产国际政策的地方视角》。该特刊在 2015 年同时以书的形式由印第安纳大学出版社出版。全书考察联合国教科文组织制定的非物质文化保护国际政策对地方社区的影响，收入的个案来自印度、日本、韩国、中国、马拉维和马其顿六个国家，重点关注于节日、舞蹈、仪式和信仰。全书阐述了地方社区在以不同方式进入联合国教科文组织的非遗保护轨道时所面临的复杂现实和诸多挑战。通过个案研究，以及由内而外的视角，全书展示了联合国教科文组织非遗保护的规范性政策如何在地方社区得以连接、协商和变化。基于三大洲六个国家的个案，全书很好地平衡了全球视角与地方经验，为理解快速全球化进程中传统与变迁的问题提供了独特的比较研究。我的非遗论文的写作大大得益于参加美国民俗学会年会以及与同仁间诸多的交流。

　　我参与灾难叙事的研究是个人未曾预想到的。2013 年 2 月，因为曲亭水库坍塌，洪洞不少村庄被淹，我做博士学位论文调查的羊獬村受灾最为严重。我在 2013 年 4 月初回到羊獬，见证了灾后村里的混乱景象和村民困苦的生活。我在美国筹集了 2522 美元的善款，兑换成差不多 15000 元人民币。但是怎么用这笔钱救灾，我一开始没有任何头绪。村子里遭难的人太多，这一点点钱连杯水车薪都算不上。后来跟村子里的朋友合作，我把 1 万多元现金分发给了 31 户受灾最严重的村民，其中 14 户的房子在水灾中坍塌了。此外，我用 3000 元钱买了各种文具分发给当地三所小学受灾的学生，最后的 2000 元钱我直接捐给羊獬村唐尧故园庙，赞助了一场蒲剧演出。我夏天不教课，没有工资，自己做研究也没有来得及申请资助。进入村子以后，我又开始不停地生病。在贫病交加的困境中，我个人对于灾民的苦难有了更深的理解。正好卡尔·林达尔发来邮件，说是范德堡大学会议之后，参会的王霄冰邀请他将自己的有关卡特里娜飓风传说的论文翻译成中文，在中国发表。他问我有没有时间和兴趣翻译他的论文，我欣然接受了翻译任务，并将林达尔的翻译酬劳用作了生活费，夏天的生计问题就此解决。

因为自己在羊獬村的经历，我对于灾难叙事这一块的研究产生了浓厚兴趣。卡尔·林达尔（2014）的研究为我立下了一个很好的研究范例，而王晓葵的著述也对我产生了重大影响。整个国际学术界近期对于灾难的关注和研究很多，有很多重要的著述纷纷出现。中国领域的很多学者也参与其中，从各个角度探索灾难的理解和应对。中国最近几年各种人为灾难和自然灾害频发，民俗学家如何记录灾民的故事，帮助他们自我疗伤并重建家园，尚有很多空间值得拓展。这一领域，是我现在和未来一段时间关注的方向。之前我所面对的理论和现实的裂缝在灾难研究的领域得以黏合，我个人一直所秉持的关注民间、传递民众声音的理念也在灾难叙事领域得以体现。

除了自己的研究领域，我从中美民俗学会的交流中方方面面得到裨益。2015 年 10 月在加州长滩召开的美国民俗学会年会上，中美民俗学会的重要学者组织专门的论坛向公众介绍两国民俗学会交流的诸多成果。在论坛上，中国民俗学会会长朝戈金说，我们中国民俗学家了解美国民俗学远远超过美国民俗学家了解中国民俗学。这句话在会上广受认同，并且被广为传播。碰巧印第安纳大学出版社的社长也在座，他迅速把这句话"推特"出去，引发热烈讨论。而他自己也决定同中国民俗学家合作，出版一些介绍中国民俗学的书籍。因为种种机缘巧合，我和张丽君得以与印大出版社合作，编辑出版一本以中英文双语形式介绍中国当下民俗学研究的专著。希望未来两三年这本书可以同中国和美国的读者见面。与此同时，我自己的博士学位论文也将由印大出版社不久出版。

我很荣幸自己身处一个充满团队合作精神的平台，一直得到很多中美同仁无私的支持与帮助。在这样一个温暖的大家庭中，我会坚持将学术的薪火传递下去。

How China-US Exchanges Influenced Me

Ziying You[*]

I entered the Department of Chinese Folk Literature at Beijing University in September 2002 to study for my master's degree. At the time, my mentor Professor Yongchao Chen was presiding over the "Youth Forum on Folk Culture." Then, in July 2003, he held the first academic conference on "Folk Culture in Modern Chinese Academics." The meeting was held online and we discussed the conference papers by several Chinese folklorists, who introduced the basic theoretical issues of Chinese folklore studies. Even after twelve years, the meeting remains as the most important stage of my academic enlightenment. Back then, I was interested in western folklore theory and applied to study abroad. Because I did not prepare enough, I was rejected the first time I applied.

In the summer of 2005, Professor Juwen Zhang lectured at Beijing University. Through his talk, I had a greater understanding of American folklore studies. After graduation, I went to the Academy Press and became an assistant editor for the journal of *Folk Culture Forum*. Later, the journal was facing possible closure, so I decided to study abroad. Because of Professor Zhang's help, I was introduced to Professor Sharon Sherman. In August 2007, I went to study film and folklore under Professor Sherman at the University of Oregon, and began shooting folklore documentaries. Because the University of Oregon's Department of English also includes folklore studies, my undergraduate and master's degree in Chinese is not very relevant. After completing my master's degree in folklore studies in June 2009, I went on to study under Professor Mark Bender at the Department of East Asian Languages and Literatures, Ohio State University.

Since 2008, I have attended the American Folklore Society's annual meeting every year. The annual meeting has attracted folklorists from all over the world and provided a platform for them to share their latest research findings. Each time I go to the annual meeting, I can see folklorists from China.

---

[*] Ziying You received her Ph. D. from Ohio State University and currently teaches at Wooster College, with a M. A. in Literature from Beijing University. She represents a new generation of folklorists who have earned degrees overseas and continued to work to develop Chinese folklore studies. They have also contributed to the development of Chinese and foreign collaborations. Ziying's experience indicates that the folklore field has continued drawing competent younger scholars.

From April 29 to May 1, 2012, I participated in the Second Sino-US Intangible Cultural Heritage Forum at Vanderbilt University in Nashville, Tennessee. At the meeting, the case studies on traditional and intangible cultural heritage protection stimulated my interest to study cultural heritage in China. One particular study by Carl Lindal and Pat Jasper on the survivors of the Hurricane Katrina struck me so much. Who would have thought that the information I learned at the meeting would determine what I would research for the next few years?

For my doctorate degree, I decided to conduct a case study in Hongtong, Shanxi. I went on-site in 2007, 2012, and 2013 to do fieldwork. Professor Yongchao Chen's research focused on understanding local myths, while I focused on traditional concepts of heritage. Hongtong customs were listed in the ICH list in 2008. After examining the local conflicts before and after the article was published, I wrote an essay titled "The Subject and Power Relations in Change: Controversies and Contradictions in Contemporary China regarding Intangible Heritage Protection." It was published in the *Journal of Folklore Research* (2015, Special Issue) with the title of "UNESCO on the Ground: Local Perspectives on Global Policy for Intangible Cultural Heritage." This special issue was edited by Michael Dylan Foster and Lisa Gilman, and was later also published in book form by Indiana University Press in 2015. Through various case studies, the book shows how UNESCO's ICH policies are connected and can be negotiated and changed.

I did not anticipate that I would be interested in studying disaster narratives. In February 2013, many villages were flooded in Hongtong because the Quting reservoir collapsed. I was doing fieldwork in Yangxie village, which was the most affected from the disaster. In April 2013, I went to the village and witnessed the chaos caused by the disaster and the hardships the villagers had to endure. I tried my best to help, so I collected $2522, about RMB 15,000, in donations from the United Studies. However, I had no idea how to use the money for disaster relief. The money was too little to help all of the affected people. Later, I distributed more than RMB 10,000 to thirty-one of the worst affected villagers; fourteen of their houses collapsed in the flood. In addition, I used RMB 3,000 to buy stationery for the students of the three local primary schools. The last RMB 2,000 was donated to the village's temple. I began to get sick once I arrived in the village. At first-hand, I understood the suffering of the flood victims.

Because of my experience in the village, my interest in studying disaster narratives increased. There has been a great deal of attention and research on disasters in the international academic community. Now, many scholars in China are also researching disasters and how to respond to them. In recent years, many man-made and natural disasters have occurred in China, so folklorists have been recording the personal stories of victims. I have been concentrating on this area in my studies. I have always been interested in and focused on the importance of the public voice in disaster narratives.

In addition to my fieldwork, I have also benefited from Sino-US Folklore collaborations. At the

2015 AFS meeting, Chinese and American scholars organized a special forum to introduce the achievements of the two countries' folklore exchanges. At the forum, Chao Gejin of the China Folklore Society stated that the Chinese folklorists' understanding of American folklore exceeds the American folklorists' understanding of Chinese folklore. This declaration was widely recognized at the meeting and was publicly spread. The Director of Indiana University Press tweeted the statement and sparked a heated discussion on Twitter. He also decided to work with Chinese folklorists to publish books on Chinese folklore. Lijun Zhang and I have been able to cooperate with the Indiana University Press to edit and publish a monograph on Chinese folklore in Chinese and English. I hope the book will be published in the next two to three years along with my own doctoral thesis.

I am honored to be part of this collaborative communication with Sino-US colleagues, from whom I have received great help and support. Undoubtedly, I will persevere to pass on this tradition.

(Translation by Erica Mao)

我与美国民俗学会年会的情缘

南快莫德格*

作为研究蒙古图瓦文化的学者，我有幸于 2010 年 11 月—2012 年 3 月到哈佛大学访学一年，并在此期间参加了我的第一次美国民俗学会年会，从此与该年会结下了不解之缘。

我是一个生长在鄂尔多斯草原上的蒙古牧民的女儿，从小在奶奶身边长大。奶奶是一个非常讲礼、节、俗的蒙古族妇女。记得我刚刚懂事起，奶奶就教我站立、坐姿、吃相到见面问候、行礼等一系列行为规范，做饭、洗衣、缝补、打扫卫生等劳动技术和规矩，再到节日节庆、祭祀、忌讳禁忌等道德规范，等等。我从小喜欢观察奶奶的言行，也喜欢模仿奶奶的言行。就这样，我在奶奶身边，耳濡目染中慢慢懂得了蒙古族日常生活的诸多民俗事项，逐渐懂得了蒙古人为人处世的道理。的确，我在生活中处处以从小习得的乡约民规即风俗习惯来约束自己，在老师和同学们中间我是个非常懂得情理的孩子。我是同龄人当中甚至比我大的人中，是懂得民俗规矩最多的人，总是会有根有据地告诉周围的人，这个应该这么做，那个应该那么做。我很受益于奶奶教给我的那么多民俗知识，使我在后来的学习中自然而然地关注各个民族的民俗文化，并终于从事了我所热爱的民俗、民族文化研究与教学工作。

去美国之前我特意找机会去了俄罗斯的图瓦共和国和蒙古国的巴音欧勒盖省和科布多省图瓦人聚居区，比较和了解三地图瓦人的情况。我自己的研究对象是新疆阿勒泰的图瓦社区。我对图瓦人的研究是从接人待物的民俗事项开始的，即从见面礼、家里的摆设、吃什么、喝什么到招待客人的用具、送别客人的礼节等入手，因为我认为民俗是了解一个陌生地方或民族时首选的最佳途径。

我第一次参加的美国民俗学会年会是于 2011 年 10 月 14—17 日在美国印第安纳大学举办的。会议通知由美国崴涞大学教授张举文博士传给我的。我认识张举文博士是 2008 年盛夏。那时他来新疆考察，我们有机会一起同车从乌鲁木齐出发，沿着天山北麓西行至伊犁，再北行至和丰、布尔津、喀纳斯，走进了图瓦人的木屋。我们沿途欣赏北疆美丽山川，一路体验各民族的饮食到服饰、礼节等风俗习惯，维吾尔的音乐、美食，哈萨克的奶茶，图瓦人

---

* 编者注：南快莫德格现任新疆师范大学教授，中央民族大学民族学博士。作为一位蒙古族学者，她所关注的是图瓦社区和文化，不仅从事着大量的学术研究，也为该族群在社会上被认知做了许多工作。目前，中国的图瓦人依然处于极度的边缘化状态。她是近年来与美国民俗学交流中不多的中国少数民族学者之一，更是长期生活在少数民族地区，研究少数民族民俗文化，以多种语言与外界交流的少数学者之一。她目前正在撰写图瓦语言文化志。

及其他独特的风俗习惯、居住的环境、社会等深深地吸引了同行的人们，在一路的欢歌笑语和关于民风民俗的探讨交流中我们结下了深厚的情谊。新疆的山水风土人情作为媒介让我结识了张博士，而在张博士的引路下我也踏入了美国民俗学年会的门槛。

此后我连续参加了五届美国民俗学会年会。记得我第一次到印第安纳大学参会时，在朋友的帮助下找到了在印第安纳大学留学的蒙古族老乡兴安和娜荷娅，他们给我解决了会议期间的住宿问题，而节省了我住宾馆的花销。在美国或去美国开会，路费不贵，贵的是住宿费。开会的第一天兴安冒雨带路送我到设在印第安纳大学的美国民俗学年会会场。那天雨天路滑，一位骑自行车的美国女孩撞倒了兴安，把兴安背在双肩包的苹果电脑给摔坏了。这成了我好几年里抹不去的一件愧疚之事。这次会议上张博士十分关照我，并介绍他在年会里的朋友们与我认识。印象最深的是印第安纳大学的苏独玉教授。苏独玉是她的中文名，她从上个世纪80年代开始研究中国青海的花儿歌曲及其文化。另一个相识的民俗学专家是俄亥俄州立大学马克·本德尔教授，他是做中国彝族研究的专家。会议期间，我还有机会去拜访了印第安纳大学内陆欧亚研究系的卡拉教授和艾特伍德教授。他们都是世界著名的蒙古学专家，蒙古语讲得就像母语一样好。和他们交流时根本不用担心我自己的英语问题，全用蒙古语交谈。在此次美国学术会议期间，我深深地感到我们要向他们学习的地方的确很多，美国专家的专业功底、田野经历和基础扎实得令人难以置信。凡是我遇到的美国的中国研究专家中文讲得都非常好，同时还掌握他所研究的中国少数民族语言，都有他所研究的中国地域的长期田野经历。在中国，涉足中国少数民族研究的专家中懂当地语言的几乎是白天找星星一样难。与他们比较，我们在学习和研究的态度、方法上以及下的功夫的程度上还存在着不小的差距。

美国民俗学会的年会在傍晚都会举办各种活动，如音乐歌曲爱好者活动，他们集聚在一起弹唱各国的民间音乐和歌曲。音乐爱好者们都会千里迢迢地带着自己的乐器来参加这样自弹自唱的活动。会议之外的这些活动在轻松愉快的气氛中加深了各国学者之间的相识相知和交流，是一种田野，是一种文化交流，为民俗学年会增添了趣味性和雅兴。我第一次参加美国民俗学年会时就被这种会上会下的交流方式所吸引，所感动。

民俗文化是不同人群之间沟通的捷径和桥梁，而语言是拉近陌生人与陌生民族之间关系的有力工具。我所工作生活的新疆自古就是一个中西文化交汇的多民族地区，语言和文化风俗各异，是歌舞之乡，是美食之乡，也是文化荟萃之乡。新疆自古就居住着许多民族。近百年的内地与边疆的经济文化交流不断繁荣，目前已有47个民族共同生活工作在新疆。但是，我所研究的图瓦人是一个特殊的群体。从民族文化风俗上来划分他们属蒙古族，而从语言上来划分他们属阿尔泰语系突厥语族。虽然我是蒙古族，但我要研究图瓦文化，图瓦语言是我必修的课。图瓦人虽然被认定为蒙古族的一个分支，但是他们有自己独立的语言。图瓦语属阿尔泰语系突厥语族东匈语支回鹘—乌古斯语组。他们在家庭内部交流时用母语-图瓦语，与外界交流时用哈萨克语，学校教育则用蒙古语。我的田野调查是从学习图瓦语和哈萨克语入手的。长达六个多月的寒冷季节里，马爬犁是他们唯一的交通工具。为了进山去牧民家访谈，我必须学会驾驭马爬犁，需要入乡随俗。在日积月累的学习与互动中，我慢慢地被他们所接纳，一步一步地融入他们的生活世界中，成为他们的一员。学语言、入乡随俗是田野调查和民族文化研究的两把剑。随俗就是尊重他者文化最重要的一步。

在美国民俗学年会期间相识的美国民俗民族文化专家们，都是游刃有余地耍着这两把剑的高手，是我学习的榜样，也是我们中国学者学习的榜样。当然，我参加美国民俗学会年会的感受不仅仅如此，还包括对民俗和民族问题的新认识。相信我今后还会继续参加美国的民俗会议，也会有更多的故事可讲。

My Love Affair with the AFS Annual Meeting

Namkamidog*

As a scholar of Mongolian Tuva culture, I was fortunate to have the opportunity to study at Harvard University from November 2010 through 2012, and attended my first AFS annual meeting in 2011. From then on, I have found myself in an inseparable connection with the AFS and American folklore studies.

I grew up in a Mongolian herdsman's family on the grassland in Ordos, raised by my grandma. She was an old-style Mongolian woman who had particular interest in various rituals and manners. As early as I could remember, she would teach me how to stand, sit, eat, greet, and behave properly. She also taught me how to cook, wash and mend clothes, and other household skills. During festivals, she would teach me the morals and taboos. I liked to imitate her, and thus learned many folklore matters in Mongolian daily life. In my own life, I have thus behaved myself based on the traditional norms learned in the herdsmen community. I was seen by my classmates and teachers as a quite mature child even in elementary school. I would even tell my little friends how to behave based on the folk knowledge from my grandma. This experience made me aware of different folklores and cultures, and eventually led me to become a folklorist, a career that I love very much.

Prior to my first trip to the US, I managed to visit the Tuva communities in the Republic of Tuva and two provinces in the Republic of Mongolia. This helped me compare the Tuva community in Altay, Xinjiang, where I have studied. I began my comparative studies from their everyday folklore matters such as how to greet, how to decorate homes, and how to receive, treat, and bid farewell to guests. I believe that folklore is the best approach to a new culture in a new place.

---

* Namkamidog is Professor of Ethnology at Xinjiang Normal University, with a Ph. D. in Ethnology from Minzu University of China. As a scholar of Mongolian origin, she focuses on the Tuva community, a subgroup of Mongols. She has been engaged not only in extensive research, but also in promoting the better recognition of Tuva culture by the broader society. The Tuva people in China are still deeply marginalized. She is one of the few scholars of minority nationalities in China who are involved in the Sino-US folkloristic communication. She is also one of the few scholars who have lived in the minority regions studying their folklores with their languages. Currently she is working on compiling an encyclopedia of Tuva language and culture.

My first AFS annual meeting was on Oct. 14 – 17, 2011 in Indiana University. It was Dr. Juwen Zhang who told me about this meeting. I met him in the summer of 2008 when he visited Xinjiang. We were together in a van of eight people, travelling from the capital city of Xinjiang, Urumqi to the western border city, Yili, then to the northern city, Burqin, and finally to the Tuva community in Kanas. It was a trip of learning new cultures, enjoying beautiful sceneries and delicious foods, and experiencing various folk customs of the Uighurs, Kazaks, and Mongols. The gorgeous landscape of Xinjiang provided the occasion to meet Dr. Zhang, who then invited me to the AFS meetings.

I have attended each annual meeting of the AFS since 2011. I remember the first conference, when a Mongolian friend who was then a visiting scholar in Indiana University helped provide me with a free room to stay. Travelling to the US for the meeting was not expensive, but lodging was. She took me to the meeting site on the first day in the rain. The sidewalk was narrow and slippery. One female student was riding a bicycle, and knocked down my friend. She fell, and the Mac computer in her backpack broke. This weighed on my conscience for several years.

At the meeting, Dr. Zhang showed me around and introduced me to many friends. Among those impressive scholars were Sue Tuohy from Indiana University, who studied the *huaer* singing fair in Qinghai, China since the 1980s, and Mark Bender from Ohio State University who studied the Yi people in China. I also had the opportunity to visit Professor Gyorgy Kara and Professsor Christopher Atwood who were world-renowned Mongol experts. I had no worries about using my English with them; Mongolian was like their native tongue.

I had a deep feeling that we had a lot to learn from those American experts who had incredible solid foundations and extensive fieldwork experiences. All those Chinese scholars whom I met speak excellent Chinese, as well as the languages of the minority nationalities that they study. In China, experts of minority nationalities can hardly speak local languages. The gap between American experts and us is quite big in terms of attitudes, methods, and efforts.

It was impressive to learn that there were various evening events during the AFS meetings such as singing and playing instruments. Those folklorists brought their instruments from faraway and enjoyed their playing and singing. Such pleasant and relaxing events deepened the communication among scholars from different countries. It is a kind of fieldwork, and a cultural communication, adding fond memories of the AFS meetings. I was deeply attracted and moved by such a way of communication.

Folklore is the bridge or short cut connecting different peoples. Language is the powerful tool to shorten the distance between strangers. The place where I work, Xinjiang, is a place where Eastern and Western cultures meet. For thousands of years it has been the home of different languages, customs, and cultures. All cultures in Xinjiang have prospered to a great extent in the past century; people of 47 different nationalities enjoy their lives there. The Tuva people whom I study, however, is a special group. In terms of culture and folklore, they belong to Mongolian nationality. From a linguistic view, they belong to Altaic Turkish family. Although I am Mongolian, I have had to learn their language in order to study their culture. The Tuva people, identified by the government as a branch of the Mongols, have their independent language. Within the Turkish language family, Tuva language is seen as part of the East Hungarian Uyghur-Ugus group. They speak their mother tongue, Tuva, at home, Kazak outside their home, and Mongolian in schools. I began my fieldwork by first studying Tuva and Kazak. For six months in the year, the Tuva people live in the snow and have little contact with the outside world. I thus learned to ride horse-sled, and eventually became a member of their community. To me, following the local customs is an important step in respecting other cultures.

The American folklorists whom I have met through AFS meetings are all examples for me, and for Chinese scholars. Of course, there are many other things that I have learned over the years, for example, my new understanding of the relationship between folklore and nationality. I will surely continue to attend the AFS meetings and will have more stories to tell.

(Translation by Juwen Zhang)

第一次参加美国民俗学年会

王均霞*

我已经参加过三次美国民俗学年会，分别是在 2010 年、2012 年和 2014 年。2010 年第一次参加的时候，我还是一名在读博士生；2012 年再参加的时候，我已经在华东师范大学任教了，已经不像初次参加时那么紧张了。然而，让我印象深刻、对我影响至深的，仍然是第一次参会时的情形。

我 2008 年秋天开始在北京师范大学跟随杨利慧老师攻读博士学位。2010 年秋天，我进入读博士的最后一年。也是在这个时候，我获得了国家留学基金委联合培养项目的资助，得以去俄亥俄州立大学访学半年，合作导师是本德尔教授。杨老师给我布置了一个任务，就是要提交论文参加美国民俗学年会。在杰斯卡·特纳的帮助下，我和俄亥俄州立大学东亚语言文学系的在读博士瑟斯顿组成了一个发言小组。我提交的论文是关于泰山进香女性的研究，瑟斯顿研究的是西藏的口头表演。杰斯卡·特纳邀请了杨利慧老师和罗什教授作为我们的论文评议人（后来罗什教授因事未能参加，北京师范大学的彭牧老师代替他完成了评议）。由于两位老师都不在美国，杰斯卡·特纳很先进地决定采用视频会议的方式来完成这次讨论。

坦率地说，这是我读书以来第一次正式参加学术会议，而且要用英文发表，心中的紧张不安盖过了将要参加学术会议的新奇与兴奋。也许本德尔老师猜到我会紧张，在我仍晕头转向的时候，他好心地提醒我提前完成发言稿，并在百忙之中帮我修改了我的发言稿。他鼓励我说，内容很有意思，一定会有很多人感兴趣的。

年会便在我紧张、忐忑的心情中如期到来。我们小组被安排在 10 月 15 日早上 8:00—10:00，我第一个发言。我总共有 30 分钟的时间，杰斯卡·特纳提醒我可以用 20 分钟介绍论文，留出 10 分钟给观众提问。我和瑟斯顿都讲完之后，杨老师和彭老师分别做了评议。我现在其实已经记不得我是怎么讲的了，也不记得二位老师评议的内容了，只记得在投影仪上看到远在北京的杨老师和彭老师觉得很亲切。也是从杨老师那里得知，不仅杨老师在中国参加了这次美国民俗学年会，研究所的同学其实也是同杨老师一起参与的。现在想起来，还

---

* 编者注：王均霞在北京师范大学获得民俗学博士学位，目前在华东师范大学任教。在读博士学位期间，她便到俄亥俄州立大学留学。后来又几次参加美国民俗学会年会，积累了与外界交往的经验。王均霞也代表了新一代高校民俗学教师，而且她的对外交往经历也在被更多的年轻学者重复着。她在此所讲述的第一次参加美国民俗学会年会的故事也体现了中国民俗学界在对外交往史上从"听者"到"说者"、从"被翻译"到"翻译自己"的过渡。

是觉得又紧张又亲切。

这次会上，除了自己做论文发表外，我也尽可能参加年会中的其他活动。我参加了东亚民俗分会的例会，亲身体验了东亚民俗分会的组织风格，还与分会同仁一起聚餐闲聊；参加了学会专为学生准备的美国民俗学会同仁招待会，招待会为来自不同学校的学生提供认识与交流的机会。

在今年（2016）的民俗学年会举行之际，重新回想起第一次参会时的点点滴滴，我庆幸自己初次参会就参加了如此高规格的会议，它对我的影响深刻。首先，我很高兴我是被作为一个研究者而不是一个学生被年会接纳。这一点我在俄亥俄州立大学学习的时候也清晰地感受到了。尽管参会时的我仍然处在紧张与不自信的情绪中，但后来慢慢反刍那段经历，我慢慢知道了如何学术地、平等地与学界同仁交流。其次，在这次年会上，我与更多的学界同仁有了更多的交流，这使得我有了以后与他们更多的学术交流与联系。在过去的6年里，我分别邀请了张举文教授、罗伯特·巴龙教授、李靖教授来华东师范大学做学术交流，张举文教授还为我们推荐了谢尔曼教授来为我们讲影视民俗学。某种程度上而言，这都得益于在那次会议上我与大家有了更多相互交流与了解的机会。再次，它让我重视参加学术会议的仪表礼仪。这次会议之后，再参加学术会议或者自己做主题演讲的时候，我都穿正装。虽然这是小细节，但它也许在无形中塑造着人们对正在参加的活动的态度呢。

My First AFS Annual Meeting

Junxia Wang[*]

I have participated in three AFS annual meetings—in 2010, 2012 and 2014. When I attended the first meeting, I was an anxious Ph. D. student at BNU. By the second meeting, I had begun teaching at ECNU. While I was not as nervous as the first time, what still impresses me the most is the memory and impact of my first meeting in 2010.

I became a doctoral student at BNU in 2008, studying under Professor Lihui Yang. In the fall of 2010, I entered the last year of my Ph. D. study. It was also at this time that I received a national government grant for a half-year of study at Ohio State University under the supervision of Professor Mark Bender. One task that Professor Yang gave me was to submit a paper about my participation in one of the AFS meetings. With the help of Jessica A. Turner, I worked with Timothy Thurston, a Ph. D. student at OSU, to form a panel, entitled "Ritual Performance and Lay Expert Knowledge in Eastern Tibet and the Shandong Peninsula." For the end product, I submitted a paper on the study of women in Mt. Tai, Thurston presented on Tibetan oral performance, and Jessica Turner invited Professors Lihui Yang and Gerald Roche as our discussants (Professor Roche was unable to attend, and Mu Peng, a teacher at BNU, took his place). Because the two discussants were not in the United States, Jessica Turner decided to Skype them in for the discussion.

Frankly speaking, that was the first time I read a paper in a formal academic conference. Furthermore, my paper was in English. My nervousness outweighed my curiosity and excitement about attending this meeting. Professor Bender saw that I was very nervous and had trouble focusing, and he kindly reminded me to finish the paper early enough so that he could help revise

---

[*] Junxia Wang received a Ph. D. in Folklore from BNU and currently teaches at ECNU. During her time as a doctoral student of folklore, she studied at the Ohio State University. Later, she deepened her connections with world folklorists through her involvement in the American Folklore Society. Wang represents a new generation of folklorists, and has begun to play an important role in international communication by inviting scholars to China from abroad. The story of her first participation in the AFS annual meeting also reflects the transition of Chinese folklore from "listeners" to "speakers" in the history of international exchange, from those "being translated" to those participating in "self-translation".

my paper. Professor Bender encouraged me by saying that the content was very interesting, and a lot of people would be very interested in the topic.

When the annual meeting arrived, I was still nervous. Our group met on October 15 from 8-10 am, and I was the first to present. I had a total of 30 minutes. Jessica Turner reminded me to use 20 minutes to read the paper, leaving 10 minutes for questions. After Thurston and I finished, Professors Yang and Peng made comments. To speak truthfully, I no longer remember what I talked about or what the professors said about my paper. All I can recall is that I felt so glad to see my teachers on the screen. Later, I learned that there were also many other students in Beijing watching me read my paper through the screen. Thinking of this event at this moment brings back two memories: the fear that I might lose face for my teachers and fellow students; the gratuity for their attention.

At the meeting, in addition to my presentation, I also participated in as many activities as possible. I participated in the Eastern Asia Folklore Section meeting to learn how the section functioned. I also ate and chatted with others, attended the graduate student reception, and got to know many people from many different places. Those were great opportunities to communicate with people from different universities.

Recalling these memories while the 2016 AFS meeting approaching, I feel that I was honored and fortunate to have attended such a meeting at the beginning of my academic career. It had great impact on me. First of all, I am glad that I was accepted as a researcher rather than a student and felt the difference of it while at OSU. Although I was nervous at first and lacked self-confidence, I learned how to communicate with others as their peers in academic and personal interaction. Secondly, at this annual meeting, I met many colleagues in the academic community and was able to share many academic interests. Furthermore, I have been able to continue communicating with them up until today. For example, in summer 2015, I invited Juwen Zhang, Robert Baron and Jing Li to come to ECNU for an academic exchange. Prof. Zhang also recommended Professor Sharon Sherman to give us lectures on film and folklore. To some extent, all of these activities were the results of my attending the AFS meeting, which established these relationships. One more thing that I learned was that I needed to pay attention to my appearance, that is, to dress properly. Since then, every time I present a paper, I would wear formal dress. Although this is a minor detail, it may potentially shape the attitude of the attendees toward what they hear and see.

(Translation by Juwen Zhang)

行走・回首・远望：中美民俗学交流之个人经历

程 鹏*

对于美国民俗学，一直有一种想象，那些在书上看到的名字和理论，使我一直对美国这个遥远的国度充满好奇。这个历史并不悠久、文化传统并不深厚的国家，其民俗学的发展却成绩斐然，诞生了许多著名的民俗学家和理论巨著。这份好奇和想象也在多年的学习过程中，不断推动着我在中美民俗学交流学习的道路上前行。

记得当初考博时，博导田兆元教授曾告诉我华东师范大学民俗学研究所一向注重对外交流，以前的多位师兄师姐都有海外访学经历。2011年5月16—25日，美国印第安纳大学的哈森教授和苏独玉教授还曾经来访，并分别开展了为期一周的交流演讲活动。2012年入学以后，所里与美国、日本等国民俗学界的交流也日渐频繁。从2013年到2015年，美国俄亥俄州立大学的本德尔教授和游自荧博士、美国俄勒冈大学的谢尔曼教授、美国威涞大学的张举文教授、美国纽约州立艺术委员会的罗伯特·巴龙先生等人都曾先后来到华东师范大学交流访问。他们的讲座为我了解美国民俗学打开了一扇窗，让我对美国民俗学研究的不同领域和方法有了更广泛的认识。如本德尔教授在研究印度东北与中国西南的生态民族志时，借助生态批评理论与民俗学理论，来探讨中国西南和印度东北的少数民族诗人及其所创作的诗歌，并将民族志诗文、宇宙志诗文以及地方民族文学的性质作为其研究潜在的主线。谢尔曼教授将影视作为弥补文本无法记录表演现场缺憾的重要研究工具，认为影视为民俗学的研究者和被研究者之间提供了互动交流的机会。罗伯特·巴龙在研究民俗旅游时，特别强调了民俗学者作为"文化经纪人"的作用，通过与社区合作、对话来推进社区以自己的话语向社区之外的人展现其传统，既为游客理解通常不对局外人开放的社区文化提供了渠道，又使社区保持了对传统的控制权。他们的研究在拓展我研究视野的同时，也让我对民俗学研究的方法及伦理等问题有了更多的反思。民俗学者怎样处理与研究对象之间的关系，怎样在研究中

---

* 编者注：程鹏在华东师范大学获得民俗学博士学位，目前在上海社会科学院文学所工作。作为新一代中国民俗学者，程鹏在读博士期间就开始了与外国学者的接触，参与邀请国外学者到暑期班讲学，并有机会到国外访学和参加会议。毫无疑问，他所代表的这一代将推动中国民俗学发展到一个新阶段。相信他在文中所提出的问题将会是新一代民俗学者在未来的交流中必将改善和提高的方面。

既有所收获又恪守伦理，这些问题都是以前所不曾思考的。

2014年7月21日至27日，华东师范大学民俗学研究所举办"民俗传统与当代社会——中美民俗研究的对话与交流"研究生暑期学校，搭建了一个国际学术交流与合作的平台，邀请中美学者讲课研讨。它不仅使我对美国民俗学学科的发展历程和主要研究议题及理论、方法有了一个整体的认识，也极大地拓展了我的学术视野。无论是美国物质文化的研究，还是新兴的"身体民俗学"，都是以前接触较少的领域。如本德尔教授对阿巴拉契亚的传统民俗和物质文化的介绍引人入胜。而之后到美国访学期间，我也有幸跟随马克教授去打猎，见识了各种打猎的工具及规矩，体验了美国的狩猎文化。

当然，与美国民俗学者的接触并不仅限于在学校里。近年来，中美民俗学界的交流合作已日益增多，如由美国民俗学会发起，中国民俗学会、中山大学、华中师范大学、云南民族博物馆等五方共同参与的中美非物质文化合作项目"中美非物质文化遗产论坛"，已经举办了多届，在专业发展、公共政策、博物馆和公共教育等方面都有着极大的成果，并且互派师生访学制度也为两国的研究人才培养做出了巨大贡献。除此之外，两国的高校和研究机构之间也开展了广泛的合作，如华中师范大学文学院与美国崴涞大学亚洲研究中心联合举办的中美民俗影像记录田野工作坊，也已举办了三届，为两国民俗学界培养了许多影像记录人才。

2014年中国民俗学会年会上，我也有幸认识了前来参会的美国民俗学会前会长比尔·艾伟先生以及美国印第安纳大学的苏独玉教授。艾伟先生率领的美国民俗学会代表团在云南大学致公堂还为大家带来了专场表演，让我们了解到美国学者在学术研究之外的精彩生活。

2015年8月我有幸获得国家留学基金委的资助，以联合培养博士生的身份赴美国俄亥俄州立大学访学，在这里不仅有幸结识了许多优秀的民俗学家，也在他们的课程和讲座中受益匪浅。如诺伊斯教授的"表演民族志"、舒曼教授的"叙事理论"、本德尔教授的"东亚表演传统"等课程使我对美国民俗学的相关理论和研究有了更深的了解。民俗研究中心每月一次的午餐交流会，还有经常举行的讲座、研讨会和读书会，也使我感受到这里浓厚的学术氛围。而在美国期间，印象最深刻的一次学术交流活动无疑是参加美国民俗学会年会。

2015年10月14日至17日，美国民俗学会年会在加州长滩的威斯汀酒店举行。酒店装修豪华，然而会议却很低调，没有横幅或者大型海报之类的宣传材料，大堂里只有一张小小的议程表，低调得让你根本看不出这里要举办大型会议。之前听说美国人办会节俭务实，由此亦可见一斑。当然，这种节俭并非是由于资金短缺。以美国学会为例，每年都会有一些机构和个人提供捐助，而学会也为参加会议的学生、国际学者还有低收入群体等人群设立了各种奖项和资助，大家不仅可以申请减免注册费，还可以申请一定的交通补贴。作为一名国外的博士生，我也非常幸运地申请到了资助，从而能够参加此次学术交流活动。

美国民俗学会已经有一百多年的历史，在机构运作、会议筹备等方面都有可资借鉴的地方。年会上，除了较为成熟的捐助和资助体系外，许多安排也都非常人性化。此外，学会还很贴心地组织了许多交流活动。会议注册时，我发现许多人的名牌下都有着不同的字条，用以标示不同的身份，我的名牌下是紫色的字条，上面写着"特约嘉宾"的字样。学会为第一次参加者尤其是国外的学生安排一位指导老师来帮助他们。担任我的指导教师是游自荧老师，她为我提供了许多建议。我所参加的小组的组织者张举文老师和主持人苏独玉老师也给了我很多帮助，尤其是苏独玉老师不厌其烦地对我的论文进行校对和润色，使我的发言增色不少。在异国他乡能得到诸位师友的帮助，真的是感激不尽。

年会上一个关于中美民俗学合作的报告就吸引了许多学者。会上中国民俗学会朝戈金会长的一句话让我记忆犹新，他提到中国的民俗学界对美国的许多民俗学者及其作品都非常熟悉，但美国民俗学界对中国的民俗学者们及其作品却知之甚少。怎样让中国民俗学走出去，是一个值得思考并努力实践的问题！

这届年会上除了各个小组的讨论之外，还组织了许多交流活动，如新会员欢迎早餐会、研究生交流会、与编辑共进午餐、与资深民俗学者共进早餐等活动。我申请参加了"与编辑共进午餐"活动，同几位来自世界各地的学生与《民俗研究》杂志的两位编辑——福斯特和巴特波一起度过了一段美好的午餐时光。两位老师不仅向大家介绍了该杂志的一些情况和电子资源，还对杂志收录论文的标准和要求进行了说明。我在席间谈到朝戈金会长讲的关于中美民俗学交流的一番话，提出中美民俗学论文的互译等问题，福斯特也表示鼓励和支持，希望可以收到更多中国学者撰写的论文，也欢迎将他们的论文译成中文。

另外，我还有幸参与了"与资深民俗学家"共进早餐的活动。这一活动邀请几位资深民俗学家与学生共进早餐，并就某一指定的话题展开讨论。我参与的是芭芭拉·克莱恩教授的小组，主题是世界各地的民俗研究。在克莱恩教授的引导下，我们一桌来自世界各地的年轻学生围绕着文化遗产、数字化等问题，就自己的研究展开了简单的探讨。

年会只有短短的四天，对美国民俗学界的认识只能说是蜻蜓点水，然而对于中美两国的交流问题却有较深的感触。朝会长提到中国学生对美国的阿兰·邓迪斯、理查德·鲍曼、丹·本-阿莫斯等学者及他们的著作都耳熟能详，我不禁反思，我们对美国民俗学真的很了解吗？由于语言的限制，长期以来我们对美国民俗学界的了解大多都是通过国内学者的译著，在范围广度和时效性等方面都远远不够。毫无疑问，交流学习是一个长期的工作，需要大家共同的努力。身为一名民俗学的博士生，我又可以为中美民俗交流做些什么呢？作为中国民俗学会的志愿者和中国民俗学论坛的版主，我和小伙伴们经常会在中国民俗学论坛上直播各类会议，或是将会议的介绍、综述等放到网上。这次参加美国民俗学会年会，我自然也不会放过这样一个好机会。我在论坛上发的主题帖《美国民俗学会2015年年会》也受到了许多国内学者的关注。

近年来，参加美国民俗学会年会的中国学者可以说是逐年增多，同时每年还有许多民俗学者和学生到美国访学深造；相比之下，来中国访学和参加中国民俗学会年会的美国学者就屈指可数了。怎样发展中国民俗学，怎样将中国民俗学界的成果翻译介绍出去，怎样吸引他国的学者前来交流学习，我们还有很长的路要走。

美国民俗学会代表团在云南大学表演后，比尔·艾伟与程鹏在舞台合影，2014年。Bill Ivey and Peng Cheng after the AFS delegates' performance at Yunnan University, 2014. Photograph courtesy of Peng Cheng.

2015年美国民俗学会年会的"与编辑共进午餐"活动. Lunch with Editors Event, AFS 2015, Long Beach, CA.（从左至右 From left to right: Anastasiya Astapova, Chad Buterbaugh, Peng Cheng, Ryo Araki, Robert Guyker, Michael Dylan Foster, Mary Sellers, and Carolyn Ware.）Photograph courtesy of Peng Cheng.

Proceeding, Retrospect, and Prospect: My Experience in the China-US Folkloristic Exchange

Peng Cheng[*]

For me, American folklore scholarship was what was in the books. So I have been curious about the distant United States, a country with a shorter history and less elaborate traditions. The development of folklore studies in China has made great progress, with the introduction of many well-known folkloristic masterpieces. Throughout my learning in the past years, my curiosity continually encourages me to explore more about the exchange of Chinese and American folk studies.

When I entered the Ph. D. program at ECNU, Professor Zhaoyuan Tian told me that the Institute of Folklore had always paid attention to international communication; many previous students had studied overseas. Professors Hasan El-Shamy and Sue Tuohy from Indiana University also visited the university from May 16th to 25th, 2011, and each gave a one-week lecture series. From 2013 to 2015, Mark Bender, Sharon Sherman, Juwen Zhang, and Robert Baron lectured at ECNU. Their lectures opened a window for my understanding of American folklore and gave me a greater appreciation of the different fields and methods of American folklore research. For example, in Professor Bender's research of ecological ethnography in northeastern India and southwestern China, he used ecocriticism theory and folklore theory to explore their poetry. Nature poetry and local literature were the main research resources. Professor Sherman also discussed how film and video could be used to for fieldwork and for communicate between scholars. In his study of folklore tourism, Robert Baron emphasized the role of folklorists as "cultural brokers" in promoting the

---

* Peng Cheng received his Ph. D. in Folklore from ECNU and is currently working in the Literature Department of the Shanghai Academy of Social Sciences. As a member of the new generation of Chinese folklorists, Cheng began contacting foreign scholars while studying for his Ph. D. He assisted in inviting foreign scholars to give lectures for the summer school in ECNU, which also brought him the opportunities to visit abroad and attend conferences. There is no doubt that his generation will develop Chinese folklore studies to a new stage. His questions in this essay will be the focus for this new generation of folklorists to improve and enhance.

community's traditions to outsiders through cooperation and dialogue. At the same time, their research expanded my vision and let me reflect more on folkloristic research methods, ethics, and other issues. There were also new problems that I did not think about, for example how folklorists should deal with the relationship between the objects of study and how to collect folklore while abiding by ethics.

From July 21st to 27th, 2014, Institute of Folklore at ECNU organized Sino-US folklore programs, creating a platform for our students to gain international awareness. These not only gave me a better understanding of American folklore research topics and methods, but also greatly contributed to my academic vision.

Of course, Chinese folklorists' contact with American folklorists is not limited to school settings. In recent years, Sino-US folklorists have increased their collaborations, which have allowed them to develop their research through museums, workshops, and other professional environments. At the annual meeting of the CFS in 2014, I was also fortunate enough to meet Bill Ivey, former AFS president, and Sue Tuohy from Indiana University.

In August 2015, I was able to receive a scholarship from the China Scholar Council to study at Ohio State University and learn from many renowned folklorists, such as Professors Dorothy Noyes and Amy Shuman. The courses I took gave me a deeper understanding of the theory and research of American folklore studies. Monthly luncheons at the Center for Folklore Studies and frequent lectures, seminars, and reading sessions also allowed me to immerse myself in the academic atmosphere. While in the United States, I attended the most impressive academic exchange event: the American Folklore Society annual meeting.

The AFS annual meeting was held at the Westin Hotel in Long Beach, California, from October 14th to 17th, 2015. The hotel was luxuriously decorated, but the meeting was very low-key with no promotional posters or banners. In the lobby, there was only one piece of paper for the meeting's agenda. At first glance, it would have looked like there was not a large-scale meeting. I have heard that Americans are frugal and pragmatic when coordinating conventions, which was evident from this event. This frugality is not due to a shortage of funds. In American educational institutions, donations from various sources enable faculty and graduate students to attend conferences and invite international scholars. For AFS meetings, international students can apply for a registration fee waiver and certain transportation subsidies. As a foreign doctoral student, I received the International Scholar Stipend to attend the meeting.

At the annual meeting, many of the arranged activities were user-friendly and used to facilitate socializing between guests. At the time of registration, I discovered that many people had ribbons at the bottom of their nametags to emphasize their roles. Mine had 'SPECIAL GUEST' on it. The Society also introduced mentors for each of the first-time attendees. In addition, Professors Juwen Zhang and Sue Tuohy gave me a lot of suggestions and help. In particular, Sue Tuohy took the trouble to proofread and refine my papers. Receiving help from the people around me in a foreign country made me really grateful.

A report on Sino-US collaboration in folklore studies attracted many scholars. At the meeting, the president of the CFS addressed the issue that Chinese folklorists often know many details about American folklore practices, while American folklorists know little about their Chinese counterparts. The problem of how to make Chinese folklore studies expand beyond China remains a challenge for us.

Besides the smaller group conversations occurring during the convention, there were several networking events. I applied for the "Lunch with the Editors" event, which allowed me to talk to several international students and two editors from the *Journal of Folklore Research*, Michael Dylan Foster and Chad Buterbaugh. The two editors introduced us to the magazine and the standards and requirements to produce it. Foster also expressed his support of Sino-US folkloristic exchanges, hoping to publish more papers written by Chinese folklorists.

I also attended the Breakfast with AFS Fellows and was put into Professor Barbro Klein's group. Her topic was folklore studies from around the world, so our group of young international students shared and discussed our personal research.

Since the meeting was only for four days, there was not enough time to deeply understand the folkloristic practices we discussed. Although the president of CFS mentioned that Chinese students are familiar with folklorists from the United States, I cannot help but wonder if we are really understanding American folklore. Our understanding of American folklore has long been translated by domestic scholars, who cannot fully convey the original meanings, which are then lost in translation.

As a doctoral student, I ask myself: what can I do for the mutual exchange of Chinese and American folklore studies? Since I am a volunteer of the CFS and a moderator of the Chinese Folklore Forum, my friends and I regularly broadcast meetings and introduce conference sessions in the forums. Because I was able to attend the AFS meeting this year, I also made posts in the forums under the topic of "2015 AFS Annual Meeting," which received a lot of attention from domestic scholars.

The number of Chinese scholars participating in the AFS annual meeting is increasing year by year. Likewise, many folklorists and students study abroad in the United States each year. In contrast, the number of American scholars that visit China and attend the CFS meetings has been very small. We still have a long way to go to promote Chinese folklore studies to the world.

(Translation by Erica Mao)

专有名称
Proper Names

  为了保持全书的统一性，参与交流的当代中国人的名字在翻译成英文时将姓氏放在名字后面，以从英文习惯。但是，历史人物则以惯例按中文习惯。英文的人名和地名按照惯例或已知译法。常用的机构和刊物名缩写如下：

  For consistency, contemporary Chinese names are translated by putting family names after their personal names, following English convention. The names of historical figures are kept in the conventional Chinese way. Place names and personal names in English are translated according to either conventional uses or extant known usages. Frequently used names of the institutions and academic journals are abbreviated as such:

  AFS = American Folklore Society 美国民俗学会
  AFC = American Folklife Center 美国民间生活中心
  CFS = China Folklore Society 中国民俗学会
  SFF = Smithsonian Folklife Festival 美国史密森民间生活节
  SI = Smithsonian Institute 史密森学会
  WSFS = Western States Folklore Society 美国西部民俗学会

  IU = Indiana University 印第安纳大学
  MUN = Memorial University of Newfoundland 纽芬兰纪念大学
  OSU = Ohio State University 俄亥俄州立大学
  UO = University of Oregon 俄勒冈大学
  UP = University of Pennsylvania 宾夕法尼亚大学
  WKU = West Kentucky University 西肯塔基大学
  WU = Willamette University 崴涞大学

  BJU = Beijing (Peking) University 北京大学
  BNU = Beijing Normal University 北京师范大学

CASS = China Academy of Social Sciences 中国社会科学院
CCNU = Central China Normal University 华中师范大学
ECNU = East China Normal University 华东师范大学
MUC = Minzu University of China 中央民族大学
SDU = Shandong University 山东大学
ZSU = Zhongshan（Sun Yat-sen）University 中山大学

GXNM = Guangxi Nationalities Museum 广西民族博物馆
GZNM = Guizhou Nationalities Museum 贵州民族博物馆
YNM = Yunnan Nationalities Museum 云南民族博物馆
MMWC = Mathers Museum of World Cultures 马瑟斯世界文化博物馆
MSUM = Michigan State University Museum 密歇根州立大学博物馆
MIFA = Museum of International Folk Art 国际民间艺术博物馆

JAF = *Journal of American Folklore*《美国民俗学刊》
WF = *Western Folklore*《西部民俗》
JFR = *Journal of Folklore Research*《民俗研究学刊》
MSYJ = *Minsu Yanjiu*（Folklore Studies, journal）《民俗研究》
MWLT = *Minjian Wenhua Luntan*（Folk Culture Forum, journal）《民间文化论坛》
WHYC = *Wenhua Yichan*（Cultural Heritage, journal）《文化遗产》

后　　记

　　2016 年，在佛罗里达州迈阿密举办的美国民俗学会年会上，张举文向宋俊华谈起中美民俗、非物质文化遗产学界近十年的交流历程，不胜感慨，说这种交流对中美民俗、非遗学界已产生了深远影响，值得记录下来。他已经组织了 30 多位学者在写他们的故事，并提议与中山大学中国非物质文化遗产研究中心共同出版一个集子，一者是记录这段历史；二者是以此为契机，推动中美民俗、非遗学术交流进一步发展。同时，他也强调了"亚民俗"的重要。宋俊华感到这个提议很妙很及时，这个新集子与正在计划出版的《文化对话：中美非物质文化遗产论坛》恰好可结为姊妹篇，成为中美学者交流的重要成果和最好见证。由此，他们携手加速促成了这个集子的问世。

　　中美民俗学会的正式交流弹指已过十年，但我们在学术交流中的点点滴滴，每一次会议、每一次讨论、每一次考察、每一次聚餐，依然历历在目。我们关于中美民俗和非遗政策、理论、方法、案例、学生培养、学科建设等的讨论，不仅使得参与其中的中美学者和学生获益，而且，相关成果通过出版物和网络传播正在让更多的人获益。从中，我们收获的不仅是学术，而且还有友谊。我们正在建立一种可持续的、平等共享的学术交流理念和机制，它将对中美民俗、非遗学界的交流发生十分深远的影响。

　　感谢热心参与并积极撰稿的中美学者；感谢参与本书中英文翻译的中美青年学者、学生；感谢 Bill Long 博士、Susan Blader 教授和 Sharon Sherman 教授对英文翻译与部分文章的校审；感谢张举文对四个部分的概述和对作者的评介。尤其要感谢美国民俗学会所承担的路思基金项目和中山大学中国非物质文化遗产研究中心对本书编撰和出版的大力支持。

　　依照中国人的传统，不论主人做出一桌多么丰盛的佳肴，都会对客人说自己做得不够好，恳请海涵；依照美国人的传统，在竞技场上不论得了什么名次，每个参赛者都可能高兴地说自己尽了最大努力，享受了过程，期待以后取得更好的成绩。我们处于两个传统之间，也许可以说，我们在此尽力做出了一桌酒席，不一定每道菜都可口，但我们尽力了，也相信以后还有机会做出更好的盛宴。的确，中美民俗、非遗学术交流才刚开始，一定还有更多有价值的故事将在续集中被记录下去。

编者
张举文，美国崴涞大学东亚系主任、教授
北京师范大学社会学院兼职教授
宋俊华，中山大学中国非物质文化遗产研究中心主任、教授
2017 年初春

Epilogue

At the 2016 AFS annual meeting in Miami, Florida, Juwen Zhang talked to Junhua Song about the previous ten years of exchanges between Chinese and American folklorists, and said that those events were meaningful and worth documenting. He had already arranged for about 30 scholars to write their stories. He suggested that this collection of stories be published by the Institute of Chinese Intangible Cultural Heritage, Sun Yat-sen University, not only as a record of the past exchanges, but also as a way to push the exchange to a higher level. Meanwhile, he emphasized the importance of "metafolklore." Junhua Song thought that it was a useful and timely idea because such a collection could, as it were, play a duet with the *Cultural Dialogue*: *Sino-US Forum on Intangible Cultural Heritage*, a volume that the Institute was preparing for publication. They agreed that these volumes would provide the best indication of collaboratve achievements by Chinese and American folklorists in the past ten years.

Though the ten years of formal Sino-US folkloristic exchanges went by quickly, our memories of each and every meeting, discussion, tour, and meal still remain vivid. We not only have a harvest of scholarship and friendship, but also, more important, have established the idea of equal academic exchange and a continuing mechanism to do so. This idea and this mechanism have laid the foundation for the current exchange and will, surely and positively, influence the future exchange on folklore and intangiable cutlural heritage studies, and even cross-cultural communication in broad sense.

We sincerely thank each and every author, young scholar and student who translated the stories. We also thank our colleagues, Dr. Bill Long, Professor Susan Blader and Professor Sharon Sherman for proofreading the English translations, and Juwen Zhang for providing a summary for each section and an introduction to each author. We thank the AFS-CFS Luce Project via American Folklore Society, and the Institute of Chinese Intangible Cultural Heritage, Sun Yat-sen University for sponsoring this publication.

In Chinese tradition, a host would plead his/her guests to tolerate the humble dishes on the table, no matter how extravagant and delicious they are. In American tradition, a competitor in a sport or game would say that he/she did his/her best and enjoyed the process and expected to do better next time, no matter what rank he/she got. Between these traditions, we may say that we have managed to provide a table of dishes and tried our best, though they may not be as delicious as expected, and that we believe there will be a chance to deliver an even better feast in the future. Indeed, the Sino-US folkloristic communication is only beginning, and many more valuable stories will take place and be recorded in future volumes.

Editors

Juwen Zheng

Professor and Chair, Dept. of Japanese and chinese, Willamette University

Visiting Professor, School of Sociology, Beijing Normal University

Junhua Song

Professor and Director, Institute of Chinese Intangible Cultural Heritage

Sun Yat-sen University

Early Spring 2017

玛莎·麦克多维尔在一次惊喜的生日庆祝晚宴上夹起长寿面,北京,2011。Marsha MacDowell picking up long-life noodles at a surprise-birthday-celebration in Beijing in 2011. Photograph by Juwen Zhang.

祝愿中美民俗学交流长存!

Long life to the Sino-US folkloristic communication!